COMPLETE BOOK OF
SHOOTING

AN OUTDOOR LIFE BOOK

CONTENTS

PART V

HUNTING WITH THE SHOTGUN / JACK O'CONNOR

PART VI

TRAP AND SKEET SHOOTING / ALEX KERR

PART VII

SAFETY AND CARE / JACK O'CONNOR

PART VIII

HANDGUN SHOOTING / JEFF COOPER

I

Fundamentals of Rifle Shooting

Jack O'Connor

1

The Rifle—An Introduction

THE RIFLE as we know it is only about 100 years old. Firearms with various types of rifled barrels were used long before that, but they were muzzle loaders and very slow to load—too slow to be of much military use. For generations the standard military firearm of the European powers was a smoothbore musket, sometimes loaded with a single ball and sometimes with a ball and three buckshot. For most of history this muzzle-loading military musket was a flintlock, and we still use expressions derived from flintlock days. When I was a child we said someone was "cocked and primed" if he was prepared to do something. If someone made a lot of noise about something but did not accomplish much what he did was known as "a flash in the pan."

The Napoleonic wars were fought with muzzle-loading flintlock muskets, but by the end of the first quarter of the nineteenth century percussion lock muskets and hunting rifles were coming into use. The American Civil War was the first major war ever fought with rifles. These were for the most part muzzle loaders primed by percussion caps and firing conical minie balls. The rifle became a practical military weapon with invention of the minie ball. It was smaller than the bore diameter and could be quickly rammed down the barrel on top of the powder charge. Then when the rifle was fired, the hollow base caused the blow of the powder gas to expand the bullet to fill the rifling.

The use of the rifle by both sides in the Civil War made it one of the bloodiest wars in history for the number of men engaged. Both Union and Confederate generals had been trained at West Point, and they had studied the musket tactics of Napoleon. These were practical in the time of the great Corsican, as a soldier with a musket had only about a 40 percent chance of hitting another at 100 yards. The American leader who told his men not to fire at their British cousins at the battle of Bunker Hill until they "could see the whites of their eyes" was giving them sound advice. But with the Civil War muzzle loader it was possible to get about 50 percent hits at 300 yards. Skilled marksmen with special rifles and telescope sights could do much better.

3

Rifles had been used in war before 1861 but by special troops. They had not been widely used by line regiments. In the Revolutionary War an American rifleman named Tim Murphy shot the British General Simon Fraser and the resultant confusion led to the defeat of Burgoyne's army.

But in the Civil War whole regiments stood up and blazed away at each other within murderous range. Army corps made frontal attacks on veteran brigades and divisions behind earthworks. At Fredericksburg, Burnside hurled the Army of the Potomac against Lee's veterans. The men in blue were slaughtered. Lee did exactly the same thing when he sent 15,000 brave Confederates against the Union center at Gettysburg. Grant tried to overwhelm Lee's Army of Northern Virginia at Cold Harbor in 1864 and sustained thousands of casualties in a few minutes. The only Civil War general who really learned the lesson early that successful frontal attacks could not be made against entrenched riflemen was James Longstreet.

The Civil War was the first war in which both breech loaders and repeating rifles were used. The Sharps rifle was used by special outfits on the Union side, notably Berdan's sharpshooters. However, the Sharps rifle of the day, although it loaded from the breech, used a linen cartridge and the charge was ignited by a percussion cap. Since it did not use a metallic cartridge case, the Sharps was not gas tight. It must have been miserable to shoot. After the Civil War the Sharps was adapted to metallic cartridges and made a great reputation as a long-range buffalo rifle.

The most radical departure in the way of military shoulder weapons during the Civil War was the Spencer carbine, the most popular of the breech-loading repeaters used during the Civil War. Others were the Burnside and the Henry. Spencer carbines were used by General Buford's cavalry to hold up the Confederate advance on the first day at the battle of Gettysburg, and they were also used by various other cavalry outfits, including Sheridan's. The Spencer was the best military weapon used during the Civil War. It was a seven-shot lever-action repeater using rimfire cartridges with heavy bullets but at low velocity. After the war hunters found the more powerful Sharps and Remington single shots better adapted to Western hunting and liked the lighter Henry (which became the Winchester Model 73) much better for the woods.

The United States government used a black-powder single-shot trapdoor Model 1873 Springfield for the .45/70 cartridge until the adoption of the .30/40 Krag in 1893. Actually some Model 1873 .45/70 rifles firing black-powder ammunition were used by volunteer regiments as late as the Spanish-American war.

The United States manufacturers turned out some memorable single-shot rifles for powerful black-powder cartridges—the Sharps, the Maynard, the Remington, the Whitney, among others. However, the typical American sporting rifle from post Civil War days until World War I was a lever action—the famous Model 1873, 1876, 1886, 1892, and 1895 Winchesters, the Marlins, the Ballards. The centerfire primer had come in, and American loading companies turned out many fine old black-powder cartridges. Most of these are gone and forgotten. About the only ones that survive are the .32/20, .44/40, the .38/55, and the .45/70. Of course, these are now loaded with smokeless powder.

At the time the American lever-action sporting rifle was developing in the last thirty years of the nineteenth century, the British were specializing in double-barreled and single-shot rifles. These were typically chambered largely for large-rimmed cartridges with heavy bullets and were designed for the game of Africa and India. The Germans, on the other hand, had begun to develop the bolt-action repeating rifles which culminated in the Model 98 Mauser, the action from which most of today's bolt-action rifles are descended.

Smokeless powder came into wide use in the early 1890's, and the character of both military and sporting cartridges changed radically. Cartridges themselves became smaller and bore diameters were likewise smaller. Velocities were stepped up with the new propellant from around 1300–1500 feet per second to about 2000. Long small-caliber bullets jacketed with cupronickel or mild steel replaced lead bullets patched with paper or lubricated by grease-filled grooves.

Military cartridges dating from the early smokeless powder era are the German 8 x 57J for the Model 88 German military rifle, the 8 mm. French Lebel, the British .303, the 7.65 Belgian Mauser, the 7 x 57 "Spanish" Mauser, the American .30/40 Krag.

The armies of the world adopted bolt-action rifles for these small-caliber, bottleneck cartridges. The Americans first selected the Danish Krag-Jorgenson action, but during the Spanish-American War, the American brass decided that the Mauser action and the 7 x 57 cartridge used by the Spanish had the edge on the Krag. In 1903 the Americans adopted the Mauser-type Model 1903 Springfield for a rimless cartridge of .30 caliber. It eventually became the famous .30/06. The Mauser-type action made the use of rimless cartridges a necessity.

Until after World War I, the lever-action rifle was the most popular type of American hunting rifle. The .30/30 cartridge for the Winchester Model 94 lever-action rifle became the most popular of all deer cartridges, and the Model 94 rifle the all-time best seller among sporting rifles. Other smokeless-powder cartridges developed for the Model 94 were the .32 Special and the .25/35. For larger game Winchester developed the .405 and .35 Winchester cartridges for the Model 95.

The British brought out powerful smokeless-powder rimmed cartridges for their doubles and single shots and also developed heavy rimless cartridges like the .375 Holland & Holland Magnum, the .404 Jeffery, and the .416 Rigby for rifles built on Mauser rifles imported from Germany. The Germans designed some heavy cartridges for the largest game, but mostly they adapted military cartridges like the 7 x 57 and 8 x 57 to hunting use.

Savage made excellent lever-action rifles for smokeless-powder cartridges, and so did Marlin. Stevens made a few. Remington, on the other hand, did not make a lever-action rifle but instead brought out the Remington-Lee bolt action and also a semiautomatic big-game rifle for Remington-designed rimless cartridges of moderate power (.35, .32, .30, and .25) and a pump (or slide) action rifle for the same cartridges. Remington also manufactured pump and semiautomatic rifles in .22 rimfire.

By the early years of this century all of the essentials of the modern big-game rifle were present—smokeless powder, centerfire primers, bottleneck cases, the strong Mauser-type actions, jacketed bullets, telescopic sights, and ultra-high velocity. Controversies developed between advocates of heavy bullets and high velocity and advocates of lighter bullets at even higher velocities.

Muzzle velocities of 3000 feet per second and above came along early in this century. The Model 1905 8 x 57 JS German military cartridge drove a sharp-pointed (spitzer) bullet weighing 154 grains at a velocity of over 2800 feet per second. The velocity of the caliber .30, Model 1906 (.30/06) 150-grain bullet was 2700. In 1910 the Canadian Sir Charles Ross brought out the sensational .280 Ross cartridge for the Model 1910 straight-pull Ross bolt-action rifle. The velocity with a 145-grain bullet was 3050 feet per second in a 28-inch barrel. The British .275 H. & H. Magnum and the .375 Magnum both came out prior to World War I, as did other British high-velocity cartridges. The .300 H. & H. Magnum appeared in the early 1920's.

The American rifle and cartridge designer Charles Newton kept American gun nuts stirred up along about the time of the first world war. He designed a whole series of high-velocity cartridges that when loaded with modern powders compare favorably with the hottest cartridges of today.

During the American participation in World War I, tens of thousands of young Americans became acquainted with bolt-action rifles. Savage brought out the Model 20 and later the Model 40, both bolt actions. Winchester designed the Model 54, which as revised later became the Model 70, and Remington converted the U.S. Model 1917 into a sporter called the Model 30. Savage introduced the .300 Savage, a .30 caliber cartridge on a shortened .30/06 case and adapted it to teh Model 99 lever action and the Model 1920 bolt rifle. Winchester designed the .270 Winchester cartridge—the .30/06 case necked down for the Model 54 rifle.

During the interval between the two world wars, the .30/06 cartridge established itself as one of the most useful and popular of the world's big game cartridges, and the .270 and the .300 Savage were also widely used. The present magnum boom began in the middle 1930's, when Winchester adapted the Model 70 rifle to the British .300 H. & H. Magnum and .375 Magnum cartridges.

Telescope sights had been used as early as the Civil War but they were optically poor, with small, dim fields of view. They were long, their mounts were frail, and they were difficult to adjust. Along in the 1920's a few bold American riflemen bought German 2½, 2¾, and 4X hunting scopes. A Californian named Rudolph Noske developed a successful side mount for some of these scopes and so did Griffin & Howe in New York. Redfield Gun Sight Company in Denver manufactured a good top mount. Noske designed 2½ and 4X scopes with internal adjustments for both windage and elevation and with eye-relief so long that the scopes could be mounted ahead of the bolt handles of Springfield and Mauser rifles. Later gunsmiths learned to alter bolt handles so scopes with shorter eye-relief could be mounted low and centrally over the bore. Then W. R. Weaver brought out his inexpensive, internally adjustable 330 and 440 scopes and inexpensive mounts. Scope sights started sprouting on all kinds of rifles. Today American scope sights are among the best in the world, and a high percentage of new big-game and varmint rifles are equipped with scopes as soon as they are purchased. Even inexpensive .22 rimfire plinking rifles are equipped with scopes. Scopes are made by Lyman, Unertl, Weaver, Redfield, and Leupold, and are also imported from Germany and Japan.

Semiautomatic or self-loading rifles and shotguns (usually called "automatics" by most sportsmen) have been around for a long time. Various systems are used (long-recoil, short-recoil, blow-back, gas) but the gas-operated action is now almost universally employed in autoloading shotguns and centerfire rifles.

The M-1 Garand .30/06 military rifle with which the United States fought World War II was a gas-operated semiautomatic, as was the little M-1 carbine. This successful use of gas seemed to set the minds of American designers to working on the problem of gas-operated automatic sporting weapons. Several gas-operated American autoloading shotguns and big-game rifles have been marketed since then.

Almost all of the famous pre-World War II rifles have either been discontinued or have been redesigned. Wherever possible machines have been substituted for hand labor. Techniques worked out in the automobile industry have been applied to gun manufacture. Barrels are rifled either by button rifling, which "irons" the rifling into the bore, or by cutting the rifling by passing a gang of broaches through the bore.

Most "engraving" is rolled on or etched. Instead of being cut by manual checkering tools, today's checkering is usually cut by computer-controlled machines. In some cases plastics are employed instead of metal, and investment castings are used instead of forgings. Much of this riles the conservatives, but rifles are produced that shoot well, are strong, and many of them have nice lines.

The wide use of telescope sights, the vast increase of hunting since the war by inexperienced and unskilled hunters, and the publicity given them, have made magnum cartridges a very hot item. Roy Weatherby, a Californian, by a combination of good design with shrewd advertising, promotion, and publicity is generally credited with having launched the magnum boom not long after the war. He introduced a series of magnum cartridges and rifles to fire them. It became the accepted thing for well-heeled Americans who had taken up big-game hunting after the war to depart to Alaska, Africa, and India loaded down with Weatherby rifles. The success of the Weatherby cartridges, along with the natural drift toward high velocity, resulted in the introduction of several new magnum cartridges by the established factories. The .300 Winchester Magnum and the .308 Norma are in a way answers to the .300 Weatherby Magnum. The .264 Winchester Magnum is similar to the .257 Weatherby, and the 7 mm. Remington Magnum is not very different from the .7 mm. Weatherby Magnum. The .338 Winchester Magnum is a powerful, flat-shooting cartridge that combines the virtues of the .300 Weatherby and the .375 Magnum. One of the most successful of the post-war magnum cartridges is the .458 Winchester, a .45 caliber cartridge on a straight, belted case. It has the same ballistics as the .470 Nitro Express, the most popular of cartridges for heavy dangerous game. The .458 has the advantage in that rifles for it are much cheaper than the classic British doubles for the .470 and the .465. The cartridge is now widely used in Africa.

Classifying Rifles

There are many ways of classifying rifles. One way is to list them by the type of action. Some are operated by bolts, some by slide handles, some by levers; some are operated automatically by recoil or by gas. In addition some rifles have two barrels and look like double-barreled shotguns and some are single shots.

Another way of classifying rifles would be by the uses to which they are put. Millions of rifles have been manufactured for military purposes. As we have seen, military rifles have long been evolving in the direction of more firepower—from muzzle loaders, to breech loaders, to various kinds of manually operated repeaters, and then to semiautomatics. The M-1 Garand with which the United States fought World War II is now obsolete. The official U.S. military rifle is the M-15 for the 5.56 mm. (.223 Remington) cartridge. The M-15, a radically different rifle designed by Armalite and manufactured by Colt, uses a high-velocity .22 caliber cartridge and fires full or semi-automatically. It was a successful combat rifle in Vietnam.

The other large classifications of rifles according to use are those used for target shooting and those used for hunting.

As we will see in the chapters on target shooting, target rifles are divided into small bores (.22 rimfires), big bores (.308 and .30/06), and into rifles designed for benchrest, military, and international competition. Other cartridges besides the .308 and the .30/06 are used for benchrest and international competition.

Rifles for hunting include inexpensive .22 rimfires used for small-game hunting and plinking. Still another class consists of special rifles used for varmint hunting and usually chambered for small-bore high-velocity cartridges. The most written about and talked about rifles and cartridges of the lot are those used on big game. Some combinations are designed for nothing more serious than deer and black bear hunting in the woods of the Eastern and Southern United States. Mostly these rifles are lever actions, pumps, and automatics for such cartridges as the .30/30, the .35 Remington, the .308.

Another class might be called the mountain rifle. Firearms of this class are most often bolt actions equipped with scope sights and chambered for cartridges running from the .270 and .30/06 to the 7 mm. Remington Magnum and .300 Winchester Magnum. These are really all-around rifles—at least for North America. They can be used on moose, on elk, and also on sheep, grizzlies, caribou, antelope, mule deer, and whitetail deer and black bear in the brush. The same rifles and cartridges do very well for most African plains game and Indian horned game. Any of the cartridges of this class will kill very neatly any thin-skinned, non-dangerous game animal if shots are well placed and proper bullets are used. This includes the largest moose, caribou, elk, large African antelope like eland, greater kudu, gemsbok, and sable. It might be argued that some of these cartridges are a bit light for dangerous game like grizzly, Alaska brown bear, lion, and tiger. Yet I know of at least three tigers that have been killed very dead with the .30/06 and many lions that have been sent to their reward with .30/06 and .270 rifles.

Another class, for which there is limited use in North America but wide use in Africa and Asia, is what the British call the medium bores. These rifles are almost always bolt actions but sometimes doubles and very rarely single shots. The most famous of these is the great .375 Magnum. Others are the .338 Winchester, the .358 Norma Magnum, the .340 Weatherby, and the 8 mm. Remington Magnum. The British formerly designed and manufactured many cartridges of this category, but except for the .375 Magnum most of them have fallen on evil days. All are characterized by bores of medium size (.323 to .375), fairly heavy bullets (200 to 300 grains), and fairly high velocity (2400 to 3000 feet per second). All can in a pinch be used on anything from small deer and antelope to elephant, and they are considered the safest cartridges to use on thin-skinned dangerous game like lion, Alaska brown bear, and tigers.

The last class of hunting rifles and cartridges is what is generally known as the big bores. These use bullets weighing from 400 to 500 grains at moderate velocities of from 2000 to 2400 feet per second. Calibers run from .40 to .45 but some obsolete British calibers took .577 and .600 caliber bullets. They produce energy of from 4000 to as much as 6000 and 7000 foot-pounds. Examples are the British .416 Rigby, the British .465 and .470 Nitro Express, the American .458 Winchester and .460 Weatherby. Rifles for these monsters are either bolt actions or doubles. They are used on large, mean, thick-skinned animals—elephants, rhinos, Cape buffalo, Indian gaur. If you are troubled with elephants in your petunias or rhinos in your potato patch, these are for you!

For the past fifty or sixty years the development of the rifle has, as we have seen, been largely a matter of refinement. Telescope sights are more practical, more reliable, better optically, easier to adjust, and better mounted. Primers have become noncorrosive so rust is no longer a bugaboo. Bullets are better designed than they used to be and it is rare that one breaks up on the surface or plows through without opening up. Velocities have gone up slowly as progressive-burning slow powders have been developed.

Ammunition is much more reliable. In the early days of smokeless powder, pierced and blown primers were common, as were stuck and broken cases, misfires, and hangfires. Now these ailments are almost unknown. Bullets are more uniform. Barrels are better. More has been learned about bedding barrels and actions. As a result of all this, accuracy is routine today that was inconceivable even twenty-five years ago. The benchrest shooter on a still day can just about put all his bullets into one hole at 200 yards, and the varmint shooter can lay them into 1½ inches at that distance. Even the mountain and plains hunter with a tuned-up, scope-sighted rifle can put all of his bullets into a hat at 300–350 yards. Never before have rifles been so reliable and so accurate!

2

Beginning with a Rifle

NINE-TENTHS OF ALL rifle shooting is very simple. All the rifleman has to do is put his sights on what he wants to hit, hold steadily, then get off his shot without disturbing his aim. If the rifle is correctly sighted and sufficiently accurate, if he can ignore trajectory (which must be taken into consideration in the case of a long shot), and if he doesn't have to figure lead (as he would on running game), that's all there is to it.

If it is all as easy as that, then, why isn't everyone a good shot?

A few little facts spoil this beautiful picture. In the first place, strictly speaking, there isn't such a thing as holding a rifle absolutely steady. Even from a benchrest, with the fore-end and butt resting on sandbags, a 20X scope will show the keen-eyed that there is still a wobble—very slight, but a wobble nonetheless—from the pulsations of the heart, or from the blood flowing through the veins perhaps.

In the second place, letting the shot off without disturbing the aim is almost as difficult as holding the rifle steady. Even under ideal conditions with a heavy rifle and a light pull delicately squeezed, the let-off undoubtedly causes some slight movement.

Knowing all this, then, acquiring skill in shooting a rifle consists largely in learning to assume quickly the steadiest position feasible under the circumstances and then controlling the trigger to get the shot off properly.

It is unfortunate, perhaps, that so many shooters are self-taught. Most of us began by getting hold of a .22 somehow, buying some ammunition, then going out and pecking away at tin cans, fence posts, rocks, or what have you. Our rifles were not properly sighted in. We knew nothing about correct positions and for that reason we couldn't hold a rifle even fairly steady. This exaggerated wobble gave us the tendency to yank the trigger. Most of us began in the offhand position, which is the most difficult of the lot. Some of us became fairly good shots, through a long process of trial and error, and through unlearning the bad habits we had picked up. Some of us did not.

The first step in learning to become a good shot is *wanting* to be one. In my own years as a professor of journalism, I found that the first requirement for learning is enthusiasm. I could teach anything, if I could make it seem interesting, dramatic, and important; but if not, I was sunk.

So it is with starting anyone out with a rifle. But sad to relate, practice with the rifle is far less dramatic than practice with a shotgun. Busting a clay target is spectacular. It gives a man something for his effort. But shooting little holes in a piece of paper is a dull business to the beginner. He wants to see things break, watch feathers fly, hear bells ring.

The ideal combination for arousing enthusiasm in the beginner would be a shooting gallery crossed with a bench rest. Our tyro—with his rifle rested solidly, so an unsteady aim would not tempt him to yank the trigger—could then shoot at iron bunnies, ducks, and whatnot. Lacking a setup like that he can be started on lumps of clay, tin cans filled with water—anything to give him a little drama.

At any rate, the beginner should start from the steadiest possible position. Since bench rests aren't too common, the next best bet is to use a sandbag and shoot prone. Granted that the rifle is correctly sighted in, the beginner can concentrate on squeezing the trigger; whereas if the rifle is unsteady (as in the offhand position) the temptation is to yank and jerk in the vain hope of getting the shot off when the sights are right.

TRIGGER CONTROL

For many years it has been taught that the way to shoot is to increase the squeeze on the trigger when the sights look right, hold it when they don't. Then, according to the theory, the gun goes off *unexpectedly when the sights are right* because that is the only time the trigger is being pressed. Theoretically all this prevents a man from flinching, because he does not know when the gun is going off. Often this method is known as "surprise fire" because presumably our shooter is astonished each time he hears a bang.

Many good shots say they always know when a rifle is going off. Equally good shots claim they never know. My own notion is that the good shot knows about when his rifle is going to fire but not exactly. The difference would be in minute fractions of a second, perhaps perceptible to some but not to others.

The ideal, then, is to squeeze that trigger with the utmost gentleness and to concentrate on the squeeze—*not* on when the gun is going off. Wild shots are usually caused not by poor aim, not by wobble, but by anticipating the recoil, yanking the trigger, and jumping. It is far better to concentrate on trigger squeeze than on aim (although both are important) because aim, I am convinced, comes more naturally than squeeze. At first, then, the beginning rifle shot should form correct habits of trigger squeeze and sight picture. Learning to hold the rifle with a fair degree of steadiness can wait. He learns that when his rifle goes off as the sights look right something happens. A clod dissolves into dust, a bottle breaks, or a tin can flies into the air.

He should quickly be taught to call his shot—to know exactly where his sights rested when the gun went off. No one who does not habitually call his shots can ever become a good shot on targets, game, or anything else. If the beginner calls a bulls-eye or a broken bottle and gets a miss, the answer is that he is yanking the trigger or flinching, which is more or less the same thing.

If our lad begins right—by shooting from the steadiest possible rest, where he can concentrate on sight picture and trigger squeeze—he will never commence yanking the trigger. And if he starts with .22 he will never develop a flinch. Proper reflexes are being formed. He has developed the habit of increasing trigger pressure when the sight picture looks right, slacking up when it doesn't. He has learned to call his shots.

The beginning shooter must learn to correlate his shooting and his breathing, as obviously he cannot get off a delicately squeezed shot when he is in the process of exhaling and inhaling. He must learn to take a deep breath, exhale part of it, and then not breathe again until he has fired. If he cannot get off his shot, he should relax, rest a moment, take another breath, and then start his squeeze again.

By this time, if he has the makings of a rifle shooter in him, our beginner should have developed enough enthusiasm to progress to a black-and-white paper target, a more revealing but less dramatic mark than a tin can. Here he can align his sights more exactly because he has a more definite aiming point. Since the paper will leave a record of his shots, he can develop more skill in calling them. He begins to learn that the *group* is the test of the rifleman's skill—not the occasional spectacular hit.

USING THE SIGHTS

Open iron sights are still standard on revolvers, and most rifles are equipped with them at the factory. The factories do not want to furnish a rifle without a sight and the open sight is cheap to manufacture. Those in charge of the factories know that except perhaps with the cheapest "plinking" rifles most of the open sights will be replaced with peep sights or scopes.

The open sight usually does not cost much and it is rugged, but otherwise it has little to recommend it, as it demands of the shooter that he focus his eye

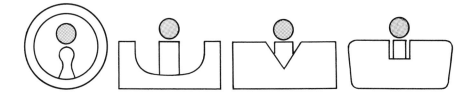

The 6 o'clock hold with four types of iron sights (l. to r.): peep, U-notch, V-notch, and patridge. The front sight must be centered in the peep and aligned with the top of the rear sight with the open sights. The bull should be seen sitting on top of the front sight, with a thin line of white between.

at the same time on rear sight, front sight, and target. Just how difficult this is is discussed in the chapter on the shooter's eyes. There are many types of open sights. The worst is the obsolete Rocky Mountain buckhorn, which has useless ears sticking up to blot out game and scenery. The fastest is the rear sight with a wide, shallow "V" such as found on British double rifles for use on dangerous game. The most accurate is the patridge type with the square front blade and the square notch for the rear sight.

There is much hocus-pocus, much folklore, about aiming with open sights. If the game is far away some try to draw a "coarse bead." Most of the time they are told to "draw a fine bead." Both terms are relative, inaccurate, and inexact, and the result is that the unskilled rifleman who uses open sights can't hit much. Furthermore, if the open rear sight has a narrow "V" or "U" notch and the rifle is sighted in with the front bead drawn fine, the shot taken in haste generally goes high since the shooter doesn't "draw down fine." With the most accurate open sight, the patridge, aim is taken with the top of the front blade even with the top of the rear sight.

The best type of iron sight and one much more accurate than the open sight is the peep or aperture. With it the rifleman naturally centers his front sight at the point of strongest light. The shooter should let his eye do his work for him. He should simply put his front sight on what he wants to hit and touch his shot off. His rear peep should be seen only as an out-of-focus blur.

Target shots who use peep or open sights generally but not always aim with the top of the blade front sight just far enough below the bull so that a white line shows between blade and bull. This is called the 6 o'clock hold and is the classic way of aiming with open sights with both rifle and revolver. However, some excellent shots always try to hold into the bull. The man who uses the 6 o'clock hold sights in his rifle so that his bullet strikes in the center of the bull.

Some big-game shots sight in so that the group forms at the top of the front sight and they aim with the top of the front sight. Others prefer to put the front sight on the game with the bullet striking where the center of the bead rests. Using the top of the bead is more accurate but one can do very well with either method.

The scope is the easiest of all sights to aim with. The shooter just puts the intersection of the crosswires, the top of the post, or perhaps the center of the dot on what he wants to hit and lets go. I once had a .270 equipped with a 2½X scope fitted with a 4-minute dot. It was a handy device. The 130-grain bullet struck just above the top of the dot at 100 and 200 yards, in center of the dot at 275, and at the bottom of the dot at about 350. However, for a quick shot at reasoanble range I just put the dot on what I wanted to hit and cut loose. Most people who use dot reticules find it more natural to aim with the center of the dot just as most users of bead front sights find it more natural to aim with the middle of the bead.

The dot reticule is no longer very popular, and neither is the once-standard crosshair. By far the most popular type today, especially for hunting, is

Two sight pictures with the peep sight for game shooting. At left, the front sight is held on the game; at right, a 6 o'clock hold with the point of impact just above the front sight.

If the front sight is seen too high above the top of the rear sight (left), the bullet will hit high; if too low, the bullet will hit low.

Rifle canted to the left, the bullet will hit left. Rifle canted to the right, bullet will hit to the right.

the dual-thickness crosswire, which consists of heavy vertical and horizontal wires that abruptly become thin near the center, where they cross. Even in dim light the outer, coarse segments of the crosswire help you get on target very quickly, but they would cover far too much of the target if they extended all the way to the center. The fine segments at the center facilitate precise aiming even at small targets. Dual-thickness reticules are marketed under many brand names: Weaver Dual X, Bushnell Multi-X, Leupold Duplex, Lyman Center Range, Redfield 4-Plex, and so on.

Two other features are now common, alone or in combination with each other and/or with the dual-thickness crosswire. One is the extra-wide objective lens, designed to provide a wide field of view to help the shooter get the crosswires on game quickly. The other is a range-finding device built into the reticule.

Range-finding devices of several kinds are marketed. The simplest is a second horizontal wire. In a fixed-power scope, the space between the two horizontal wires "sandwiches" a known measurement—an amount of the target—at a given distance. At 100 yards, for instance, it may sandwich six inches of target. If the shooter knows the approximate size of the game or target, he can estimate range from how much of it fits between the wires. In a variable-power scope of the same type, the space between horizontal wires

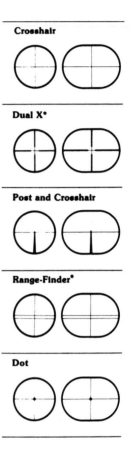

Five reticules offered in Weaver scopes, each in a standard and wide-view model. These are the most popular types and are available from most manufacturers.

functions the same way—as a given measurement such as six inches at 100 yards—when the power ring is turned to the highest setting.

Some variable-power scopes employ a more sophisticated rangefinder with a numbered yardage scale. The power ring is turned, changing the apparent size of the target—say a deer, whose body is generally about 18 inches deep—until it is bracketed by the two wires. The scale number that appears at the top or bottom of the reticule shows the yardage when game of that size is sandwiched between the two wires.

One other change has occurred in recent years. The optics and construction of variable-power scopes have been greatly improved, making them lighter, smaller, and more durable and reliable than they used to be, and also providing a brighter and bigger field of view at the higher power settings. With or without the other features described here, variable magnification now seems to be more popular than fixed power.

Whatever type of sight is used, the rifleman should avoid canting (leaning his rifle to one side or the other) if possible. If sighted in with sights straight up and down, the rifle will shoot to one side or the other if canted. Most riflemen cant their rifles slightly one way or another, but if their cant is consistent and if they are sighted in for it this doesn't make much difference. Canted to the right the rifle shoots to the right. Canted to the left it shoots to the left. A cheekpiece that is too thick will make a rifleman cant his piece to the right generally, and too thin a cheekpiece or none at all may make him cant it a bit to the left.

SHOOTING POSITIONS

By now the beginner is ready to master the shooting positions, those arrangements of the human anatomy by which a mass of wobbling joints, quivering muscles, and throbbing veins can become a fairly satisfactory shooting platform.

Prone

Because prone is the steadiest of all positions he should perfect it first. The photos of this position will give the beginner the main idea, though of course personal coaching from a skilled rifle shot will be even better. Principal things to remember are to get the left elbow directly under the rifle, and to have the body axis slant away from the rifle at an angle of about 45 degrees.

Much target shooting, probably too much, is done from prone, and many a .22 caliber "small bore" shooter does competitive shooting in no other position. Some of those lads are so skilled as to be human machine rests. But we are assuming that our beginner wants to become a good *game* shot; and for that, alas, the prone position is the least useful of all. In game country it is rare to find a piece of ground level enough to lie down on or free enough from high grass or brush so the prone position can be used.

However, the hunter should do some practicing from prone because occasionally he will use it, say in shooting *up* a steep hillside—something that can't be done from the sit. Again, in the high Rockies above timberline the hunter can often assume a good prone position to shoot caribou, sheep, goats, or grizzlies in a basin below. Then, too, since antelope are usually shot in open, rolling country, and at rather long range, prone is a natural for them.

Almost all shooting at small "varmints" such as woodchucks, ground squirrels, and predatory hawks is done prone from a rest, as this is the only way the shooter can come close to realizing the accuracy potential of his rifle, cartridge, and sights. Any shot at big game at much beyond about 250 yards should also be taken from a rest—and also generally from the prone position.

The professionals who hunted buffalo for their hides shot prone from rests whenever possible. They used two sticks tied together and sharpened at one end so they could be stuck into the ground. They knew that killing power was largely a matter of precision shooting. Today several rests are manufactured for varmint hunters, some adjustable and some not. With them, a good rifle-

Prone position is assumed with the shooter's body at about a 45-degree angle to the line of aim. The legs are extended and spread, the feet lie flat on the ground. If the sling is used, it should be tight and give ample support. The left elbow should be under the rifle, acting as a brace, and as a pivot in shifting the aim.

man can shoot almost as well as he can from a bench rest. Some hunters take them along to use on big-game hunts. If the character of the country is such that prone shots can be taken the idea is not a bad one. I know one hunter who lay down on an Alaskan beach, used his varmint rest, and killed a giant brown bear dead in his tracks at 300 yards. Since the bear was only a few yards from heavy timber, he would not have shot unless he could have taken that solid rest.

A thing to remember is never to rest the rifle, particularly the barrel, over anything hard or the rifle will recoil away from it and the shot will fly high. When I rest a rifle over stones or logs, I pad the object with a jacket, a hat, or anything soft.

The Sitting Position

On the plains and in the mountains, the sitting position is the most useful of them all when you're after big game. It isn't quite as steady as the prone, so your shooting will be a little less accurate. It isn't quite as fast as the offhand when you have an easy-to-hit target, but it's a lot faster for a *precise* shot at a difficult mark. It doesn't put the line of sight quite as high above the ground as the kneeling position, but is a great deal steadier. Finally, it can be used under a greater variety of conditions than any other reasonably steady position.

The sitting position is not only fast and fairly steady but, best of all, it can be used—unlike prone or kneeling—to shoot across or down a hillside. For mountain hunting it is the business. In plains hunting it is very useful for a steady shot when no rest is available and you can't lie prone because grass and weeds are too high or because cactus, thorns, or sharp rocks make lying down hazardous.

Just how accurately can a lightweight, scope-sighted hunting rifle be shot from the sit? A good rifleman should be able to keep three-fourths of his shots inside a 10-inch bull at 300 yards. Now and then he'll score a possible, but or-

Two ways to assume the sitting position. Shooter faces about 45-degrees from the line of aim. By leaning well forward, and putting the flat of the left elbow against the flat of the left knee, a solid shooting platform is created. Legs may be spread or crossed, which ever is more comfortable.

dinarily from one to three or four shots out of ten will wander out of the black. They should not, however, be *far* out.

Holding an 8- or 9½-pound hunting rifle steady is harder than holding down a 10½- or 11½-pound target rifle. At 200 yards, if our boy is holding and squeezing well, practically *all* the shots should be pretty well centered in the 10-inch black.

A good shot with a 4X scope on an accurate rifle will kill more jackrabbits and woodchucks at 200 yards from the sit than he'll miss. And even at 300 yards, with a scope of 8X or 10X, he'll make a surprising proportion of one-shot kills. Since errors of aim from the sitting position tend to be horizontal rather than vertical, there is more leeway on a big-game animal than on a varmint, so it's no astounding feat to place all shots in the forward half of an elk or caribou at 400 yards.

In shooting game—be it jackrabbit, woodchuck, whitetail deer, grizzly bear, or what have you—there are no close 4's. Only the 5's count. It is better by far to get in one well-aimed, well-held, well-placed shot from the sit than to get in three or four poorly aimed, poorly held, poorly placed shots or misses offhand. No time to sit? I have seen many a man miss three or four shots at standing game that he could have killed dead if he'd taken a second to plant his posterior on the earth.

When the uninstructed beginner first tries the sitting position, he almost always makes one principal mistake. He sits up too straight and puts his wobbly elbows right on his wobbly kneecaps. That position is little steadier, if any, than offhand. The secret of a good sitting position is to lean forward and put the flat of the left arm, just above the elbow, against the flat of the shin just below the left knee. Feet should be well apart and feet and ankles relaxed. I have often read that "the heels should be dug into the ground." That's the poorest advice I know of, since the digging induces a tremor. The only time the rifleman should jam his heels into the ground is when he's shooting from a steep hillside and has to dig in to keep from skidding.

Everyone, I believe, has to work out the minor details of his own sitting position for himself. A man with a paunch, for instance, cannot bend forward as far as a flat-bellied youth. Some riflemen prefer crossed legs rather than outstretched ones. For me, though, the key to a good solid sitting position is the relationship of left arm and shin, as described above. The upper right arm likewise rests against the right shin but what happens to it is relatively unimportant, just so the position feels comfortable and *relaxed*. The natural tension of the back muscles will pull the upper arms against the shin and bring equilibrium and relative steadiness.

In no position should a rifleman try to hold by main strength. He should always feel relaxed. The harder a man tries to hold, the more tense he becomes; and the more tension, the greater the wobble.

My own besetting sin is tenseness. I often catch myself bearing down, determined to hold that damned rifle steady if I have to squeeze it in two at the grip—and when I hold like that, the old musket wobbles all over the target. Then I must *deliberately* loosen up.

I am convinced that the difference between the ordinary good rifleman and the superlative one is not that the latter has better eyes or muscles, or is smarter or better-looking, but simply that he can relax, even when picking off the biggest buck he ever saw at 350 yards or firing the last shot in a string when a 5 will mean a win and a 4 a tie. The more relaxed the rifle shot is, the steadier he tends to be and the more he can concentrate on a gentle trigger squeeze.

If a man misses a standing buck from the sitting position up to 250 yards, it's not because he couldn't hold properly but because he yanked his shot. Really wild shots always come from a yank. Sometimes, of course, a shot may "get away" from a shooter; that's because the rifle goes off when the squeeze is in progress, but not at the precise moment the shooter wants it to. Such a shot hits out of the black on the target range, or out of the vital area on game, but the deviation won't be very wide. The lad who misses his game by feet or who knocks out 3's and 2's on a target, or misses it completely, does so *not* because he cannot hold steady but because he is yanking the trigger. Under any conditions, it must always be squeezed gently. A good rifleman may squeeze it *fast,* but he squeezes it, never yanks it!

Offhand

It is a curious fact that 75 percent—maybe 90 percent—of all rifle shooting is done in the unsteadiest of all positions: offhand, or standing, or "shooting off your hind legs like a man," as the late Harry Pope, dean of barrelmakers, used to describe it.

Prone is the easiest position in which to shoot accurately, sitting is next. Kneeling is fairly tough, and offhand is the toughest of all. It is the position for the expert, and yet it is the one that the beginner will instinctively use if he does not have the advice of a more experienced shooter.

Offhand, then, is the position of the cool, precise, skillful shot—and also the position of the tyro. A man is usually pretty good at offhand—or pretty bad.

While shooting on the hind legs is a tough position, a man who cannot do it pretty well is not a good all-around shot. On one hand, it is a highly specialized position for competitive target shooting; on the other, an exceedingly useful position for the big-game hunter. I am a firm believer in never taking a shot at game offhand if it is possible to plant the posterior firmly on mother earth and take a shot from the much steadier sitting position. Nevertheless, mixed big-game hunting abounds in situations where the shot must be taken from the hind legs or not at all.

In many cases there is no time to get into a steadier position. Very often high grass or low brush makes it impossible to see when sitting or even kneeling. In forest and jungle hunting, the great majority of shots are taken from the hind legs. Even on the plains and in relatively open mountain and canyon country, situations often arise where the hunter has no choice but to shoot offhand. Thus it's in order for anyone who wants to be an adequate game shot to learn to shoot on his hind legs.

The offhand shooter finds that he faces two tough problems. The first, of course, is holding his musket with some degree of steadiness. Obviously the steadier a rifle is, the easier it is to shoot. If a rifle did not wobble at all and if the trigger could be let off without introducing any movement, accurate shooting would be very easy. Sad to say, though, no one can hold a rifle with absolute steadiness, even from a good prone position with tight sling—or even a 15-pound rifle on a bench rest. I said *absolute* steadiness.

Offhand is the least steady of all positions because the rifle has from 4 to 5 feet of wobbling, quivering, throbbing human muscles and nerves between it and the ground. Anyone who begins offhand practice under the illusion that he can hold the rifle still is in for some bitter disillusionment, because he'll soon find out his sights wobble and sway like a tree in the wind.

The best the offhand shooter can do is hold his rifle *fairly* steady, so as to slow down and tame the oscillations of the muzzle, because, obviously, the narrower the arc of the swing, the smaller the group on the target.

The old-time schuetzen and the present-day free-rifle shooters licked this swinging-muzzle business by using a very heavy (and also muzzle-heavy) rifle and firing it from a hip rest. The rifle with the long, heavy barrel swings more slowly and in a smaller arc than the light sporting rifle that is also muzzle-light. Some of the old-time schuetzen men who had ponderous .32/40's and .38/55's, with palm rests and special offhand stocks, shot groups at 200 yards that would knock your eye out. I have seen groups made with iron sights that would compare favorably with the best made by a crack shot from the sitting position with a modern, scope-sighted big-game rifle with tight sling.

However, no hunter will want to lug around a 12- or 14-pound free rifle equipped with a palm rest, nor will he favor the old hip-rest position that is still used in free-rifle competition and four-position small-bore shooting. You might use the hip rest once in a great while for a long offhand shot at game, but it is an exceedingly inflexible position, useless for a moving target. I'd call it a position strictly for target work, and the game hunter without target ambitions should not spend much time practicing it.

Beginners in offhand shooting make some basic mistakes in position. For one thing, they hold the left hand too far out on the fore-end and usually to one side, instead of underneath. That's like trying to carry a tray of dishes at arm's length—a tiring, unsteady, even painful position. The steadiest offhand position is with the *heel* of the palm just forward of the trigger guard on the magazine floorplate, and with the left elbow under the rifle. Then the weight of the rifle is supported on a straight line, much as a waiter's up-thrust arm supports a heavy tray. Such a position supports the rifle as steadily as it is possible to do so *offhand*—making the weight hang forward and slowing down the rate of oscillation.

In the offhand position, shooter stands almost facing the target, legs spread comfortably apart, weight balanced against that of the rifle. The left hand supports the rifle with the heel of the palm. The left elbow is directly under the rifle. The upper arm should be horizontal and the elbow level with the top of the shoulder. Southpaw shooters simply read "left" for "right" in these instructions, as shown in the photo at right.

For quick shooting at nearby game or at any running animal the left hand should be moved farther out—perhaps 9 or 10 inches in front of the trigger guard; then it's not necessary to get the elbow clear under the fore-end. Such a hold gives more leverage and enables the shooter to swing faster. But it is *never* necessary for the left hand to grasp the rifle clear out near the fore-end tip.

The upper right arm should be horizontal and the elbow level with the top of the shoulder. The butt should rest on the pad of muscle formed at the junction of the shoulder and the upper arm when the arm is lifted, and not down on the collar bone. The rifle merely rests on the left hand, with the right hand on the pistol grip holding the butt firmly against the shoulder. Your weight should be evenly distributed on your two feet; an imaginary line drawn across the toes would point slightly to the left of the target.

The rifleman should stand in an easy, *relaxed* position, with his weight bal-

anced against that of the rifle. If he is tense, if he tries to stop the swing and
the wobble of the rifle by main strength, he will introduce new shakes and
tremors. To be relaxed is of utmost importance in any position, but nowhere is
it more important than in the offhand.

Many uninstructed rifle shots make the mistake of trying to let the shot off
with the *tip* of the index finger. That is O.K. with a hair or set trigger. But
with the ordinary single trigger, use the pad of muscle between the first and
second joints.

Good offhand shooting is half good position, half good trigger control. If a
man could hold his rifle with absolute steadiness, the control of his trigger
would not be of much importance as long as he could get the shot off without
disturbing the aim. On the other hand, if a man had perfect trigger control
and could let his shot off *exactly* when he wished, position would not be so important; while his sights might swing all over the place he would shoot only
when they were aligned on the target.

The beginner should squeeze his trigger so gradually that he doesn't know
when his rifle is going off; so should the lad with the tendency to flinch. Many
fine shooters claim they are always surprised when their rifles go off, even from
the offhand position—that they simply increase the pressure when the sights
look right and hold it when they don't. One Army training manual says that
the man who doesn't know when his rifle is going off is always a good shot, the
man who does know is a bum shot and a flincher.

A great many citizens, including your correspondent, are skeptical about
this. In the first place, the free-rifle competitors, the world's greatest offhand
target shots, use set triggers that will be touched off if a man who has been
eating onions breathes on them from 6 feet away. It's a cinch that these free-
rifle men know when their muskets are going off. In the second place, I believe
most people who do much shooting can quickly feel out a trigger, so that
about the third time they let it off they *know* the exact amount of pressure required to send it. For my part, I cannot shoot offhand worth a hoot unless I
know when the rifle's going off.

The good offhand shot is the lad who can squeeze out all the pull but two
or three ounces and then, when his sights hang momentarily in the right
place, let off the balance. This fine trigger control—this ability to make the
rifle go off at the right moment without disturbing the aim—is what distin-
guishes the crack offhand shooter from the ordinary one. It is something that
can be acquired only by practice, by constantly squeezing off from a good position and *calling the shot*—remembering exactly where the sights rested when
the trigger finally let go and the firing pin fell. The nice part of it is that about
90 percent of this skill can be obtained by dry firing.

The Kneeling Position

Kneeling is one of the standard positions in target shooting, but it is a position that does not have much to recommend it to the hunter. As I write this I

cannot remember a single head of game I have shot from the kneeling position in many years.

Kneeling does have the advantage of putting the muzzle of the rifle and the eye of the shooter about one foot higher than does the much steadier sitting position. In low bushes (such as the sage that grows on the antelope flats of Wyoming) this might be an advantage for a quick shot. Another advantage to kneeling is that on ground covered by thorns or sharp stones it enables the rifleman to assume a position somewhat steadier than offhand without injuring his posterior.

The kneeling position is quicker to assume than the sitting position, particularly for the man who isn't used to going into the sit fast. Still another advantage is that in combat a man can rise quicker to defend himself or to move than he can from the sit.

The good kneeling position puts the shooter lower than the position most untrained men assume. The buttock rests on the right heel and the left arm is hooked over the left knee.

The late Capt. E. C. Crossman, rifle columnist for *Outdoor Life,* who died in 1939, says of the kneeling position in *Military and Sporting Rifle Shooting*—"A position nearly without merit, but more steady than offhand, offers less target in war, permits seeing over higher obstacles than sitting and is a bit more quickly assumed. Inferior in nearly every respect to sitting except for one foot of height and a slightly greater speed of assuming."

Back in the 1930's when my wife used to hunt jackrabbits with me on the Arizona desert, she often assumed an odd position called squatting. From time to time this has been taught in the navy and, I believe, during World War II in the army. The shooter keeps his feet flat on the ground, keeps his fanny off the ground, and rests his elbows on his knees. I could never hit much from this position, but my wife shot well from it. In it the shooter is precariously balanced and often recoil knocks him backward. This is a freak position.

If shooting from a benchrest is rated 100 percent in that a good bench-rest shot can get about 100 percent of the accuracy out of a rifle and the cartridge that is in it, prone could be rated about 80 percent (with some prone experts better), sitting perhaps 60 percent, kneeling about 45–50 percent, and offhand maybe 35–40 percent. These figures are to give a general idea. Some people are better in one position than in others. My wife, as I have said, used to do very good shooting in the squatting position. She would probably rate it not far under sitting. My own shooting from the squat would be about like offhand.

The skillful rifleman should be able to combine any of these positions with a rest. I have used the aid of stones and trees in the standing position, stones and limbs from kneeling and sitting, stones padded with down jackets, hats, bed rolls, binocular cases, and all manner of things from prone.

The longest shot I ever made at a game animal at a distance measured off by pacing was at an elk. I rested a scope-sighted .270 over a rock padded by a

To assume the kneeling position, the shooter faces half right from the target and gets down on his right knee (if he's right-handed), and sits on the heel or inside of his right foot. The left elbow rests across the right knee (in the photo, recoil has pushed it slightly back), and should be under the barrel for a firm support.

Whenever possible, use a rest when shooting game. Here the author gains steadiness by supporting his rifle on a log with a rolled jacket for padding. Never rest the fore-end on a hard surface.

When padding is not available, the rifle should be supported by the left hand, and the forearm rested on the rock or log.

Some varmint hunters and other long-range riflemen install a foldable bipod under the rifle's fore-end so they'll always have a steady shooting rest. There are bipods with telescoping legs to be used from either the prone or sitting position. When not in use, the bipod folds almost flat against the stock.

down jacket and sat on another rock. It was like shooting from a bench rest. As near as two companions and I could determine by pacing over a fairly level basin, the elk was about 600 yards from the point where I shot. At any rate I held for 600 yards and hit the elk.

The experienced big-game shot always tries to place his shot exactly and his ideal is to kill with one shot. To do this he assumes the steadiest possible position. He never shoots from the standing position if he can sit, and he never sits if he can shoot prone or from a rest.

The man who takes the steadiest position open to him seldom gets into trouble with dangerous game. Let's illustrate: Of two Alaskan brown bears I have shot one was killed as I lay in the rain on a beach while the great bear walked toward me. I was using a standard prone position for steadiness as well as to be inconspicuous. The bear was 65 yards away. My second brown bear was shot prone with a rest over a log at probably about 240 yards. Of the four African lions I have shot one was taken from the standing position with a rest over an ant hill at about 100 yards, another from the sitting position with a rest over a low limb of a small tree, another from the sitting position, and the fourth running like a rabbit and from offhand. Of the dozen or so grizzlies I have knocked over eleven were shot from the sitting position and one from offhand. The experienced hunter tries never to give the game a chance. By that I mean a chance to escape wounded and to die after long suffering. The expert hunter tries to assume the steadiest possible position and to kill cleanly and quickly with one shot.

Shooting with a Sling

There are three types of rifle slings in use in this country—the two-piece, the one-piece adjustable, and the single carrying strap. The two-piece sling is simply a narrow edition of the military sling. The front portion forms the loop into which the upper arm is inserted. It consists of a strip of leather about 45 inches long, with two "keepers" and a claw hook. The rear portion of the sling is 23 inches in length and is known as the tail or tailpiece. It likewise has a claw hook for adjustment, and it is attached to the front or "loop" portion with a metal loop which is a part of it.

The adjustable one-piece sling is a single strip of leather usually about 52 inches in length with a sliding buckle or claw hook at one end. The sling also has one or two leather keepers and sometimes a leather lacing. This type is very popular. Often, the part of the sling that rides on the rifleman's shoulder as he walks flares out, the way the hood of a cobra snake flares. A "cobra" sling is comfortable and helps to keep the rifle from slipping, especially if the inner surface of the wide over-the-shoulder portion is faced with rough leather or some other non-slip material.

The carrying strap is just that and nothing more—a strip of leather for carrying the rifle. The length is not readily adjustable.

Slings are attached to the rifles by swivels on the fore-end and on the buttstock. Some factory rifles come equipped with permanent swivel-bows, which are perfectly all right except that you can't take the sling off the rifle without a lot of work.

With quick-detachable swivels—such as are furnished on many factory and most custom rifles—the sling can be quickly removed. Then the rifle can be carried in a saddle scabbard with no chance of the sling's catching on a snag and yanking the rifle out. It is also convenient to remove the sling when the rifle is put away in the gun cabinet.

Another advantage of quick-detachable swivels is that the same sling with the same adjustment can be used on several rifles, provided the swivel bases are the same distance apart.

Adjust a sling—and carry it that way—so that it is right not only for carrying but also for shooting from sitting, which in open-country and mountain hunting is the most generally used position. When so adjusted, the sling is from 33 to 36 inches long, depending on how far the swivels are apart. (This length is for the sling strap itself in case of permanent swivels, or for strap *and* swivels, in the case of the quick-detachable outfit.) The sling can quickly be lengthened or shortened, of course, by sliding the buckle or casting loose the claw hook and putting it in another set of holes. This length, however, is about right for carrying.

How far the end of the two-piece sling's loop should be from the forward swivel depends on the shooter's build. The loop should be adjusted exactly right. If the loop is too tight it is difficult to get into and clumsy to use. If it is too loose, it is not of much help in firm holding.

Some experimenting will show just how much loop you need. At first, adjust it so that in the sitting position it is almost necessary, when the arm is in

HOW TO USE A SLING

Using a two-piece Whelen-type hunting sling in the tight-sling position, Jack O'Connor turns loop to the left and puts his arm through.

Loop is slid high on the left arm and is tightened there by pulling the leather keeper close to the arm.

Shooter puts left hand under sling and slides it hard against the front swivel. Fore-end rests in the palm of the hand.

Sling should be so tight that the butt has to be lifted to the right shoulder with the right hand.

Sitting position with a sling is rock steady. Both elbows should be over the knees with the flats of upper arms against flats of shins.

the loop, to seat the buttplate at the right shoulder with the right hand. For target shooting, this is the correct adjustment; but for sporting use the loop should be a shade looser for the sake of speed.

In the two-piece "Whelen-type" sling, the loop is adjusted by putting the claw hook in the proper pair of holes until the length is just right. Sometimes it is necessary to punch new holes for absolute comfort and perfection. For sporting use, it is also a pious idea to lace the loop portion of the sling together just behind the hook, for the hook sometimes has a way of falling out. Length overall is, of course, obtained by placement of the claw hook in the holes in the tailpiece of the sling.

To use this tight-sling position when on the sit, first hold the rifle up, then give the loop a full quarter turn to the left. Now thrust the left arm through the loop, between the keepers, as far as it will go. With the loop high around the upper arm, tighten the keepers until the loop is snug. Now bring the left hand around to the left of the sling and up against the forward swivel, with the fore-end right against the palm. Now, with the right hand either at the grip or at the toe of the stock, thrust the butt up against the right shoulder. Sit facing at an angle of about 45 degrees away from the target, with body well forward, and the left elbow well over the left knee, so the shin is against the bottom of the upper arm.

The position may at first seem a bit strained, particularly if the loop is too tight. If so, it will feel that way and your back will be too nearly upright; you should shift your lacings to a set of holes farther back. If the loop is too loose, the position will feel wobbly, and you should move the lacings forward.

With the sling correctly adjusted, the position should feel very steady even with the right hand completely away from the grip and the left hand against the front swivel but not grasping the fore-end.

Tremor is introduced, and the best shooting absolutely cannot be done unless the left hand is always *hard* against the swivel—so hard that in a long match a big shooting glove has to be worn to protect the hand from a bad beating. For hunting, however, the shooting glove is of course unnecessary. Place the swivel farther back, if you cannot get the hand hard against it.

From such a position a good shot with a scope-sighted rifle who is willing to do some practicing but who makes no pretense at being a superman should keep three out of four shots in a 10-inch circle at 300 yards, and the others close. To a shooter like that a standing deer at 300 yards is simply cold turkey, as he will almost never miss the large chest area. Likewise the chance that a chuck or a jackrabbit at that distance will live to see his great-grandchildren are definitely not too good.

The one-piece adjustable sling is something else again. The overall length is obtained, of course, by the position of the buckle or claw hook. With this sling, too, you can adjust the loop for tight-sling shooting, but few hunters bother these days because it takes a fair bit of time to get into this target-shooting position. Most hunters who use the sling at all for offhand shots employ the

To use the hasty-sling shooting position, thrust your left arm (or right arm if you're a southpaw) between sling and rifle, then back around and through the sling. In effect, you've wrapped the sling around your "off" (forward) arm and when you push that hand toward the front swivel, the sling will tighten, creating a steadying tension.

so-called "hasty" sling position. It isn't quite as steady as tight-sling shooting but it lets you make a shot very quickly.

To use the hasty sling, hold the rifle up with your right hand, letting the sling dangle. Thrust your left arm between sling and rifle from left to right. Then bring your left hand around and back through the sling, and grasp the rifle's fore-end. Push your left hand forward toward the swivel, and the sling will tighten, creating a tension that steadies the rifle.

3

Sighting In the Rifle

MANY RIFLE USERS look on the adjustment of sights as something beyond the ability of the ordinary man—an art requiring superior technical skill and knowledge, a mysterious task to be accomplished at the factory or by a gunsmith. I know many fairly successful hunters who would no more attempt to sight in their own rifles than try to overhaul an automobile motor.

It is true that some rifles are carefully sighted in at the factory. All would be well then *if* the user were content to shoot the same weight of bullet and the same powder charge, over the same range, for the rest of his life . . . and *if* the rifle never changed its point of impact . . . and *if* the rifle owner and the factory expert both saw the sight and held the rifle alike.

What actually happens? First off, bullets of different makes but of the same weight and velocity tend to group differently—hit at a different place on the target. Different bullet weight complicates things further. A .30/06, for example, may put one weight of bullet as much as 2 feet lower at 200 yards than another. *Usually* the heavier, slower bullet will strike lower, but sometimes, with a freakishly vibrating barrel, it will strike higher. I have seen rifles sighted in with the 150-grain M-2 .30/06 military load (at a muzzle velocity of about 2800 foot-seconds) that threw the commercial 150-grain bullets (loaded to something over 2900) far enough from point of aim to miss a buck at 200 yards.

For the most part, factory big-game rifles are sighted to hit point of aim at 100 yards. A man who hunts the open mountains of the West isn't going to do much good with a rifle so sighted—and neither is the chap trying to knock over a deer across a ravine through thin timber and leafless brush, when shooting from one Pennsylvania hillside to another.

No two men will see their sights precisely alike, either. With open sights one man may habitually take a fine bead, another a coarse one. With a peep sight, one may prefer to aim with the top of his front bead, whereas another likes to aim so that his bullet strikes where the center of the bead rests.

This difference in the way two people "see" their sights is most marked with open sights, least so with a scope. Actually, with a scope of good definition and no parallax, two people will aim about the same. But with open sights two good shots will often get very different points of impact.

This phenomenon—where the same rifle shoots to different points of impact when used by different people—is partly due to the way the sights are used. It is also partly due to the way the rifle is held. One chap may habitually cant his rifle a bit to the right, the next a bit to the left. A third man may keep it precisely straight up and down, as all shooters are supposed to do. All this affects point of impact. Likewise one chap may hold his weapon loosely, another tightly.

Optical collimator houses a lens and grid, and is affixed over the muzzle by slipping a mandrel into the bore. Adjust the scope or rear sight so you're lined up properly on the grid, then remove the collimator and your first shot will be on the paper. Shown here is a Tasco collimator; other models are supplied by several manufacturers, including Bushnell and Redfield.

All this dull stuff adds up to this: there is but one person who can do an absolutely 100 percent job of sighting in a rifle and that is the chap who is going to use it. He should do so when he acquires a new rifle or when he installs new sights on an old one—and he should also check his sights before every hunting season. It is entirely possible for a warping fore-end to throw the point of impact far enough off to cause a miss even at relatively short range. It is also possible for a shift in brand of ammunition, powder charge, or bullet weight to cause the point of impact to vary and result in a miss.

Every big-game rifle should be sighted in, with the exact load that will be used on game, for the most useful range. And it should be finally checked in the position that will be used in the field. The man who sights in from prone with a tight sling may be in for some unpleasant surprises if he has to try to knock off a trophy buck from the offhand position at 200 yards.

Let's see how we go about this sighting-in business. If a new receiver sight or scope has been installed, probably the first thing to do is to try the simple but mysterious-sounding stunt called "bore-sighting"—that is, if you own a bolt-action rifle from which the bolt can be removed, letting you look right down the barrel. You can't bore-sight a pump or a lever-action rifle without an optical collimator. This handy device is used by gunsmiths and by many shooters for bore-sighting. It's a tubular or rectangular housing with a lens and a grid, and it fits over the rifle's muzzle by means of a short, adjustable mandrel that slides into the bore and is then tightened in place so the grid won't shift. Expandable or interchangeable mandrels permit use with various calibers. In effect, the grid substitutes for a target as you would see it through the bore with the bolt removed. You adjust your scope or rear sight to align on a central vertical grid line for windage and on one of several horizontal lines for elevation at a given distance.

The use of a collimator doesn't replace the entire procedure of sighting in; it's not that precise, as a rule. But it will put your first shot on the paper, thus saving a lot of time and ammunition. After that, only minor adjustments will be needed. Several scope manufacturers market collimators, and they're not expensive.

The way to bore-sight without an optical collimator is to remove the bolt, then put the rifle in a vise or on a box with V's cut into it. Next adjust it so that some prominent object can be seen right in the middle of the bore as you look through it. Once you get the object lined up, adjust the receiver sight or scope until it too lines up exactly with the object.

Now, working this way, a man can align the reticule of a scope on a .30/06 rifle so that it rests about 3 inches below the spot at which the bore points and (theoretically) be pretty well sighted-in for 200 yards. *But* the old devil barrel whip, or vibration, usually throws the sighting off. Sometimes a bore-sighted rifle will be right on the button, but usually one cannot expect anything better than to be on the paper of a 100-yard small-bore target at, let us say, 100 yards.

That's the point: the bore-sighted rifle will be on the paper—and you'll have put it there without burning up any cartridges at 70 cents a burn. From then on you need only to refine your sighting.

The next step with a bolt-action rifle, and the *first* step with a lever or pump, is to shoot at a distance short enough to insure the bullets' hitting the target. Nothing will drive a man to the bottle quicker than to put up a target at 100 or 200 yards, fire a string of shots, and then discover that he had not connected once—and knows exactly as much as when he started out. He should do the preliminary shooting at short range, so that no matter how cockeyed the sights are, he'll hit the target somewhere and have some idea whether his rifle is shooting high or low, right or left.

Because the bullet starts out *below* the line of sight, crosses it rising, and crosses it once more coming down, it is wise to choose the range at which the bullet first crosses the line of sight for preliminary sighting. With an iron-sighted rifle, this distance is 12½ yards; with a scope-sighted job, it's 25 yards. So do your preliminary sighting at 12½-yard range with the first, at 25 yards with the second.

Let us suppose that we have just put a new scope on a bolt-action big-game rifle. As the first step, we have bore-sighted it and know the scope and barrel are looking pretty much in the same direction. Now we set up a target of some sort. It should be large enough to catch all shots, even though the sight may be poorly lined up. It should also have a definite aiming point. A target 24 x 24 inches with a 1-inch bull will do.

I usually shoot this course from the sitting position, firing two shots as carefully as I can. If they hit close together, I take the midpoint between them as the point of impact. If they do not I suspect a flinch, fire another shot, and take as the point of impact a spot midway between the closer hits. Usually, if a man is a fairly good shot, his first two shots at 25 yards should almost touch.

Now we look at the target. In this case, the bullets have struck 1 inch low and 3 inches to the right. Now we have got somewhere—we have established the point of impact. Often after bore-sighting, we find that we are very close to the point of aim. But sometimes, because of barrel vibration, we are off. Now the thing to do is to make the point of impact identical with the point of aim.

With a telescopic sight, or with a receiver sight calibrated in minutes of angle or in fractions thereof, this operation is simple.

A minute of angle (for all practical purposes) represents a spread of 1 inch at 100 yards, 2 inches at 200 yards, etc. At 25 yards—the range at which we have been shooting—a minute of angle has a value of ¼ inch, since 25 yards is one fourth of 100. Similarly, at 50 yards a minute of angle is worth ½ inch. (If we were tuning up an iron-sighted rifle at 12½ yards, the minute of angle would have a value of ⅛ inch.)

Now for adjustments. All modern American hunting-type scopes with internal adjustments for windage and elevation are graduated on the adjustment dials in minutes of angle and are marked for the direction the point of impact will move—U or UP for the direction the dial must be turned to raise

Adjusting the elevation dial on a telescope sight with a coin. Telescope sights with adjustments for elevation and windage have dials graduated in minutes of angle and fractions thereof. Each minute of angle represents a spread of 1 inch at 100 yards, 2 inches at 200 yards, etc.

the point of impact. It is obvious that turning the dial in the opposite direction will lower the point of impact. The "windage" dial for horizontal adjustment of the point of impact is always marked with an arrow for direction—R for right, L for left.

Some hunting-type scopes "click" in half or quarter minutes of angle. Others do not. All are graduated in minutes of angle. Some foreign scopes are neither marked for direction nor graduated in minutes of angle, and these make sighting in difficult.

At one time, target scopes (like very old-fashioned hunting scopes) had no internal adjustments. The rear portions of mounts for these target scopes had micrometer adjustment knobs, which were turned to move the scope tube. Anyone using an old scope and mount of this type must remember the sighting-in rule: the point of impact moves the direction the rear sight is moved, opposite to the way the front sight is moved. In the case of the target scope the ocular end of the scope acts like the rear sight. So if you turn the windage knob of the target mount clockwise the rear of the scope tube is moved to the left and the point of impact moves to the left. If you turn the elevation knob clockwise, the rear of the scope tube is depressed and the point of impact is lowered.

In the past, some hunting-type scopes were made with no internal adjustments. These were used with adjustable mounts. At one time hunting scopes were made in this country and imported from Europe with adjustment for elevation only. These required mounts with provision for lateral adjustment. The now obsolete but excellent Tilden mounts and the currently manufactured Redfield Jr., Leupold and Buehler have opposite screws in the rear portion of the base which make lateral (windage) adjustment possible. But nearly all modern scopes employ internal adjustments, a much more desirable arrangement.

Receiver sights are also graduated in minutes of angle. The Lyman 48 has ¼ minute clicks, as do most other receiver sights. Each manufacturer's literature tells the shooter how his particular sight is graduated.

Now, for the sake of illustration, let us go back to the target we have shot at. We have found that at 25 yards our bullets average striking 1 inch low and 3 inches to the right. Correction is very simple. We must move *up* 4 minutes of angle and *left* twelve minutes (again, at 25 yards a minute of angle is worth ¼ inch).

If we were using an iron-sighted rifle and shooting at 12½ yards, we would have to double our correction, because at that distance the minute would be worth only ⅛ inch. We would come up 8 minutes, to the left 24 minutes.

But suppose that our rifle wears an open factory sight which is rigid laterally, preventing easy right or left adjustment, and has only notches in a slide for elevation. Precise sight adjustment now becomes difficult indeed. If the musket is shooting to the right, all one can do is take a hammer and a punch and knock the rear sight over to the left in its slot, remembering again the old rule that one moves the rear sight in the same direction one wants the point of

Receiver sights also have windage and elevation adjustments graduated in minutes of angle. A screwdriver is required to adjust this Lyman 48 sight.

impact to move, or moves the front sight in the opposite direction. That holds, too, when the shooter wants the bullet to strike higher on the target; he raises the rear sight or lowers the front one.

This crude open arrangement is a sorry excuse for a sight, and the most expensive of all sights to line up properly. Often the rifle will shoot too high with the rear sight in one notch, too low with it in the next. Then all one can do is file down the higher notch. It is not unusual for a rifle to shoot too high with the rear sight in the lowest notch. Then the only thing to do is buy a higher front sight. Meanwhile, round after round of expensive ammunition is used up.

I have seen fancy foreign rifles with a whole parade of open leaf sights as unadjustable as the Statue of Liberty and marked 100, 200, and 300. Such a gimmick makes me crawl into a corner and have a good cry. Presumably the leaves are marked for hundreds of yards. But with what weight of bullet? At what velocity? With what person shooting?

How any real rifleman could endure such a sight I cannot say. It may look as exotic as all get out. It will get by for short-range shooting at large and patient mammals, but for any precision or long-range shooting it is almost worthless.

We have seen that no two shooters see their sights (particularly open sights) exactly alike. We have seen that no two shooters hold just alike. We have also seen that rifles shoot to different points of impact with different bullet weights, different powder charges, and that with the same load the point of impact may change if the fore-end warps up against the barrel.

So the best investment a rifleman can make is an easily adjustable sight, be it scope or receiver sight. He'll save its cost many times over in ammunition if he really wants to keep his rifle hitting on the button.

But to get back to our scope-sighted rifle. Now we have it hitting right at point of aim at 25 yards (or our iron-sighted job laying them in at 12½ yards). Our next step is to check this sighting at a longer range—100 yards, let us say—and if necessary to refine it further, since an error made at 25 yards (and not particularly noticeable) is multiplied four times at 100 yards. (If it's made at 12½ yards it is multiplied eight times.)

The man who is a pretty good prone or sitting shot can do his 100-yard shooting in one of those positions. But he'll do better from a sandbagged bench rest or from the prone with the fore-end of his rifle resting on something soft, such as a rolled-up sleeping bag. When sighting in, you want to remove as much human error as possible.

A scope-sighted .270 firing the 130-grain factory load at a muzzle velocity of 3110 foot-seconds and putting bullets to point of aim at 25 yards, will send them 3 inches high at 100 yards, about 4 inches high at 200, on the button at 275, and about 2 inches low at 300. Point of impact of the 150-grain .30/06 bullet first crossing the line of aim at 25 yards, is almost 3 inches high at 100 yards, a bit over 2 inches high at 200, at point of aim (for the second time) at 250. With loads in the 2700 foot-seconds bracket, like the 180-grain .30/06 or 165-grain .308 Winchester, the bullet crosses the line of aim the second time at about 225.

The iron-sighted rifle in the 2000–2200 foot-seconds class, like the .30/30, .35 Remington, or .375 Winchester, and sighted in to put its bullets at point of aim the first time at 12½ yards, will group about 2 inches high at 100 yards, be at point of aim again at 150, and 4 or 5 inches low at 200.

The sight-ins I've given for scope-sighted rifles are about right for fairly open country, where the shots run long. Those for the iron-sighted rifles are suitable for wooded country, where shots tend to be at short and medium ranges.

A rise in trajectory at midrange of even 4 inches is not excessive, since even a small deer or antelope measures from 14 to 16 inches from top of shoulder to bottom of chest. A 2-inch rise at midrange can absolutely be disregarded for woods hunting; not one man in a thousand can shoot well enough offhand to know if his rifle is hitting 1 inch high at 100 yards or not.

But if the average range for deer is about 100 yards in wooded country, why have a rifle sighted in for 150? Well, now and then any hunter will have to take a shot across a ravine at 200 yards or so. If our .30/30 man is sighted in for 100 yards and he shoots right at his deer, his bullet will fall about 8 inches at 200 yards and he'll probably miss. But if he is sighted for 150, his bullet will fall only 4 inches at 200 and he'll hit.

Special types of hunting require different adjustment. The chap who hunts African elephants in heavy brush and wants to drive his bullet into the brain, and has to shoot into an area about the size of his palm, should be very carefully sighted in for 50 yards. With cartridges of the 2000–2200 foot-sec-

For final sighting in at 100 yards, it is advisable to support the rifle on an improvised rest or, better yet, a sandbagged pedestal on a benchrest.

onds class used on elephants the bullet will be slightly above the line of bore up to 50 yards, slightly below to 100 yards. Such a hunter would probably never shoot at over 100 yards.

The varmint man, even with a cartridge of ultra-high velocity like the .220 Swift, should probably never have a trajectory rise of over 2 inches, because most varmints are small marks and powerfully easy to miss. Some skilled varmint hunters limit midrange rise to 1 inch.

Once the rifleman is pretty well sighted in and knows where he is hitting, he should by all means do some practicing—the more the better. In the open, mountainous West, he probably ought to specialize in the sitting position because it is relatively steady, quick to assume, and practical for shooting from hillside to hillside. In the East he probably should do most of his practice on his hind legs, because that's the way he'll shoot in the woods.

THE CHANGING POINT OF IMPACT

Any change of alignment of the sights, either iron or glass, will of course change the point of impact, often sufficiently to cause a miss on even a large and close-by target. One chap I talked to last season missed his dream buck because in pulling his rifle from the scabbard he wound the windage screw of his receiver sight out. The buck was running away from him and every shot went to one side. He found out what had happened, corrected his windage by bore sighting, then went on and got himself a trophy very nearly as good as the one he missed.

If Old Betsy starts shooting off, the first thing to examine is the sights. Have they been damaged by a fall? Have they been moved? Are they loose?

A joker to watch out for in a bolt-action rifle is the loosening up of the guard screws. You should always keep them tight, and always check the front screw *first*. It is surprising how much loose ones will change the point of impact.

Another unpredictable little item that changes point of impact is the warping of the wooden stock. A sporting-weight barrel is very flexible, by the way. Put one in a vise and you can bend it perceptibly with a finger. What a wooden fore-end that warps after you've sighted in does to it is plenty. Warped hard *against* the barrel, the fore-end makes the rifle shoot high. Warped *away* from the barrel, it makes the rifle shoot low.

Stock blanks should always be cut so that the grain does not run parallel to the barrel, but at an angle. This weakens the fore-end so that it cannot exert so much upward pressure.

Warping stocks are responsible for most of the stories one hears about rifles changing their point of impact with changes in altitude. The sportsman lives in a nice, dry, steam-heated apartment, where he keeps his rifle in the closet in the spare bedroom. He takes a trip to the mountains of British Columbia, where the base camp is beside a trout stream and just across from a muskeg meadow. Humidity is much greater than in his city apartment, and the fore-end warps up against the barrel. When he shoots his musket he finds that the bullets fly high.

Now and then a telescope sight with internal adjustments for both windage and elevation will go haywire, for such adjustments are of necessity complicated and often flimsy. When that happens in the hunting field, you're really behind the 8 ball.

The citizen who invests important money in a hunting trip is what is known as a chump if he dashes forth with but one set of sights on his artillery. If but one rifle is to be taken, it is a very pertinent idea to have some provision for auxiliary sights. Some scope mounts have auxiliary peeps. Open sights can be left on the rifle when swing-away or quick-detachable mounts are used, and even receiver sights are perfectly practical. Also available are raised "see-through" mounts that let you peer under the scope to use the iron sights. With such mounts you must cock your head up slightly to aim through the scope and down slightly for the iron sights. Still, the arrangement works well enough if you don't mind a high-riding scope and can keep your cheek pressed down against the comb.

Another possibility is to have two scopes for the same rifle—something which is possible with a good many mounts.

Even better is the notion of taking a spare rifle, for then the hunter is protected not only against sights going sour but against changes of point of impact that result from warpage in the stock.

While we are on this subject, let's not forget that switching bullet weights, amount and kind of powder, and sometimes even brands of ammunition can sometimes result in surprising changes in point of impact. The man who blithely changes bullet weights will more often than not let himself in for some surprising misses.

Some calibers are very poor in maintaining the same point of impact with different bullet weights. On the other hand, certain individual rifles in some calibers will shoot almost any reasonable full-power load to approximately the same point of impact up to 200 yards. Why? I don't know.

Let's lay down a few rules to take the sting out of this tendency rifles have to stop shooting where they look.

1. Never start off on a trip without carefully sighting in.

2. Never change ammunition without checking point of impact.

3. Always keep screws tight.

4. Never let the rifle lie around where the stock can absorb moisture.

5. Always check the point of impact at the end of a long trip into hunting country.

6. If you have but one rifle, see that it is equipped with auxiliary sights.

7. Always take a spare rifle on a long and expensive trip.

8. If you miss an easy shot that you have called as being good, find out at once what is wrong. It may be you, but then again it may be the rifle!

4

Trajectory and Range Estimation

WHEN A BULLET leaves the barrel of a rifle it immediately begins to fall from the *line of bore,* although at the same time it is rising toward the *line of sight.* All bullets are acted on by the force of gravity. A 150-grain 7 mm. Magnum bullet dropped from the hand will hit the ground at exactly the same time as the same bullet fired from a rifle with a muzzle velocity approaching 3200 foot-seconds, for both are free-falling bodies of the same weight and shape. If the same 7 mm. bullet could be speeded up to 4000 or even to 5000 foot-seconds it would also hit the ground at the same time. However, the faster the bullet travels the farther it goes in the interval that gravity is acting upon it.

The faster a bullet is traveling, the "flatter" the path of travel—that is, the less it falls for every foot of forward travel. No bullet flies flat, no matter how fast it is traveling, because all the time it is moving foward gravity is also pulling it down.

So the answer to the often-asked question as to how far such-and-such a bullet will travel without dropping is, "No distance at all." Near the muzzle where velocity is high the drop is very slight, but it is there just the same.

"Flatness" of trajectory depends on the initial velocity coupled with the shape and sectional density of the bullet. A long sharp-pointed bullet loses velocity more slowly than a short round-nosed bullet and hence shoots "flatter." And that last word, by the way, should read "more nearly flat" or "with a less-pronounced curve." To employ another popular term which doesn't mean much, such a bullet "carries up" better. A baseball thrown with the same speed as a tennis ball has a less curved trajectory because it has superior sectional density.

To get down to concrete instances, Remington used to load a round-nosed 110-grain bullet in .30/06 caliber at a muzzle velocity of 3350 foot-seconds. In spite of its high velocity this bullet had a more curved trajectory over 300 yards than did the Remington 150-grain Bronze Point bullet which left the muzzle at a velocity of about 400 foot-seconds less. The latter had better shape and sectional density—or, to employ a fancy term, a better ballistic coefficient. This is why using a lighter but faster bullet of the same caliber does not always pay off. In a given caliber, the shorter the bullet is the faster it loses velocity and the more pronounced its trajectory curve is.

Because gravity remains constant whereas velocity is not always falling off, the path of a bullet is a curve known as a parabola—NOT the arc of a circle as is often imagined. Consequently, the high point of the trajectory over any given range is not halfway but somewhat beyond. It is at about 110 yards over a 200-yard range, and at about 165 yards over 300 yards. The farther the bullet travels, the greater the drop.

This all may be on the technical side, but it shows three things: 1. Bullets are always falling. 2. Strictly speaking, no rifle is really "flat shooting." 3. High muzzle velocity is just one of the factors in a comparatively flat trajectory.

Trajectory curve of the .22 Long Rifle bullet in a rifle zeroed in at 75 yards. Bullet crosses line of sight at 10 yards, again at 75 yards. At 50 yards bullet is 1.3 inches above line of sight; at 100 yards it has dropped 4 inches below line of sight.

In order to compensate for the drop of the bullet, the rifle that's properly sighted in has the bore pointed *up*, as the rear sight is higher than the front sight. The line of sight, then, is an imaginary line running straight to the target. The line of bore is another imaginary straight line which intersects the line of sight and continues on. The trajectory curve is the path actually taken by the bullet. It crosses the line of sight once near the muzzle and once again at a considerable distance, but it never goes above the line of bore because the bullet falls continuously after it leaves the muzzle.

If a rifle is fired with its line of bore exactly horizontal, the bullet drop at 100 yards is amazing. Here are some figures: the .22 Long Rifle bullet, at standard muzzle velocity of 1140 foot-seconds, has a drop, or total fall below the line of bore, of 15 inches. The high-velocity version of the same bullet at 1280 foot-seconds has a total fall of 13 inches. Even the 170-grain .30/30 bullet, which steps along at the much faster rate of 2200 foot-seconds, falls 4 inches. The 180-grain .30/06 bullet is traveling at 2700 foot-seconds when it leaves the muzzle and drops 3 inches. Speed the bullet up to 3110 (as in the case with the 150-grain 7 mm. Remington Magnum bullet or the 130-grain .270) and the drop is only about 2 inches. Speed it up still more, until it is traveling like the .220 Swift or the 100-grain .270, and the total fall is only about 1 inch. *The faster a bullet travels the less it falls over a given range, because the less time gravity has to work on it.*

Now let's look at the total fall from line of bore of those bullets over 200 yards, at which distance they are slowing up more and gravity has had more chance to get in its dirty work:

.22 Long Rifle (standard speed) .... 55 in.
.22 Long Rifle (high velocity) .... 50 in.
.30/30 (170 gr.) .... 18 in.
.30/06 (180 gr.) .... 11 in.
.270 (130 gr.) .... 8 in.
.220 Swift (48 gr.) .... 4 in.

The thing to do in sighting in a rifle, then, is to jockey these figures of total fall, line of sight, and line of bore around until we have a useful combination. We tame this trajectory business and *learn* it thoroughly.

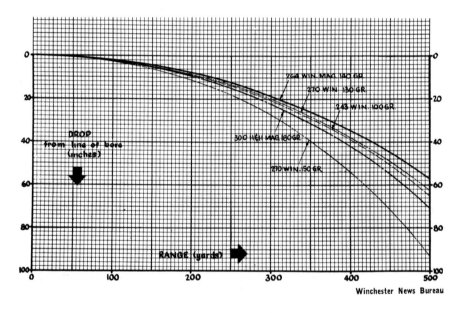

Winchester News Bureau

Game Cartridges: Drop from line of bore at different ranges.

In the case of the .22 with high-speed ammunition, for example, we learn that we tame the trajectory curve a bit by hoisting it above the line of sight, then letting it drop again. In a bore-sighted .22, at only 50 yards the total fall of the high-velocity Long Rifle bullet is 3 inches, and at that range you'd miss the head of a squirrel; but if you line up its iron sights on a point 50 yards away, the bullet will hit the point of aim—and it will rise only about ½ inch above the line of sight at 30 yards.

Even when zeroed at 75 yards, the low-velocity .22 Long Rifle bullet from an iron-sighted rifle will cross the line of aim *first* at 10 yards, climb 1.3 inches above the line of sight at 50 yards, cross the line of aim again at 75 yards (the distance at which it is said to be sighted in for or zeroed at), and fall 4 inches below the line of sight at 100 yards—a far cry indeed from the appalling total fall of 12 inches at that distance, if the bore were horizontal instead of tilting slightly up.

Anywhere along the way from the muzzle to 85 yards, the bullet would not deviate from line of sight enough to miss the head of a cottontail—or, in most cases, the head of a squirrel.

With the scope-sighted .22 the range can be stretched a bit with the same maximum trajectory height above the line of sight of 1.3 inches. In this case the low-velocity Long Rifle bullet will first cross the line of aim at 12½ yards, cross again at 85 yards, and be only 2 inches low at 100. Even with that sighting, though, the bullet, because of its low velocity, is 7 inches low at 125 yards and 15 inches low at 150 yards. All of which explains why the finest scope in the world won't make up for the shortcomings of a .22 Long Rifle on varmints at long range! Gravity simply has too much time to work on the bullet.

To me it seems sheer folly to sight in a rifle for some short distance simply because most game is killed at that range. I once read a very good hunting tale by a man who used a scope-sighted .270 which he zeroed for 100 yards because he had it doped out that he would probably shoot his deer at that distance. Now suppose our hunter had got a quick shot at 250 yards and he had held dead on. The 150-grain bullet would have fallen 10 inches below point of aim and he probably would have missed his buck.

On the other hand, if he had sighted in for 225 yards the bullet would have been only 3 inches high at 100 and 150 yards, and only 2 inches low at 250. Unless you plan to go around shooting deer in the eye, a 3-inch deviation from line of sight surely is not excessive!

With the standard .270 factory loads with the 130-grain bullet, I do the preliminary sighting in at 25 yards and adjust the scope to hit the point of aim at that distance. The bullet then strikes 3 inches high at 100 yards, 4 inches high at 150 and 200 yards, at point of aim the second time at 275, and only 2 inches low at 300. At 325 yards the bullet is about 4 inches below the point of aim. For shooting big game—even deer and antelope measuring from 14 to 17 inches from top of shoulder to bottom of chest—this is not excessive deviation, and the point-blank range of a .270 so sighted is 325 yards.

Sighted for 200 yards, on the other hand, the point-blank range is only about 260 yards because at that distance the bullet falls 4 inches below point of aim.

Let's apply the same formula to the scope-sighted .30/06 with the factory 150-grain load at a muzzle velocity of 2910 foot-seconds, sighting in so the path of the bullet first crosses the line of aim at 25 yards and strikes 3 inches high at 100 yards. At 150 yards the bullet strikes 4 inches high; at 200 yards it's 3 inches high; at 250 yards it is at point of aim the second time; and the bullet does not fall more than 4 inches below point of aim until it has passed the 290-yard mark. Such a sighting makes the .30/06 a pretty good long-range sheep and antelope rifle!

With the slower 180-grain bullet at a muzzle velocity of 2700 foot-seconds and the same formula of the scope-sighted rifle—laying them at point of aim at 25 yards the first time and putting them 3 inches high at 100 yards—the range is stretched to 225 yards, where the bullet crosses the line of sight the second time. It does not drop more than 4 inches until it has passed the 260-yard mark.

Now let's take a look at the ordinary deer rifle—say an iron-sighted .30/30 using a 170-grain bullet with a muzzle velocity of 2200 foot-seconds. If you sight one of these in for 100 yards, at 200 yards the bullet fall below the line of bore will be about 10 inches—enough to miss even a big white-tail buck with a center-of-the-chest hold. On the other hand, if the rifle is sighted in for 150 yards the bullet will fall only 5 inches at 200 yards, and a hit with no allowance for drop is probable. What's more, at 100 yards the bullet is only 2 inches above the line of sight, and that is so little deviation as to be negligible. The bullet will cross the line of sight the first time at about 12½ yards, a handy thing to remember when a grouse perches up in the tree. Substantially the same trajectory applies to any of the other so-called deer cartridges—including the .32 Special, .35 Remington and .375 Winchester.

The iron-sighted rifle using a cartridge with a velocity of from 2400 to 2500 foot-seconds can well be sighted in for 175 yards. This will include the .30/40 Krag, the .303 British as loaded in Canada, and the .300 Savage—all with the 180-grain bullet; also the .358 Winchester with the 200-grain bullet, the .30/06 with the 220-grain bullet, and the 7 mm. Mauser with the 175-grain bullet. With any of these the bullet will first cross the line of iron sight at from 10 to 12½ yards. At 100 yards it will be 2½ or 3 inches high, at point of aim again at 175 yards, and only 2 or 3 inches low at 200 yards.

When such rifles are scope-sighted, the trajectory is apparently flattened out a bit, and they can be zeroed for 200 yards. In that case the bullet will first cross the line of sight at 25 yards. At 100 yards it will be 3 inches high, and at 250 only about 5 inches low—all of which means that with the 180-grain bullet and a scope sight even the old .30/40 Krag can stretch right out there.

How much mid-range trajectory height above line of sight can be permitted? That depends a good deal on the size of the game. The squirrel hunter, for instance, who usually aims at the head, cannot have much more than an inch. The varmint hunter too shoots at small targets, and in his case a 2½-inch deviation is the most he can work with. I prefer a mid-range trajectory of no more than 1½ inches for varmint shooting.

The hunter of big game, on the other hand, has much larger marks—from the small deer measuring 14 inches from chest to withers, to the huge moose of from 35 to 40 inches. A 4-inch deviation is peanuts even on a medium-size animal like a bighorn ram or a mule deer.

Knowledge of trajectory and the practical application of this knowledge is enormously useful to the hunter. It will enable him to snap off the head of an ugly-looking rattlesnake at 10 feet, knock down a grouse with a big-game rifle at 25 yards, or collect the fat buck that is standing and looking at him a long way across the canyon.

So by all means the hunter should memorize the trajectory of his rifle. If worst comes to worst, and he doesn't trust his memory, he can copy off the dope from a trajectory table and affix to the buttstock of the rifle with Scotch tape. Then it would be right there when it's needed.

JUDGMENT OF RANGE

Over the years ammunition and shooting equipment have improved vastly. Velocity of bullets for big-game hunting has been stepped up from the 2000 feet per second of the first smokeless powder big game cartridges to the 3100 and 3200 that is fairly common today. Barrels and bullets are more uniform and capable of much better accuracy than was possible a generation ago. The wide use of the telescopic sight has made better holding and more exact shot placement easier.

But the weak link in the shooting combination is the shooter himself. Human ingenuity has produced superb equipment but nature goes on producing imperfect human bodies that are poorly designed as shooting platforms. The knees wobble, the hands shake, the chests heave, the eyes water. The jittery human brain creates dragons in the path, is prone to buck fever, jitters, and other ailments of the mind.

All of this adds up to the fact that few hunters have any business shooting at big game at very long range and that they do not have much need for instruction in range judgment. What they need instead is someone to convince them that they should get close enough so that they are SURE of a hit or not shoot.

The "point blank" range of a modern high-velocity big-game rifle properly sighted in with a telescopic sight, as we have seen above, is something around 300 yards. By "point blank" range I mean the distance over which the bullet does not rise or fall more than 4 inches from the point of aim. The .270 with the 130-grain bullet was the first American cartridge with this flat trajectory, but when the .30/06 with the 150-grain bullet was stepped up to give a velocity of something over 2,900, it was not too far behind.

In the 1980's many such cartridges are in common use—the .25/06 Remington with the 120-grain bullet, the .264 Winchester with the 140-grain bullet, and the 7 mm. Express Remington and 7 mm. Remington Magnum with the 150-grain bullet, the .300 Winchester Magnum, the .338 Winchester Magnum and the various cartridges of the Weatherby line. With any of these a dead-on hold halfway down from the top of the shoulder in line with the foreleg will result in a killing hit to over 300 yards. A crack shot shooting from a solid rest may be justified in holding on the top of the shoulder. In this case (if all goes well) a solid hit will result, depending on the particular trajectory and the size of the animal, out to the neighborhood of 400 yards.

The fact is that hunters armed with modern high-velocity rifles do not have much need for elaborate instructions on the judgment of range. They should learn what the combination of their skill and equipment makes possible and then stay within those limits. If the rifleman is no better than a 200-yard shot even under ideal conditions from a sitting position at standing game, he should pass up more distant and more difficult targets. If he has learned to use a rest or has mastered the prone position with sling and can stay within a 10- or 12-inch circle at 400 yards he is justified in occasionally shooting from that distance.

In the days of black-powder rifles and velocities of from 1300 to 1500 feet per second, judgment of range was very important unless a hunter was willing to confine his shooting to modest distances. The .270 Winchester cartridge with the 130-grain bullet, the 7 mm. Remington Magnum with the 150-grain bullet, and other cartridges of the 3100–3150 feet per second class have mid-range trajectories of about 2 inches over 200 yards and about 5 inches over 300 yards.

The experienced hunter who has been in the open a lot and has seen much game can generally tell about how far an animal is away—but not always. It is difficult to judge range over a flat surface with the eyes close to the ground. Things appear closer in bright light, farther away in poor light. The brilliantly marked pronghorn antelope is apt to look closer than the drab colored deer.

Inexperienced hunters with their imagination stimulated by buck fever make some wonderful mistakes in range judgment. I once tried to show an inexperienced hunter a desert bighorn ram about 200 yards away and he started shooting at a rock as big as a small house and about 800 yards away. Another chap I knew thought a sitting jackrabbit at 40 or 50 yards was a deer at 300.

Various hunters have their pet ways of determining practical range. Old duck hunters say that when you cannot see the markings on a mallard drake clearly he is too far away to shoot at. I have just read a book written by an Englishman during the black-powder days. He said he did not like to shoot anything with his .500 Express unless he could see the animal's eye clearly. That isn't very far away!

If an animal is at long and undetermined range and if the hunter has plenty of time it helps to divide the distance off mentally into 100-yard units. Also helpful is to compare the depths of an animal's body with a scope reticule of known value—a 4-minute dot, for example, or the known distance at 100 yards between two horizontal stadia wires on some rangefinder reticules—a 6-minute space, for instance. With one of the range-finding variable-power scopes, you just turn the power ring ahead of the eyepiece until the stadia wires bracket the animal's brisket, then read the range on a numerical display in the reticule. Some scopes also have trajectory-compensating elevation dials which can then be set to place the bullet at point of aim at the distance shown in the reticule.

Such devices are helpful but not exact, as animals vary considerably in size. However, the range-finding reticule can head off some pretty bad guesses. I make a practice of measuring game animals on a straight line from the top of the shoulder to the bottom of the brisket. An antelope or a small deer measures about 14 inches. A good buck mule deer measures around 18 inches. A Rocky Mountain goat or a large ram will measure from 22 to 24 inches, an elk from 24 to 30 inches and a big bull moose from 36 to 40 inches.

Keeping these rough figures in mind and using them to compare the depths of animals' bodies with various range-finding reticules will often show the most experienced hunter that he isn't the world's best judge of distance.

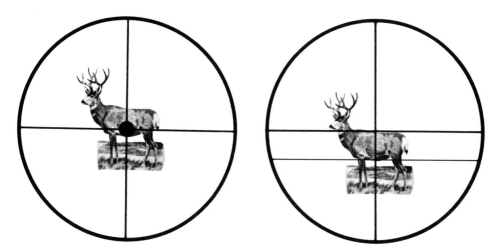

Reticules in telescope sights aid in range finding. If a dot reticule (left), designed to subtend 3 inches at 100 yards covers half the body of an average-sized deer (18 inches from back to brisket), the deer would be 300 yards away. Horizontal stadia hairs of rangefinder reticule (right) are spaced apart a distance covering 6 inches on the target at 100 yards. If hairs bracket a deer of average size, it is 300 yards away.

5

Light, Mirage, and Wind

LIGHT

Those who shoot must have light. It may be furnished by the sun, by a powerful flashlight—even by the moon. But light there must be. It may be the flat gray light of dawn and dusk, or the hard, bright, contrasty light of midday.

The character of the light is more important to the target competitor than to the big-game hunter because the hunter seldom shoots at the longer ranges where light can get in its dirty licks to fool the target rifleman.

Yet light, and its source the sun, can bother even the simple deer hunter. Many years ago a companion and I were driving along a wandering track in the Sonora desert when a lone buck antelope popped up from behind a bush not 20 feet from our automobile. I jumped out with a .30/06 equipped with a Lyman 48 receiver sight in my hand. But the antelope was running right into the setting sun and every time I tried to aim, bits of lint in the peep flared so badly from the rays of the sun that I could not see.

Flare like this used to bother the scope user, but since World War II the universal use of coated optics has taken the bite out and it is now possible to shoot almost directly into the sun without being bothered by flare.

Today, a very high proportion of varmint and big-game rifles are equipped with telescope sights. As a consequence, many young riflemen have never encountered the iron-sight phenomenon of "shooting away from the light." Let us suppose that the sun was from the left. Then the rifle will shoot to the right. The reason for this is that the bright sun forms a false center on the front sight. The rifleman aims by it instead of the true center. Since the false center is toward the sun on the left, the effect is the same as moving the front sight to the left—and the rifle shoots to the right. This shooting away from the light is the most marked in round or pointed gold beads, but it is present even with a flat blade or patridge-type front sight. It is also present, though to a lesser extent, with steel blade front sights that have been heavily smoked by a burning kitchen match or by a camphor flame.

Many years ago I used a now obsolete front sight called the Sheard Gold Bead spark sight or something of the sort. It was pointed and presumably the light would always be seen as a spark at the point. However, this baby really shot away from the light. I have long since lost my notes but as I remember it, a bright 3 o'clock or 9 o'clock light would make the rifle shoot off several inches (3 or 4 perhaps) at 100 yards.

Even the rough-and-tumble deer hunter must take light into consideration. Sometimes light is so poor (particularly early in the morning and late in the afternoon) when deer hunting is apt to be at its best that the hunter can see the deer after a fashion but cannot see to aim properly. In addition it is indifferent light combined with the natural spookiness of the hunter that makes so many shots at deer with open sights fly high. The explanation for this phenomenon is that the hunter aims hastily at a running deer or one that he thinks is about to take off. The light is not too good anyway and the farther he puts that front bead down into the narrow "V" or the rear sight the poorer the light is. So he doesn't "draw down fine enough," as hunters used to say when I was a kid, and as a consequence he overshoots. That is why the peep sight is optically so much better than the open sight. The eye naturally centers the front bead at the point of strongest light. This is the middle of the peep and it is as it should be.

Because the peep sight properly used for hunting with no screw-in disk is so easy to look through, passes so much light, and so much can be seen through it, many hunters feel that its use is practically immoral. They do not realize that the eye naturally centers the bead and the size of the aperture makes very little difference as far as accuracy goes. I made that mistake with the first peep sight I ever used on a hunting rifle. I screwed in the target disk and when just at sundown I had a chance to shoot a juicy young buck standing back in the timber 100 yards or so away I could not see him through the small, dim hole in the disk.

The best iron rear sight for bad light is one which is almost never seen now—a peep mounted on the cocking piece of a bolt-action rifle or on the tang of a lever action. These are close to the eye, do not cut off light. All outdoors can be seen through them, and the only problem is to have a front sight that can be seen. A good open sight for poor light is the British shallow "V" with a narrow platinum line running from the bottom of the sight base to the bottom of the "V." Most front beads on British double rifles, even those in large calibers and intended for dangerous game, are too small and are difficult to pick up quickly. However, the British used to make (and will no doubt make today if their palms are crossed with sufficient shillings) what they called "folding moon sights." These were large gold or ivory beads that folded down into the ramp front sight base when not in use, but flipped up against the smaller bead when it was needed. The British used these "folding moon sights" for fast shooting at dangerous game in brush and jungle and for shooting at tigers from machans by electric torches—or what we call flashlights.

The best of all sights when light is poor is the scope—and the best scope for dusk and night shooting is one of fairly low power with a large objective. In giving specifications for telescope sights and binoculars manufacturers generally list one called "relative brightness." This is derived from the power and the size of clear aperture of the objective lens—in other words, the hole that lets the light into the instrument. The larger the clear aperture is, the greater the brightness. The lower the power is the greater the brightness. Considerable magnification in a scope with a small objective means a scope that seems bright only in very good light when the pupil of the eye is contracted. In bad light such a scope is poor. That is why good telescope sights in powers from 4X up have enlarged objectives—in other words, the objective end of the scope is larger than the tube.

It is possible to tell something about the relative brightness of a scope or of a pair of binoculars by holding them at arms length. Then you can see the size of the light pencil. I have a pair of 7 x 35 binoculars and also a pair of 9 x 35's. As one would expect the diameter of the light pencil of the 7X glass is considerably larger than that of the 9X glass. In bright light the 9X looks just as bright as the 7X but in poor light the 7X with its larger light pencil is definitely superior. True night glasses have even larger objectives. The standard night glass of the U.S. Navy is a 7 x 50.

The pupil of the human eye will expand only so much in poor light and it does no good if the light pencil is larger than the pupil. That is why a 9 x 35 looks just as bright in good light as a 7 x 35. The pupil has closed up so that it cannot even use all the light in the 9 x 35 light pencil. In scopes the size of the light pencil has another function in that the larger the light pencil the less critical eye relief is. A "non-critical eye relief" means that the eye has more latitude to be up or down, forward or back and still get the full field of the scope. To state it another way, the eye does not have to be in the same place all the time in order to get the full field of view. A non-critical eye relief is of enormous importance in a big-game scope, but not nearly so important in a scope to be used on stationary targets.

A bright hunting scope with a good reticule is the best of all sights to use by artificial light and by moonlight. A most excellent one I once used was a 2½X German Ajax with a very coarse crosswire. However, any good hunting scope with a coarse or medium crosswire reticule is good. The crosswire is the best reticule because it is not necessary to see the intersection of the crosswires to know where it is if the shooter can see four, three, or even two wires leading into the target. For shooting in poor light the post is not very good because the tip will be lost against the target, and the floating dot is worthless.

Another characteristic of light is that game animals look nearer on bright days, farther away on dark overcast days. This is particularly true of brightly marked, conspicuous animals like antelope, elk in tan and brown fall coats, or Dall sheep. It is also true of animals against a contrasting background—a black bear against the yellow frost-cured grass of a hillside, for example. A neutral-colored animal seen on an overcast day against a neutral-colored background (a mule deer against gray slide rock, for example) seems farther away than he is.

All things considered, the scope remains the best all-around rifle sight available. Little wonder, then, that it's so universally used by hunters today.

MIRAGE

The condition called "mirage" is present when sun warms the ground more than it does the air above it. The ground in turn heats the air immediately adjacent to it. This layer of air rises and cooler air flows in to take its place. The result is that the light between the rifleman and his target is bent. The effect is something like trying to spear a fish from above the surface of the water. The fish isn't where he looks as if he should be and the spear looks crooked.

Mirage gives some queer effects. In the Arizona desert, where I grew up, a common manifestation of mirage is what appears to be a pool of blue water a half-mile or so away down a paved road. Lakes can be seen between the viewer and the mountains and sometimes one can make out trees and bushes beside the blue waters of these lakes.

I have heard of mirages that were complete with houses and whatnot, mirages that showed actual cities hundreds of miles away. I have never seen one.

To the shooter the commonest manifestation of mirage is a boiling or flowing of light between him and his target. It looks a bit like very clear water flowing over pebbles of some lovely mountain trout stream. If there is no wind, mirage boils straight up. If there is it flows to the right or left in the direction the wind is blowing. With mirage boiling up from below, the bull looks larger than it would in clear air and it also appears elongated. When the mirage is flowing from left to right or vice versa, the elongated bull leans in the direction the mirage is flowing.

Target shooters find mirage helpful for doping wind through high-power target scopes and through spotting scopes, but they also find that mirage causes sour shots because of the displaced image of the target.

Mirage can cause big-game hunters to misjudge range and even misjudge species of game. Once when I was hunting desert game in the Sahara I saw what I thought was a whole line of camels on the horizon. The "camels" turned out to be dama gazelles magnified and distorted by mirage. A dama weighs about 125 pounds.

The closer the shooter is to the ground the more anything he sees is distorted by mirage. Once I made a long sneak on a black buck in the blistering hot, sun-baked plains of India north of Delhi. Since there was no cover it was necessary for me to creep along on my knees and elbows. Finally I got within what I thought was about 150 yards of the blackbuck made swirling and indistinct by mirage. I shot and the blackbuck took off. I jumped to my feet and instantly I could see that he was well over 300 yards away.

WIND

Wind affects the rifle shooter in two ways. The most obvious is that if there is much wind it blows against shooter and rifle, moves the rifle and makes it difficult for him to shoot accurately. The less obvious effect is that it affects the path of his bullet. Under ordinary circumstances this is of no great moment to the big-game hunter, as big-game animals are large and generally are not shot at such great range that the wind has a chance to get in many of its dirty licks. Wind effect is much more important to the varmint shooter, who aims at very small marks at considerable distance (a woodchuck at 350–400 yards, for example) and to the target shooter. The big-bore target shooter at 600 and 1,000 yards must be able to dope wind if he is to score well and so must the small-bore shooter at 200. In either case an unexpected gust can blow the best aimed bullet out of the bull and sometimes off the target.

As far as bullet drift in a crosswind goes, it would be simple and logical to assume that the faster the bullet gets to the target the less it is affected by wind. But that ain't so. Over fifty years ago (about 1931, in fact) when high-speed .22 Long Rifle ammunition first came out, small-bore shooters thought that with its velocity of about 1335 feet per second and shorter elapsed time from muzzle to target that the bullet would be less affected by wind than the old low-speed match ammunition at about 1050. They were shocked to discover that the fast stuff drifted more than the slow.

How come? The answer is that the drift is proportional to the delay of the bullet over the range at which it is fired. "Delay" means the difference between the actual time it takes the bullet to get to target and the time it would have taken had the bullet been fired in a vacuum. Air resistance is different at different speeds, and when the bullet breaks the sound barrier it encounters terrific resistance. The speed of sound at sea-level is 1080 feet per second at 68° Fahrenheit and at an atmospheric pressure of 29.92 inches of mercury. The speed of .22 match ammunition runs slightly below that of sound and as a consequence it does not encounter this resistance, has less delay, and less drift. Anyone who has been around much .22 shooting has noticed that if high-speed .22 ammunition is shot in his direction he will hear both the crack of the bullet and the report. This is because he hears the crack of the bullet as it breaks the sound barrier and he hears this sharp crack first since the bullet travels faster than sound. Since match ammunition is loaded below the speed of sound, one hears only the report of the rifle. Silencers, which were once widely used, are now illegal in the United States. They actually silenced .22 rifles with low-speed ammunition, but they cannot silence any rifle using ammunition with bullets traveling faster than sound. Some ordinary low-speed .22 ammunition is loaded to just about the speed of sound. Those just above the critical velocity crack, and those below do not.

At 100 yards in a crosswind with a velocity of 10 feet per second the time of flight for a .22 match bullet with a muzzle velocity of 1050 feet per second is 0.30834 second and that of a high-velocity .22 bullet is 0.26364 second. Nevertheless, the drift of the faster bullet is 3.768 inches whereas that of the slower match bullet is 2.594 inches. This doesn't seem to make sense but there she is! At 100 yards, the allowance for drift must be increased 45 percent for the faster bullet.

The factors in wind drift then are the speed of the wind, the direction of the wind, the distance to the target, and the delay or "lag" of the bullet over the given range.

The worst bullets for blowing hither and yon are the short, blunt bullets driven at very high velocity like the old 110-grain bullets loaded for the .30/06 at very high (about 3380 feet per second) velocity. The better the ballistic coefficient of the bullet, the more slowly it loses its velocity and the less wind sensitive it is. A 200-grain .30 caliber match bullet with a spitzer (sharp) nose and a boattail base has an excellent ballistic coefficient and drifts much less when loaded to only about 2550 feet per second and the flat-base 150-grain .30 caliber bullet loaded to around 2910.

A headwind will make a bullet strike low, a tail wind will make it strike high because the headwind increases air resistance and the tail wind decreases it. This is exactly like the jet plane that flies to Europe faster with a tail wind. This is important to the long-range target shot, but makes little difference to the big-game hunter. With the M-2 .30/06 military cartridge with the 152-grain bullet a 10-mile-per-hour tail wind would make the bullet strike 24 inches higher at 1000 yards. If it were a headwind the bullet would strike 24 inches lower. But at game ranges (up to 400 yards) the difference is negligible (less than 2 inches difference between point of impact with headwind, tail wind, and no wind).

Here are some figures worked out years ago by Wallace H. Coxe, du Pont ballistician, of wind drift over 100 yards with a 10-mile-an-hour wind with various bullets:

Cartridge	Bullet Weight	Muzzle Velocity	Velocity at 100 yd.	Drift
.22 Long Rifle	40 grains	1070 f.p.s.	932	3.29 in.
.250/200 Savage	100 grains	2850	2589	.52
.270 Winchester	130 grains	3160	2358	.32
.30/06	180 grains	2700	2463	.52
.30/30	170 grains	2000	1722	1.97

Sad to say, complete windage tables so far as I know do not exist for anything but the popular target cartridges such as the .22 Long Rifle, the .30/06 with the 150- and 172-grain bullets, and the .308 with the 150-grain bullet. Long-range match shooters who use special target cartridges similar to the .300 Weatherby and the .30/338 must have approximate tables but I have never run across them.

The better the ballistic coefficient and the smaller the velocity loss the less the drift. Here are the figures for a 10-mile wind at 3 o'clock or 9 o'clock at the practical hunting range of 300 yards for four types of bullets: the old .45/70 with a 500-grain bullet at a velocity of about 1200 feet per second—25 inches; the .30/40 Krag with a 220-grain round nose bullet at 2200 feet per second— 15.5; the 150-grain .30/06 flat-base spitzer bullet at 2700 feet per second—8; the 172-grain .30/06 spitzer boattail at about 2650—5.8.

As far as really long-range shooting goes 300 yards is practically next door, but the 2-foot drift of the .45/70 would mean the difference between a well placed shot and a poor one. The drift of the more efficient and modern bullets are not to be ignored. Even the user of the .30/06 with the very efficient 180-grain spitzer should allow for drift by holding slightly into the wind at 300 yards.

At 500 yards, with the same wind, the .45/70 would drift 55 inches, the .30/40, 46.2 inches, the .30/06 with the 150-grain bullet, 25 inches, and the .30/06 with the 172-grain bullet, 17 inches. A 10-mile-an-hour wind is a fairly strong breeze, but not a rip-snorter by any means, and hunters on the plains of Wyoming and other windy places will encounter harder winds as a matter of routine.

Drift with a 5-mile-an-hour wind would be half as much, with a 20-mile-an-hour wind twice as much. A 5-mile wind might be described as a pleasant zephyr, a 20-mile wind as a hard, annoying wind but not a gale.

Those who need most to study wind, then, are the 600 and 1000-yard .30 caliber match shooters, the 200-yard small-bore shooters, the varmint hunters, and the long-range big-game hunters. A .22 Long Rifle match bullet will drift 16 inches at 200 yards with a 10-mile-an-hour crosswind, and wind will push a .30 caliber bullet clear off the target at 1000 yards if no allowance is made for it. The varmint shooter who doesn't allow for wind when he is shooting at a woodchuck at 300 yards won't hit many, and the Wyoming antelope hunter had better hold well into the wind at 300 yards if he is going to bring home the venison!

6

The Shooter's Eyes

THERE ARE THREE principal eye defects: nearsightedness or myopia; farsightedness or hyperopia; and astigmatism, a condition which is the result of cockeyed curves of the cornea. The astigmatic eye cannot focus horizontal and vertical lines perfectly, and it is astigmatism which causes the most discomfort. Without astigmatism a nearsighted or a farsighted person can get along without eyestrain and headaches. The nearsighted man simply cannot see well at a distance and the farsighted man cannot see things close by.

Most members of the human race are afflicted to some extent with one or another of these eye defects. Possibly a majority of the human race is somewhat farsighted, but most of the young people one sees wearing glasses do so because they are nearsighted and astigmatic. Some are mostly astigmatic and only slightly near or farsighted. Slight astigmatism does not bother most people unduly.

The reason the myope is nearsighted is that his eye is like a camera with the lens racked out so as to bring close objects into sharp focus. Many people are born with eye lenses of that shape. Sometimes the condition can be brought about from measles in childhood. The hyperope's eye lens is like that of a camera focused for infinity. He sees distant objects clearly but when he is young his power of accommodation enables him to yank his eyeballs into shape so he can see things close by.

Another ailment of the eye is known as presbyopia—the flattening and stiffening of the eyeball which comes with age. Then the naturally farsighted person becomes more farsighted and his ageing muscles cannot pull his eye lens into proper position for him to see anything that is close by. The person of normal vision finds that his eyes are permanently focused for "infinity"—say from 10 feet on up. As middle age and its accompanying presbyopia sets in, the person who has had normal vision and has never needed glasses to read with or to see at a distance with now finds that he simply cannot focus his eye on near objects. He holds a newspaper or a restaurant menu farther and farther away until he finally finds that his arms aren't long enough.

If the middle-aged person has good vision except for presbyopia (old sight), he can get by simply with glasses for close work—"reading glasses." If it is too much trouble to take them off and put them on he uses bifocals with the lower part corrected for close vision, the upper part with little or no correction. The man or woman with a little vanity can use glasses corrected for close work only and then simply use them when the occasion arises. Many men carry their reading glasses in the breast pockets of their jackets. Women carry theirs in their purses. Sometimes they use lorgnettes. A friend of mine uses a pair of glasses that contains only the reading portion and nothing above.

The middle-aged or elderly myope (if he doesn't have much astigmatism) needs glasses for distant vision, but when he wants to read, his stiff eye lenses are fixed for close work. The eyes of most healthy people retain some power of accommodation. In middle age, they wear bifocal glasses with the upper part right for from 5 to 6 feet out to infinity and with the lower part at their usual reading distance, which is, let us say, about 15 or 16 inches. If he wants to gaze into the violet eyes of a beautiful girl (something no man of his age has any business doing, incidentally) he still has enough power of accommodation left usually to bring her into fair focus at 2 feet. Some people who have pretty well lost the power of accommodation wear tri-focal glasses, using the top part for distance vision, the middle part for seeing things at from 4 to 6 feet, and the bottom part for reading.

The nearsighted man needs a concave lens in his spectacles. When the condition is extreme, the lenses give the eyes a wild and froggy look. A far-sighted man has to have a convex lens to make things look right. Contact lenses have been a great boon to many, particularly to pretty women with some congenital sight defect and to athletes who find the wearing of glasses not feasible. Incidentally, it is not necessary to put correction for astigmatism into contact lenses as the lenses shape up and correct the eye lens for the defect.

The eye and a camera are very much alike. Actually it could be said that the human eye is a sort of a camera that registers on nerves and brains instead of on film. The pupil of the eye closes up in bright light and opens in dim light, exactly like the diaphragm in a modern camera that is controlled by photo-electric cells. Also like the camera lens, the eye has greater depth of focus at a small aperture than at a large one. That is why the person who is a bit farsighted finds it easier to read in bright light than in dim. The iris of his eye has closed up and gives greater depth of focus. It is also why some ageing shooters hang a gadget with a little hole in it on the lens of the spectacle they use for aiming. Then because they are aiming through a small aperture, everything—rear sight, front sight, and target—is sharp like a picture taken by a camera with the lens aperture set at F.22. It is instructive to look into the ground glass of a view or portrait camera with the camera focused lens wide open at one distance. Then as the opening is closed up to a small F stop, more and more things come into sharp focus.

The human eye has great depth of focus because it has a short focal length.

It also has a wide field of view—and optically it is like one of the wide-angle lenses used on miniature cameras. Much stuff written about shooting does not take this into consideration. Shotgun writers who say the shooter should hold his head up, see his target but not his barrel, are asking the impossible, since the wide-angle lens of the eye can't help seeing the barrel as well as the target.

The human eye is certainly one of the best, if not the best eye in the world of mammals. If any eyes are as good they are to be found among our relatives the apes and monkeys. The fact that our eyes are set in the front of our heads cuts down on our side vision, but it gives us the priceless advantage of binocular vision. This in turn enables us to judge distance—something our tree-dwelling ancestors had to have if they didn't want to break their necks leaping from branch to branch. Judgment of distance is about as important to a shooter as it is to an orangoutan—and that is why it is important to shoot with both eyes open.

Of the two eyes, one is the master. Generally but not always the right eye of the right-handed man is the master. It is easy for anyone to tell which is his master eye. Here is a test: Point your finger at some nearby object with both eyes open. Close your left eye. The finger should not move if you are right-handed and right-eyed. However, if you are right-handed and right-eyed and close the right eye the left eye takes over and the finger moves, appearing to be at the right of the object at which it was pointed.

Suppose someone is right-handed and left-eyed because he is just naturally that way or because he has injured his right eye. What can he do? If he has good vision in his right eye, he can simply close his left eye and let his right take over. This is a handicap but it can be borne. If he has poor vision in his right eye he can learn to shoot left-handed or he can use a "cross-eyed" stock with which he puts the gun to his right shoulder but shoots with his left eye. This is a tough choice. I do not know which I'd choose if I had to.

The eye has great depth of focus, but not enough to focus at the same time on an open rear sight 15 inches or so from the eye, the front sight 30–36 inches from the eye, and the target 200 or 300 yards away. The quick-focusing eyes of the young can skip back and forth from one object to another so rapidly that they can fool themselves into believing that they are in focus on all three at once. This is impossible. Open sights (which are pretty primitive sights at best) are young man's sights.

The man in the grip of presbyopia as middle age clutches him with its icy fingers finds that he can no longer see the rear sight clearly. He can, however, see the front sight and the target. The thing for him to do then is to go to the optically superior peep sight. One does not need to "see" a peep sight clearly. He simply looks through it and is vaguely conscious of it as only a fuzzy ring. He puts the front bead on what he wants to hit, makes no effort to center the bead, as his eye naturally does that for him.

It is instinctive to put the front bead at the point of strongest light, which is the center of the aperture. For this reason there is no tendency to shoot high as there is with an open rear sight. With such a sight the hunter in poor light or in haste has a tendency not to get the front bead down in the dark bottom of the notch. He cuts loose with too coarse a bead and shoots high.

●

To determine which is your shooting eye, extend your arm and, with both eyes open, sight over your index finger at a spot on the wall. Now close your right eye. If your finger moves to the right, it means your right eye is your shooting eye. If your finger remains on the spot, close your left eye. Most likely your finger will jump to the left, indicating that your left eye is your shooting eye.

At first the farsighted man has trouble seeing his open rear sight. Eventually many cannot even focus on the front sight, although the target is clear. Then the only cure is to go to the scope sight focused for the shooter's eye. Then he sees everything in the same focal plane—which means target and aiming reticule. So equipped the old man suffering from presbyopia can see like a kid again—and often outshoots the kid since he has skill and experience behind him.

GLASSES FOR THE SHOOTER

It is best for anyone who needs optical aid in the form of glasses to go to a professional who is well prepared to serve him. There are two classes of professionals licensed to fit glasses. One is the oculist. He is an M.D. with a general medical education who has taken post-graduate training in the treatment of ailments of the eye, including defects in vision. The optometrist is not a physician, does not treat diseases of the eye, but only fits glasses. Professionals belonging to either category will do a competent job of fitting glasses.

Old books on glasses for shooters recommended "toric" or curved lenses for spectacles rather than flat lenses, because with the toric lenses the user always looks through his correction, something he does not do with the flat lenses. I can remember when one had a choice between flat and curved lenses, with the curved lenses costing more. Whether the flat lenses are made today or not I cannot say.

The lenses should be sufficiently large so that the shooter, particularly the shotgun shooter, does not see the rims. If a bifocal portion is worn it should not interfere. Amber-tinted glasses diminish glare to some extent, sharpen up the target, make game stand out more clearly in the few minutes before darkness when game and forest tend to merge in the gathering grayness. Some skeet and trap shooters like amber-colored glasses and feel that these sharpen up the clay targets for them. For wear in snow on bright days and in the glare of sandy deserts, green-tinted glasses are probably better than amber. At least I like them better. My eyes are not unduly sensitive to light. I have a pair of spectacles with green lenses ground to my prescription, bifocal and all, and I wear them on bright days when there is snow on the ground and in the glare of sun on desert sands or at sea. An extra pair of spectacles with tinted lenses also serve as a spare on a hunting trip to the habitual spectacle wearer.

Actually anyone who shoots should wear glasses to protect his eyes even if he does not need them to sharpen up his vision. I learned that the hard way back in the early 1930's. I had at that time a fine custom-made 7 x 57 Mauser and for practice I was shooting some bargain military ammunition with 175-grain full metal jacketed bullets made by the old U.S. Cartridge Company. How old the stuff was I cannot say but the story was that someone had bought it to run across the border to Pancho Villa, the Mexican bandit general, about 1915 or twenty years before. I inspected the cartridges, threw away all those that showed neck cracks or a great deal of corrosion.

I was shooting prone one day when there was a tremendous explosion in my face. My face was marked by unburned powder grains and bits of brass, my eyebrows were singed, the lenses of my glasses were covered with oily smoke and fragments of brass. *But my eyes were not damaged.* If I had not been wearing glasses I probably would have lost my eyesight. Incidentally, the case had come in two right at the extractor groove and when I opened the bolt, the dime-size head of the case came out. The trouble was not excess headspace but old and defective brass.

Primer leaks and blown primers may squirt gas back into the eye, and blown out rims of .22's can do the same thing. I know a man who lost the sight of an eye when he was struck by spent shot fired by a gunner who was not even aware of his presence. Fragments of clay targets have damaged many unguarded eyes on skeet fields.

Actually even for the hunter the wearing of spectacles is not much of an annoyance. When I am hunting out in the mountains I wear a broadbrimmed hat to keep the rain off of my glasses, and I always make certain that I have a clean handkerchief in my trousers' pocket so I can wipe them off if necessary. Because the wearing of spectacles puts the eyes farther away from the ocular lenses of binoculars, the spectacle wearer should order binoculars with flat eyepieces, something all optical manufacturers furnish as optional equipment. Some spectacle wearers who do not have binoculars equipped with flat eye cups push their glasses up and use binoculars without them. They can focus binoculars to compensate for near or farsightedness, but not for astigmatism, and if astigmatic eyes uncorrected by spectacles are used for a long time with binoculars severe eyestrain will result.

Many men who find it necessary to wear glasses all the time have special shooting glasses made. Generally they have the bifocal section left out since they will not use them to read with. They also have them made extra large, as many shooters are annoyed by the shadowy presence of frames, just as they are annoyed by the bifocal portion. Pistol shooters often have their glasses made to let them see their sights sharp, even if the target is fuzzy. But every shooter should wear glasses in front of his eyes for protection—even if he does not need their help in seeing.

Just how much it helps to "rest" the eyes I cannot say. Target shooters are convinced that the day before a match they should use their eyes for close work as little as possible.

Good vision is one of the things that go with good general health, and loss of sleep or the excessive use of tobacco, alcohol, or sleeping pills never made anyone see any better!

7

Women and Shooting

I HAVE BEEN TOLD that men are natural warriors and killers and that women are naturally kind, natural mothers, the protectors of stray cats and waifs. I have further been told (or maybe I read it somewhere) that if you put a little boy about a year old and a little girl about the same age in a room with a gun and a doll the little boy would make a beeline for the gun and the little girl for the doll, the little boy would start slaying dragons or something with the gun and the little girl would start cuddling the doll.

This all may be true but believe me I have known some exceptions to both rules. Once when I was laid up for some weeks in a hospital one of my regular visitors was a handsome nurse who was a deer, elk, and bear hunter, a gun nut, a skillful horsewoman, a handloader, a trap shooter, and a low-handicap golfer who could belt a drive 240 yards. She used to come around to see me to talk guns and hunting. Her husband took not the slightest interest in either subject and in the fall when she took off to the tall timber for her annual big game hunt he stayed at home, watered the flowers and took care of her bird dogs.

I knew another gal, also quite pretty, who grew up on a ranch and who for more than a decade worked two or three months each fall as a guide on elk, deer, and bear hunts.

Osa Johnson, the wife of Martin Johnson, the pioneer African motion picture photographer in the golden days of British East Africa back in the 1920's and early thirties, used to protect her husband when he was photgraphing dangerous game like lions and rhinos. No Johnson movie was complete without some footage of 5-foot, 100-pound Osa bowling over a charging rhino or a lion a few yards from the camera.

I've known quite a few skillful and intrepid sportswomen like Marge Hopkins of Spokane, Washington, and Katie Batten of Racine, Wisconsin—veterans of African safaris, and Indian shikars. Many women have distinguished themselves with shotgun and handgun. More than a generation ago, a beautiful young blonde named Patricia Lorison was one of the finest skeet shots in

America. Carol Lombard, the famous actress, was very handy with a skeet gun, too. Among today's top NRA competitors, women's names are too numerous to list. And in the 1970's and '80's an impressive number of women have been among the winners of gold, silver, and bronze medals in Olympic and Pan American shooting events and in the World Shooting Championships (international competitions held in the "off" years, between Olympic matches). In the early '80's, top trap competitors included names like Nora Martin, Lou Ann Munson, Lynn Magnuson, Sandy Latham, Sheryl Gorres, Sunny Palmer, and Rosemary Edmondson—to name just a few.

There isn't any reason why women should not be excellent shots. In its various forms shooting is one of the few sports in which women can compete on equal terms with men. Brute strength and bulging muscles are great for weight lifters, shot putters, and football linemen, but no one needs bulging muscles in order to shoot well. Instead one needs good eyesight, steady nerves, fine muscular co-ordination. These things women are endowed with just as men are.

No woman can hit a golf ball as far as Arnold Palmer or Jack Nicklaus can or crack a tennis ball as hard as Jimmy Connors. Women simply do not have the size and the muscles, but there are probably quite a few women golfers who can pitch and putt right along with any male golfers. These departments of the game require good eyes, delicacy of touch, coordination—just as shooting does.

If women can compete on even terms with men in the various branches of shooting, why, then, are there not more women bird hunters, big-game hunters, skeet and trap shooters?

Undoubtedly we must blame instinct to some extent. Anthropologists now believe that human beings have been on this earth for around one million years, and for almost all of that time the male of the human species has had to hunt in order to exist. It is now generally believed by anthropologists that as the frost-free belt of central and southern Africa dried up during the Pliocene, the forests retreated and more and more of the country became grassy plains and scrub. The apes who followed the retreating forests into the west were the ancestors of the gorilla and the chimpanzee. Since they lived in the trees their legs became small, their arms long so they could swing from branch to branch.

The ancestors of man learned to live on the plains. To survive they had to learn to eat meat, to hunt small, slow and harmless creatures. They learned to throw stones, to belt small animals like porcupines or the young of antelope with clubs and bones. Later primitive human beings learned to make axes and spears, bows and arrows, to hunt large and dangerous game. So skillful did primitive hunters become that they are believed to have been responsible for the extermination of the mammoth, that big hairy relative of the Indian elephant—at least in northern Europe. Whole tribes based their economy on mammoths, as archaeologists excavating in Czechoslovakia and Poland have discovered. They ate mammoth meat, wore clothing made of mammoth skins, and lived in huts of mammoth skins draped over frameworks of mammoth ribs.

The point of all this is that the male variety of mankind has been a hunter a long, long time. If he is interested in weapons and if mysterious urges impel him to go back into the boondocks and shoot at something each November, he came by it naturally.

In that million or so years from the time that pre-men started learning to live in the grasslands and supplement their diet with meat until the development of herding and agriculture, women had to keep the fires burning, to mind the young, to pick up fruit and seeds. She may not have the instinctive urge to go out and chase animals around, but we must remember that every girl has a father as well as a mother to inherit instincts from. We must also remember that little girls identify with their mothers, just as little boys identify with their fathers. Mamma usually doesn't grab a .30/06 and go out and shoot an elk, so it never occurs to daughter to think she ought to do it.

In the great majority of cases where a girl gets interested in shooting and hunting she has been encouraged to go into it by some man—generally her father if she starts young or her husband if she starts later. Gloria Jacobs' father was a law enforcement officer and a handgun enthusiast. He used to keep his co-ordination in tune by going out to the city dump at Sacramento and shooting rats with a .38 Special. One day when Gloria was around 12 (as I remember the story) she asked if she could go along. She thought rat shooting looked interesting and asked her father if she might try to hit one. He told her how to aim, how to squeeze, and handed her his revolver. Gloria knocked off four rats with her first six shots. Her father knew he had a natural on his hands and Gloria herself was hooked. He coached her and encouraged her, took her around to tournaments, and she became the greatest woman pistol shot of her day.

The big-game hunting nurse I spoke of earlier got into shooting and hunting the same way. Her father had a small Montana cattle ranch and no sons. He treated her like a boy, taught her to ride, to shoot, to break broncos. My gal guide likewise grew up on a ranch, rode ten miles each way five days a week to a country school, learned to pack, rope, chase cougars and black bears with hounds, shoot deer and elk for the winter's meat.

Another lady hunter I knew was Babe Dickson, daughter of Tom Dickson, pioneer Yukon mounted policeman and big-game outfitter. Babe was a fine cook who was also a crack shot, a skillful trapper, a good packer, a good sheep and grizzly hunter, one of the best dog-team drivers in the Yukon. Babe went along to cook for my wife and me at my request on my last Yukon hunt. Her father and her brothers made a hunter out of her. Babe died of a heart attack after a dog race in 1965.

My wife Eleanor had a hunting father but it had never occurred to him to take his daughter along on a hunt and when I married her she had not fired so much as a cap pistol. Not long after we got married, I started her shooting a

.22 rifle and she developed considerable skill with it. Presently I raised enough scratch to acquire for her an Ithaca 20-gauge double with 26-inch barrels. Her first big-game rifle was a bolt-action Model 30 Remington in .25 Remington caliber, an obsolete cartridge with about the ballistics of a .25/35 Winchester. She graduated to a .257 Roberts not long after that cartridge came out and used it for years on javelina, antelope, mule deer and whitetail deer. The first time she went to Africa I got her a custom-made 7 x 57 Mauser and she did very well with it. When we planned to go to India for a tiger shoot in 1965, I thought she might use still a bit more power and had Len Brownell restock and remodel a Winchester Model 70 .30/06 Featherweight for her. She knocked off a couple of tigers, two big antelope called nilgai, chital (spotted Axis deer), and a little antelope called a chinkara, or ravine deer, with it. In more than thirty-five years Eleanor hunted from Sonora to the Yukon, from Washington to India, and in six countries in Africa.

Some women who are introduced to hunting by their husbands smile, keep a stiff upper lip, try to be good sports and yet are bored to tears by the whole business. They go along only because they want to be pals to their husbands or maybe because they want to keep the old boy under surveillance.

But many women (perhaps the majority) get so they love the woods and the mountains. They are interested in the game and in shooting, and they are happy to be able to share one of their husbands' enthusiasms. Women who do become genuinely interested in shooting and hunting more often than not become better shots than the average man. Most of them can't climb like their husbands, can't carry loads as heavy, wouldn't be caught dead taking the insides out of a deer. But when the chips are down, when someone has to lay a bullet in just the right place, these gals usually deliver.

I think the reason for this odd phenomenon is psychological. A man's hunting is all tied up with his masculine ego, his picture of himself as a real he-guy. Getting his limit of quail or ducks, shooting his annual whitetail buck, getting a big 6-point bull elk, stalking and collecting a 44-inch ram, shooting an elephant with 100-pound tusks—all of these prove to the hunter himself that he is all man. For this reason he often tends to become overeager, too anxious to prove himself, and he may be unhinged by a spectacular trophy or an unexpected chance.

Mamma, on the other hand, doesn't have to prove a darned thing. She has already proved her femininity by catching and taming a wild and elusive male and by having children. She has proved herself a good sport and an ever-loving wife by going along with the big slob. When, as often happens, she shoots the most quail, kills the biggest ram, the first elk, or the most tigers, it is all very well but her ego does not depend on it. The woman hunter can't lose. If she misses something, the men along say: "What the hell! She's only a dame." If she delivers, they say: "What do you know about that! This little pint-size woman knocked that bull moose off with her first shot!"

I believe my wife's first buck illustrated this. We had heard some shooting on the other side of an Arizona hill and thought something might come by us.

About a dozen deer clattered out of the brush and started to run by us at about 200 yards. One was a perfectly magnificent buck, one of the finest I have ever seen.

I got excited, and instead of swinging along with the buck, I got tense, stopped my swing, and shot behind. Eleanor very coolly plinked it right behind the shoulder with her pip-squeak .25 Remington. I heard the bullet strike. We went over and found it quickly. It was stone dead. When I congratulated her on her fine shot she answered with perfect logic that any deer was easier to hit at that distance than a rabbit and the larger the deer the easier he was to hit.

Men hate to admit that recoil bothers them. Again they feel that if getting belted by some hard-kicking gun bruises them and shakes them up they are lacking in masculinity. I have seen men who were so afraid of their magnum rifles that they closed their eyes, jerked the trigger, and couldn't hit a wash tub at 100 yards. Yet they denied that they flinched and claimed that they were such stout fellas that they actually loved recoil.

But not women. If a gal finds shooting a certain rifle or shotgun unpleasant, she says to hell with it. Eventually most of them can get used to recoil. The crack lady skeet and trap shots all use 12-gauge guns. Katie Batten shot her Indian tiger, bear and leopard with a .450/400 double rifle which kicks like the devil. When Marge Hopkins was doing a lot of African hunting her favorite all-around rifle was a powerful and hard-kicking wildcat called the .333 Belted, a cartridge about like the .338 Winchester. Little Osa Johnson used a .470 double rifle and a .405 Winchester lever action, neither of them exactly air rifles.

But from what I have seen of lady shooters, I'd be willing to bet that all of them worked up to those cannons. Not long after we were married, my wife shot my Model 54 Winchester .270—once. She handed it back to me and announced she would never shoot it again.

I think that the man who wants to get his wife interested in shooting and hunting should start her out with something pretty mild. She should learn the mechanics of sight alignment, breathing, and trigger control with a .22. Then when she shifts to a deer rifle it should be something rather mild. The obsolescent .250/3000 Savage and .257 Roberts cartridges were excellent for women. Today's .243 Winchester and 6 mm. Remington do very well for deer and antelope.

The best all-around big-game cartridge to start a woman off on is, I believe, the 7 x 57 Mauser. This fine old cartridge is loaded by Norma with a 150-grain bullet that chronographs about 2750 in a 24-inch barrel. American companies load 175-grain bullets at about 2450 in the same barrel length. The light bullet is sufficiently flat-shooting for open country deer and antelope and the 175-grain bullet is fine medicine in the woods. In Mozambique my wife once collected seventeen head of game with nineteen shots fired. She used the 7 mm. with a 160-grain bullet handloaded to about 2675. At the time this was the record for the most game with the fewest shots on the Save River concession. She put three shots into a big bull kudu that was dead on his feet but wouldn't fall over. A kudu is as heavy as a big bull elk and a waterbuck or a sable is about the size of a spike bull. She also shot bear, mountain sheep, mountain goats, mule deer, and elk with the same rifle and the same load.

I know men who have started their wives and daughters out with full choke .410 shotguns, but too often the gals find the guns hard to hit with. They get discouraged and give up. The best compromise between recoil and pattern is a skeet-bored 20 gauge or a 20-gauge pump or automatic fitted with a variable choke device used wide open. Especially in shotgun shooting, it is very important to get the beginner to breaking his targets as quickly as possible. Hitting leads to more hitting, missing to more missing. Later the woman shooter can use more choke and a larger gauge if she wants to. Whatever the gauge, the woman's gun should be kept light, as a 110-pound gal cannot carry as much as a 180-pound man.

Women apparently have tenderer hides than men, and I believe their rifles and shotguns should be equipped with rubber recoil pads. The stocks of their guns should be shorter. An American factory-built shotgun has a length of pull of 14 inches from the center of the trigger to the center of the buttplate. Any normally built man from 5 feet 7 inches tall to 6 feet 1 inch can make a pretty fair stab at adapting himself to it. It is, however, a bit long for even a rather rangy girl. Gun stocks used by women for general hunting should run from 13 inches for shorties to about 13¾ inches for tall women. Rifle stocks should, of course, run even shorter. The stocks on my wife's 7 x 57 and her .30/06 measured 12¾ inches from center of trigger to center of buttplate to fit her 5-foot 2-inch frame. The stock on her 16-gauge Model 21 had a pull of 13½.

Men often dress like indigents when they go hunting. They may drive out in $20,000 cars and shoot $1,000 guns, but they wear dirty, blood-stained, and ragged clothes. But women like to be smartly attired, and as more women take up big-game and bird shooting smarter hunting clothes for women are available. Large sporting goods stores stock very handsome clothes for women hunters and lady bird shooters. So do mail order concerns like Norm Thompson in Portland and Eddie Bauer in Seattle.

Sportswomen are an ornament to the hunting scene. A few women just go along for the ride, but those that take their shooting seriously can make most men look to their laurels.

Hunting with
the Rifle

Jack O'Connor

Varmint Shooting

CARTRIDGES AND RIFLES

TO MANY RIFLEMEN varmint shooting is the most fascinating of all shooting and the most demanding. Certain predatory species—such as the coyote and bobcat—are most often lured into close range with a predator call, but some of them, especially coyotes in open country, are also shot at long range in the classic manner of varmint hunting. Most of the mammals and the few birds known collectively as "varmints" are much smaller. And, being wary, they generally must be taken at long range and they require very precise shooting. The varmint hunter must be right in the X-ring or he has made a miss.

The woodchuck of the Middle West and East is the most famous of the varmints. With his cousins, the rockchuck of the Northwest and the hoary marmot of the high Rockies, he has been worth hundreds of thousands of dollars to the manufacturers of bullets, telescope sights, precision rifles. The crow and the magpie are also popular varmints in some areas, and difficult targets, as are prairie dogs and Columbian ground squirrels.

Varmint hunting has changed considerably in recent years as a result of changing attitudes and regulations. In regions where prairie dogs are scarce or are classified as a threatened species, they are fully protected. The word "varmint" is derived from "vermin," but no longer are all varmints unprotected or killed for bounties. You must check your state regulations, because some of these animals are now classified as game species or furbearers. The bobcat may be unprotected in one state and a protected furbearer in another. Even where there's no closed season on a particular species, you may want to forego hunting it at certain times of year. Take the woodchuck, for instance. You can't tell a male from a female, and if you kill a female before the end of June you'll probably be killing a nursing mother—thus destroying her entire litter of four young, still in the burrow and totally dependent on her.

With crows and magpies, the laws are complicated. Legally they are no

longer varmints but are now classified as migratory birds, like waterfowl, and
can be hunted only within protective federal guidelines. They can't be hunted
during breeding season, and in some states they can't be hunted at all. Nowhere can the open season on crows run more than 124 days (consecutively or
split) although exceptions may be made in some states, such as Oklahoma,
where large concentrations can damage crops or trees or cause a potential hazard to human health. Some states have bag limits and some, such as New Jer-
sey, impose "rest days" during the annually set open season. Magpies never
were as avidly hunted as crows, and now almost no one shoots them because
the combined federal and state laws are too restrictive; more often than not,
it's just plain illegal to kill magpies.

The mammalian varmints such as chucks and prairie dogs still provide
much sport, however. Usually they're shot when they're sitting or standing
still, and at a considerable distance. The shooting is generally done from a
prone or sitting position, and often from a rest of some sort. Rifles, cartridges,
scopes, and other equipment for this type of shooting are quite specialized.

Until the early 1930's, there was hardly such a thing as a specialized factory varmint cartridge. Many used the .25/20 and the .32/30 cartridges, but
these were not much better than .22 rimfires. The rifles made for them were
too light. They were not particularly accurate, and in some cases they were
unsuited for scope mounting. Winchester made the Model 1892 lever-action
rifle for these cartridges. Marlin and Remington made pumps, and Savage
chambered the Model 23 series bolt-action rifles for them. Of the lot the most
accurate rifle was the Savage, but the accuracy of both cartridges was mediocre and this combined with their curved trajectories made them no better
than 125-yard varmint outfits at best.

It is a characteristic of varmint hunters that they become fascinated by
long-range precision shooting, and that they are never quite content with any
cartridge-rifle-scope combination, no matter how good. If they have good
outfits they are looking for something better. The varmint hunter is the man
who kept handloading alive from the black-powder days to these days of
widespread popularity. He is also the original experimenter and developer of
wildcat cartridges, the man whose patronage enabled gunsmiths to eat during
the Depression and who made it possible for scope and bullet manufacturers
to start their businesses.

Typically the varmint hunter started then (and probably starts today)
plinking away at crows and woodchucks with a .22 rimfire and iron sights. He
finds that he can almost never hit anything at over 75 yards. He tries .22 Long
Rifle high-velocity ammunition, but discovers he cannot hit much farther
with it. He then gets a scope for his .22. He can make hits perhaps 25 or 35
yards farther because he can see better, but beyond that distance the curved
trajectory of the rimfire .22 has him whipped.

Not long after World War I the more particular varmint hunters began to
grow unhappy with the .25/20 and the .32/20. If the varmint hunter was a
sophisticated and knowledgeable rifleman he might have a custom-made rifle

for a wildcat cartridge built. The .25/06 (the .30/06 case necked down to take a .25 caliber bullet) was developed prior to World War I by chuck hunters. It was originally called the .25 Niedner, the .25 High Power, or the .25 Whelen. The .25 Krag (the .30/40 case necked to .25) was probably developed a little earlier, and rifles for it were built on Krag and various single-shot actions.

But custom rifles are expensive, so the average woodchuck hunter who had grown discontented with .22 rimfires had to improve on existing calibers by handloading. In the 1920's the Director of Civilian Marksmanship sold to members of the National Rifle Association good military, national match, and sporting Springfields in .30/06 caliber at quite modest prices. The D.C.M. also sold cases, powder, primers, and bullets. It was these cheap rifles and components that gradually revived handloading, an art which had been popular during the days of black powder but which had almost died out after the introduction of smokeless powder.

These handloading varmint hunters used .30/06 rifles, very often N.R.A. Springfield sporters, but sometimes Model 30 Remingtons or Model 54 Winchesters. They wanted flat-shooting loads with bullets that would expand rapidly on light game and that would go to pieces when they struck the ground and not ricochet. They loaded 93-grain bullets made for the .30 Luger pistol, the 80- and 100-grain .32/20 bullets (as the .32/20 is actually an oversize .30 caliber) and they often tried cast lead bullets with gas checks to protect their bases. Remington brought out a 110-grain bullet to use on varmints in the .30/06 and loaded it to about 3300 foot-seconds.

The .30/06 is a fine big-game cartridge, a good target cartridge, and a good military cartridge, but it left much to be desired for use on varmints. For one thing, it was too noisy. For another it gave too much recoil, and for yet another none of these early varmint loads for the .30/06 were staggeringly accurate.

Varmint shooters wanted a quieter, more accurate cartridge with less recoil. They got it in the little .22 Hornet, which is once again regaining popularity in spite of its advanced years. This was originally a wildcat developed by the late Capt. Grosvynor Wotkyns. It was simply a modernization of an old and obsolete black-powder cartridge—the .22 Winchester Center Fire, a cartridge that had been mildly popular in the Winchester Model 85 single-shot rifle. Wotkyns substituted modern smokeless powder for black powder and .22 caliber jacketed bullets made for a European pistol cartridge called the .22 Velo Dog, and the result was the .22 Hornet. Original ballistics gave a 45-grain bullet a velocity of 2450 and a trajectory that made 150–175-yard hits possible. Accuracy was much better than the old .30/06 handloads with makeshift bullets.

Wotkyns got technicians at the Springfield arsenal interested in the cartridge. Some .22 Springfield rifles were chambered and adapted to it. Winchester brought out .22 Hornet ammunition, and Savage brought out a Model 23 rifle for it and Winchester a Model 54. The factory ballistics of the cartridge were stepped up to 2650.

The success of the .22 Hornet resulted in many .22 factory and wildcat varmint cartridges. The .220 Swift, for which the Model 54 Winchester (and later the Model 70) was chambered, appeared in 1936 with a 48-grain bullet at 4140, the highest muzzle velocity ever given an American factory cartridge. The .219 Zipper (the .25/35 Winchester case necked down to .22) came out in 1938 and the .218 Bee in 1939. Both cartridges appeared originally in lever-action rifles. They were not particularly accurate, and although both cartridges are still loaded no rifles are made for them and they are only feebly alive. The Swift is also a near orphan, as only Ruger has recently chambered rifles for it.

Another good but dying cartridge is the .257 Roberts, the 7 mm. x 57 Mauser case necked to .25 caliber. It was introduced as a factory cartridge in 1934 and Winchester Model 54 and Model 70 and Remington Model 30 and Model 722 rifles have been made for it. Its sales dropped off so badly after the introduction of the .243 Winchester and the .244 Remington that rifles in .257 caliber were dropped from manufacture until the early part of this decade, when Ruger, Remington and Winchester revived this chambering.

Along in the middle 1930's a 100-grain bullet was introduced for the .270 Winchester, a cartridge that had come out in the Model 54 Winchester in 1925. This was and is a fine varmint cartridge, particularly for the long-range chuck shot. Velocity is over 3500 and with some bullets accuracy is very good. Recoil and report are both too great to be ideal.

Between the introduction of the .22 Hornet and the outbreak of World War II, dozens of wildcat varmint cartridges were introduced. Few of them offered anything outstanding and almost all are now forgotten.

Among the most popular of today's varmint cartridges are the .222 Remington, the .223 Remington, and the .22/250. Unlike many other new cartridges the .222 Remington was not based on any existing case. Instead it was designed from scratch. In many respects it is the ideal varmint cartridge. It is very accurate. Recoil is almost nonexistent. The report is sharp but light. It is flatter-shooting than such cartridges as the .22 Hornet and the old .218 Bee. Since it doesn't use much powder, it is not expensive to load and it is easy on barrels. The .222 as factory loaded drives a 55-grain bullet along at 3000 foot-seconds and produces a mid-range trajectory over 200 yards of only 2.5 inches. It is a good 225-yard varmint cartridge, and very few varmint shooters have the skill to hit beyond that range. A number of bolt rifles have been chambered for the .222 Remington, including the Remington 700, the Savage 340, and the excellent Finnish Sako.

The .222 Remington Magnum is a little more potent than the .222 but it has never achieved the same popularity. The .223 Remington, which is the 5.56 mm. military round in civilian guise, exhibits the same ballistics and is vastly more popular. Both fire a 55-grain bullet at 3240 feet per second. The .223 chambering is available in a wide array of popular sporting rifles.

Three .22 caliber varmint cartridges, the .22/250 Remington, the .225 Winchester, and the .224 Weatherby Varmintmaster were introduced along about the same time in the middle 1960's. The .22/250 is simply the old

.22/250 wildcat or "Varminter." It is the wildcat from which the .220 Swift was developed, and it has been around 30 years. It is the .250/3000 Savage case necked down to .22 and given a 28 degree shoulder. It pushes a 35-grain bullet along at about 3650 foot-seconds in a 24-inch barrel. The .22/250 has always been an excellent cartridge giving long barrel life, good accuracy, and flat trajectory. It should have been a factory cartridge long before it was. Remington makes the Model 700 in .22/250 and also in the 40-X. Savage, Winchester, Ruger, Sako and Browning all chamber bolt-action rifles for it.

The .225 Winchester came out in the new Model 70 Winchester rifle in the spring of 1964 to replace the .220 Swift. The factory load gives a 55-grain bullet 3650 foot-seconds at the muzzle. The popularity of Remington's .22/250, introduced a year later, has about killed the .225.

The .224 Weatherby is, like the .222 Remington, an entirely new cartridge on a case designed from scratch. The rifle for which it is chambered has a short Weatherby Mark V action. Factory ballistics for the .224 show a 50-grain bullet at 3800 and a 55-grain at 3600. The mid-range trajectory over 200 yards is 1.7 inches. In powder capacity the .224 is about like the 225 Winchester. In equally good rifles it would take an astute shooter to tell any important difference between the .22/250, the .225, and the .224.

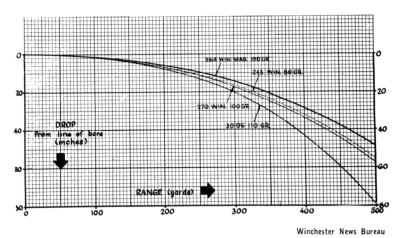

Varmint Cartridges: Drop from line of bore at different ranges.

When the 6 mm. cartridges (the .243 Winchester and the .244 Remington) broke on the breathless world in 1955, many assumed that this 6 mm. business was something new. Actually the U.S. Navy was using a straight-pull 6 mm. Lee rifle back in Spanish-American War days and the British firm of Holland & Holland made a 6 mm., the .240 H. & H., on a small, belted case long before the last war started. Fred Huntington, the R.C.B.S. tool and die man, was the father of the current 6 mm. fad. He necked down the .257 Roberts case to

6 mm., changed the shoulder angle and called it the .243 Rockchucker. It was brought out in a slightly different form by Remington as the .244 Remington. Winchester necked down the .308 Winchester case to 6 mm. and called it the .243 Winchester. The .243 became immensely popular as it had a 1–10 twist and gave good accuracy with sharp-pointed bullets as heavy as 105 grains and

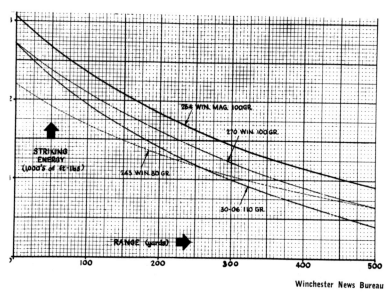

Winchester News Bureau

Varmint Cartridges: Striking energy at different ranges.

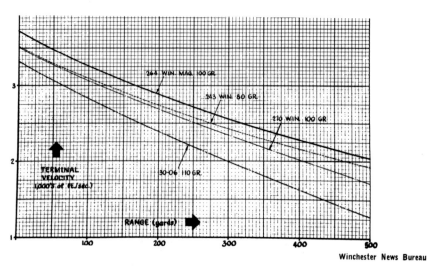

Winchester News Bureau

Varmint Cartridges: Terminal velocity at different ranges.

was regularly loaded with 100-grain bullets at 2960 in a 24-inch barrel, as well as an 80-grain bullet at 3350, also in a 24-inch barrel.

The rifle buyers chose the .243 over the .244 because the .243 had a faster twist and could handle heavier bullets. With its 1–12 twist the heaviest factory bullet furnished by Remington weighed 90 grains. The lads wanted rifles that would use heavier bullets and would do for deer as well as varmints. The .244 fell on its face. It was renamed the 6 mm. Remington and cartridges were loaded under that name with a 100-grain bullet at 3130 in a 24-inch barrel.

Rifle buyers are bemused when they cast an eye on the voluptuous factory ballistics of the two cartridges. However, these are taken in a 24-inch barrel and the big seller in the Winchester Model 70 was always the Featherweight with the 22-inch barrel. The Model 700 Remington in 6 mm. is also sold in a 22-inch barrel. In a 22-inch barrel the velocity of the .243 with the 100-grain bullet runs from 2900 to 2950 and with the 80-grain it runs from 3200 to 3300. What the velocity of the 6 mm. Remington is in a 22-inch barrel I cannot say.

Just as the .222 killed off the .22 Hornet, the .219 Zipper, and the .218 Bee, so did the .243 and the 6 mm. all but kill off the excellent .257 Roberts. The .257 is the 7 x 57 Mauser case necked to .25 caliber just as the 6 mm. is the .257 case necked down a bit to .244. The .257 is one of the most useful cartridges ever designed, more useful and more versatile than either the .243 or Remington's 6 mm. Since bullets weighing up to 125–130 grains can be used in the .257, it will do for everything from ground squirrels to elk. It is accurate, mild of recoil, and flat-shooting enough.

SCOPES

The first successful varmint scopes were simply target scopes mounted on the barrel or on the barrel and receiver with scope blocks. The scopes had no internal adjustments for windage and elevation, but instead were sighted in by micrometer adjustments in the rear scope mount. The scopes moved with recoil and had to be pulled back to battery with each shot. Fecker, Unertl, and Lyman target scopes were of that type. Unertl still makes these target-type scopes in powers from 8 to 36. For serious woodchuck shooting 10 or 12X is about right and some use scopes of 15X. The higher powers are for benchrest and target shooting.

Most of these old scopes were heavy, not too beautiful, and rather fragilely mounted. The best were superb optically and the adjustments were very exact. Now, however, most varmint shooters have abandoned them for internal-adjustment scopes of fairly high power—6 to 18. Silhouette shooters use similar scopes with oversized adjustment knobs. Redfield, Weaver, Leupold, Bushnell, and Burris also make variable-power models—4–12X and higher magnification for varmint and target shooting.

It is axiomatic that no one, no matter how steadily he can hold a rifle and no matter how gently he can squeeze, can shoot any better than he can see. If the chuck or crow hunter has a rifle-cartridge combination flat shooting and

accurate enough to reach out and knock off a crow or a chuck at 300 yards or
more he needs a scope which will enable him to aim properly at whatever he is
shooting at. When I first moved to Idaho I went out to shoot rockchucks with
a very accurate .270 mounted with a 4X scope. The rockchucks were the same
color as the scab rock country they inhabited. Many times I would locate a
chuck with my 9 x 35 binocular, but when I tried to aim through the scope I
was lost. I even shot at rocks instead of chucks.

The good varmint scope for precision shooting at long range should have
what is known as resolving power—and resolving power comes from a combination of fairly high magnification with a large objective. Magnification
without the large objective simply gives a larger image without detail. Resolving power enables the shooter to tell a chuck from a rock, a feeding ground
squirrel from a dead weed being moved by the wind.

But there has to be a compromise somewhere. A large objective makes a
scope rather homely looking. It raises the line of sight, and adds to the weight.
The higher the power of the scope, the smaller the field of view, the more critical the eye relief, and the shallower the depth of focus. The best power for the
scope sight is the lowest that will do the work satisfactorily.

I am convinced that no one has ever needed more than 6X for a .22 Hornet rifle, and for most conditions 6X is entirely satisfactory on a .222, although
for the man who wants to shoot out to the limits of the .222 trajectory an 8X is
all right. For something like the .243, the 6 mm. Remington, the .22/250, the
.220 Swift, or the .25/06, I think a 10X is about right for the chuck shooter,
and no one needs more power than 12. I owned a chuck rifle mounted with a
15X Unertl Ultra Varmint scope. It was a beautiful optical instrument, but
was long, heavy, bulky, and awkward. The depth of focus was very critical
and the field of view so small that it was sometimes difficult to pick the target
up quickly. I could see to aim nicely with it on chucks and crows farther than I
could hit them consistently. It was too much scope for me or for any of my
varmint rifles.

The varmint cartridge, then, should be very accurate, very flat shooting,
and the bullet should be so constructed that it will blow up in the carcass of a
small varmint or disintegrate when it strikes the ground. If in addition this
cartridge gives a light report and little recoil, so much the better. Not only
does light report make the varmint hunter more welcome (or less unwelcome)
in settled communities but the varmint hunter usually shoots better when his
rifle does not buck and bellow.

Varmint rifles themselves vary almost as much as varmint cartridges.
Winchester makes a heavier than average rifle in varmint calibers, and woodchuck hunters generally want their rifles to be a good deal heavier than
sporters used for woods and mountain hunting of big game. Probably the rifle
weighing complete with scope about 10–11 pounds is about right. The chuck
hunter usually doesn't carry his rifle far, and the heavy rifle is generally a bit
more accurate and easier to shoot accurately than the lighter rifle.

SHOOTING TECHNIQUES

The hunter of woodchucks, crows, and predatory hawks almost always shoots from a rest—across a stone wall, over the hood of a car (where it is legal to shoot from country roads) with his rifle resting on a stone padded by a jacket. Various portable rests are available. An excellent shooter's bipod is made by Harris Engineering, Inc., of Barlow, Ky. It attaches easily to a rifle's fore-end at the forward sling swivel, and the legs fold up alongside the barrel when not in use.

The shooting of the livelier varmints like the jackrabbits, coyotes, and bobcats of the West is something entirely different. These animals do not linger. If they are shot standing still they generally have to be shot quickly before they move on. Often they are shot on the run. The best hunting for these lively varmints is found far from roads and the hunter must walk long distances. It is seldom possible to shoot at these creatures from the prone position, as most of the country in which these animals are found is covered with low bushes which block out the view from prone and the country is covered with sharp rocks and thorns which make the sitting position hazardous and the prone position impossible.

For jackrabbit and coyote shooting, I have most often used the same light sporters I have used for deer, mountain sheep, and antelope. I have hunted

Winchester News Bureau

Varmint shooter using the hood of a jeep as a rifle rest. Padding under the fore-end prevents the rifle from jumping and shooting high.

Two types of portable rests. Left, the author using a bipod with a padded fork to support the fore-end; right, a forked-stick model which clamps around the barrel.

with rifles in caliber from .22 Hornet to .270 and .30/06. I have done most of my hunting of this type with 4X scopes and I would not want one with more power than 6. Scopes of higher power do not have enough field of view and enough latitude of eye relief to be practical for shooting running game.

The use of varmint callers has become very popular. When skillfully blown, these will bring almost any meat eater running, as they sound like rabbits in distress and the coyote or bobcat thinks he is about to fall heir to an easy meal. Calls that sound like a fawn in distress will bring up deer. One chap took such a varmint caller to India some years ago and called up a tiger!

I once asked a famous Alberta guide and outfitter who were the best rifle shots that came out to hunt with him. He told me they were the woodchuck hunters. Unlike those who shot only on black and white targets, he said, they were used to seeing small, neutral-colored animals in surroundings that partially camouflaged them and they had no difficulty picking up game. They were used to assuming steady positions and shooting accurately from improvised rests. They were used to shooting quickly and estimating distances under hunting conditions. "Give me a varmint shooter and my guiding job is easy!" he told me.

9

Hitting Running Game

THERE ARE two extreme views about shooting at moving game with a rifle. Those who are ultra-conservative say that under no circumstances is anyone justified in shooting at a running animal. If an animal is on the move, they say, the rifleman should wait until it stops. If it does not stop he should pass it up. In direct contrast are those who blaze away at any game animal they see as long as they can see it in the hope that they can kill it or at least slow it down. I have seen western deer and antelope hunters stand on their hind legs and pump bullets at running animals as long as they were in sight. I have never seen any figures on the percentage of antelope that get away wounded to die after these bombardments, but it must be quite high.

Once I was making a stalk on a bunch of antelope that had a nice buck in it. I was sneaking along the bottom of a ravine (or coulee, as they call it in Wyoming) when I heard a bullet crack over my head. A moment later I heard the boom—and I knew that the hunters doing the shooting were on the other side and I was between them and the antelope. I was hearing the crack of the bullet going through the air before I heard the report of the rifle. A whole fusillade followed that first shot, and I ducked down behind the cut bank to get out of the line of fire. When the antelope disappeared over the skyline the firing stopped. When it began the hunters were at least 600 yards from me and 800 yards from the antelope.

In contrast to such hopeful fellows, there are those who feel that shooting at a running animal at *any* distance is immoral, cruel, reckless. I was once taken to task by a reader because I related how I took a pop at a running ram at about 150 yards. He thought I was setting a bad example for my readers and leading the youth of America into the paths of sin.

Well, maybe!

Was I justified in shooting or wasn't I?

This ram was a very good ram, the best I had an opportunity to take a shot at, and the hunt was nearing the end. The ram was running broadside in the open at a moderate range. I had killed much game under similar circumstances and was quite sure I could hit the ram solidly. Actually I did hit the ram, though a bit far back. It ran 100 to 150 yards, fell, and rolled over a little cliff 10 or 15 feet high. It was dead when we got to it.

I felt then and still feel that under the circumstances I was justified in taking that shot.

I was hunting lions in Tanganyika in 1959 when a big male popped his head out of the grass at what afterwards proved to be 140 paces. I had an expensive lion license. Lions were not plentiful. If I did not get this lion, I would probably not get another shot, and in fact in the next two weeks until the trip was over I did not see another lion. The shot was almost exactly like the shot I took later at the ram. I swung the .375 along with the horizontal wire traveling along his yellow body. When the intersection of the crosswires was well ahead of his chest (about 1½ to 2 feet as I remember it) the sight picture looked so pretty I couldn't keep from squeezing the trigger. The lion let out the half-growl, half-roar that signifies a hit on any of the great cats. Then he disappeared into high grass.

Luckily I had put a 300-grain .375 Silvertip right through the lion's heart. It had run perhaps 35 or 40 yards into the tall grass and had died. Was I justified in taking the shot?

I doubt it. I was quite certain of hitting it somewhere, but I certainly wouldn't have bet any money that I would shoot it through the heart. A mountain ram is a harmless animal. If I had wounded that ram and we had followed it up, he would not have turned on me. On the other hand, if I had gut-shot that lion he might have killed me, the professional hunter or a gun bearer if we had followed him up in tall grass where all the advantage was on the side of the lion. My professional hunter on this trip was John Kingsley-Heath, who a year or so later was badly mauled and almost killed by a wounded lion. Would I take the same shot again if it were offered? I don't know. I'll be perfectly honest and say that it would depend on the state of my blood pressure. When people are hunting they are excited, and even the most experienced hunter will sometimes take shots the cold light of reason later tells him are unjustified. As I think about it, I don't think I should have taken the shot. The money I had spent for a lion license and the satisfaction of owning another lion trophy did not balance the very grave risk I ran.

Many years ago a great and experienced hunter wrote that any hit on a running animal at any distance is a first-class shot. I wouldn't say a first-class shot under all circumstances but I'd say a satisfactory shot. I have missed fast-jumping deer in heavy brush almost within spitting range, and I think most hunters who are honest and who have done much brush hunting will admit they have done the same.

Hitting running big game, particularly hitting it in the right place, is by no means easy, yet on the other hand it is not as difficult as it might seem. A running animal at 100 yards or at whatever distance he is shot at offers just as big a target as if he were standing. He generally isn't moving very fast. He generally looks as if he is going fast because our excitement makes us think he is going fast. Probably the average running deer, elk, or sheep isn't going over 15 miles an hour. A thoroughly frightened deer chased by an automobile can probably go 25 miles an hour, possibly 30. A scared coyote cannot travel at over 35, and I don't think a fat old bighorn ram can run as fast over level ground as a reasonably frisky man. Once many years ago in Sonora I was driving along an old mine road when I saw an old, heavy desert bighorn ram feeding on cholla fruit. I decided to see how fast he could run. I jumped out of the car and took after him. By the time I was out of wind I was almost close enough to slap him on the fanny and he had got the fright of his life. The antelope is the real speedster and has been clocked by automobile speedometers at 55 and 60 miles an hour.

Any small skill I may have developed at shooting running game I owe to two wonderful animals—the jackrabbit and the Arizona whitetail deer. Most of the time I lived in Tucson, Arizona, blacktail and antelope jackrabbits were very plentiful. I made it a rule not to shoot at a sitting rabbit at under 150 yards. If I couldn't get one to run I'd shoot at him offhand. My favorite target was the big antelope or "white side" jackrabbit. He ran more smoothly and was generally found in more open country than the smaller blacktail. My hunting partner most of the time was a fine shot and gun nut named Carroll Lemon. For twelve or fourteen years we must have averaged one jackrabbit hunt a week, and in the course of a year we would blunder into and bump off quite a few running coyotes. Often I have left the car with fifty rounds of ammunition and when I returned I'd have not a cartridge.

The Arizona whitetail (*Odocoileus couesi*), which is also called the fantail and the Sonora whitetail, is for my money the most beautiful of all American deer. In much of his range he is found in semi-open country where the draws are full of trees and brush, but the grassy hillsides spotted with evergreen oaks are open enough for running shooting. The mule deer can generally be depended on to stop for a backward look before he gets out of sight, even if he has been shot at. But not the Arizona whitetail. Once he has located and identified the hunter, he blasts off like a scared cottontail and keeps picking them up and laying them down until he is on the other side of the ridge or in the depths of a canyon.

It is entirely feasible in many areas to hunt these fine little deer from horseback. The hunter rides along the side of a canyon watching for a deer to move below him or on the other side. If he sees a buck he bounces off his horse, yanks his rifle out of the scabbard, and starts shooting. The deer like to bed down in the heavy brush at the foot of a cliff where the talus slope of soil and rocks broken off the cliff begins. In such brushy, rocky country conventional still-hunting is impossible. The country is so noisy that a caterpillar couldn't go across it without sounding like a bulldozer. Southwestern whitetail hunters get deer out of that country by getting on the cliff above a likely looking place and throwing stones into the brush. Even the smartest buck can take this only so long before his nerves are shot. Then he comes tearing out of there, and it is up to the hunter to cut him down on the run.

Another good method of getting a crack at these elusive little creatures is for one hunter to ride or walk on one side of a canyon and another hunter to take the other. Then each hunter will get a shot at the bucks the other hunter across the canyon has moved.

A good still-hunter who gets out early enough so that the deer are still feeding and moving around can often get standing shots at bucks. The year my son Bradford was thirteen, he was pretty small and too inexperienced in riding and shooting to leap off a horse and belt a running buck. I acted as his guide and we still-hunted for the little deer. He got two, one in Arizona and one in Sonora. He got the Sonora buck in his bed, something that almost never happens with this wary little whitetail.

The same principles apply to shooting running game as apply to shooting flying game with a shotgun. The chief differences are that big game shot with a rifle is generally shot at a greater distance and the hunter must depend on one bullet instead of a cloud of shot. He has to be more precise, but otherwise the techniques are the same.

Depending on circumstances the man who shoots game on the run will spot shoot, employ the fast swing, or use the sustained lead, a technique also called "pointing out."

By spot shooting or snap shooting, I mean throwing up the rifle, aiming at a spot where the target (the vital part of the animal) will be when the bullet gets there and then shooting with a stationary rifle. This is exactly the technique used for some types of shotgun shooting. Most gunners kill quartering birds by aiming at the spot ahead where the bird will be when the shot gets there. I do not swing down on the No. 1 high house target at skeet. Instead I shoot at a spot about 2 feet below it.

If a deer is climbing out of a canyon going directly away, hold above it, or if it is angling as it climbs, hold above and to one side so he'll run into the bullet. In other words, "spot shoot" it. If the animal is on the same level and going directly away from you, shoot right at it (trying to break the spine at the root of the tail or to drive the bullet between the hams) as no lead is required. If a charging animal such as a lion, a tiger, or grizzly bear is coming directly toward the hunter, the aim should be low so the animal will be led.

The great majority of running shots that the hunter in heavy brush and forest must take will be of the spot-shooting variety. The distance will be short, the angle gentle. The hunter should put his aiming point where he thinks the part of the animal he wants to hit will be and touch her off. As in shotgun shooting, he should fire the *instant* the sight looks right. If he hesitates he'll be behind.

If the game is moving at anything but a gentle angle, the shot must be taken with a moving rifle, just as a crossing bird must be shot with a moving shotgun. At any distance the aim must be well ahead of the target. If the hunter swings fast and has a slow reaction time *and* if the distance is short (50 yards or so), he may be able to aim for the spot he wants to hit and not be far from it. However, even under those circumstances he is apt to hit behind.

Every year tens of thousands of deer and antelope are gut-shot by hunters who did not get far enough in front.

When the 7 mm. Remington Magnum cartridge first came out, a gun nut at a luncheon party announced to one and all that the sustained velocity of the 7 mm. Magnum cartridge with the 150-grain bullet was so great that it was not necessary to lead running game with it up to 300 yards. In my usual tactful way I told him he was full of prunes—that I had shot hundreds of running jackrabbits with .270's using the 100-grain bullet and .220 Swifts using the 50- and 55-grain bullets (all of which would get to 100 yards faster than the 150-grain 7 mm. Magnum bullet) and that even at 100 yards and with a moving rifle if you shot right at a running jack you'd miss him every time. Depending, of course, how fast the jack is running the bullet will be from 1 foot to 2 feet behind the jack at 100 yards even if the sights are right on the jack and moving apparently as fast as the jack. If the shot is taken with a stationary rifle at a jack running broadside at 100 yards the bullet will land at least 3 feet and maybe 6 feet behind.

In the years when I lived in southern Arizona and hunted jackrabbits regularly, I developed a fair degree of skill in shooting running game with a rifle. Carroll Lemon and I got so that if a running jack was tearing along on an open hillside we never missed it far, and a fair percentage of the time we could roll a jackrabbit over if he were not over 200 yards away and we could fire

Most shots at deer in heavy brush will be at short range and at a gentle angle. Hunter must aim slightly ahead of running deer and fire the instant the sight looks right.

four or five shots as he ran along. I suppose we could keep our shots within about a 2-foot circle around the jack. We'd have unlucky streaks where four or five running jacks in succession might get away and lucky streaks where we'd knock over three or four in succession.

I remember one occasion when Lemon and I were hunting together. As we left the car I told him I was having a feud with a jack that lived under a bush across a wide draw on the other side of the first ridge, that he'd probably jump as soon as we got in sight. I said I had missed him three days in succession and wanted to take a crack at him. Sure enough, the jack was under his usual bush and he took off running broadside. I sat down, swung about 3 feet ahead, shot, and the jack simply blew up. As the rifle went off, another jack came barreling out and down it went. In the next draw I bounced another galloping jack with my second shot. Lucky day!

Practice on running jacks is the finest I know for shooting running big game. Lemon and I got so sharp with all this practice that running deer and coyotes were generally cold turkey. Before the Fish & Wildlife Service went on a poisoning rampage, there were a good many coyotes in the deserts around Tucson. They occasionally killed fawns but for the most part they lived on jackrabbits, cottontails, and packrats. In the course of a year, I'd get 9 or 10. Generally they would be moving slowly, but some I shot going flat out. I remember one, so help me, that must have been at least 300 and maybe 350 yards away. I killed him on the second shot and I must have led him around 25 feet. A shot like that is not entirely luck but it has a lot of luck in it.

In the same period I hunted deer a lot in Mexico and shot a whitetail every year in Arizona. I remember one stretch of four seasons where I hunted every year on the Siebold ranch near Patagonia. I fired 6 shots and killed 4 bucks, all were running at from 150 yards to perhaps 250. The Siebolds will remember this. I couldn't do that well now.

Fred Huntington, the R.C.B.S. tycoon, will remember this shot. We were hunting in Wyoming and Fred had already got an antelope. As we headed back home a bunch of antelope circled around and cut across in front of the car. I sat down, swung the .275 H. & H. Magnum I was using with the horizontal crosswire moving along the middle of the buck's body. When the vertical wire looked to be about 3 to 3½ lengths ahead, I touched off the shot. A moment later we heard the sound of a striking bullet and an instant later the buck slid on his nose. We paced the distance off over absolutely level ground and got 285 paces. I got a big assist from luck on that one.

Those who do not live in jackrabbit country but who want to acquire a fair degree of skill in running shooting are in luck if they have access to a rifle club that has a running deer target. Running-boar shoots are popular in Europe, and there are some ranges now in this country where this animated target sport can be practiced. If it does nothing else such targets will show the shooter that he has to get well out in front with a moving rifle if he is going to hit anything. I have seen a lot of people shooting at running deer targets and I have yet to see anyone miss by shooting in front.

At longer ranges, when the game is moving directly across the line of sight, hunter can swing with the animal and fire when his lead looks right. At 100 yards, lead should be a bit ahead of brisket.

At 150 yards a lead of about 3 or 4 feet is called for.

At 200 yards the rifleman's lead increases to 6 to 8 feet.

Some years ago, I went with a friend out to a rifle club near Mexico City. The boys were practicing on a moving target at 300 meters (well over 300 yards). Beginners were often missing the target by 40 or 50 yards. Some of the old-timers were surprisingly good, hitting on or near the target with each shot. I asked one very good shot how much he was leading the target and he said about 30 meters. I asked another and he said he shot right at it. So much for having others tell you how much to lead.

If there are no running jacks and no running deer or boar target, it helps the hunter to shoot cottontails with a .22 rimfire rifle and the same type of sights he uses for big game. You can also take turns with a partner, rolling an old tire with a cardboard target in its center downhill. This is a sporty, hard-to-hit mark that provides fine pre-hunt practice. Just make sure to exercise all safety precautions.

For woods hunting most shots will be fast snaps at deer going directly away or at gentle angles. But even in the woods one will get an occasional broadside running shot that requires swing and lead. On such shots remember to get ahead and keep the rifle moving.

For open-country running shooting such as is often done on antelope, Arizona whitetail, and mule deer, the rifleman should sit, as sitting is a much steadier position than offhand and much more flexible than prone. Some excellent running shots tell me that they use the fast swing. As with the shotgun that means that they start behind the running animal, swing faster than the animal, then touch off the shot with what looks like the right lead.

I like that method only at short ranges. If an animal is in open or fairly open country, I prefer the sustained lead. I swing the rifle along ahead of the animal with the aiming point traveling apparently as fast as the animal. Keeping the rifle swinging I squeeze off. If you stop your swing when the trigger is pulled, you'll probably miss. Follow-through is important.

How far should the running target be led? That depends on a good many factors. About the least of these is the speed of the bullet. I think it makes almost no difference if the bullet leaves the muzzle at 2500 or 3500 foot-seconds. I have shot running jacks on alternate days with a .257 and a bullet traveling at 2900 at the muzzle and a Swift with a bullet that left the muzzle at 4100. As far as I could tell there wasn't a dime's worth of difference in necessary lead.

The important factors are how fast the rifleman swings, how fast the animal is moving, and how far the animal is away. I have seen tables of necessary lead published. I think they are worthless. They are based on bullets fired from a stationary rifle at animals at known speeds and distances. This is theoretical lead. As is the case with shotgun shooting, practical lead with a swinging rifle is about half of theoretical lead. Like the shotgunner, the rifleman thinks he shoots instantly but he does not. While his rifle is swinging the firing pin falls, the primer goes off and ignites the powder. Powder gas pushes the bullet up the barrel and out after the game. All that time the rifle is moving.

The running shot should remember to shoot as quickly as he can and not to dawdle. To keep his rifle moving and never to slow or to stop his swing. He should remember to sit and never to try anything but a short running shot from unsteady offhand. He should watch for the dust thrown by his bullets and correct his lead. To do this he must know exactly where his sights were when the rifle went off.

People miss running shots because they are excited. They don't really aim. They just point in the general direction of the game and shoot. They miss running shots because they shoot right at a crossing animal. He who does that gut shoots the animal or misses him. They also miss because overanxiety makes them stop or slow their swings. As is the case with flying game, running animals are most often missed by shooting behind.

How much to lead? Here are some leads that work for me. If a deer is running across in front of me at about 100 yards, I'd swing along with it and let off the shot a bit ahead of the brisket. If it were an antelope at 100 yards and making knots, I'd swing about 2 feet ahead.

If the deer was about 150 yards running broadside I'd try to be 3 or 4 feet in front of his brisket, and at 200 yards I'd try to be 6 or 8 feet ahead.

Every individual must find out his own leads by shooting, by watching the spurts of dust, by missing and by hitting. As is the case with the shotgun, one man's lead is another man's poison.

10

Shooting at Long Range

ANYONE who lulls himself into slumberland every night as I do by reading a hunting tale will run into some eye-popping accounts of game knocked off at fantastic ranges. In one story a writer shot a ram at 600 yards, and in his next he knocked off a bear at the same distance. In both cases the animals were running. I wish the guy would quit it; the suspense is bad for my heart.

I hate to be a pessimist, but I suspect that either our boy was not letting a good tale get any the worse in the telling or he is not the best judge of distances that ever lived.

Once upon a time (just once!) I killed an elk at what actually seemed to be about 600 yards. I had two companions with me, and, as the basin in which I killed the elk was fairly level, we made a pretty good stab at pacing off the distance to the spot where the elk lay. We had all the time in the world, and the comparison of the depth of the elk's body with the 4-minute dot in the scope I was using made 600 yards the most likely estimate. I held for 600 yards and hit the elk twice, so the guess wasn't too far wrong. When I shot I was sitting on a rock and resting the fore-end of my rifle over a larger rock padded with a down jacket. My hold was as steady as if I had been shooting from a bench rest.

I strongly suspect that most 600-yard shots are about 300, or maybe 250. That elk looked a long, long distance away, and my original guess (before I compared the depth of his body with the size of the dot) was over 800 yards. He was a very big six-pointer, and he was standing in the shade and I could not see his long and heavy antlers through the 2½X scope I was using. He was with a bunch of cows. I had to get him well located in relation to a large boulder with 8X binoculars in order not to shoot a cow by mistake.

In that particular case I may have been justified in shooting at 600 yards. However, I am inclined to doubt it. The bull was in a big, open timberline basin, and I could get no nearer because the one good line of approach was blocked by several lesser bulls. The basin was so open that I could have shot a whole box of cartridges at the bull if I had wounded him. I had a perfect place to shoot from, a good idea of the range, and I was well informed as to the trajectory of my rifle. Furthermore an elk is a large animal that is easier to hit than a sheep, deer, or black bear.

A score of years ago I had an amigo who was what he liked to call a practical big-game shot. I suppose the fact that I did a lot of paper punching made me an impractical big-game shot in his eyes. Anyway, this lad used to regale me with tales of the long-range shots he made with his iron-sighted .30/06. For him a deer running like a scared rabbit at 500 yards was cold turkey.

One day I persuaded him to come with me out to the range of the rifle club to which I belonged. At the 400-yard shooting point I stopped the car and suggested that we get out and unload rifles and spotting scopes, then go on and put up some targets. "Hells bells," he said. "You don't expect me to shoot from here, do you? That's half a mile away." After a time he decided that maybe those deer had been only 300 yards away—or maybe 250.

I used to take more shots at long range than I do now. Part of it was the natural ebullience of youth, but some of it was due to the fact that I grew up in the Southwest where most of my hunting was done in hilly and mountainous open country where ranges were long and where the deer usually saw the hunter first.

Much of the hunting in the Southwest is done on horseback, and generally the deer will either lie low and let the hunter ride by or take off at 200 to 300 yards. Then the hunter gets off and smokes up the deer. I have seen quite a few bucks killed running (or at least moving) at around an honest 300 yards, and I have likewise seen many deer shot at (most at) farther off than that.

The more I hunted deer in those Arizona hills the more convinced I was that under most circumstances about 300 yards was the longest range at which the hunter should shoot at them—even a good, unflustered rifleman with a 4X scope on a flat-shooting, accurate rifle. Beyond that distance, there is simply too much chance of a poorly placed shot and a wounded animal.

Wild sheep and goats are traditionally supposed to be shot at long range, but for my part I have seldom had to take long shots. Sometimes sheep will be found in big open basins or in rolling hills where a close approach is impossible. Generally, though, they are found in cut-up country of sharp ridges, bluffs, and deep canyons where they can be approached from behind a ridge. I have shot three Rocky Mountain goats and a couple of ibex, and most were shot at less than 200 yards. Of the 35 or 40 mountain sheep I have shot on three continents, I have killed more at under 200 yards than over. The last desert sheep I shot was not over 35 yards from the muzzle of my rifle, and the last wild sheep I shot was spotted at over a mile and stalked to about 150 yards.

Many antelope are killed at long range, but the average is probably around 200 yards, and perhaps more are shot at ranges under 200 than over. However, much needless wild shooting is done at antelope. Too many hunters start bombarding them the moment they see them instead of taking their time and planning and executing a skillful stalk. The result is, of course, that many antelope escape wounded.

Most of us habitually overestimate range—at birds, varmints, or big game. I know that I have missed far more game by overestimating the range and overshooting than I have by undershooting. As the years calmed my natural exuberance, I found that I took fewer long shots than I once did. I believe this conservatism goes hand in hand with age and experience. The more a man hunts, the more he hates to wound and lose an animal, and the greater the pride he takes in killing cleanly with one shot.

Over the years I made a series of rules for myself, rules I rarely violated.

For one thing, I tried never to take a shot at long range if I had a reasonable chance of getting closer. Generally it was possible to stalk closer. I have had many chances to blast a mountain sheep 400 and 500 yards away, but I learned to restrain myself.

Even if an animal sees the hunter, he generally won't leave the country if he is not shot at. He may be suspicious, but he is not badly frightened. If he doesn't shoot, the hunter may be able to come up on the animal later—or even next day. On several occasions I have been within long shooting range of rams at a time when there wasn't enough light left to complete a stalk and bring me safely back to camp. Then the question was whether to gamble on a long shot, and possibly a wounded animal, or to leave the rams alone and take a chance on finding them next day. Experience has taught me that it is the better bet to forget the itching trigger finger and to come back the next day and try to locate them.

A deer that has been frightened will run around on the other side of a hill and brush up. A frightened elk will often go miles. One time on Arizona's Mogollon Rim I took a 500-yard shot at a big six-point bull. I could have gotten closer, and I also could have taken more time to get into a more solid position. But I was new to elk hunting then and I was excited. I missed the elk but decided to follow him up. As near as I could figure out from a forest service map, I followed him fifteen miles. I never saw him again.

Sheep that have been shot up will likewise put a lot of country behind them. On one occasion years ago another hombre and I were hunting in the San Francisco mountains of northern Sonora—a group of very steep and rugged granite mountains rising from 1,500 to possibly 3,000 feet above the desert plain. We had separated in the morning and I had not seen him again. Then, late in the afternoon, I heard him open up about a mile away. Presently I located him with binoculars.

He was shooting at a small bunch of rams (three or four, if I remember correctly). He spotted them below him on a point and, instead of trying to stalk closer, he had started smoking them up at about 400 yards. He didn't get a hair. I watched the rams run off the mountain, across a mile or so of flat desert, up another mountain, and out of sight over the top. Neither of us saw them again. The next day I found where they had left the San Franciscos and were headed for another range fifteen miles or so away.

The ability to make a reasonably correct decision whether to shoot or not to shoot is the product of a lot of experience. If the animal is not frightened, if time and terrain make a closer approach possible, or if the shot is beyond the hunter's skill, then the thing the hunter should do is pass up the shot. He should likewise think twice, even if there is a pretty good chance that he can make a hit, if the animal is in such a position that it can move out of sight after one shot. An animal standing at the edge of thick brush can often disappear before the hunter can tell whether he hit or missed. So can an animal on the skyline.

One time I was hunting on horseback in Sonora when I saw a deer moving through thin brush far across a canyon. I got off my horse, sat down, and got him in the field of view of my 9X binoculars. I could see he was a big buck. He was aware of my presence and didn't like my looks. Wary but not panicky, he was simply planning to put a ridge between us. I got into a good sitting position and sat watching him through the scope. I hoped he would stop for a moment when he got to the top of the ridge. I estimated that he was under 400 yards, over 300. I was using a .270 with the 130-grain bullet sighted to hit the point of aim at 275 yards. When the rifle recoiled, the horizontal crosswire looked to be a touch above the top of the buck's shoulder.

One jump took the buck out of sight. I hadn't heard the bullet hit, didn't see the buck flinch or sag, saw no dust fly. I decided that the buck was not as far away as I had thought and that I had shot over him. Getting over to the top of the other ridge would be pretty tough, as the country was steep and rough. I was about to decide to ride on and try to scare up another buck when a cruising crow came wheeling down the ridge. When he got just above the spot where the buck had disappeared, he did a double take, circled, and announced to the world in crow language that he had just seen something very interesting. It took me over half an hour to get across the canyon, but when I did so I found that the buck had been shot squarely through the lungs and hadn't traveled over 30 feet. If it hadn't been for the tattletale crow I would have lost some very nice venison.

A long-range shot is generally justified only when the animal has been spooked and when the lay of the land makes it impossible to get closer, when the country is such that several shots can be taken if the first misses or wounds, and when the hunter is convinced that he can kill the animal before it gets out of sight. He should not simply *hope* he can get the game down, he should *know* it. Self-confidence makes for a steadier hand and eye.

Back in 1955 I was hunting the lively little Persian red sheep in the Zagros Mountains of Iran with Prince Abdorreza Pahlavi. We were at about 12,500 feet elevation, and now and then in the soil between the rocks we would see very fresh ram tracks. Then we saw the rams—about a dozen of them. They had been in a basin just ahead of us, and apparently the shifting, vagrant wind had brought them a whiff of man scent.

I decided to shoot because (1) the rams were spooked and were moving out; (2) because they were in the open, had about 200 yards to travel before they'd be out of sight; and (3) because past experience told me that I had a 10-1 chance of killing one of them before they could cover that 200 yards. I was by no means certain of the range, as the Persian red sheep is a little fellow smaller than the smallest of the North American sheep. Furthermore, there was nothing in the scenery to help me judge range. However, I guessed that the ram of my choice was out at 300 yards or more.

Since I, like anyone else, am a bit more apt to overestimate the range than underestimate, I held the first shot dead on and right behind the shoulder. The Prince had his binoculars on the ram and called the shot just under the chest. I held the next above the shoulder. I heard the bullet plunk, and in a few seconds the ram began rolling down the hillside. He was probably well over 300 yards away.

Judging range is a pretty baffling business. Animals seen in bright light look closer than if seen on an overcast day. Animals seen above and below seem smaller and farther away. Animals outlined against the skyline seem closer than they are. In hot desert country, mirage can make an animal seem twice as large as normal and therefore closer. An animal with the lower part of its body hidden by tall grass generally seems smaller and farther away.

Because the human hunter is not equipped with a built-in rangefinder, the man who does much shooting at the longer ranges should use a relatively flat-shooting rifle and sight it in for the longest distance that will not cause mid-range misses. I have done more plains and mountain hunting with a .270 than with anything else. I generally use the 130-grain bullet at about 3140 foot-seconds and sight in to put the bullet 3 inches above line of scope sight at 100 yards. The bullet then lands 2 inches high at 200, 4 inches low at 300, 8 inches low at 350, and 18 inches low at 400. With this system, and with a cartridge with approximately the .270 trajectory, the point-blank range is about 325 yards, even on a smallish deer or antelope. Other cartridges with approximately the same trajectory are the .264 Winchester with the 140-grain bullet, the .300 Weatherby with the 180-grain bullet, the .300 Winchester Magnum with the 150-grain bullet, and the 7 mm. Weatherby with the 140-grain bullet. The 7 mm. Express Remington, .308 Winchester and the .30/06 with the 150-grain bullets are a bit less flat, and so is the 7 x 57 with the 140-grain bullet.

Plenty of missing from holding too high has taught me that it is generally the wisest thing to hold dead on for the first shot if there is any doubt about the range. A low shot is generally easier to see and tells the rifleman more than a high one. If the hunter is convinced that the animal is well over 300 yards away, then he can hedge his bets by holding on the top of the shoulder.

If the animal is 350 yards away, the hold will drop the bullet squarely into the chest cavity. Even if the animal is 400 yards away, a hit on a fairly large animal will generally result. My own feeling is that generally if an animal can't be hit with a flat-shooting rifle and a top-of-the-shoulder hold, he is too far away to shoot at. By following this system of sighting in and holding, most hunters will cut down on their long-range misses. Using a range-finding scope can also cut down on guesswork, but these devices aren't infallible. At 400 yards, an animal is too far away for most shooters. Almost always, the best tactic is to try to get closer.

Range judgment is tough at best, and the more the hunter pins his faith to a flat-shooting rifle and the less he relies on his faulty estimates the better off he is. Some bum judgments on range are ludicrous. I once had an innocent pal who mistook a jackrabbit at about 75 yards for a deer at 300, and another who opened up on a porcupine at 100 yards thinking it was a grizzly at long range.

But who am I to scoff? One time in northern British Columbia I saw two bears far above me on a hillside. I was carrying a .30/06 loaded with the factory stuff giving a 180-grain bullet about 2700. My rifle was sighted for 200 yards, and the bullet would drop 9 inches at 300, 24 inches at 400. My guide and I decided that the bears were at least 400 yards away and possibly something over 500. I took a good rest and opened up. I never got close enough to bother the bears much, and the damp, grassy hillside kept us from seeing any spurts of dust.

The guide and I were both puzzled by the business. A check at camp showed that my rifle was sighted in properly and that my cartridges came complete with bullets, primers, and powder. The fact that the bears had been so little bothered by the shooting gave me a clue. Generally a low shot will throw stones or dirt on an animal and it will react. These bears weren't bothered. I finally decided that the only explanation was that these were not adult black bears at 400–500 yards, but cubs at about 200.

I remember another very bum guess. My son Bradford and I were hunting mule deer in the mountains overlooking Idaho's Salmon River when I spied a buck standing by a yellow pine across a canyon and looking right at us. Again I had a .30/06 in my hands. I took an expert glance at the buck. "My lad," I said to Bradford, "yonder buck is not far from 400 yards away. I'll hold right on his nose and drop the bullet right into his chest."

I shot. The buck went down in his tracks. "Behold, my son," quoth I, "and observe your father's skill."

But alas, the buck was hit through the neck right below the point of the chin. Instead of being 400 yards away he was not much over 200.

I have made some fairly good guesses on range in my day, but I have also made some pretty sour ones. As the years have slipped by I have learned that the more I depend on the trajectory of a flat-shooting rifle and the less I depend on my very fallible guesser the better off I am. Experience has taught me that I (along with most other hunters I know) miss more shots at long and undetermined range by overestimating the distance than by underestimating, and by overshooting rather than by undershooting. Experience has also taught me that if an animal is too far away to hit with a flat-shooting rifle and a hold at the top of the shoulder, he is generally too darned far away to shoot at. Experience has also taught me that more often than not, the smart thing to do is avoid opening up at long and undetermined range, as usually the animal can be stalked closer—or even hunted the following day. Experience also taught me that when I shot at an animal and knew I'd hit him, I almost always did. When I was not sure I generally missed.

These 600-yard shots at fleeing stags and galloping bears make pretty exciting reading, but the absolutely cold-turkey shot at sure range fired by a good rifleman who knows he is going to hit puts more trophies on the wall of the rumpus room and more meat in the locker.

Target Shooting

Roy Dunlap

11

Small-Bore Match Shooting

SMALL BORE, or .22 rimfire target shooting has existed since the end of muzzle loading and the beginning of breech loading a hundred years ago. It reached a specialized form around 1890 when riflemen called for matching equipment to their large-caliber schuetzen rifles. These were single-shot off-hand, or standing position, types made on various falling-block lever actions, often quite heavy, with set triggers and good sights. Use was mostly indoors during winter months. World War I ended the era—millions of men were trained with bolt-action rifles and the Germanic-flavored schuetzen game died.

Modern small-bore shooting began as training for big-bore: Military authorities had long used special equipment—Krags with special .22 barrels, 1903 Springfields with several different conversions—but not until the end of World War I was the true bolt-action .22 target rifle really conceived, and still as rehearsal arms for the Springfield service rifle. In 1919 the Savage Arms Company brought out the Model 19 NRA Match Rifle, a 7-pound full-military stocked job. Also in 1919 Winchester introduced the fine Model 52 series—discontinued long ago, to the chagrin of many shooters. It was made to same weight and buttstock dimensions as the 1903 Springfield and with the same double-pull 3-pound military trigger, though not the full stock. Military designers were also at work and in 1922 produced the U.S. Springfield .22 M1922M1, a small-bore target rifle for training purposes, and made it available to civilian members of the National Rifle Association. Winchester had already, in 1920, developed the first .22 match cartridge, soon followed by other firms, and shooters now had a choice of good rifles and good ammunition.

By 1925 small-bore target shooting began to shape into a field of its own, no longer limited to military training procedures, targets, and courses, but basically influenced by the military trend of much prone practice and the 3-pound trigger pull. Heavy custom barrels, better sights, telescopic equipment, good single-stage triggers (no military "take-up" of slack), special stocks, every possible accessory helpful to shooting, and improved match ammunition ap-

99

peared in the next decade. Indoor .22 shooting rose at the same time with the same equipment, but from the start retained the military training positions—prone, sitting, kneeling, and standing. After World War II Americans again became interested in international competitions, the Olympic and International Shooting Union matches, which call for, or rather, allow, specialized rifles evolved from the old schuetzen arms and feature shooting in standing, prone, and kneeling positions. The United States up until the 1930 Depression had been a leader in world shooting but was unable to again send teams until 1948. Harry Renshaw of Arizona was high man in Rome in 1930—and it was thirty-two years later that Gary Anderson of Nebraska became world champion at Cairo. His victory increased interest in the international courses and equipment so that today outdoor position shooting is very popular, in many areas drawing more competitors than the now long-established strictly prone tournaments.

RIFLES FOR SMALL-BORE SHOOTING

As in photography or fishing, equipment for shooting is as much what you want as what you need. A man can have a complete separate outfit for each of the four forms of small-bore competition—prone, international, gallery, and outdoor position. Few shooters of course have several rifles although many have two, one for prone competition and a second equipped for position matches. Any inferiority in rifle, sights, or ammunition means defeat in prone competition almost 100 percent of the time. In position shooting, the human element carries much more weight, but a bad trigger, a poorly-designed stock or a rifle too light or too heavy are also nearly insurmountable handicaps.

For "beginner" target rifles, we are in a sad state today—only Remington makes a model suitable for youngsters or small adults, the 540-XR Jr. We have many thousands of junior shooters struggling along with obsolete and inferior old rifles handed down. Most of these are barely good enough for basic 50-foot training and, with their poor sights and triggers, are pretty discouraging to the kids. A boy, or girl, ten to twelve years old, when he is most interested in learning to shoot, has a hard time. His hands are small so they can't get much strength into the trigger because of the big grips on the stocks, most triggers are overweight, and a perfect 3-pound pull is as heavy to them as 8 pounds to a normal adult. How the sub-juniors (under 13) do as well as they do is hard to understand.

Other moderately priced rimfire target rifles include the full-size Remington 540-XR, the Mossberg Model 144, the Harrington & Richardson Model 5200 Match Rifle, and the Anschutz Mark 2000. These are high-quality rifles, popular with feminine shooters as well as teenagers.

In the heavy first-line category we have a much better selection, aimed at the adult who wants the best and can pay for it. Many such rifles are restocked and altered for position use by individual shooters and gunsmiths. Remington's entry is the 40-XR, built on a modified single-shot version of their short

Anschutz Model 1808ED Super is a precision .22 target rifle designed for international running-target competition.

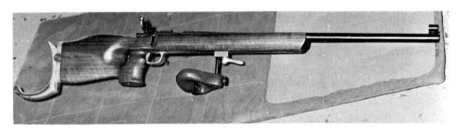

Remington Model 40-XR rimfire position rifle, with adjustable hand stop and two-way vertically adjustable buttplates.

Custom-built Finnish .22 free rifle with hook and palm rest for standing. The barrel is very long and heavy, sights are offset to the left, and the trigger can be adjusted at a very light setting.

Anschutz Model 64-MS is specifically designed for rimfire silhouette shooting, an astonishingly fast-growing target sport that originated in Mexico.

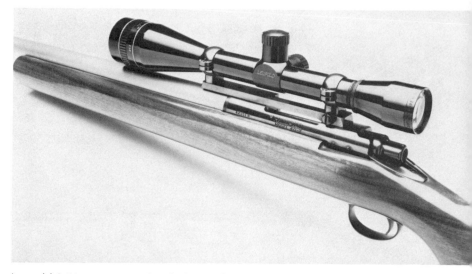

Leupold 24X target scope has locking adjustment dials for windage and elevation, and a focusing objective lens. Only in recent years have high-power target scopes been made this compact.

centerfire sporting rifle action. It is available with prone stock or, at considerably higher price, in an international model with thumbhole stock, palm rest, light trigger, etc. The heavy Anschutz Model 1800 series, offering several variations and stock styles, is quite popular. Position and international-minded shooters have a choice of Walther, Finnish Lion, Feinwerkbau, Anschutz and Kirco. The Oregon firm of Kimber also manufactures a limited number of high-quality target rimfires. Kimber, Anschutz and other makers also produce specialized rifles for rimfire game-silhouette matches.

The American .22 prone shooter, concentrating on prone position only, demands perfection in performance. At 100 yards he shoots at a 2-inch 10-ring, with a 1-inch X-ring in the center to break ties—and he'd better keep nearly all his bullet holes inside that X-ring to win anything. In any 40-shot match in good weather there will be many perfect 400 scores turned in and the man with most X's wins. So, he wants barrels and ammunition capable of grouping well under 1 inch at 100 yards, for a bit of leeway. Good as they are, the American-made rifles in unaltered factory style are almost never used by topflight marksmen. Custom barrels, tested and retested, special stocks, special triggers and selected sights are the rule rather than the exception. Great care is given to selection and testing of match ammunition by the shooters as it always varies slightly due to manufacturing processes. The match barrels vary also—one may shoot one type of ammunition better than others, and the prone shooter works constantly to keep a supply of "hot ammo" for his rifle. A good percentage of the first-rank competitors now use special actions made to order by individual machine shops or gunsmiths. These are designed to be more rigid and take a longer threaded shank of barrel in hope of further increasing accuracy or maintaining it as the rifle heats up in long matches.

AMMUNITION

Only the .22 Long Rifle cartridge is ever used. Indeed, by rule, no longer case, or larger diameter, or heavier bullet than the normal factory standard can be fired in competition. The .22 Short and Long are never used—the Short's case doesn't fill the match chamber and the Long has an inaccurate bullet. This is a shame really, for the long rifle case is now unnecessary. It was designed long ago, to take a case full of black powder—which hasn't been used for many years. Now only a tiny pinch of smokeless powder is necessary, which practically gets lost in the case. How the powder lies in the loaded cartridge at time of firing can affect ignition and therefore accuracy, and requires careful seating of bullets. If one bullet requires more pressure to jar it loose than the next, accuracy is radically affected. An arms and ammunition expert for one of the large firms says that they could load the long rifle match bullet to desired match velocity (just under the speed of sound) in the .22 Short case—or one even smaller—and equal if not surpass the current long rifle match ammunition performance. He believes manufacture would be cheaper and production more uniform. However, the long rifle is so firmly established people wouldn't consider any alternate, and of course rifles would have to be chambered for the short cartridges.

SIGHTS

Target rifle sights are like the steering gear on a car—if not perfect, better not enter any races. The rear sight is a micrometer-screw adjusting type with ball-bearings or plungers spring-loaded to retain positions. Most are ¼-minute adjustment, each click moving the point of aim ¼ inch per 100 yards of range—⅛ at 50 yards, ¼ at 100, ½ at 200, etc. Redfield also makes a sight adjusting to ⅛-inch at 100 yards, ¹⁄₁₆ at 50, etc. These are generally used by shooters who fire on the critical ISU international targets rather than the easier-scoring NRA. The sight must positively move a certain distance, no more, no less, for each adjustment. Redfield and Lyman are the only firms we have now commercially producing match sights.

Shading attachments, light filters, adjustable iris and selective-hole apertures are commonly used with the rear sights. Front sights come in all sizes, prone shooters often using very long and large-diameter tubular types, seeking the perfect sight-picture—a clearly defined bull's-eye and sight reticule, the latter usually a ring type with clear or tinted plastic having an outlined hole in the exact center, interchangeable so that various sizes can be inserted for different-sized bulls or light conditions. Position and international shooting calls for smaller globe-fronts, some men using post inserts rather than ring types. Shooting glasses are nearly always worn, with prescription lenses for those who need correction. The American type has always been just a modified sunglass, with green or yellow lens, but the European styles of specialized shooting glasses are now very popular. They are designed to hold lenses at correct angle and position when actually sighting the rifle rather than forcing the shooter to look through the northwest corner of his lens at an angle to the line of sight.

International rules specify metallic sights (no magnifying lenses) but in prone, gallery, and outdoor position matches, at least 50 percent of firing is with the U.S.-developed target telescopic sight. Rimfire game silhouette competition also allows the use of scope sights—indeed, the scope is a must for anyone even halfway serious about the sport. The target riflescope is high power—up to 30 power being used, though most prone men stay 20X or under, position and gallery less. Exterior micrometer adjustments give the same ¼ minute elevation and windage changes that the rear sight provides. Quality 6-18X variable scopes are made by Burris, Redfield and Leupold, but their weight and higher cost have limited popularity. The scope reticule is most often a fine crosswire, with a fair number of shooters using the crosswires with a center dot on them. The high power of these scopes makes it necessary to focus carefully for each range used.

SPOTTING SCOPES

Spotting telescopes, for seeing bullet holes in the target and watching wind conditions—interpreting the "mirage" or heat waves in the air—are prismatic types, 20 to 30 power, with objectives 2 inches or more in diameter. They are held by tripods or other stands in position so that the shooter has only to move his head a few inches from firing position to view his target. A couple of "zoom"type of focusing and variable-power scopes are now available, but most rely on screw focusing and change of eyepiece to change power. The optical glass and size of ocular (eye piece) are keys to quality. A large objective means little if the back end isn't right too. Many of the cheap imported spotting scopes are weak here. It is also nice to have prisms in your prismatic scope instead of mirrors. A good scope should be able to pick up all .22 bullet holes at 100 yards under all light conditions except near total darkness, at 20, 24 or 25X, and .30 bullet holes at 200 yards under all average conditions. B & L, Unertl, and Bushnell are the most popular makes used.

SMALL-BORE COMPETITION

The position shooter isn't quite so concerned with ultra-precision barrels as the prone specialist, though his must be very good, since his longest range is 50 yards and prone only a fourth of his shooting, at most one third. He wants an accurate rifle and ammunition, but also must practice his positions. His rifle must shoot well and be reasonably comfortable prone, but also and more important, handle perfectly when standing. It doesn't help much to have a perfect prone score then lose five points in one shot standing. The prone rifle has a long buttstock with high comb, and wide, shallow fore-end, all for comfort while firing long prone matches. The position rifle must have a shorter buttstock, with an adjustable buttplate set having hook and prone type plates, so that it will fit in four body positions; the comb or cheekpiece should be fairly high and straight so that the eye is in line with the sight whether the face is forward or back, and a fore-end rather deep for best control in kneeling position. Most shooters hold the rifle fore-end when kneeling, rather than just letting it lie in the palm against sling tension as in prone and sitting. The prone shooter may have any type of sling setup, heavy padded leather cuffs around the arm being common, while the position man usually has a narrower cuff, less padding, for a more flexible unit, since it must be changed often for the different positions.

The prone man fires 40-shot matches, 20 at a target, 5 on each bull at 50 yards, 10 on each bull at 100 yards, usually changing targets after each 20-shot stage. NRA 50-meter shooting is the same as the 50-yard. In competition, target frames are built to hold a backing target, a plain piece of target paper approximately 7 inches behind the target at 50 yards and 15 inches at 100 yards. The bullet passes through both targets and, owing to the distance between, and the slight angle, locates differently on the backing target. Two bullets may go through one hole in the target, making it appear that the shooter didn't fire all his shots, but the backer will show that he did. Also, if a person cross-fires on another's target, the scorers not only know it, they can tell who did it by the angle of displacement from the group fired by the proper shooter.

Time limit for prone is one minute per shot, including sighters. The targets have an extra bull, for sighting in, and shooters may fire as many shots as they wish at it, so long as they get twenty shots in their record bulls in twenty minutes. For the standing, kneeling, and sitting positions, a minute and a half is allowed, though gallery shooting usually limits the time to one minute a shot because ranges are always crowded with people waiting to shoot. For this reason some of the features of the international rifles—free rifles—are not too practical for gallery and outdoor position matches—competitors just don't have time to use accessories requiring several minutes to attach and adjust. However, a position shooter with a good rifle is not limited—he can shoot prone or international without feeling much handicapped, whereas the prone man with his specialized prone stock is liable to be pretty uncomfortable anywhere but prone, and the international-rifle owner may have to tear his rifle apart to get the trigger to meet NRA rules. For years the NRA insisted on the 3-pound trigger for all regular competitions, which handicapped our international program as candidates for Olympic and World teams could not use the set or very light match triggers allowed in such matches, which are a vast advantage. It amounted to forcing our people to learn a difficult technique in a hurry, which didn't work.

Around 1955 the U.S. Army set up a service marksmanship unit and worked with the free rifle equipment. The program produced Puckel, Wright, Anderson, Pool and the other Americans whose names are now well-known in countries that never heard of Reggie Jackson or Arnold Palmer. In 1964 the NRA put a new rule in the small-bore book which allows a match sponsor to specify in his program what will be followed in trigger limitation and a new .22 rifle class designation, not requiring the 3-pound trigger, so that now most matches will allow use of any safe trigger.

The International Small Bore rules cover two regular matches, a 60-shot prone match and a 120-shot three-position match, 40 shots each, prone, standing, and kneeling. The rifle must be .22 Long Rifle caliber, not weigh over 17.6 lbs., have metallic sights. That's all. The targets have a large black bull, but very small scoring rings. Rifles ordinarily weigh from 14 to 16 pounds, have everything possible adjustable so that the rifleman can be comfortable in all positions. Some have triggers that can be moved back and forth to suit length of finger, adjustable shelves on the side of the grip on which to rest the hand, buttplates that move in and out to give a short stock for standing, long for prone, and also move up and down and pivot to the side somewhat. Palm rests to hold up the heavy rifles when standing come in many shapes and types; swivel and handstop sling attachments give complete control of slings, which is vital in prone and kneeling. Much time is allowed—six hours for the 120-shot course.

Free rifles must be as accurate as possible, with triggers to suit the individual rifleman. Some men like double-set "hair" triggers, others the light European-type "match" trigger having a slack or take-up stage before feeling a light stop or resistance, then a crisp final pull of from 4 to 10 ounces. Fast-action light triggers which hold up under much use are wanted, and a really good trigger can cost as much to make as the rest of the rifle.

Where the prone shooter is easily satisfied with any sort of cloth shooting jacket with any sort of padding, the free rifle and position shooter wants a heavy leather shooting coat, usually wearing it with two or three sweatshirts underneath. Such an outfit is pretty hot to wear, but the higher scores prove its worth. A cylindrical cushion is used in the kneeling position under the instep of the foot, helping to take some weight off the toe as the shooter sits on one heel. Stiff shoes or low boots are worn, ski boots being ideal. In free rifle shooting, equipment is made as perfect as possible, to eliminate everything except the human error. Through much practice the best men become almost unbelievably expert—they can shoot as well standing as many good shooters can prone.

Because the various courses and targets call for a specified number of shots an important accessory is the loading block, or cartridge box, usually wood, with holes for cartridges to be held ready for individual loading and firing. Even the best men can lose track of the number of shots fired, particularly if they have bullet holes cutting into each other, or through the same hole. The block, holding cartridges in rows of five, tells the shooter at a glance where he is, and how many to go. An extra open box of ammo beside the block is used for sighters—in NRA .22 shooting sighters may be taken any time, to check setting or wind drift, etc. In ISU, the sighters are limited and must be taken before starting any 10-shot record string, which must be completed before any additional sighters can be fired.

In recent years, a new form of target competition has grown popular, first in Mexico, then in the United States and elsewhere. Called metallic silhouette (or sometimes game silhouette), it consists of shooting at steel cutouts of prairie chickens, wild pigs, turkeys, and sheep. Hitting these targets doesn't look very hard—nor is it. But to score, you must *knock the target over*, which means you have to hit it in just the right area, and that isn't one bit easy. It's reminiscent of the line of little metal ducks and animals at the old-fashioned shooting galleries in amusement parks, but it's a lot harder and a lot more fun.

There are both rimfire and centerfire matches. In the rimfire version, five chicken silhouettes are set in a line at 40 meters, five pigs at 60 meters, five turkeys at 77 meters, and five sheep at 100 meters. You shoot at the targets in left-to-right order, trying to knock over the silhouettes in each line in their proper turn. For use at these rimfire distances, the silhouettes are cut to ⅕ scale.

TARGETS

There are many different targets in use, for various ranges and courses of fire, the most commonly used being the 50-foot indoor, with one sighting bull and ten record bulls, one shot to be fired on each, the 10-ring being .150 inch in diameter (yes, smaller than the .22 bullet), black through the 7-ring, 1.150 inches. The 50-yard target: X-ring .39 inch, 10-ring .89 inch, taking the 8-ring in black, 2.89 inch. At 100 yards, the X is 1 inch, 10-ring 2 inches, black bull 6 inches. Most shooters would like to see the size of the black increased and the scoring rings decreased. A step in this direction was the military decision to train with ISU type targets. All Reserve, Guard and ROTC now use a 50-foot indoor target with twelve bulls, two for sighting, having a 10-ring just a dot .008 inch in diameter, 9-ring .193 inch, and a black of 1.395 inches. The standard 50-meter outdoor international target has an X-ring which is just a 1 mm. white dot, a 10-ring which is almost a half-inch thick, and about 4½ inches of black out to the 3-ring. Fifty meters is about 55 yards, so you have a big, black bull you can see well, but you have to hit it in the middle to get a good score.

Many variations of these targets are available—paper and tagboard (very light cardboard) with one, two, three, or five bull's-eyes printed on single sheets. The material must be made so that a .22 bullet will cut a reasonably clean hole, with edges defined, as on the target the shooter gets the higher score if his bullet-hole cuts the next higher scoring ring, and there are lots of close ones. Magnifying gauges are used in matches to insure uniformity in scoring.

Smallbore shooting is done wherever men can find a place—indoors in

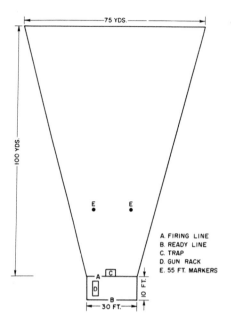

A. FIRING LINE
B. READY LINE
C. TRAP
D. GUN RACK
E. 55 FT. MARKERS

Dimensions of an outdoor 100-yard small-bore target range.

A bullet stop for pellets and .22 rimfires can be easily assembled from a 24- to 30-inch stack of large magazines and a corrugated box that will hold them tightly packed and standing on end. A .22 rimfire standard-velocity bullet will go about 10 inches into the magazines.

city basements, outdoors in safe and legal areas. A .22 bullet will travel a long way, and as target shooters are ultra-sensitive about safety, ranges are a problem. Many are now being constructed with firing lines and shooting shelters baffled, to prevent a bullet being fired over the backstop accidently. The shooters have no worries about such things, but have to do everything possible to appease the authorities and the public.

12

Big-Bore Match Shooting

TARGET SHOOTING has always existed; there are organized shooting clubs in Europe over five-hundred years old, started when the arms were bows and crossbows, and they didn't hesitate taking up firearms. A shooting magazine had on one of their covers last year a 15th-century woodcut showing a shooting match. And, even to the unhappy contestant being marked a wide shot, the range flags, target setup, and target-marking procedure were basically the same as used today.

By 1700 shooting was almost a universal sport, and later, from the set-trigger long rifles of the American frontiersman and the shorter but similar rifles of the German Jaegers (hunters) developed the standing, later schuetzen, target sport. This was entirely a civilian field and went smoothly from muzzle loading to cartridge rifles—and many schuetzen men loaded a blank cartridge and then seated a bullet from the muzzle, for best accuracy. At the same time, with the advent and rapid improvement of the metallic cartridge, the military target program developed from service training courses and was entered by civilian shooters interested mainly in long-range prone competition. However, they didn't limit themselves to anything in particular—every man was interested, experts were as well known as baseball stars are today. Most men in the West could shoot, and, unmentioned by television, many of the famed pistoleros were also very fine riflemen. Hickok was a top rifleman, as was Wyatt Earp, a capable buffalo hunter. Billy the Kid was deadly, whether using a saddle carbine on running antelope or the custom Mannlicher he handled in the Lincoln County War. Dodge City brings to mind only quick-draw gunfights, but at the same time had a town rifle team willing to bet big money against any group wanting to shoot against them. During this time, the late 1870's, Eastern long-range teams were firing against English and Irish teams, using large-caliber black-powder rifles of course.

By 1890 the bottle-necked small-caliber high-velocity military cartridge and smokeless powder appeared, for repeating rifles, and target shooting began a new era. Formal establishment of annual National Matches by Con-

109

gress in 1903, and the adoption of the 1903 Springfield rifle greatly encouraged military rifle shooting and this interest in competition by both military and civilian personnel aided considerably in development of rifles and
ammunition. Until World War I the various ammunition companies competed each year to furnish the National Match ammunition—whoever furnished the best by test got the contract. However, the war left the government
with much excess ammunition and greatly expanded facilities, so all ammo
from 1919 on was made at Frankfort Arsenal, until 1940 and World War II. In
1957 National Match ammunition manufacture was resumed, with both
Frankfort and Lake City loading plants in business. Today it is generally understood that any caliber over .25 is considered "big bore," and customarily
means any .30 caliber.

BIG-BORE RIFLES

Between the wars big-bore target shooting was strictly military in form,
dominated by the National Match Model 1903 Springfield rifle, a specially
made version of the service rifle, with smoother action and selected barrel.
The only other range arm having any popularity was the "bullgun" (for
shooting "bulls" or bull's-eyes, not male bovines). This descended from the
old long-range black-powder rifle, having a long, heavy barrel, bases for telescopic sights, almost always stocked for prone comfort only. Springfield even
produced the Type T Springfield, a bullgun for use of the service people in
long-range matches, most of these allowing any sights, and fired 800 through
1,000 yards, prone. The .30/06 caliber ruled until 1931 when Ben Comfort, a
civilian, turned up with a bullgun chambered for the .300 H & H Magnum
and handloaded ammunition. It wiped out the .30/06 bullgun, and since then
the rifles have been made for all types and calibers, the increased-capacity
magnums in .30 caliber coming to the top. Today, the .300 Winchester and
the .30 338, made by necking down the .338 Magnum case, are favored.

Adoption of the semiautomatic Garand, the M1 rifle, followed by World
War II, ended the Springfield. When big-bore target shooting again got underway in 1947, the service rifle was the M1 and not then available to the civilians. The Springfield was no longer the standard and shooters no longer restricted to its use as issued. Big-bore shooting branched into the service-rifle
class and the match-rifle class now set up for bolt-action rifles. Courses fired
were the same—standing and sitting rapid-fire at 200 yards, rapid fire prone
at 300, and slow-fire at 600 yards. The old 1,000-yard stage was dropped in
most localities as ranges were no longer available. The service rifle was gradually improved until by 1957 a match-grade M1 and National Match ammunition was available to both service and civilian marksmen. In the meantime,
the bolt-action match rifle evolved into a precision arm; barrels became longer
and heavier, fine sights were developed, essentially the same as small-bore
types, stocks were engineered to fit the man, match ammunition components
were available and accuracy was on the market. The Winchester Model 70 ac-

Remington Model 40XB centerfire target rifle, a quality single-shot bolt-action for serious big-bore marksmen.

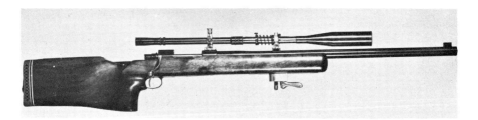

A magnum long-range prone rifle, often called a "bullgun," equipped with a telescope sight.

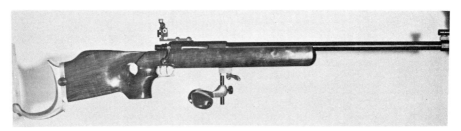

A custom 300-meter free rifle with a single-shot heavy action, double set triggers, offset sights, hook buttplate, and palm rest for firing in the standing position. Caliber is 7.62 mm. NATO, or .308 Winchester.

The modern big-bore match rifle: Winchester Model 70 bolt action with custom stock and barrel, Redfield International sights.

tion became the standard because of its fine single-stage trigger, fast firing-pin action and smooth bolt functioning. The factory target rifle, or long-barrelled custom-stocked match rifles using the M70 actions now hold literally all shooting records.

High Power Shooting, as the NRA terms it, at present encompasses not only the three phases mentioned—service rifle, match rifle, and bullgun, or long range—but also the 300 Meter International class of competition, using rifles of the same type, weight, design, and rule limitations as the small-bore free rifle, and allowing the same accessories. Further, the service rifle now is the M14, the M1 being obsolescent. Civilians may own the M1, not the M14. Only at the National Matches at Camp Perry, Ohio, may they draw and use the new rifle. For all other service-rifle shooting they may possess the M1. The M1 is .30/06 caliber, the M14, 7.62 mm. NATO, essentially the .308 Winchester.

A recent change of rule eliminates the old military standing position and the arm supporting the rifle may now be brought back against the body for added support. This has already influenced the match rifle. Barrels as long and heavy as on some bullguns are used in the standing matches. As only the military calibers are legal for match competition, either the .30/06 or .308 can be used. The manually operated rifle gets ten seconds more time in each stage of rapid or "sustained" fire than the military autos—sixty seconds sitting, seventy seconds for the 300 prone rapid. Time starts when the targets appear out of the pits with shooters in standing position. Slow fire allows one minute per shot, except at 1,000 yards it's a minute and a half. The big-bore shooter gets a total of two sighting shots at each range during a tournament, and many matches allow no sighters at all. Any crossfire is a complete miss. Match rifles must have a three-pound trigger, service rifles, 4½ lbs. It isn't the easiest sport to take up.

The long-range rifles are not limited as to caliber or trigger weight, now usually have bases for both telescopic sight and match metallic sights, use good prone stocks and weigh from 13 to 16 pounds. The long and heavy barrel gives a long sight-radius (distance between front and rear), radiates heat more evenly, and the extra weight makes for less movement and helps resist recoil. Heavy bullets and maximum loads are the rule, and you need all the help you can get to handle the outfit. Set triggers are seldom used, a two- or three-pound single-stage trigger being easily controlled in the prone position. Ammunition is always handloaded. Two-hundred grain boattail match bullets, .30 caliber, are most popular, followed by 190-grain types. The old 180-grain match bullet is not considered equal to the heavier ones at 1,000 yards.

The International big-bore program is ruled by the International Shooting Union Rules. The free rifle and small-bore free rifle must meet the same rules except for caliber—the big bore may be any not over 8 mm., or .32. Firing is at 300 meters—327 yards—but slightly reduced targets are printed in the U.S. for 300-yard ranges, and a proportionately reduced one for 200 yards.

It is a difficult target in any form—the tie-breaking X-ring is 1.968 inch, 10-ring, 3.937 inches, black through the 5-ring, 23.622 inches.

In the centerfire version of metallic silhouette shooting, our fastest-growing target sport, rifles must have a bore size of 6 mm. (.243) or larger. The 7 x 57 mm. and .308 Winchester are popular choices. The rifle and sights combined must weigh no more than 10 pounds 2 ounces, but there are no limitations on the type of sights. Most competitors use high-power scopes with oversized adjustment knobs. Silhouette matches have attracted such a large following that some gun manufacturers now supply rifles specifically designed for the sport, and optical companies provide special scopes.

Some manufacturers provide rifles specially designed or modified for game silhouette shooting. Pictured here is the Savage 110-S Metallic Silhouette Rifle.

Only the unsupported offhand position is permitted—no sling, no hand stop, no specialized shooting jacket. Each shooter tries to topple four lines of five steel silhouettes each: a total of 20 lifesize game targets. The chickens are placed at 200 meters, pigs at 300, turkeys at 385, and sheep at 500. This is a very demanding sport. It takes a powerful load and a well placed bullet to topple a 55-pound steel sheep silhouette at 500 meters.

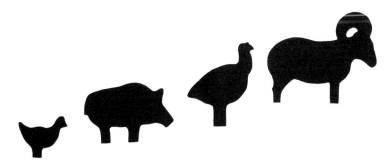

These are the metallic targets used in silhouette matches.

AMMUNITION

Ammunition is the big-bore shooter's problem. Commercial .30/06 match ammunition—Remington's Palma and Western's Super-match—costs too much for most people, in view of the great number of rounds needed for competition and practice. So, handloading is almost universal among .30-caliber riflemen. Many good match bullets are obtainable today, with also a wide choice of primers and powder. A shooter can tailor his ammunition to his taste—if he wants a light-recoil load for standing or rapid-fire, he can put together an accurate cartridge. The National Match ammunition made for the National Matches has not been sold to civilians for several years now, though sometimes issued for state team try-outs and special matches if available. The .30/06 NM is based on the old M1 NM ammunition of the 1930's, with velocity reduced to 2650 feet per second (for best performance in the M1 rifle). Though it is very accurate, most bolt-action match rifle competitors prefer to load a heavier bullet at higher velocity for ranges beyond 300 yards. The National Match 7.62 mm. cartridge uses the same 173-grain boattail bullet loaded to 2550 feet per second muzzle velocity.

SIGHTS AND ACCESSORIES

The big-bore competitor's accessories are basically the same as the small-bore man needs: he uses the same rear sight, usually the Redfield International model with one-quarter minute adjustments, a shorter front sight using apertures, able to take either post or ring inserts, and the same spotting scope, prismatic, 20 to 30X. His telescopic sight for testing and long-range shooting will be the 1½-inch type 14 to 20X, though some men prefer slightly smaller and lighter scopes. The target telescope is free to slide in its spring-loaded micrometer mounts and of course the inertial movement under recoil is less with a light scope. Shooters usually return it to position by hand, not using the return-springs the small-bore shooter relies on. (If close to a scope with spring set, on a big rifle, it'll return too fast and strike glasses or eyebrow.)

Clothing and allied items are very important to the rifleman. For sitting rapid-fire, his trousers must be of nonslip so his elbows will not slide. Boots or heavy shoes with good heels are important for standing—a run-over heel can really hurt you in the score as well as the ankle. Slings are sometimes the flexible-cuff target types as used by position and free-rifle shooters, but more often will be the old military leather loop sling, the same as was used with the Springfield. The shooting coat is primarily to keep the rifle and rifleman from slipping, more than to provide padding against recoil and firing point. The big-bore man wants a coat that supports his body, won't pull out of position, won't let the butt slip on his shoulder, elbows, legs, or knees in rapid fire, not restrict his arm movement in prone rapid, or get out of place when he goes from standing to sitting or prone. Some of the good men are now going to the leather international coats for shooting the standing stages only, changing to fitted fabric coats for other stages of fire.

Courses of Fire

Military courses of fire are generally followed by civilian clubs, using the same targets, range procedure, and types of ranges. The National Match Course consists of 10 shots standing, and 10 shots rapid-fire, standing to sitting, at 200 yards, followed by 10 shots rapid at 300 yards, standing to prone, then 20 shots prone slow-fire at 600 yards. Of course, all variations of these stages and combinations of them are used to make up match programs. The

The following photos are of John A. Clerke, National Match Rifle Champion of the United States in 1965. The explanations of the shooting positions are in Clerke's own words.

OFFHAND POSITON: "I stand with my feet close together (heels about 9 inches apart), weight evenly distributed on both feet. The high right arm supports almost the entire weight of the rifle. The left hand is used as a guide and provides very little support. I find I can get much better trigger control when using a 3-pound trigger if I hold the rifle with my right hand. The head should be held as straight as possible. The rifle and the arms form two triangles—the upper right arm, buttstock, and lower right arm forming one triangle and the left arm and fore-end of the rifle forming the other, much like a truss frame. (Note diagram.) In forming these triangles, the upper left arm almost appears to be an extension of the lower right arm."

ideal range will allow shooting up to 600 yards and face north, for best light during a full day of shooting. Few 1,000 yard ranges are now in operation by individual clubs, but large tournaments are often held at military installations having them, so long range shooting remains popular. Unfortunately, in many parts of the nation sufficient area is not available and many clubs must content themselves with short courses, some ranges being limited to only 200 yards. Targets are contained in a pit, or trench, or behind a built-up bank of earth, and are raised and lowered by mechanical carriers operated by pit personnel—"target pullers." In slow fire, the target is pulled down after each shot, a cardboard disc with bullet-sized peg is placed in the hole, target raised and value of shot signalled from pit. The disc, or spotter, is used because bullet holes can't be seen reliably beyond 200 yards; and besides, the hole must be

SITTING POSITION: "I use this position because it fits my physical conformation. It is basically sound and allows for rapid operation of the bolt. Both elbows are in contact with the legs, not with the knees. Supporting the elbows on the kneecaps is an open invitation to low scores. The knees are low, bringing the entire silhouette close to the ground where there is less wind velocity. The bolt can be operated without moving the elbow from the leg. The left hand is against the fore-end stop, the stop being adjusted backward or forward to raise or lower the muzzle."

protected against the next bullet and the shooter must know where the hit was. After each shot, the spotter is moved to a new hole, and the old one is pasted up. In rapid fire, the target remains up for each 10-shot string, then is marked, small spotters sometimes being used to show the group, often no spotters at all. Pit and firing lines are connected by field telephones for general communication. Each target has a large number-board in front, which is important, for in big-bore, unlike small-bore, a shot on the wrong target is a complete miss. In small-bore, the firer gets the value of the shot, less one penalty point.

PRONE POSITION: "This is a modified form of the Estonian prone position. The body is extended straight behind the gun, and the right knee is drawn up. The right side is off the ground, supported by the right elbow and the right leg. The left hand is up against the fore-end stop; the left elbow is well under the rifle. The head, which is held back just enough to keep from being hit with the rear sight, is sandwiched between the left shoulder and the stock. I use this position in both rapid fire and slow fire."

TARGETS

The targets are the military types, the short-range being the "A" with 4-inch tie-breaking ring, called "V" (instead of X), and a 12-inch black bull, value 5. Only a 4-ring, and a 36-inch 3-ring remain on the target—outside the ring is a miss. This is used at 200 and 300 yards, perfect scores being common, and shooting is ruled by the V-ring—the man with most V's wins, of course. At 600 yards, the "B" target is used, with 12-inch V-ring and 20-inch black bull (5), 40-inch 4-ring and 60-inch 3-ring, remainder of target a miss. The over-all target size is 48 x 72 inches for A, 72 inches square for the B, and for the C, the 1,000-yard target which has a 20-inch V-ring, 36-inch black bull, and a 54-inch 4-ring—remainder of target is worth three points. The scoring areas sound big, compared with small-bore and international targets. The .22 100-yard target has a 6-inch black aiming point. Scale down the 600- and 1,000-yard targets to 100-yard size and they are just over 3½ inches. And distance doesn't enlarge it any. The .30-caliber competitor has only a vague, tiny bull's-eye to aim at and in poor light it can be very trying. Even so, in any normal match, the winner is almost always determined only by the V-count, as many perfect scores are fired.

One of the permissible standing positions in military competition with the M14 service rifle. The left elbow rests against the hip and the left hand supports the rifle under the ammunition clip. Note that the shooter's stool is positioned so that he need not move his feet when sitting to rest between shots, and that the spotting scope is set up to view the target when he is sitting on the stool.

Standing position with the free rifle, which is similar to the military position. Shooter is wearing special Swiss rifle glasses having the right lens raised and angled so that it is 90 degrees to the line of sight.

For a good many years new targets have been needed and many experimental types tried in an effort to find one incorporating a larger black bull which would be more visible yet have smaller scoring rings and still allow an uncomplicated system of pit-scoring. Only a few distinctly separate signals by large marking paddles are possible so that targets with rings from 10 down to 1 would mean confusion and incorrect scores. Also, the bull and rings should be figured to relate to the minute-of-angle, so that rifle sights can be adjusted correctly. A modern target should appear before long.

Big-bore shooting is about 95 percent with metallic sights. A good number, probably the majority, of civilian marksmen do not have particularly good eyesight and would like to do more firing with telescopic sights. There is a series of NRA targets for use up to 600 yards, scaled-up from the 100-yard small-bore target and called the Decimal targets. These are suitable for any-sight matches but have never seen much use, although the 200-yard type is fairly popular. This one is also used for the now-rare 200 yard .22 matches. A new target series would in all probability create added interest and competition for all riflemen.

THE NRA

To understand target shooting in the United States, it is necessary to know something about the organization of the riflemen, The National Rifle Association. To quote from my membership certificate: "A patriotic organization organized in 1871 for the purpose of promoting and encouraging rifle shooting among the citizens of the United States."

The National Rifle Association is today a large body with many functions, perhaps the most important being to resist the anti-firearms laws proposed by politicians.

We are, however, talking about target shooting, and the NRA governs it. Elected members make rules for all forms of competition, representing the United States in the International Shooting Union and Olympic meetings, working with the Armed Services in presenting the National Matches each year, keeping vast records on all competitors to classify them as to ability and improvement so they will compete against others of their own level of skill, publishing much literature to help clubs, junior shooters, and promote safety in firearms handling. Training films and even trained instructors are found for all who want or need them.

Almost every community in the country of any size, and many of no size at all, has a rifle club, or pistol club, or one for both, affiliated with The National Rifle Association. Any group meeting normal standards of good citizenship is welcome. Affiliated clubs are eligible for aid from the Director of Civilian Marksmanship, a military official, using a senior officer of the regular army appointed by the Department of Defense, and his office, a government organization dedicated to aiding civilian marksmanship and training. Clubs may qualify for military (M1) rifles to be issued them for use of members and re-

ceive an annual issue of ammunition without charge except for transportation, also small-bore rifles and ammunition, components for loading ammunition, range supplies, targets, spare parts for arms, and any other equipment
not normally available through other sources. Since DCM supplies are dependent on surpluses in Armed Forces equipment, not all items are available
at all times, but every effort is made to aid the civilian marksman. Individual
members of the NRA are eligible to purchase military arms, ammunition, and
components when allowed by law, as well as surplus and obsolete arms at low
prices as they become obtainable by the DCM. Only rifles, pistols, and carbines may be purchased, of course.

The NRA provides rules, standards of conduct in scheduling matches, and
a qualified referee for rifle and pistol matches sponsored by clubs and state associations. It registers matches and scores for all types of competitions to
maintain a uniform nation-wide sport.

NRA headquarters in Washington, D.C. publishes the monthly journal
The American Rifleman, which covers all types of firearms activities and new developments, including changes in targets, rules, and courses of fire.

13

Benchrest Shooting

SHOOTING FROM A TABLE or bench has no doubt always been done, as gunmakers and owners always want to know how well their firearms shoot when held steady. In the early years of the United States informal matches were held for turkeys, money, or other prizes. The riflemen shot prone, with the rifle or hand resting on a log. The "beef shoots" were sort of a gambling proposition—a group of settlers would chip in to buy a cow, then shoot at a mark for choice of meat, one shot each. The shot closest to center got first choice, and so on. Shooting from a rest offset the skill of the experts, who could beat their neighbors in standing or kneeling positions.

In later years rest shooting for sport alone claimed a few adherents, and from 1840 to 1880 benchrests and rifles made especially for the purpose appeared, some of the rifles weighing around 50 pounds. Telescopic sights and precision loading developed. Experiments were made in lead-bullet design and manufacture, and straight-line tools to seat bullets down the barrels. The very heavy rifles disappeared, but the benchrest, a heavy, rigid table, usually with three legs, was used for testing purposes. Many of the schuetzen riflemen used benchrests constantly. Remaining on an individual basis through the 1930's, the first attempt at organization came in the Pacific Northwest around the time of World War II, in the form of the "Sniper's Congress" shoots. After the war Eastern shooters became interested and in a few years formed the National Benchrest Shooter's Association, with present headquarters at Minerva, Ohio.

Clubs now exist over most of the country; the association has its journal in the magazine *Precision Shooting*, carrying information on all types of shooting as well as benchrest. Originally organized simply to achieve interchange of information on loading and rifle construction directed solely toward increasing accuracy, the association rapidly developed home bullet-making techniques and tools, and the spirit of competition arose. Standard courses evolved, rules were made defining classes of rifles, national records recognized, and finally annual National Benchrest Matches established. The exchange of information has been quite important, not only in the benchrest field, but in all other fields of shooting.

Today benchrest shooting exists on a somewhat competitive base. I would say that very few of the shooters do not compete to some extent. Clubs ordinarily have small memberships, compared to big-bore and small-bore groups, as the form of shooting appeals to a different personality—the man (or woman) fascinated by the fine points of accuracy and the equipment to produce it. He is much more interested in how well he can make his rifles shoot and his bullets group than how he physically can handle a match rifle of any type. The benches and rifle rests take care of the holding. Do not take this to mean that the game doesn't require skill. Anyone who thinks all he has to do is put his rifle on a couple of sandbags to shoot little groups is mistaken. I am a master class competitive rifleman, my business is making match rifles. I've used a bench for over thirty years in testing—and I have trouble getting off five out of ten shots exactly to same point of aim.

Benchrest rules are quite simple: four classes of rifle are specified; all barrels must be 18 inches or longer, all rifles must have a manually operated firing mechanism—no electric or hydraulic trigger systems. The Bench rifle has no other restrictions. Any caliber, type of action, barrel, or stock is allowed. Many have little resemblance to conventional rifles. Next is the Heavy Varmint Rifle class, weight limited to 13½ pounds including sight, always telescopic, stock not more than 3 inches wide, barrel not more than .900 inch diameter at muzzle or 1¼ inches, 4 inches ahead of the receiver. The Light Varmint Rifle has the same maximum limitations but must not weigh more than 10½ pounds complete. Last is the Sporter Rifle, same limits as light varmint, but must be larger than .22 caliber.

Excepting the sporter class, various .22 centerfire cartridges are predominant. Most shooting being at 100 and 200 yards, the smaller ones such as .222 Remington and its variations have come to the fore, although the .219 Wasp, a larger rimmed "wildcat" based on the .25/35 or .30/30 case is still popular. Literally all .22 centerfire cartridge cases have been experimented with in the past fifteen years. Larger calibers, with greater recoil and bullet-making problems have not yet shown up in any numbers. The 6 mm. (.24 caliber) is in fair use, usually in modified shapes of the Winchester .243 and Remington .244 cartridges. Remington now calls the .244 the 6 mm., incidentally. One top benchrest man has made the .308 Winchester perform well in benchrest competition.

Ammunition is the heart of the game, and men go to unbelievable lengths to achieve perfect cartridges. Bullets are the most variable factor, and the shooters usually make them themselves in expensive precision dies, observing great care in every stage of manufacture. Jackets are checked in every way possible for uniformity in all things, sometimes reamed in special machines to make thickness uniform. Lead cores are swaged, weighed and bullets assembled as carefully and uniformly as can be done. Finished bullets are checked and rechecked, spun for concentricity and handled very carefully to avoid

The benchrest rifle (side and front views), on unrestricted fully adjustable rests, sighted with a 2-inch
Unertl scope. Stock is fitted with metal plates which
match steel guide rails in the machined rest supports.
The bedding of this rifle is the monobloc—rifle and scope are supported entirely
by the steel block around the barrel, which is the only contact with the stock.
Rifle is a .219 caliber made on the custom Weber action.

dents or scratches. Cartridge cases are selected for weight, same-size primer
pockets and usually necks reamed or turned, to get perfectly concentric seating and bullet pull. A shooter can have from a hundred to a thousand dollars
in loading equipment and be ready to buy, make or have made anything at all
he thinks just might make his groups smaller.

Benchrest rifles are usually based on massive custom actions, or a
strengthened standard type, having steel sleeves over the entire receiver, or
plates attached to top or bottom. Stocks are often huge, with square, or specially shaped fore-end and buttstock, sometimes with grooves, V-ways, or a
track system to engage matching fittings in the rest used. No two rifles are ever
exactly alike. Great pains in chambering and throating the heavy barrels for
exact headspacing and bullet-seating are taken, and of course carefully made

A heavy varmint rifle on a benchrest. This is also a .219, made on a Shilen action
and equipped with a 2-inch Unertl scope. The mahogany stock is flat at the bottom
of the fore-end. The rest has a vertical adjustment only at the front; sandbags are
used at the rear.

barrels are used, and tested to prove quality before the rifle is completed. Stainless-steel barrels are at present most favored. Triggers are usually light single-stage or set types. Stocks can be of any material.

Due to the weight limitation, the varmint and sporter-class bench rifles use more or less conventional actions and stocks, and there is constant conversation among the shooters as to limiting the power of the telescopic sights, to keep within the spirit of the competition. Obviously, a 2-inch Unertl riflescope weighing about 3 pounds and 24 power isn't appropriate to a sporting rifle, and it runs the weight up anyway. At the same time, it is what the big unlimited bench rifle needs, though I think the next size down is probably more popular.

The benches are simply heavy tables, often set in concrete or the ground, constructed so they can be used by either right- or left-handed people. The rests have become very elaborate. The unrestricted rest may incorporate precision adjustments, guide rails, V-ways, or other means of holding specially designed rifles and allowing them to be returned to exactly the same position after each shot. These require only joining of the front and rear rests to be actually machine-rests.

Next is the restricted rest with adjustment in the front rest only and no means of controlling or guiding the rifle, and the third and last class of rest is the sandbag, actually meaning bags of any material having some yield to hand pressure, and also allowing blocks of rubber, plastic, or similar material.

Targets are entirely different from those used for any other form of shooting. The bench target has small scoring rings only, without value: the 100-yard target has a ½-inch 10 ring, and larger rings ½-inch apart, with a heavy black aiming square at 12 o'clock, tangent to the 9-ring, for the scopes to aim at. Rings and square are contained in a heavy black border 3½ by 4¾ inches. The object is to fire five or ten shots in a group inside the border regardless of scoring rings—the size of the group is what counts. At 200 yards, the border is 7 by 7 inches, rings and square double the 100-yard size, and at 300 meters, seldom fired, the border is 17 by 17 inches, with larger rings and aiming point, of course.

Groups are usually small. The 100-yard groups are often only a ragged-looking bullet hole, and 200-yard groups can usually be covered by a quarter. A moving backing target strip is used to register the shots fired and prove the competitor did fire ten bullets through that hole. This mechanized paper strip moves very slowly behind the target so that bullet holes appear in a row. Scoring is done by optical tools, the Sweany Reticule Rule being the official instrument, measuring groups in thousandths of an inch, figured from a zero center to center of the shot-hole farthest from that center. It may sound incredible, but the 100-yard record group is about half the diameter of a .22 bullet.

Tournaments are groups of matches, involve many targets at both 100 and 200 yards, with the over-all winner the man having the best average of all matches.

A light varmint or sporter-class rifle on a benchrest. A 6 mm. made on a Hart action, it is fitted with a Lyman Supertargetspot scope which is mounted on an extension bracket extending from the receiver so that the barrel may be free.

Competitive benchrest shooting is expensive and will take all your spare time, but nobody starts at the top. All shooters get their equipment a piece at a time and enjoy working their way up. Bench shooting also provides a pastime and sport for men physically unable to do conventional target shooting but who still want to fire a rifle and put bullet holes together.

IV

Fundamentals of Shotgun Shooting

Jack O'Connor

14

An Introduction to the Shotgun

THE RIFLE is the primary weapon of warfare and the basic unit of all the armies of the world is the infantryman armed with a rifle. The shotgun, on the other hand, is almost entirely a sporting weapon used on game birds, to some extent on deer and other non-flying game, and in competitive games in which "clay" targets are broken. Shotguns are used to some extent by law enforcement officers and have also been used in trench and jungle warfare, but at least 99 percent of all shotguns are sporting weapons.

Unlike the rifle, the shotgun is a short-range weapon. Skilled riflemen do competitive target shooting at 600 and 1,000 yards and a good shot can lay all his bullets into the 36-inch bull's-eye at that distance. Compared to this the range of the shotgun is modest indeed. Most game killed with a shotgun is taken within 40 yards, and even the tightest-choked duck guns firing the heaviest loads are not reliable at over 60–65 yards. With rifled slugs and a shotgun especially bored for them and equipped with telescopic or iron rifle sights, a shotgun is accurate enough for deer at an outside limit of about 100 yards. All in all, the shotgun is no long-range weapon.

The basic difference between the shotgun and the rifle is that the shotgun bore is smooth and that of the rifle has spiral grooves cut in it. The smooth bore of the shotgun is primarily designed to handle multiple missiles called shot. The charge fired by the shotgun may consist of from nine to two dozen large shot designed for big game and called buckshot, or many hundreds of small shot called bird shot. The rifle barrel, on the other hand, is designed to handle one bullet accurately. The rifling spins this bullet, keeps it point on, and makes it accurate. The slugs fired in shotguns do not spin like rifle bullets. Instead they fly with fair accuracy because they are heavy at the front end. When slugs are used, the shotgun is not properly a shotgun at all but simply a rather poor substitute for a rifle.

A shotgun barrel is a long cylinder. The breech end is enlarged to receive what is called the "shell" in the United States and the "cartridge" in Britain. The bore of the shotgun is a true cylinder from the end of the forcing cone of

129

the chamber to a point within a few inches of the muzzle. There it narrows down into some sort of choke. The amount that is narrows depends on the purpose to which the shotgun is to be put—from $\frac{3}{1000}$ inch for skeet shooting and close-range upland hunting to as much as $\frac{40}{1000}$ inch for long-range waterfowl shooting. These figures are for 12-gauge shotguns.

Shotguns are classified by "gauges" and the gauge was originally determined by the number of round balls of the bore diameter of the particular gun there were to the pound. Shotguns have been made in 4, 6, 8, 10, 12, 14, 16, 20, 24, 28, 32, and .410 gauge. Actually the .410 is not a gauge but a caliber.

At one time 4-, 6-, and 8-gauge guns were fairly popular for waterfowl shooting, and the 10 gauge was the all-around gauge. Today no shotguns of a gauge larger than 10 are made in the United States and no shells of a gauge larger than 10 are loaded.

Here are the bore diameters of the various gauges:

10-Gauge	.775-inch	20-Gauge	.615-inch
12-Gauge	.729-inch	28-Gauge	.550-inch
16-Gauge	.662-inch	.410-Gauge	.410-inch

About 50 percent of all shotguns sold are in 12 gauge. The next most popular gauge is the 20, followed distantly by the .410. Some 24- and 32-gauge guns have been built in the United States and ammunition is still loaded in these gauges in Europe.

The degree of choke in a shotgun barrel is classified by the percentage of shot in the charge that it will put into a 30-inch circle at 40 yards. If the barrel patterns 70 percent or more, it is a full choke. If it patterns more than 60 percent but less than 70 percent it is generally called an "improved modified." If it patterns from 55 to 60 percent it is known as "modified" or sometimes "half choke." A barrel that will pattern around 45-50 percent is an "improved cylinder" or "quarter choke." A cylinder-bore will generally pattern somewhere between 30 and 40 percent. Skeet No. 1 boring is about like cylinder and Skeet No. 2 varies between improved cylinder and modified. These pattern percentages are all taken in a 30-inch circle at 40 yards in gauges from 28 to 10. Patterns of the .410 gauge are taken at 30 yards.

The usual method of taking shot patterns is to use a paper target approximately 4 feet square, mounted on a frame. The shooter stands off to a distance where the muzzle of his gun is 40 yards from the target, after placing a black paster or bull's-eye in the center of the target to assist in aiming. After the shot is fired, a 30-inch circle is drawn to enclose the greatest number of shot holes. The total number of pellets in the shot charge can be used as a basis to determine the pattern percentage in rating the choke of a shotgun.

The use of the various degrees of choke are as follows:

Full Choke: Pass shooting at waterfowl, handicap shooting at traps.

Improved Modified: All-around trap shooting, waterfowl shooting.

Modified: Waterfowl shooting over decoys, doves, pheasants, chukar partridges. Skeet No. 2 about the same.

Improved Cylinder: Most upland shooting—quail, grouse, woodcock, pheasants over dogs, skeet.

Cylinder: Skeet, rifled slugs.

Skeet No. 1: Skeet, upland shooting.

The best shot size to use on game birds is the smallest size that will give sufficient penetration, as the killing power of shot largely depends on multiple hits. The greater the number of shot that hits a bird the greater the chance that one will hit in a vital area—brain, heart, spine, lungs.

Here is a list of recommended shot sizes from a Winchester handbook. Recommending shot sizes is one of the world's easiest ways to stir up an argument, but this will do as well as any:

For Upland Shooting

Shot Sizes

Snipe, woodcock, rail, quail in early season and small shore birds	8 or 9
Dove, quail in late season, large shore birds, and small winged pests	7, 7½ or 8
Pheasant, prairie chicken, grouse, rabbit and squirrel	4, 5, 6 or 7
Turkey and large furred vermin	BB, 2 or 4

For Wildfowl Shooting

Duck shooting over decoys	5 or 6 (lead)
	4 (steel)
All other duck shooting	4 (lead)
	2 or 4 (steel)
Goose shooting	BB, 2 or 4 (lead)
	BB, 1 or 2 (steel)

For Trap Shooting

16-yard singles and first barrel of doubles	7½ or 8
Second barrel of doubles and handicap targets	7½ or 8

For Skeet Shooting

For any skeet shooting	9

At one time shotguns were made with barrels 36 and 40 inches long, but such barrels are rare these days. Many ill-informed people think that the longer a shotgun barrel is the harder it shoots and the farther it kills. This notion, like many other gunning notions, is a holdover from black-powder days. With modern smokeless powders full velocity is developed in barrels of from 24 to 26 inches in length and if longer barrels are chosen it should be because of balance, steadiness of swing, and a longer sighting plane.

Just as there is a slow drift toward smaller gauges and more open chokes there is also a drift toward shorter barrels. At one time the one-gun man usually had a 30-inch barrel, but today the 28-inch barrel is the best seller in pump and automatic shotguns. Guns with 30-inch barrels are the most popular for trap shooting and for pass shooting at wildfowl. Skeet shooters who use pumps and automatics generally want 26-inch barrels and if they use doubles they want 26- or 28-inch barrels. Upland guns generally have 26-inch barrels, but some upland hunters are equipping pumps and automatics with variable choke devices fitted to give over-all barrel lengths of 22 and 24 inches.

The dominant type of shotgun in Europe has long been the side-by-side double barrel. Such guns are made all over Europe, from England to Hungary and from Italy to Sweden. Many cheap shotguns are made in Spain and some very good ones. Belgium, Italy, Germany, Japan and England all produce doubles, some good and some indifferent. In Europe the over-and-under shotgun is gaining in popularity, and many excellent pump and self-loading (automatic) shotguns are made in Japan, Italy, Belgium, and France.

In the United States the American-made double-barreled shotgun is almost a thing of the past, and the shift to repeaters has been under way for over 70 years. The reason for this is that the manufacture of a good, smoothworking, reliable double-barreled gun requires so much handwork that guns produced by workers paid American wages are so expensive that few can buy them. As an example, a Model 21 Winchester with single trigger, automatic ejectors, and beavertail fore-end cost a little over $100 in 1940. Today it costs $10,000. Ruger manufactures an excellent and moderately priced over-and-under double, and Savage continues to offer budget-priced side-by-side shotguns made in this country. But the trend is definitely toward magazine-fed repeaters.

The dominant type of American shotgun is the pump gun operated by a slide handle, but the self-loader, which in the United States is almost universally called the automatic, is gaining in popularity. Cheaper types are the single-barrel, break-open guns of all gauges from .410 to 10 and bolt actions. An increasing number of double-barreled shotguns, both side-by-side and over-and-under, are being imported from Europe and from Japan. The famed Browning over-and-under is manufactured in Belgium and the Winchester Model 101, another over-and-under, is made by a Winchester subsidiary in Japan.

Rifle ballistics have changed enormously in the past 100 years. In the last days of muzzle-loading rifles bullets were generally either spherical or conical with hollow bases. They were made of pure, soft lead and velocity ran from 1300 to 1500 feet per second. Today rifle bullets are jacketed in gliding metal or mild steel, are constructed so they open against slight resistance and yet hold together in tough muscle and against bone, and they are driven at velocities of from 2500 to as much as 4000 feet per second.

Smokeless powders have stepped up shotgun velocities a little and choke boring and shotshell improvements have tightened up patterns and increased range somewhat. Basically, however, the shotgun is still a short-range weapon. An 1825 British gunner with a muzzle-loading Joseph Manton fowling piece and an 1885 American gunner using a Parker with black-powder shells could do about anything the 1980's American or European shotgunner with the most modern equipment can do today. In 1825 most game birds were killed at under 40 yards and they are killed at under 40 yards today.

The most important changes that have taken place in the field of the shotgun in the past twenty years have been in the shotshell and its manufacture. Progressive-burning powders that give a longer push and reach peak pressures farther up the barrel came along in the early 1920's. These made possible such shotshells as Super-X (Western) and Nitro Express (Remington) that carried heavier charges of shot. Since that time shotgun powders have continued to improve, and as they have grown more progressive in character they have made heavier shot charges possible in all gauges. Another improvement in shotshells that came along in the 1920's was the use of copper-plated shot. This was harder, and as a result fewer shot were deformed by contact with the forcing cones and the bore and the shot gave tighter patterns. Prior to the last war the use of the "star" or "pie crimp" instead of an "over shot" or top wad to hold the shot in the shell came in. This improved pattern percentages as the top wad occasionally got in the way of the shot charge and caused a hole in the pattern.

The next improvement to come along was the use of "gas seal wads" and "cup wads." These were used as "over powder" wads and served to seal the gas behind the wads and keep it out of the shot charge. If gas gets by hard, dried-out wads it disrupts the pattern and sometimes even fuses the shot.

Now almost entirely replaced by the modern plastic shell, the classic shotshell was made of a waxed or lacquered cardboard tube with a brass head with a hole in it for the primer. It was reinforced with a cardboard coil called the base wad. Then above the base wad was the powder charge and on top of that a cardboard "over powder" wad. Then there were a couple of filler wads, often of greased felt but sometimes cork or fibre. Then came the shot charge and above that the top wad, or "over shot" wad. The mouth of the shell was crimped around the top wad to hold the wad in place.

As we have seen in the late 1930's the pie or star crimp began to replace the top wad. Then came plastic wads used over the powder and taking the place of the cardboard gas seal wads and a filler wad. Then the use of plastics came in with a bang. Winchester-Western introduced a plastic shot protector, a sort of a bandage around the shot charge that protected the shot from deformation against the bore and against the forcing cones. About that time Remington introduced plastic shell tubes with copperplated steel heads. Then came plastic wad column-shot protectors. The rear portion of the gimmicks takes the place of over powder wad and filler wads and the front portion is a shot protector. All major American loading companies now make and use these plastic wad columns.

Today all of the loading companies are turning out plastic shotshells. Some are all molded plastic—base wad, primer pocket, the works. Some have plastic tubes and brass or copper-plated steel heads. The molded plastic shell with the plastic wad column does not swell when it gets wet. It functions nicely in any shotgun. It can be reloaded many times and it is simpler and cheaper to make.

The ammunition loaded with buckshot and slugs for use on deer and other large game will be discussed in the chapter on that subject. Other types of shotshells are those designed to give relatively light recoil and uniform patterns for use on clay targets. These are loaded with No. 7½ and No. 8 shot for trap shooting and No. 9 for skeet. Powder charges are fairly light. They are usually called "target loads." Almost all trap shooting is done with 12-gauge guns, but skeet shooting is divided into various classes and 12, 20, 28, and .410 guns are used at skeet. Target loads with No. 7½ and No. 8 shot make very good upland game loads. No. 9 shot is too small for anything except small birds at short range.

"Field loads" are characterized by moderate amounts of powder and shot, generally 1⅛ ounces of shot in the 12 gauge, 1 or 1⅛ ounces in the 16, and ⅞ and 1 ounce in the 20. These loads are generally pleasant to shoot and entirely adequate in a suitable gauge for about 95 percent of all shooting.

The old maximum loads like Remington "Express" and Winchester Super-X carry more powder and shot. The 12-gauge duck load that has been used for about forty years has 3¾ drams equivalent of powder behind 1¼ ounces of shot. This load for the 16 is 3¼ drams and 1⅛ ounces of shot and for the 20 it is 2¾ drams and 1 ounce. For the little gauges it is 2¾ drams and ¾ ounce for the 28 and with the 3-inch .410 it is ¾ ounce of shot in front of an unstated amount of some rifle powder such as No. 4327 or No. 2400.

The use of "steel" shot (actually soft iron) is now mandated in some waterfowl areas as a result of studies showing significant numbers of ducks and geese dying from lead poisoning when they ingest lead pellets as they pick grit and feed. Since these steel pellets are less dense than lead, the same volume will have less weight. Standard 12-gauge Express loads carry only 1⅛ ounce of steel shot.

The short (2¾-inch) Magnum loads use heavy charges of shot in shells of standard length. This is made possible by the use of dense, slow-burning powder, and by cutting down on the length of the wad column. The 12-gauge short Magnum is loaded with 1½ ounces of shot in front of the equivalent of 4 drams of powder. "Baby Magnum" steel-shot loads have 3¾-dram equivalents and 1¼ ounces of the lighter-weight pellets. The 16-gauge short Magnum uses 3½ drams and 1¼ ounces of shot, the 20 gauge 3-1⅛, and the 28 gauge 2¾ drams and 1 ounce—the same load as used to be considered maximum in the 20. As can be seen by these figures, the various gauges are treading on each other's heels.

The next class of shotshell loads might be called the super magnums—shells with extra-long cases. The 10-gauge 3½-inch Magnum shell uses 5 drams of powder and 2 ounces of shot, the 12-gauge 3-inch Magnum 4½ drams and 1⅞ ounces, and the 3-inch 20-gauge 3¼ drams and 1¼ ounces of shot. This 20-gauge 3-inch Magnum load makes the magnum 20 a good bet for long-range cornfield pheasant shooting and for all-around duck shooting. The big-bump 12- and 10-gauge Magnum loads should be used only for long-range pass shooting.

The various plastic shot protectors tend to reduce the size of the patterns and increase pattern density. The use of the star crimp tightens up patterns and so does the use of plated shot and hard alloyed shot. As a consequence it is not unusual to find a barrel marked "modified" throwing a full choke pattern and an improved cylinder barrel throwing a modified or an improved modified pattern. It must not be forgotten that the shotgun pattern is the product not only of the choke in the barrel but the shell.

Another type of shell is the "brush load" or "scatter load" which is designed to open up and scatter the shot charge and to give approximately improved cylinder patterns when used in a full choke barrel. In these the shot charge is divided by several thin horizontal wads or it is split by vertical wads into four pieces like a pie. These don't throw the evenest patterns imaginable, but they will make a grouse or quail gun out of a gun with a full-choke barrel. As a historical note, two of these shells used to be furnished with every box of skeet loads and specially marked. They were supposed to be used to break the No. 8 station targets. At this writing, commercial brush loads are no longer manufactured, but some handloaders make their own.

Shotguns kill a bit farther than they did a generation or two ago, but they do so because they put more shot in a given area. As we have seen this is made possible by the use of heavier shot charges, slower-burning powders, harder shot, more efficient over powder pads, the star crimp, plastic shot protectors. Each of these improvements might be called minor but together they add up to considerably more efficient ammunition.

It must not be forgotten, however, that the range and killing power of the shotgun is determined by the pattern density with shot of suitable size. Pattern density is in turn determined by the degree of choke, by the amount of shot in the shell, and by the efficiency of the shell. The velocity of the shot pellet at the muzzle is relatively a minor factor. For one thing higher velocity means higher pressure and pressures must be kept comparatively low in shotshells or the following gases will blow and scatter the shot charge. For another, the round pellet of shot is inefficient ballistically and loses its velocity rapidly. Much is made in advertising of "high-speed" and "high-velocity" loads, but shotgun velocities are modest and there isn't too much difference between that turned up by low-brass and high-brass shells.

The muzzle velocity of the 12-gauge 2¾-inch Magnum load with 1½ ounces of shot is 1315 feet per second, and that of the mild 12-gauge trap load with 1⅛ ounces of shot is 1200 feet per second. The difference in range and killing power lies in the amount of shot put in a given area. Incidentally, the larger the shot the better they retain their velocity. A pellet of No. 2 that leaves the muzzle at 1330 feet per second arrives at 40 yards with a retained velocity of 730, whereas a pellet of No. 7½ that starts out at the same velocity is going at only 580. The difference in killing power and range between a 12 gauge and a .410 is that the 12 gauge gets there with more shot.

15

Design and Fit of the Shotgun Stock

THE PRIMARY FUNCTION of the shotgun stock is to enable the gunner to shoot faster and more accurately. Another function is for the stock to keep the left hand (of a right-handed man) from getting burned on the barrels. Still another function of the stock is to lend an air of beauty and elegance to the gun.

It takes all kinds of people to make up the world of gun enthusiasts. Some love to shoot but are completely indifferent to the appearance of a gun. Others are primarily interested in collecting and hoarding handsome guns and care but little about shooting them. Most gun owners like to shoot them, but also take some pride in their appearance.

The classic shotgun stock evolved in England in the last years of the eighteenth century and the early part of the nineteenth. It had a straight or "English" grip, a rather wide, flat butt to cut down on apparent recoil, and a small, narrow fore-end.

This type of stock was carried over to the British-made breech loaders, and the fine and famous London-made doubles such as those turned out by Purdey, Boss, and Holland & Holland have these straight grips, small fore-ends (which Americans sometimes call "splinter"), scroll engraving, checkering in diamond patterns. Grips of rifle stocks tend to be about round in cross-section, but the straight grips of fine British guns are generally shaped like long ovals or even like rounded diamonds for firmer holding. British stock design has been followed by the best Spanish, Belgian, and Italian makers.

Manufacturers of German shotguns have generally used pistol grips, sometimes "full" pistol grips, sometimes "half" pistol grips. Like the British they go in for the "splinter" fore-ends, but unlike the British they favor more ornate checkering and engraving. An expensive German shotgun is generally carved as well as checkered at grip and fore-end with acorns, oak leaves, and whatnot. German engravers favor pictures of birds, animals, and hunting scenes cut into the metal. Sometimes the birds and animals are made of gold and inlaid into the steel of the frame just as gold inlays are put in teeth. A fine British, Belgian, Italian, or Spanish side-by-side double generally has a lean and racy look, but for whatever the reason German doubles often look a bit bulbous.

American stocks for double guns were influenced both by the British and by the Germans, but more pistol grips were used than straight grips and in the higher grades American checkering and decoration tended to look more like the German than the British. Instead of using chaste diamond patterns, Americans liked fancy ones with lots of curlicues and instead of scroll engraving they went in for ducks and bird dogs and whatnot.

Winchester Model 21 double-barrel shotgun combines the classic British straight grip and the American beavertail fore-end.

Remington Model 870 pump-action shotgun has a pistol grip and a husky fore-end.

Trapshooting and skeet have affected shotgun stock design in the United States, and a fairly early development in trapshooting was the beavertail fore-end, a large flat fore-end which kept the trapshooter's hand away from the hot barrels and gave him a greater degree of control over his gun. Double-barrel guns designed for skeet and made by American makers also featured beavertails. I do not think there is any doubt but that a well-designed pistol grip is an aid in gun control and quick pointing at either trap or skeet. For many years almost all American shotguns have been made with pistol grips.

Today the American-made side-by-side double gun is just about a thing of the past. It has been shot down by changing public taste and expense of manufacture. A good, smooth-working double gun needs many hours of skilled hand labor for its completion, as the double contains many small and intricate parts which must be closely fitted and polished. It simply isn't in the cards to turn out a finely-fitted and smooth-working double-barrel shotgun at a moderate price if labor is paid $15 an hour. The only very high-class double-barrel shotgun manufactured in the United States today is the custom-made Winchester 21, and the prices are astronomical.

The American market has largely been taken over by the automatic (self-loading) and pump shotguns, and even these have been redesigned to lend themselves to mass production with a minimum of hand labor. Almost all of these American repeaters are made with pistol grip buttstocks, rather large fore-ends to house the repeating mechanisms if the guns are automatics or to serve as slide handles if the guns are pumps. All American shotgun stocks have thicker and more rounded combs than do most European guns.

American stock dimensions are just about the same: Length of pull for a field gun, 14 inches; drop at comb from $1\frac{1}{2}$ to $1\frac{5}{8}$ inches; drop at heel, $2\frac{1}{2}$ inches. These are the dimensions of a reasonably straight stock and they are a pretty good compromise. Anyone from 5 feet, 8 inches to 6 feet, 1 inch can adjust himself to one of these standard American stocks and make a pretty good stab at shooting it.

These dimensions started coming along in the early years of this century. In the 1880's and 1890's stocks were much more "crooked," had much more drop at comb and heel. Some old guns sometimes had 2 inches or more drop at comb and $3\frac{1}{2}$ inches or more at heel. Apparently the old-timers who used them were a stiff-necked lot who hated to bend their heads. These old crooked-stocked guns were slow to point and tended to pattern low. If shot with heavy loads they kicked like the devil.

Most people think they want shorter and more crooked stocks when they first start shooting than they like later. An old rule is that the longer a man shoots the longer and the straighter he likes his stock. That is true after a fashion.

As we have seen, the dimensions of field stocks run about $1\frac{5}{8} \times 2\frac{1}{2} \times 14$. Since trapshooters mount their guns before they call for their targets, and since they always shoot at rapidly rising targets, and also because recoil is felt less with a staight stock, guns used in trapshooting have dimensions about like this: drop at comb—$1\frac{1}{4}$–$1\frac{3}{8}$; drop at heel, $1\frac{3}{4}$–2; length of pull, $14\frac{1}{4}$–$14\frac{3}{4}$. The gun with the straight stock points more rapidly and gives less apparent recoil.

The trapshooter always shoots at a rising target, but the skeet shooter more often than not shoots at a target that is falling. It is now legal in American skeet shooting to mount the gun before the target takes off, but many skeet shooters still keep their guns in field position. Guns must likewise be kept down when shooting international skeet. Consequently the skeet shooter takes a shorter stock with more drop than the trapshooter.

In England much ado is made about having the shotgun fitted to the individual with the use of a try-gun by a professional gun fitter and shooting coach. The professional with the try-gun is supposed to watch the customer mount his gun and shoot, then make adjustments here and there in height of comb, of heel, in length, pitch, and cast-off. Finally this expert gun fitter is presumed to come up with stock dimensions that just about make the gun self-pointing.

Those who have patronized the British gunmakers in the past have been rich Britishers and continentals who actually know little about guns and who are used to having most things done for them. Servants clean and put away their guns for them after each day's shoot. Beaters put up their game. Their rifle maker sights their rifles for them, and the gun fitter works out the measurements of their shotgun stocks.

I take all this gun fitting business with a grain of salt. A friend of mine on the continent is a keen shot but not frightfully knowledgeable about the technical aspect of guns. He had a matched pair of handsome British doubles but he never used them. When he shot birds he always left his matched pair in the rack and came out with an old Browning 12-gauge automatic. When I asked him why he used that old automatic instead of his handsome doubles, he told me that he could hit things with the automatic but did very poorly with the double. He and I have similar builds. I mounted one of his doubles a couple of times and then told him I was sure the reason he found it difficult to shoot them was that the stocks were too long for him and the combs were too high. Apparently the guns had been built for driven bird shooting—and for nothing else.

He assured me that the guns *did* fit him, as his dimensions had been specified by an expert with a try-gun. I finally demonstrated to him why he was missing and he returned the guns to the maker and asked for a lower comb and a shorter pull. Once the dimensions were changed he did well with the matched pair. Another hunter I knew had a top-grade British rifle. It was fitted with a detachable scope sight and iron sights. He never used the scope, said his rifle was not "accurate" with the scope. I sighted it in for him to put the 150-grain .300 Magnum bullet 3 inches high at 100 yards and on at about 275. It almost drove him mad to see that the elevation dial showed the rifle was sighted in for 100 yards. I finally convinced him that the figures on the dial meant nothing—that what counted was whether he could hit or not.

And so it is with the fit of the shotgun stock. I am convinced that there is only one person in the world who can tell a shooter if a shotgun stock fits him or not—and that is the shooter himself, but only if he has done enough shooting to know how a gun should handle, mount, and point. I believe also that only one person can tell if a pair of shoes fits—and that is the guy who has to wear them.

So let us take a look at the various stock dimensions to see what their functions are and how the gunner should be fitted for all-around use. The height of comb is right if it puts the right eye (of a right-handed man, of course) in line with the rib. He should be able to look right down the rib with his cheek pressed firmly against the comb. When he is actually shooting, he doesn't press his cheek quite so firmly. He sees his target just above the end of his barrel, shoots "up" at it slightly, and hits it. If the comb is too high and he sees a great deal of barrel, the gun will shoot high, and he will shoot over the bird going dead away or rising at a gentle angle. The trapshooter wants a highshooting gun as the targets he shoots are all rising sharply. The upland gun should shoot a bit high in the field, as most upland game birds are also rising.

The height of the comb is a very important stock measurement. The rear sight of the shotgun is the eye of the shooter, and the comb is the mechanism that elevates it. If the comb is so high that the shooter cannot look down the rib with his cheek pressed firmly against it, the shot charge will fly high. If the comb is so low that the shooter does not have contact with his cheek, he tends to shoot low and he finds it difficult to swing with his arms instead of rotating his whole body. If the comb hurts his cheekbone, it is too high or too sharp or both. Many continental guns have sharp combs and often these combs are likewise pretty high. Then they can really beat a shooter to death—particularly if the high, sharp comb is combined with considerable drop at heel. When I was hunting desert game in the southern Sahara some years ago, I rented a 16-gauge French double to use in shooting guinea fowl and francolin for the pot. That was the most miserable shotgun I have ever tried to use. Trigger pulls were about 20 pounds, and the gun had a high sharp comb that beat me to death. When I had shot it five or six times I had a bump on my cheekbone that was as large as a walnut and that throbbed like an ulcerated tooth.

Another very important dimension is the length of pull. If the stock is too short the shooter gets his nose pumped by his right thumb. If it is too long he finds the gun clumsy to mount. The butt catches in his clothes and slows him up.

The drop at heel is not a particularly important measurement. A difference of ⅛ inch in drop at comb is important but it is neither here nor there in drop at heel. I *think* I am most comfortable with a drop at heel of 2¼ inches, but I do equally well with a 2-inch drop or a 2½-inch drop. More than 2½ inches seems clumsy to me. The less the drop at heel, the less the apparent recoil since the gun comes back on a straight line. Guns with excessive heel drop recoil upward as well as backward and bruise the cheekbone.

Pitch is simply the angle of the butt and is measured by setting the gun with the butt flat against the floor and the breech against the wall. The pitch is determined by measuring the distance from the muzzle to the wall. If the muzzle is against the wall the gun is said to have zero pitch. If it is 2 inches from the wall it is said that the gun has a pitch down of 2 inches. Obviously the longer the barrel, the greater the pitch measurement will be even though the angle of the butt is the same. As a consequence the man who is ordering a custom stock for a shotgun should always specify pitch from a certain barrel length. It is even more certain to specify the measurement wanted from center of trigger to the heel of the stock and from the center of trigger to the toe. I fancy myself happiest with a pitch down of 1 inch on a double with 26-inch barrels. The function of pitch is to keep the butt firmly and comfortably against the shoulder. Too little pitch down (zero pitch or pitch up) has a ten-

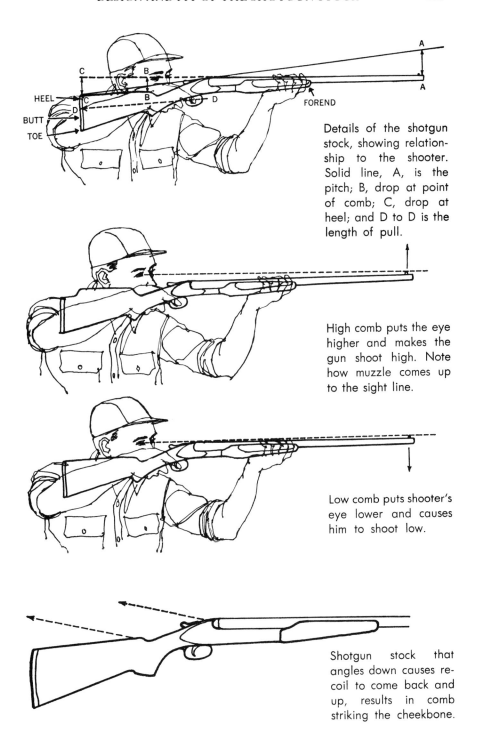

Details of the shotgun stock, showing relationship to the shooter. Solid line, A, is the pitch; B, drop at point of comb; C, drop at heel; and D to D is the length of pull.

High comb puts the eye higher and makes the gun shoot high. Note how muzzle comes up to the sight line.

Low comb puts shooter's eye lower and causes him to shoot low.

Shotgun stock that angles down causes recoil to come back and up, results in comb striking the cheekbone.

dency to make the butt of the gun slip down under the armpit and cause the gun to throw its charge high. Too much pitch down has just the opposite effect.

British guns are almost always made with what is called "cast-off." This means that the stock for the right-handed man when seen from above inclines slightly at the butt toward his right shoulder. Generally this cast-off is no more than ½ inch. The British claim that cast-off makes the gun easier to mount and faster to line up. American guns have seldom been made with cast-off and I am skeptical of its value.

These days few people have shotgun stocks custom made to their specifications. Instead they make-do with factory guns. Suppose they want to change the stock dimensions on a factory pump or automatic. What can be done? Pitch can be changed by loosening buttplate screws and inserting cardboard at toe or heel. Cardboard at toe reduces pitch down and cardboard at heel increases it. Length of pull can be changed by fitting a rubber recoil pad to desired dimensions. Drop at heel can be decreased and comb raised slightly by having a good gunsmith bend the stock to give desired dimensions. If the comb is too high, too sharp, or too thick (as factory combs sometimes are if a man has very wide cheekbones) the comb can be worked over to desired dimensions by scraping with a piece of broken glass, then smoothing up with sandpaper, and refinishing.

The fore-end of an automatic and the slide handle of a pump serve the same function as a beavertail fore-end on the double—they keep the hand away from the hot barrel and they help the shooter to control his piece. Americans generally demand some form of beavertail fore-end on side-by-side doubles, but Britishers and continentals seldom use them. Instead they often use fiber handguard on the barrels ahead of the splinter fore-ends. They can get their left hands farther ahead and control their guns better.

Theoretically, right hand and left hand should be on line. If the left hand is higher than the right the theory is that the gunner will have a tendency to shoot high. If his left hand is lower, the tendency is to shoot low. Precisely how much water this theory holds I cannot say. Fore-ends of most automatics and some over-and-unders put the left hand lower than the right. Side-by-side doubles tend to put the left hand high. Probably the best hand alignment is with shallow-frame over-and-under shotguns such as those made by Holland & Holland and Boss in England and Beretta in Italy. Several Japanese firms also make shallow-frame "stackbarrels."

Checkering on the grip and fore-end are ornamental and also useful in that they keep the hands from slipping and give a firmer grip. Today, most checkering on American repeating shotguns is cut by machine, although the top-quality guns still feature hand-checkered stocks.

A well-designed and good-fitting stock makes the shotgun easier to mount, quicker to point, and more comfortable to shoot; but, alas, no one has yet invented a stock which would prevent a man from slowing or stopping his swing by giving a warning buzzer or that gave him an electric shock if he took his cheek off the comb. When such a stock is invented I'll stand in line to buy it.

16

Beginning with the Shotgun

LEARNING TO BECOME reasonably skillfull with a shotgun is not difficult. It is, I am convinced, far easier to learn to break 25 (a perfect score) at skeet or traps with fair regularity than to become proficient enough at golf to break 80.

To be a superlative shot—a chap who can break 150 straight at skeet or traps and perform spectacularly on flying game—a gunner must have fine muscular co-ordination, keen eyesight, and a competitive temperament. The very best shots (like the best golfers, the best tennis players, the best baseball players) are those who are keyed up by competition but not made jittery by it.

Actually the difference in the very good performers and the superstars in any sport is not so much a matter of skill as of temperament—not of muscles but of nerves. There are dozens of golfers who are mechanically just about perfect. The difference between them and the Arnold Palmers and Jack Nicklauses is that the superstars, the big money winners, generally do their best under pressure and the also-rans do not.

Below the shooters who are at the top physically and emotionally and those who are first class physically but not emotionally are those of us of average physical and emotional endowment. We are the 85-95 shooters in golf, the Class B and C skeet and trap shooters, and because there are so many of us we are the guys who keep up the gun clubs and the golf courses. The hotshots may win the medals and the money, but I do not think they have more fun.

Just about anyone, then, can become a reasonably good hand with the shotgun. He can learn to do well enough on clay targets to have fun, shoot well enough in the field so that he gets his share of birds and looks pretty good. But let us face it. Unless we are born with the eyes, the muscular co-ordination, the temperament we will not be experts no matter how much we practice.

Since most of us cannot hope to become top-flight performers with a shotgun, let us learn from the gifted ones.

The superb shotgun shot always makes shooting look easy and he is almost always a very fast shot.

The not-so-good gunner makes shooting look like hard work—and for him it is hard work. He falls into the habit of assuming exaggerated stances. Often

143

they are crouches. He grips his gun so hard the sweat breaks out on his brow. The good shot stands naturally, relaxed but alert.

PROPER STANCE

So let's start from the beginning. The gunner should stand with his feet far enough apart so that he is in balance, close enough together so he can move hips and shoulders freely. The stance is as important in shotgun shooting as it is in golf and boxing—and for exactly the same reason. If a man's feet are too close together he loses balance and if they are too far apart he is inflexible.

He should face away from the direction of his aim at about a 45-degree angle. His knees should be slightly bent for flexibility, just as the knees of a golfer are bent, but he should not be in the sort of a crouch that one sometimes sees assumed by trap and skeet shooters. The gunner should lean a bit forward into the shot so that recoil will not disturb his balance. Some very good skeet shooters lean so far forward that all their weight is on their left legs and they are definitely off balance. Many of these chaps are good shots not because of their exaggerated stance but in spite of it. Such a stance would be poison in the field because the gunner would be off balance and it would be difficult for him to transfer his weight from one leg to another. As a right-handed man swings from right to left he transfers his weight to his right leg. If he cannot transfer his weight he tends to be an arms swinger instead of rotating his hips. The swing from left to right is made with most of the weight on the left leg. If poor stance has the gunner's hips locked or if he is off balance, he simply cannot swing freely and he shoots behind.

MOUNTING AND AIMING THE GUN

It is an old saying among shotgunners that the good shot puts his gun to his face, the poor shot his face to his gun. As the good shot sees the bird his head goes down and inclines to the right in the position in which it will be when he shoots. His right shoulder goes up a bit. He pushes his gun out and back in a straight line, and when the butt hits his shoulder his right eye is in line with his barrel. In effect as he steps into the shot and brings his head down into position he has already to a large extent "aimed" or "pointed" his gun by aiming himself.

When he mounts his gun his right elbow is down at an angle of about 45 degrees, his right shoulder elevated a trifle, his left hand is out on the fore-end or slide handle so he can have more control.

The good shot shoots with both eyes open. This gives him binocular vision which in turn gives better judgment of range. It also gives him a wider field of view. The only time a good shot shoots with one eye closed is when his master eye is on the wrong side. Some right-handed men have left master eyes. In that case the unfortunate gunner must learn to shoot left-handed or he must close his left eye or shoot with a patch over it. Blocking off the vision of the master

To mount shotgun, keep your eye on the target, push the gun out, pull it straight back.

eye on the wrong side is much the easier of the two solutions. Yet another solution, although it is costly and not very satisfactory, is to use a cross-eyed stock—a stock so bent that the gun can be held at the right shoulder but the left eye is in line with the barrel or the rib. The same solution is used when a right-handed man has defective vision in his right eye.

The terms "aiming" and "pointing" are both used in reference to lining up shotgun barrel with the target. They are used interchangeably, but properly speaking aiming means the exact alignment of two sights with the target as with a rifle or the exact alignment of the reticule of a telescope sight with the target. "Pointing" means the quick and approximate alignment of the muzzle or muzzles of the shotgun with the target. Even when a shotgun barrel has a front bead and a smaller bead halfway down the barrel, the good shot never tries to line up the two beads or "aim." Generally he is not conscious of his front bead. He aims or points with the muzzle of the gun. Actually the muzzle is the front sight and his eye is the rear sight. If his eye is too low he undershoots. If it is too high he overshoots. The elevating mechanism of the rear sight (his eye) should be the comb of his stock. His cheek against the comb should control the position of his eye. That is why one of the principal sins of the shotgunner is not getting his cheek down on the comb. When he does not his eye is too high and he overshoots.

The beginner with a shotgun does everything all wrong just as the beginner with a tennis racket or a golf club does everything all wrong. He does not elevate his right shoulder and lift his right elbow midway between belt and shoulder. He does not put his head down. Instead he generally keeps his elbow down by his side, his left hand too close to the trigger guard. He does not put his head forward by running his neck out. Instead he gives an exaggerated cock to his head so he can see down the barrel. In addition he almost always closes his left eye. The first time anyone tries to mount a gun he looks about as much at home with it as he would be with a pair of chopsticks. The eyes of our beginner are often so concentrated on his gun barrel that when a clay target is thrown he does not see it.

The good American shotgun shot is target conscious. He concentrates on the target instead of on his barrel, but he sees the end of his barrel in relation to the target. He knows about how far he was ahead of the target when the gun went off. His eyes are focused on the bird or the target but he is also conscious of the end of that barrel. We might say that the target is in sharp focus of both vision and attention but the shooter is conscious of the end of the barrel. It may be a bit out of focus but he sees it. He calls his shot. In other words he knows where the muzzle was in relation to the bird or target when the gun went off. Many times when I have missed a bird with a one-foot lead, let us say, I have swung farther ahead and have hit it with the second shot.

The skilled shot does not look exactly down the barrel or rib, hold the front bead right in the middle of his target and cut loose, as one would do if he wanted to shoot a deer in the heart with a rifle. Instead good shots have found that they have more success by seeing the entire barrel foreshortened with the bird or the target above it. The method of looking down the barrel and cutting the target in half with the bead is actually aiming. The man who sees his barrel foreshortened with the bird above it is pointing—in effect shooting up at the target.

The British school of shotgunnery holds that the shooter should keep his head up, with eye well above the rib. They say he should not even see the barrels but only the bird. They likewise say that he simply should see the bird or target, point at it with his left hand, and pull the trigger. They likewise say that it is bad form, my dear fellows, to give any bird or target conscious lead, that giving conscious lead tends to make the gunner slow and pokey.

Now there is something to this. It is not absolutely necessary to see the gun barrel. I have seen trick shots do a pretty fair job of breaking skeet targets by shooting from the hip. I also knew a chap with a set of gifted muscles who astonished the natives by knocking off flushing pheasants quite regularly by shooting from the hip.

A man used to shooting can hit tin cans quite regularly with a .22 rifle by shooting with head erect and not looking at his sights or even by shooting from the hip. No one really aims when he sinks a ball in the basket when playing basketball, when he hits a golf or tennis ball, or when he heaves a forward pass into the hands of an end rushing 40 yards or so down field.

An interesting experiment is to point at a picture or some other object on the wall with a flashlight with a focused beam. Then turn on the light. With a little practice most people can learn to put the beam on or close to what they point at—even from the hip.

All this is complicated by the fact that many fine shots are inarticulate about their shooting technique. Often they have no idea what they do. They just shoot and hit.

I once went out to a London shooting school where I was coached in this

In the field, hunter carries his shotgun ready to go into action—butt forward, muzzle high, trigger guard to front.

When game is sighted, he brings the gun down with his right hand as his left comes up to grasp the fore-end.

Eye on the game, the gunner is ready to mount his gun.

Pushing gun out and back in a straight line, he brings the butt to his shoulder. As butt hits his shoulder, his right eye is in line with the barrel.

heads-up,   never-see-the-barrel,   shoot-the-instant-the-butt-touches-your-shoulder. In spite of the fact that it went against my habits, my instinct, and my reason, I could have done worse.

Nevertheless, I see no point in the British system. To me it makes no sense to shoot right at a crossing bird at 20 yards and also at 40 yards. I am sure many Britishers shoot well by the method, particularly on birds flushing in front of dogs and on Scotch grouse. These are incomers at gentle angles—about like the No. 1 and No. 2 low house birds at skeet.

The American skeet and trap shooters are certainly as good as any in the world and almost without exception they look down the barrel and see the end of the barrel in relation to their targets. I have seen but one trap shooter who used the heads-up-no-seeum barrel method. He was very fast and when he was hot he was quite good. When he was bad he didn't do so well.

The good American shotgun shot swings by rotating his hips. He does not horse his gun around with his arms. His cheek is firm against the comb of his stock. He looks right down the barrel and he sees the end of it in relation to the bird he hopes to bring down or the target he hopes to break. When he has to take a crossing bird, he swings with it, passes it, shoots when the muzzle looks the right distance ahead.

In rifle shooting the trigger is squeezed and in handgun shooting it is squeezed to the nth degree. The trigger of the shotgun is "slapped" or "jerked." The swinging gun and the big cloud of shot more than compensate for a bit of disturbance by the trigger let off.

Learning to Shoot

The best way for the beginner to learn to shoot is to go out to a gun club or a shooting school and put himself in the hands of an instructor. He then starts off right. But most young Americans start off as I did. I was given a single-barrel 20 gauge gun, some shells, and told to go to it. The result was that in learning to shoot I formed bad habits which I found difficult to break and some of which still haunt me at times. The beginner who starts out with a coach is lucky indeed.

If the beginning shooter lives in an area where there is no formal instruction in shooting, he can learn from books and magazine articles and he can also learn from watching good shots perform.

The man who wants to shoot well must practice—and he must practice on clay targets. The day when a lad could pick up a shotgun, stuff some shells in his pocket and go out and learn to shoot on feathered game is over. Almost any shooting is helpful. Skill acquired at trap and skeet shooting is quickly transferred to field shooting. If these shooting games are not available, it is always possible for a couple of gunners to buy a handtrap and a case of clay targets and go out into a field somewhere to practice.

The reason there are so many fantastically poor field shots is that so many gunners never pop a cap except at something that sheds feathers and leaks blood. This is as if a golfer never hit a ball except when the tournament for the club championship rolled around. Practice may not make us perfect, but it certainly makes us better! Reading and thinking about shooting is no substitute for practice—but it helps.

17

Shooting Muzzleloaders

by Clair Rees

THE MODERN SPORTSMAN, with his breechloading firearms loaded with smokeless-powder cartridges, enjoys shooting convenience unknown a century and a half ago. His guns are easier to load and shoot, and much easier to care for than the muzzleloading charcoal burners of great grandfather's day.

In spite of these facts, many hunters continue to go afield armed with aging front-stuffers or newly manufactured replicas of these guns. Why? Nostalgia has a lot to do with today's popularity of muzzleloading rifles, handguns and shotguns. Shooting a blackpowder firearm gives the sportsman a brief look at yesteryear. There's no denying the romance of stepping back in time.

Like the bowhunter, the sportsman who limits his armament to muzzleloading single-shots is intentionally making things more difficult for himself. He (or she) is adding excitement to an already exciting sport, and when a buck falls to a Hawken ball it provides even greater satisfaction than a deer harvested with a modern, scope-sighted repeater.

Shooters in the 1840's regarded the lengthy, messy task of cleaning the black-powder residue from their guns as an onerous and tedious chore. The modern muzzleloading fan even manages to find pleasure in this pastime, for this too is a way of stepping back in time and sharing the experiences of hunters in another age.

Because hunting with muzzleloaders has become so popular, many states now offer a special, early season for sportsmen who use front-stuffing rifles. Archers are accorded similarly privileged treatment.

Black-powder guns fall into two general categories: flintlocks and percussion-lock guns. In the flintlock, the propellant charge in the barrel is ignited by a relatively complicated chain of events. The hammer, which carries a piece of flint locked in a set of adjustable jaws, is first pulled back to the cocked position. A charge of finely granulated powder is poured into the priming pan, which rides alongside the barrel.

When the target is sighted, the trigger is pulled to release the hammer. As

It's just as important to sight in muzzleloaders as to sight in cartridge arms. Clair Rees is shown checking zero of his Thompson/Center Cougar, a replica of the Hawken percussion rifle with stainless-steel fittings.

the hammer falls forward under spring pressure, the flint rubs along a curved striking plate, producing sparks. These sparks fall into the priming pan, igniting the priming charge. This charge, in turn, burns through a small port in the barrel to ignite the much larger charge of coarser black powder behind the ball. As you can see, there is a small but noticeable time lag once the trigger is pulled before the ball is forced out the bore.

A later development, the percussion lock is more reliable and faster. In place of the unwieldy loose priming charge and flint, ignition is provided by a metallic percussion cap placed on a hollow anvil. The falling hammer strikes the cap, exploding the fulminate compound inside. The resulting flash is transmitted through the touchhole to the propellant charge.

Except for the method of priming, all muzzleloading rifles are loaded the same way. First, the lock mechanism is examined to make sure there's no priming charge or percussion cap in place. This is an important safety step, as the firearm is necessarily loaded from the muzzle end. An accidental discharge could have disastrous effects on the person loading the rifle.

Next, if the gun isn't being reloaded immediately after firing, a ramrod is dropped down the bore to measure its empty length and ensure that an unfired charge isn't already in place. Double-charging a muzzleloader can create dangerous pressures that could result in damage to both the gun and the shooter.

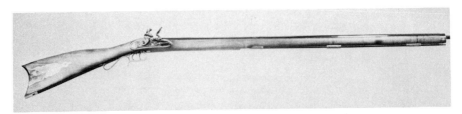

Flintlock Lancaster County Rifle, built from kit supplied by Dixie Gun Works. Caplock version of this Pennsylvania rifle also comes in kit for do-it-yourself hobbyists.

Thompson/Center Arms markets this optional accessory pack for its .45 and .50 Hawken replica rifles. Pack includes Lyman bullet mold, 100 patches, nipple wrench, Hoppe's No. 9 Plus Black Powder Solvent, short starter, spare nipple, and four powder scoops (for different charges).

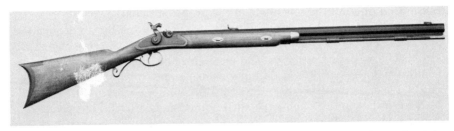

Browning offers black-powder guns as well as modern repeaters. This is the John Browning Mountain Rifle, a modern counterpart of a 19th-century percussion rifle.

Although round balls are patched for use in muzzleloading shoulder arms, elongated cast slugs like these .54 caliber Maxi-Balls are loaded without patches. Cast rings help hold lubricant and engage the rifling as the bullet moves through the bore.

Then the powder charge is measured out and poured down the bore. This powder should be of the proper granulation; fine-grain powder used in pistol charges burns too fast for rifle use. Black powder or its modern substitute, Pyrodex, is always measured by volume, never by weight. The correct charge should be determined by consulting black-powder loading manuals or the instructions that come packed with most modern muzzleloaders. Tapping the rifle butt lightly against the ground settles the charge.

Both patched, round balls and elongated, cast slugs are used in black-powder rifles. If a round ball is used, a cloth patch is first cut to size—large enough to wrap nearly around the ball, but not large enough to create seating

Short starter is used to force lubricated Maxi-Ball into rifling at the muzzle. Full-length ramrod will then be used to push the slug home, seating it over powder charge. See text for full loading procedure.

Small-bore black-powder rifles like this Mowrey percussion .36 are popular for hunting small game.

problems. The patch is then greased with Spit Patch or some other suitable lubricant.

The lubricated patch is placed on the muzzle, and the ball pressed into it from above. Then a short, sturdy ramrod called the "short starter" is used to force the patched ball a short way down the bore. Elongated "Maxi-Ball" type slugs are greased and used without patches.

A full-length ramrod is then employed to push the ball all the way down the bore until it's seated firmly over the powder charge. Again, the ramrod is used to make sure the ball is at the proper depth. An air space between ball and powder can create dangerously high pressures. Then remove the ramrod—this is a step a surprising number of shooters sometimes forget, and many a ramrod has disappeared forever after being shot downrange.

Finally, place the priming cap—or if a flintlock is used, the priming powder—and the rifle is fully charged and ready to go.

A similar procedure is used for loading black-powder shotguns. The primary difference is that cut cardboard wads are used in place of the patching material, and loose shot pellets replace the ball. A cardboard wad is seated over the powder charge, then the shot pellets are poured down the bore. A second wad card is then seated to keep the shot from rolling down and out of the barrel when the gun is tipped forward.

Most black-powder aficionados use shoulder arms, but muzzleloading side arms have also become very popular. They're used for target shooting and plinking, of course, and to some extent for hunting. Many of us particularly enjoy hunting small game with a muzzleloading handgun. For that matter, you can take deer and big game, too, with one of the large-bore black-powder handguns. Actually, you can do as the bowhunters do: Try for whatever you feel up to hunting, simply bearing in mind that the range must be short and you're operating under self-imposed limitations that don't apply to the pursuit of game with modern, often scope-sighted handguns.

These restrictions are all the more severe if you choose a single-shot pistol. Such guns are supplied in flintlock and percussion versions by Navy, Dixie, Connecticut Valley Arms, Thompson/Center, and Tingle, among others. Some models are rather precise replicas of antique arms; some are not actually replicas but are rather closely modeled after dueling pistols, saddle pistols, or howdah pistols, and some are modern in design.

The revolvers are cap-and-ball guns, of course. An outstanding one is a non-replica, a modern design utilizing an antique ignition and loading system. It's the .44 Ruger Old Army Model, which has adjustable target sights and is popular among top target competitors. Obviously, such a gun is also an excellent hunting choice.

Truly authentic replicas of the Colts used from 1850 to about 1870—one of the most exciting eras of American history—have been available recently from the original maker. Among these models are the Colt 1851 Navy, the Colt Dragoons, and the Colt 1860 Army, all fine revolvers. Another popular revolver is the Navy Arms .44 Model 1858 Remington Army, and still another

Brass Barrel Kentucky Pistol from Navy Arms is reminiscent of the Queen Anne era of gunmaking. It has oil-finished walnut stock, highly polished brass furniture, color case-hardened lock, and solid-brass octagonal barrel. Most such guns were English or European, but a few were made by early American gunsmiths. This one has a rifled .44 bore.

Another Navy Arms Kentucky Pistol is this .44 percussion model. Except for its blued steel barrel and caplock ignition, it's very much like the Navy Arms Brass Barrel flintlock.

Lyman's New Model Navy .36 is modeled after early Remington percussion six-guns. Unlike many early caplock revolvers, this Remington design has a topstrap over the cylinder, providing extra frame strength.

is Lyman's Squareback Navy .36. Quite a few replicas of other 19th-century percussion revolvers are imported by the same companies that market replica shoulder arms. Among both shoulder arms and side arms, some models are available either in finished form or assembly kits for do-it-yourselfers. The Lyman Navy, for example, can be bought as a kit. Assembly of these guns requires care but isn't at all difficult. Of course, how they function and look depends on how well the hobbyist fits, polishes, and finishes them.

A flintlock single-shot pistol is loaded like a flintlock rifle, except that the charge will be considerably lighter than for a rifle of the same bore size. Again, consult a loading manual or the instructions furnished with the gun. The same caution applies to percussion handguns, which are not loaded the same way as caplock shoulder arms.

Before loading a percussion handgun, clean all the oil from the bore (and from the cylinder if you're using a revolver). Fire a couple of caps to take out any oil residue and to clear the nipple (or, in the case of a revolver, all the nipples).

With a single-shot percussion pistol, place the hammer at half-cock and make sure there's no cap on the nipple. Then pour the correct charge of Pyrodex or FFFg black powder down the bore. Now start a patched ball. By the way, tightly woven cotton .015-inch thick is excellent material for patches. After using the starter, seat the ball all the way with the ramrod, doing it firmly but without pounding. Then seat a cap on the nipple and the gun is ready to fire.

With a revolver, after you're cleaned out the oil and cleared the nipples by

In Civil War "skirmish" regalia, Val Forgett, Jr., of Navy Arms, uses a replica powder flask with a built-in measure to charge one of the chambers in his cap-and-ball .44.

popping caps, move the hammer back to half-cock and the cylinder can then be turned by hand. Drop the correct powder charge into one chamber and place an unpatched ball over it, at the chamber's mouth. A caplock revolver has a built-in rammer that pivots back under the barrel. Turn the cylinder to align the loaded chamber with the rammer, then lower the rammer to seat the ball against the powder. Repeat the procedure with each chamber. When finished, fill the mouths of all the chambers with one of the commercial lubricants sold for the purpose, or with ordinary automotive water-pump grease or vegetable shortening. Plugging the chambers with grease softens the fouling and—far more important—prevents a multiple discharge. As you can imagine, multiple discharge in a revolver is an extremely dangerous occurrence, so this safety precaution is vital. Once the chambers are grease-plugged, you can cap the nipples and your revolver is ready to fire. If you're going to be carrying the gun rather than firing all your shots immediately at a target, don't load all six chambers. For safety, the chamber under the hammer should be empty. As with black-powder shoulder arms, a thorough cleaning is needed after a firing session or a day's hunting.

A revolver must be taken down; that is, the cylinder must be removed from the frame and barrel assembly. The method of doing this, though fast and simple, varies slightly from one model to another, so you must read the instructions furnished with the gun. After disassembly, scrub the parts with hot, soapy water. Use soap, not detergent. Then flush the parts well with hot rinse water and wipe thoroughly. A good trick to ensure complete drying is to place each part on a sheet of aluminum foil and put them in an oven at 200 degrees for 10 minutes. This will not harm your gun. When the parts are good and dry, oil them lightly and reassemble the gun.

Single-shot black-powder pistols, like muzzleloading rifles and shotguns, have "hooked" barrels that can be lifted out of the stock for cleaning. The barrels are locked in place by a metal wedge (often brass) located in the fore-end. With this wedge drifted out, your gun's barrel is easily detached.

I can't emphasize too strongly the importance of cleaning muzzleloaders thoroughly after use. Black-powder residue is highly corrosive and will cause rust in short order. With a single-shot muzzleloading pistol or a muzzleloading rifle or shotgun, the traditional procedure is to scrub the bore with hot, soapy water. Except for the method of disassembly, you do pretty much the same thing as with cap-and-ball revolvers—only you don't have the chore of scrubbing all those chambers.

Soap—not detergent—should be dissolved in boiling water, and a patched ramrod used to swab the bore. Michaels of Oregon offers a handy cleaning kit that consists of a special nipple (to replace the percussion nipple), a length of surgical tubing, and some solvent-soaked disposable pieces of cloth. The cleaning nipple has "O"-rings to make a tight seal; once in place, the surgical tubing is attached to the nipple, while the other end of the tubing is placed in a container of hot, soapy water. A cloth patch is fitted to the ramrod, and the road is stroked back and forth in the bore. This creates a pumping action that forces the hot water in and out of the bore, taking the black-powder residue with it.

When properly done, this procedure heats the steel barrel to the point that the water quickly evaporates. The dry metal is then swabbed or wiped with an oiled patch to prevent oxidation.

There are commercial black-powder solvents on the market that can be substituted for hot, soapy water, but none are more effective than this homely mixture. As a matter of fact, soapy water near the boiling point is probably the best cleaning agent you can use for these guns.

If Pyrodex is used as the propellant powder, prompt cleaning is less imperative. The cleaning must be done, but neglecting this chore overnight won't cause the gun any harm. Pyrodex is a modern black-powder substitute, and is measured on the same volume basis. It's considered less volatile—and therefore safer—than black powder, and it's also less corrosive.

Because there's always a bit of oil left in the bore of a properly cleaned muzzleloader, a couple of percussion caps should be snapped on the nipple to burn out this lubricant just before the gun is to be loaded. If any oil remains, it will foul the powder charge and cause a misfire. If this happens, snap a few more caps. If the gun still refuses to fire, unscrew the percussion nipple and use a straightened paper clip or some other tool to scrape out the oil-soaked part of the charge. Pour in some fresh powder, replace the nipple and try again.

A similar procedure is used to dislodge a ball or shot charge seated in the bore without benefit of a powder charge beneath it. Unscrew the nipple, pour in some powder (this takes a little patience, as the orifice is small), replace the nipple, cap it, and shoot the obstruction free.

Muzzleloading shotguns are available in standard gauges from 10 to 28, and even some in-between sizes. Cardboard wads are purchased commercially or simply cut to fit, while some shooters take advantage of modern shotshell technology and use plastic sleeve-wad combinations to contain the shot. Most muzzleloading scatterguns feature straight cylinder bores and are best employed at ranges of 30 yards or less. At that distance, these guns can perform just about as well as their modern counterparts, and throw deadly patterns.

Black-powder rifles, too, are offered in many bore sizes, the most popular being .32, .36, .45, .50, .54 and .58 caliber. For hunting small game, .32 and .36 caliber rifles are used, while anything in .45 caliber or larger is suitable for taking deer. A .50 or .54 slug or round ball is highly effective on large game, and just about any game that walks has been successfully hunted with muzzleloading firearms.

Because the open sights employed on most muzzleloading rifles are too coarse to allow precise long-distance shooting, the smart deer hunter will limit his range to 125 yards or less when shooting black powder. The rifles themselves may be capable of longer-range accuracy, but their primitive sights simply don't lend themselves to distant marksmanship. Also, the heavy, round balls describe a rainbow trajectory, and this is another limiting factor.

Anyone interested in black-powder shooting ought to contact the National Muzzle Loading Rifle Association, which publishes its own magazine and provides members with news and information about products, matches, gun shows, and various activities. You can write to the NMLRA at Box 67, Friendship, IN 47021.

Shooting black-powder firearms is fun. You may have to step aside after you shoot, or wait for the wind to blow the billowing white smoke cloud away so that you can see if you hit what you were aiming at. And you'll have to make that first shot count. But all that is part of the attraction for the increasing number of sportsmen who are turning to muzzleloaders for at least part of their hunting fun.

V

Hunting with the Shotgun

Jack O'Connor

18

Upland Guns and Upland Gunning

IT WOULD BE very pleasant indeed and life would be much more simple if one gun, one shot size, and one loading would do for all game shot in the uplands.

The sad fact is that the terms "upland game" and "upland hunting" take in an enormous amount of territory. A proper gun, the right degree of choke, and the best shot size for one bird and one set of hunting conditions may not be much good for another.

The term *upland hunting* applies to all bird hunting except the shooting of waterfowl—to New England grouse and woodcock shooting, where birds are taken at from 10 to 25 yards, as well as to mourning and whitewing dove shooting on some Southwestern pass, where shots are taken at from 30 to 55 yards. The term upland game applies to the close-lying bobwhite of the grassy Georgia pine forests and to the fast-running, wild-flushing scaled and Gambel's quail of West Texas, Arizona, and New Mexico. The rock-dwelling chukar partridge in the hills and canyons of the Northwest is an upland game bird and so are the prairie-dwelling Hungarian and the gaudy cornfield pheasant of the Middle West.

Far more upland game than waterfowl is taken in the United States. There are many reasons for this. Most important is that upland game birds are more numerous than ducks and geese. Yet another is that more and more of the best waterfowl hunting areas are coming under the control of private clubs.

For many years more shotshells were fired at the humble cottontail rabbit (which is certainly upland game) than at any other target (including all the clay targets broken or missed at skeet or traps) but in recent years it is the mourning dove that is responsible for the greatest expenditure of ammunition.

It is an odd fact that this most shot at of all the upland game birds has many points in common with waterfowl, and of all the upland game he can be shot most successfully with a duck gun. Like the duck or the goose the dove (and also his Southwestern and Mexican cousin, the whitewing) comes to the

163

hunter. Generally, the dove hunter finds a pass where the birds fly between feed and water or between feeding ground and roosting area. Then he finds some sort of complete or partial concealment and shoots at birds that come by within what he considers the range of his gun and his skill.

Sometimes the dove hunter builds a blind by a water hole or near a feeding area such as a wheat field, a weed patch or a field of peas or peanuts. He may even set out dove decoys—some perched happily in nearby trees, others on the ground, presumably feeding.

Dove shooting of this type is much easier than pass shooting. Birds are not flying nearly so fast and if the gunner remains concealed they are unsuspicious. They come in to water or to feed with their flaps down and are not difficult to hit.

The patient, reasonably competent gunners shooting from a blind with an open-bored gun should get at least three doves out of five, possibly four out of five. It is much like shooting puddle ducks from a blind, except that it is easier, as the dove comes in more slowly and lands more gently than the duck.

On many occasions when shooting at the water hole I have averaged from 75 to 90 percent on doves, but I have taken my time and I have used an open-bored gun.

Walking up doves that are feeding in wheat fields or weed patches is also not difficult. The birds are generally quartering away at easy angles and with an open-bored gun they are not hard to grass.

But pass shooting at doves is something else again. It is surely one of the world's most difficult types of field shooting. The dove is a fast flier and since he has a low wing loading he is very maneuverable. I have heard that shooting driven grouse in Scotland was an acid test of the shotgunner's skill, but I found grouse much easier than doves on a flyway.

The red grouse of Scotland is a fast bird, but I doubt if he is as fast as a dove and since he has a high wing loading he is not nearly so maneuverable. The grouse will swerve or "jink," as the British say, when the gunner rises from concealment to salute the incoming birds, but his best is simple as compared to the confusing gyrations of which a dove is capable. Many a time I have let doves pass without shooting simply because the bird could twist and turn faster than I could follow him with my gun and I never felt sure enough of them to fire.

In most states where doves are hunted there are well-known flyways and since the birds are creatures of habit, their flights occur about the same time every morning and every afternoon. Then the dove hunters go out with everything from a canteen of lukewarm water to a container full of bottled beer in cracked ice. Generally they have something to sit on—a camp chair, a wooden box, even a British shooting stick. Most of them take a shot at everything that comes by in what they consider possible range—anywhere from 50 to 65 yards.

Many times I have seen gunners shooting on a pass burn up a box of shells and get no more than a bird or two. Many won't agree with me but I think that for the average hunter one bird in the hand for five shells expended is not bad shooting.

Years ago I asked two groups of scatter gunners—one composed of ordinary run-of-the-mill gunners and the other of crack skeet and trap shots who did a lot of shooting—to keep track for me of doves in the hand to shells expended and to report at the end of the day. The so-so shots averaged one dove in the hand to 8–9 shots, the good shots reported one bird for 3–3½ shells. Both groups said they could not understand it. They had never done such lousy shooting in their lives. Years later I asked one of the best shotgun shots in the United States what his average on doves was if he shot on a pass and took everything within a range. He said he picked up about one dove for three shells. That is excellent shooting!

The dove is a tender, fragile bird and hits that a quail would carry off will bring him down. When he falls wounded he lies there instead of crawling off to hide like a quail or a pheasant. Since the gunner who shoots on a flight does little walking his gun can be fairly heavy—if he likes a heavy gun. Most hunters are overgunned with a full choke. They may kill a few birds out around 55 yards they would only wound otherwise but they will miss a lot of close ones because of patterns that are too small. Because most doves are shot in level flight like ducks the gun should shoot where it looks at 40 yards, not high like most upland guns. A good bet is a 12-gauge pump or automatic with a 26–28 inch barrel throwing a 50 percent pattern with No. 7½ shot. To maintain the same pattern density a 20 gauge should be bored about 60 percent.

Most dove hunters use too much choke and loads that are too heavy. Since it requires from three to eight shots to put a dove in the pot the heavy loads shake the gunner up too much. Best record I ever made on a dove flyway was with an improved cylinder 12, but I simply did not shoot at anything I thought was over 35 yards away.

Most upland shooting is very different from the flight shooting of doves. The gunner has to walk long distances. Almost all of his shooting is within 35 yards and most of it within 25 yards. Almost all the birds he shoots at are rising and most of them are at birds going directly away or flying at a gentle angle. The wildfowl hunter or the man gunning for doves in flight generally has his target in sight for some time before he has to pull the trigger. But since most upland game is shot while it is going away, the hunter must shoot quickly with his open-bored gun or the game will be beyond range.

This quick shooting at close range at rising birds requires a light, open-bored, fast-handling gun that throws its patterns somewhat high. The gun should balance about four inches in front of the trigger, which means that it should be a bit muzzle light, since in upland shooting it is more important that it come up fast than that it swing steady.

The versatile 12 gauge is the best choice for waterfowl, for trap and skeet shooting, for wild turkeys, for deer with rifled slugs. The 12 can also be used for upland game, but the smaller gauges do just as well and are a bit more pleasant to carry and shoot. For most upland shooting 1 or 1⅛ ounce is plenty of shot—and if 1⅛ ounce is enough it doesn't matter much whether it is shot from a 20 gauge in the form of the 2¾-inch Magnum shell or from a 12-gauge gun in the form of the low-brass field load. I like a 16 gauge for the uplands, and actually a 16 can be used with anything from 1 ounce to 1¼ ounces of shot. Although the Magnum 20 has displaced it in national popularity, the 16 is still liked for quail and doves in the deep South.

It is the 20, however, that is the queen of the upland gauges. A light 20 gauge with 1 ounce of shot is very pleasant to shoot. The report is a sharp crack instead of a bellow like that of the 12. Recoil is light and the ammunition weighs less than that of the 12.

An improved cylinder 20 gauge with 1 ounce of No. 7½ or No. 8 will kill quail nicely at 30 yards and to a little over that (perhaps 33 yards) with the 1⅛-ounce, 2¾-inch 20-gauge Magnum load. Since 90 percent of all upland game is shot within 30 yards, a light 20 has plenty of range.

Ever since the end of World War II, guns chambered for the 3-inch 20-gauge Magnum shell have become increasingly popular. The long shells make a duck gun out of a 20 gauge. It was the advent of the 20-gauge Magnum shell that moved the 20 greatly ahead of the 16 in gun and ammunition sales.

The 28 gauge was never anything but an upland gauge. It was developed by the Parker Gun Company in the early years of this century. For a time the 28 was mildly popular among quail and dove shooters and double guns were made for the shell by Ithaca as well as Parker. Shells were variously made in lengths of 2½ inches, 2⅞ inches, and 2¾ inches. Now shells and chambers are standardized as 2¾-inch. At first the 28 was loaded with ⅝ ounce of shot, then ¾ ounce. Since the 3-inch .410 shell would handle ¾ ounce of shot, there wasn't much percentage in owning a 28. The war killed off the Parker, and Ithaca quit making doubles not long after the war was over. Winchester brought out the Model 12 in 28 gauge in 1934 and made pumps in that gauge until about 1937. The 28-gauge Model 12's were generally seen in the form of skeet guns and actually it was the game of skeet which kept the 28 gauge alive. The gauge is legal and widely used in small-bore skeet shooting with ¾ ounce of shot, as the 28 patterns better than the .410 with the same amount of shot. Remington offers lightweight 28-gauge versions of the Model 870 pump and 1100 autoloader. These are fine little guns to shoot.

The Browning Superposed (over-and-under) and Citori shotguns are available in 28 and Harrington & Richardson makes a 28-gauge single shot. Some 28-gauge doubles have been imported from Japan, Spain, and Belgium. I have never heard of a 28 being made in England, Germany, or Italy.

The .410 is a pleasant little gun to shoot, and it is very popular. More than 10 percent of all the guns and shotshells sold each year in the United States are in .410. Browning furnishes the stackbarreled Citori in .410 for sub-small bore skeet shooters and Remington makes the 870 and 1100 models in .410. Savage makes its over-and-under combination gun in .22-.410. Winchester dropped its excellent Model 42 pump in .410 at the time the company was shooting down many fine old models which could apparently no longer be manufactured profitably. There is a place for the .410, but I can think of better upland guns.

The classic gun for the uplands is the side-by-side double. On most of the continent it is a 16 gauge. In England it is almost always a light 12. The British upland load contains only 1¹⁄₁₆ ounces of shot and is pleasant to shoot even in a 6½- or 7-pound gun. The standard British "game cartridge" is 2½ inches long, but the British also use 12-gauge shells as short as 2 inches and with as little as ¹³⁄₁₆ ounce of shot.

A generation ago the classic upland gun was generally made with 28-inch barrels, but today most upland doubles being built by Europe's fine gun makers have 26- or 27-inch barrels. The British firm of Churchill has long made a specialty of light 12-gauge guns with 25-inch barrels. Particularly lovely upland guns for those who can afford them are the slim shallow-frame over-and-unders which have locks on the sides of the barrels instead of under bolts. Examples are the British Holland & Holland (under-and-over), the Boss, and the Woodward, which is built by Purdey. Fine over-and-unders of this shallow-frame type are the high-grade Italian Berettas and Spanish AyA's. The handsome over-and-under Berettas are made in both sidelock and boxlock style and in 20 and 12 gauge. The Beretta Models S O 3 EL and the S O 3 EE LL are about as handsome and finely made shotguns as you can get anywhere. In 20 gauge and with 26-inch barrels these shallow-frame guns weigh right around 6 pounds and if there are faster-handling guns made anywhere I have not run across them.

The Browning Citori Superlight 20 gauge with 26-inch barrels is another fast-handling 6-pounder. The Superlight 12 weighs 6 pounds 9 ounces with 26-inch barrels, the weight of an Italian Franchi 12-gauge over-and-under I have. My 28-gauge Arizaga double weighs 6 pounds, my 20 gauge of the same make 6½, my Winchester Model 21 20 gauge, 7 pounds. I wouldn't have an upland gun that weighed over 7 pounds and I'd rather have one that went 6.

There are many American-made pump and automatic shotguns that do nicely for the uplands, weigh about the same as the flossiest European double, and cost a fraction as much. The 12-gauge Winchester Model 1500XTR with 28-inch barrel is a fast-handling gun and because of its non-recoiling barrel doesn't kick much. The Remington Model 1100, and the 878 pump, the Ithaca Model 37 pump, the Browning and Smith & Wesson pumps and autos in 20 gauge do very well in the uplands. Most of them would be improved in balance and handling qualities if they had 23- or 24-inch barrels. I know of many gunners who have attached variable choke devices to give such an over-all length and they would not go back to longer barrels.

The American factory pump or automatic is stocked with a drop at the comb of 1½-1⅝ inches and drop at the heel of 2½. The length of pull (center of trigger to center of butt-plate) is 14 inches. These dimensions fit the average man quite well, but for upland use I prefer a stock a little straighter. A full, well-rounded comb with a drop of 1½ inches gets me very nicely. I like a drop at heel of 2-2½ inches and a length of pull of 14½ inches. Men with thinner faces can take a drop at comb of 1⅜ or even 1¼. Those over 6 feet, 1 inch can take longer stocks up to 14¾ inches.

The upland gun should center its patterns about 1 foot high at 40 yards and a straight stock with a high comb is what puts them there. Then the upland gunner who mounts his gun and shoots fast can hold right on a rising pheasant or quail and nail it.

For bobwhite quail, ruffed grouse, and woodcock the best boring for a double is improved cylinder or Skeet No. 1 and modified or Skeet No. 2. For quail and woodcock the best shot are No. 8 and No. 7½, for ruffed grouse, No. 7½ or No. 6.

Full choke guns are generally recommended for shooting pheasants in the Dakota and Nebraska cornfields. I used to shoot most of my pheasants in wheat stubble, along brushy creek bottoms, and on grassy sidehills. In a 12 gauge I always liked a modified boring if the gun was a pump or auto, but quarter choke (50 percent) and modified (60 percent) if a double. Long experience taught me that I could kill a pheasant to 40 yards with a 50 percent 12, but that he was hard to kill clean at 45 yards with anything. The man who has a good pointing dog and will pass up the longer shots can kill plenty of pheasants with an improved cylinder 20. The poorer pheasant shot will wound fewer birds with an improved cylinder or skeet bored 12 because he will hit them nearer to the center of his wide even pattern and with more shot. With a full choke he is apt to catch his birds on the thin edge of his pattern. The pheasant is a tough bird and needs to be hit hard. For that reason I generally used 20-gauge doubles bored modified and full.

Hungarian partridges, chukars, and such Western quail as the California valley, the scaled, and the Gambel are tougher birds than bobwhite and tend to rise wilder. For these a modified 20 is about right, but the very fast shot or the man with enough moral fiber to pass up anything beyond 25 or 30 yards can do very well with an improved cylinder 16 or 20 gauge.

However, the quail of the West are more often than not found in overgrazed cattle country where there is little cover. They seldom lie well for dog or hunter and when they are knocked down they will hide in a pack rat's nest or run down a burrow as long as they have strength to move. For that reason they should be hit with more shot than the bobwhite.

The chukar partridge likes rocky hills and canyons, seldom lies well for a dog, and flushes wild. Neither species should be shot with anything with less authority than a 50 percent 12 gauge or a modified 20.

Shooting ruffed, blue grouse, and woodcock generally requires very fast shooting with light, open-bored guns at short ranges. The pump or automatic can be one of the light 12's, a 16, or a 20 and used with one of the variable choke devices wide open or with a skeet choke. For this fast, short-range shooting the gunner needs all the pattern he can get.

19

Wildfowl Shooting

MOST OF US THINK of a duck or goose gun as being heavy, long of barrel, tightly choked, and using the heaviest possible loads. Such guns are used for waterfowl, but they are indicated for only a small proportion of waterfowl shooting. These big berthas are actually specialized guns for pass shooting, where ducks and geese are taken at from 50 to 65 yards or so. Some ducks and geese are shot on passes, but far more ducks are shot at under 40 yards than over—and for 30–40-yard shooting no one needs a 30- or 32-inch barrel and a 3-inch 12-gauge shell throwing 1⅞ ounces of shot.

A great deal of duck shooting and most duck killing (if we count the birds in the bag instead of the birds merely shot at) is actually shot at upland game ranges and can be taken quite well with upland guns. For such shooting the long-barreled, heavy "duck" gun is actually a handicap.

We almost always overestimate the range if a bird is above us against the sky, just as we generally overestimate the range of anything above us or below us. The steel worker high on a girder of a new building looks far, far away, whereas he is within easy rifle shot or perhaps even within the range of a shotgun. If we look down on people below us from the window of a tall building they seem very small and very far away.

Once I was killing ducks regularly with a 20-gauge shotgun and 1 ounce of shot as they flew over a certain lone pine tree enroute from one lake to another. I got the reputation of being a wicked shot who owned the "hardest shooting" 20-gauge shotgun in the area. Then an engineer figured out by triangulation at about how far I was killing the ducks. They were from 30 to 35 yards away, and killing them at that range was certainly no great feat—either for the gun or for me.

Another time a companion and I were in a blind waiting for some ducks to come into our decoys. In another blind on a point about 100 yards from us was a lone hunter. Every time a duck came over this chap enroute to our decoys, this character would down it. My companion was furious. "That guy is using a 10 gauge," he said. At that time the 10 was illegal, so my friend was

169

hopping mad. "He's killing those ducks 75 yards up!" I insisted that I knew the hunter and his gun. He was using a Winchester Model 21 skeet gun in 12-gauge bored Skeet No. 1 and Skeet No. 2. We later found out that he was knocking his ducks down with trap loads of 1⅛ ounces of No. 7½ shot and he was killing them at 75 feet, not yards.

At Nilo, an experimental game management farm, near Alton, Illinois, mallard ducks are raised and fed on a pond. Then when someone wants some shooting they are taken to a tower about half a mile from the lake and released. The ducks then fly back to the lake. Some of the blinds are in deep little ravines and the ducks flash overhead, the most distant not over 25 yards away. The gunners must shoot fast or not at all. The first time I shot there I used a full choke automatic with a 30-inch barrel. Trying to swing the long barrel and get the small pattern on those speedy ducks was pretty tough. My ratio of ducks to shells expended was certainly not distinguished.

The next year I spied in the gun room at the club house a Winchester Model 21 skeet gun. John Amber, then editor of the *Gun Digest,* was my companion in the blind. With the shorter barrel, the more open borings, and the larger patterns I did quite well and picked up at least one duck for every two shells expended.

Ducks that come into decoys are commonly shot at 30 yards or less, and almost any upland gun from 20 to 12 bored improved cylinder or modified is much better than a full choke. One decoy shooter I know says the deadliest combination he knows of is a skeet-bored gun used with 1½ ounces of shot—the 2¾-inch 12-gauge magnum load.

In my home area of Idaho there is often good jump shooting along small streams. To do this type of hunting one simply pussyfoots along the stream bank. Now and then a few mallards will come hurtling up over the tops of willows. They are usually killed at from 25 to 30 yards and I've generally hunted them with a 20-gauge double bored modified and full. Most of the time I've used the 3-inch magnum shells in the 20 gauge and for all practical purposes these make a 12 gauge out of it.

Mallards are fairly large birds (very large as compared to doves and quail) and many gunners simply cannot wait to let them come all the way into a blind. Instead they blast away at them at too great a distance and miss. Unskillful and excitable hunters not only ruin their own hunting by shooting at waterfowl out of range but they also ruin everyone else's. I have been on marshes when the ducks were flying, but few were bagged because hunters would not let them get within gunshot. Instead they would blast away at ducks a good 200 yards away.

Geese are very large birds and they fool the excitable beginner even worse than ducks do. I believe I have seen hunters shoot at geese that were at least 300 yards away—even when the geese were headed toward their blinds.

The larger the bird, the closer it looks. A Canada goose at 50 yards looks so close that the inexperienced gunner thinks he is almost close enough so that he can grab him and wring his neck. A mallard the same distance from the gun seems much farther away, and a green-wing teal farther yet. A quail at 50 yards seems almost microscopic, and gunners who would blast off at a goose at 100 won't shoot at a quail at 50.

How can the gunner tell if a bird is within range? There is no genuinely easy and exact way. Many, many years ago I found out that if I *hoped* a deer or an antelope had an exceptional head and thought it *might* it never did. If I *knew* the head was a good one it always was. And so it is with ducks. When I hope they are in range, they never are. When I *know* they are in range they are.

The bird that is in range generally looks large and the markings can be seen. I can see the markings on a mallard drake plainly at 40–45 yards—and I am about a 40–45 yard mallard shooter. If a duck is so far away no distinguishing markings can be seen he is too far away to shoot at. However, on foggy, heavily overcast days it is often difficult to distinguish markings and birds seem farther away, just as a gray day makes big game seem farther away.

How far to lead a duck? That is a problem to make a computer blow a fuse. Let us look at the factors that have to be considered: the distance from gun to duck, the angle at which the duck is traveling, the mean velocity of the shot charge, the speed of the gunner's swing, the gunner's reaction time (how long it takes from the time the gunner's brain tells him he should pull the trigger until he actually does), and the mechanical lag (the time interval that is occupied by the falling of the firing pin, the igniting of powder charge by the primer, and the passage of the shot charge up the barrel). Feed all of this into a computer and you'll get the correct answer. But in the meantime the duck is several miles away.

The "theoretical" lead one sometimes reads about might better be called "actual" lead, as the actual lead is the distance the gun must be pointed in front of a bird at a certain distance and traveling at a certain speed in order to hit it. The actual lead simply has to be there. It is a matter of mathematics. A mallard, for example, travels along at about 70 feet per second and if he is to be hit at 40 yards the muzzle has to be pointing between 8 and 9 feet in front of him if his flight and that of the shot charge are going to connect. But at 40 yards few gunners should lead a mallard that far. Their "practical" lead, then, would be less than the actual lead. The reason for this is that the gun is swinging while the impulse to slap the trigger is traveling from the gunner's brain to his finger, the finger is pulling the trigger, the firing pin is falling, the primer fires the powder up, the gas expands to push the shot out of the barrel, and the shot wings its way to its rendezvous with the mallard. If the gunner, who in a way is a sort of a flesh-and-blood computer, has operated properly, down comes the duck. He probably thinks he had lead the duck 4 or 5 feet. A canvasback has a faster cruising speed than a mallard. The actual lead on a can at 40 yards should be about 12 feet, but the apparent lead is generally about 6 feet. Teal fly about like a canvasback and require about the same lead, but because they are smaller they appear to be flying faster. The cruising speed of a Canada goose is actually about that of the teal and the goose requires the same lead, but the goose with his large size and slow wing beat appears to be loafing along, whereas the little teal with his twinkling wings appears to be traveling like the famous bat out of hell. The tendency is to overlead a teal and underlead a goose.

There are two methods of leading crossing ducks. One is called the fast swing. The gunner starts with the muzzle of his gun behind the bird, swings much faster than the bird is moving (three times faster, let us say) and fires when the muzzle appears to be the proper distance ahead. For many reasons no two men will say they are exactly the same distance ahead when the gun goes off. I have known men who say they shoot right at ducks crossing at 40 yards and I have known men who say they lead a duck at 40 yards 10 feet. They both hit ducks. Who is right? Both are.

There are many reasons for this difference in testimonial evidence. One is the difference in individual reaction time. It is entirely possible for a very fast swinger with a slow reaction time to be able to hit a duck he does not consciously lead at 40 yards. However, do not forget that the actual lead has to be there or the duck and the shot charge do not connect. Remember also that the fast swinger (the man who starts behind his bird, swings apparently faster than the bird, gets ahead and slaps the trigger) requires less lead than the man who uses the sustained lead. Those who use this last method decide, let us say, that they want to lead this particular duck 10 feet. So they swing along with their ducks with the muzzle at what looks like 10 feet ahead. A mallard is about a foot long, so the sustained leader or pointer-outer should try to keep his muzzle 10 lengths ahead of his bird and traveling as fast as the bird. With either method any slowing or stopping of the swing will cause a miss.

What is the best method? I would say that most absolutely top shots are fast swingers. These are men with keen vision, quick-focusing eyes, and fast reflexes. They swing fast and shoot fast and the faster a man swings and shoots, the less apt he is to slow or stop his swing. However, all of us have our natural timing. Some of us have quick muscles and eyes, just as some of us have quick and analytical brains. Some of us are not so quick and not so smart and some who are very smart are also very slow. Likewise some who are very quick are not very smart. The man who tries to shoot faster than his natural timing will come to grief. Generally (and roughly) the pointer-outer will need from half again to twice as much lead as the fast swinger and often the actual textbook-computer lead and the practical lead of the pointer-outer won't be so different.

Another reason that people do not agree on how much they lead is that what looks like 10 feet to one man may look like 5 feet to another and 2 feet to a third. Often in the same skeet squad the estimates of good shots as to how far they lead, let us say, the right-angling No. 5 high house target will vary from 6 inches to 6 feet. Every gunner must learn his own lead and if he hits it is right for him. But no matter how anyone shoots he MUST get ahead of his target and he MUST keep his gun swinging even after the gun goes off. Follow through is as important in wing shooting as it is in golf and tennis.

For shooting waterfowl over decoys and for jump shooting along a stream an upland gun does very well. But guns for pass shooting are something else again—and so are loads. By "pass shooting" we mean knocking off waterfowl that are not coming into decoys, not bouncing out of a stream, but waterfowl that are going from somewhere to somewhere else. Now and then traveling ducks and geese are shot at short range. Once some years ago I was out early one morning on a drizzly, overcast day. Flock after flock of mallard were taking off from a stretch of river that was in a game preserve and flying off to the wheat fields where they got their breakfasts. They were barely clearing a high bluff and staying just below the clouds. I could almost spit in their eyes as they came over and I got my limit very easily.

But mostly waterfowl on passes are shot at from 50 to 65 yards. Occasionally one is scratched down at 75 or even farther. For these long shots the open bored gun is worthless. The pass shooter wants all the choke and all the shot he can handle. The limitations of most of us being what they are, I doubt if many of us are undergunned with a full choke 12 or a full choke 20-gauge Magnum and 1¼ ounces of shot. If we lead our birds right with that combination we should be able to hit a mallard with from 4 to 6 No. 4 shot to kill him regularly at 50 yards and sometimes at 55. For many years the standard "heavy duck load" or "high velocity" load used by wildfowlers in full choke 12-gauge guns was 1¼ ounces of No. 4's, No. 5's, or sometimes No. 6's in front of 3¾ drams of progressive burning powder. Winchester's Super X was a pioneer shotshell of this type—and so was Remington Nitro Express. Both shells are still loaded.

Along in the 1920's a few bold souls had long-chambered, overbored, long-barreled, and heavy, "long-range" 12-gauge Magnum double guns built. These were turned out by the Hunter Arms Company of Fulton, N.Y. in L. C. Smith brand, by the A. H. Fox Company of Philadelphia, by Parker, and by Ithaca. These were called long-range wildfowl guns, and then the British term "magnum" was tacked on to them. At first the maximum load for these special 3-inch shells was only 1⅜ ounces of shot. Great tales were told of this. Then along in the 1930's, the load was stepped up to 1⅝ ounces of BB, No. 2, 4, 5, or No. 6 shot.

At one time the 10 gauge had been the standard waterfowl gauge, but interest in the 10 had died down—and no wonder since the standard 10-gauge load was 4¼ drams of powder and only 1¼ ounces of shot, the same amount of shot as in the standard 12-gauge duck load. But the loading companies came out with 1⅝ ounces of shot in the 2⅞-inch 10-gauge case. This made the 10-bore lovers smell blood. Then Western Cartrdige Company and the Ithaca Gun Company cooperated to bring out a 3½-inch magnum shell throwing 2 ounces of shot (the load of the old 8 gauge which was prohibited by federal law) and a big, heavy double to shoot it. Ithaca made just 1,000 of these big 10-gauge guns, I have been told. They are collector's items today. Parker also made some 10-gauge magnums, but how many I cannot say. I doubt if 100 were built.

These big 10's gave rise to a sort of a cult. One citizen I knew even hunted pheasants with one of these monsters. I cannot imagine a worse pheasant gun. I once borrowed one from Ithaca, but since its use was then illegal in Arizona on wildfowl, the only thing I ever shot with it was jackrabbits. The big gun weighed about 11 pounds, had 32-inch barrels, and was about as handy to swing as a vaulting pole.

Today, Ithaca manufactures the Mag-10, the only 10-gauge autoloader in existence. Because its gas-operated action buffers recoil, this is a pleasant gun to shoot. It's popular with pass-shooting waterfowlers—especially goose hunters—and with turkey hunters.

Some magnum 10's have been made in Europe and imported into this country but I do not think they have taken the market by storm. Actually there isn't anything much they can do that the 12-gauge Magnum with (ugh!) 1⅞ ounces of shot cannot do.

In these days of heavy hunting and diminishing wildfowl water many gunners get only rather long shots at ducks. They install themselves in a blind near the boundary of a game sanctuary, let us say, and then at their scheduled time the ducks start coming out. Ducks are not stupid. They know where the borders of the sanctuary are and they also know that when they reach them they are going to be shot at. They likewise have a pretty good notion as to the range of a shotgun. When they come over they are just out of range—tantalizingly so.

Down below our gunners keep banging away. Mostly they don't even get a feather, but now and then a gut-shot bird slants off and lands heavily a half-mile away. Occasionally a bird tumbles from a lucky hit with a large shot in the head or neck.

Our gunner thinks he could reach those birds if he just had a little more powerful gun—a 12 gauge with 32-inch barrel shooting the 2¾-inch Magnum shell with 1½ ounces of lead or 1¼ ounces of steel shot, a 12-gauge for the 3-inch Magnum with 1⅞ ounces of lead shot or 1⅜ ounces of steel, or a 10-gauge Magnum handling the 3½-inch shell with 2 ounces of lead or 1⅝ ounces of steel shot. But alas, the limitations not only lie with the gun but also with the gunner.

Once some other citizens and I were hiding in a corn field and trying to bushwhack mallards that were flying over us out of a reserve. We were mostly using automatic shotguns with the lead 1½-ounce 2¾-inch magnum load. The results were about as I have described. Then for some reason known only to the ducks the flocks started crossing lower. The mallards started falling like hail. Not only were the birds within range of our guns but they were within the limits of our skill.

What kills ducks is pattern density, so long as the shot are heavy enough and traveling fast enough to give sufficient penetration to get into the vitals. If a mallard is hit by four No. 4 shot he will come down, no matter whether the shot were fired from a 20-gauge or a Magnum 12. The distance that a combination of gun and load will always put that many shot into a mallard is the range at which it is effective. A lucky hit may kill farther but it cannot be counted on.

The shot generally chosen for shooting over decoys is No. 6, although some swear by No. 7½. Either of these shot sizes will take teal. No. 4 is generally considered the medicine for large ducks like mallards and canvasbacks, particularly on a pass. For decoyed ducks anything from 20 gauge with as little as 1 ounce of shot up to a 12 will do. For pass shooting, the gunner should go to a 12 with from 1¼ to 1½ ounces of No. 4 shot. The pumps and automatics have pretty well put doubles out of business as wildfowl guns. Gas-operated automatics have noticeably less recoil than pumps. The gun for pass shooting should have a 28- or 30-inch barrel and many like a ventilated rib.

Most goose hunters use No. 2 lead or No. 1 or BB steel shot, but there is a school of gunners who claim that because you'll get a greater number of hits with No. 4 lead shot or No. 2 steel pellets you'll get a higher percentage of kills. There is yet another school of goose hunters, who use small shot, who never shoot unless the goose is within 40 yards, and who ty to hit the birds in the head and neck. Something I have learned in pass shooting at geese is that the best way to bring one down no matter what you use is to pick one bird out of a flock and keep pouring it to him until he falls. A goose is a pretty tough old bird in more ways than one.

The shotgun is still a short-range weapon, but over the years the range of the standard 12 gauge has been extended little by little. Choke boring back in the 1870's helped. So did progressive burning powders, plated shot, the use of heavier charges of shot, gas seal wads, and now plastic shot protectors. But even today with all these wonders the man who kills a duck cleanly at 60 yards is getting all he can expect out of his gun and his load. And if he's using steel shot, 50 yards is definitely stretching things.

Wing-Shooting

ONE OF THE FIRST THINGS anyone trying to learn to handle a scattergun discovers is that for the majority of shots he has to shoot in a direction away from his game. He points "where they ain't." At first his reward is a monotonous series of misses. Then one day a bird actually runs into a shot charge, more by accident than by good management, and our hero is launched into his career as a wing-shot. Hitting leads to more hitting, and as time passes, the gunner gets so he can hit flying game with some degree of regularity. He has begun to master this thing called lead.

It is depressing to record that no mortal man has completely mastered lead. There are too many variables connected with wing-shooting—far more than with most rifle shooting. The simplest form of rifle shooting is at a stationary mark, with a rifle as dead still as one can manage to hold it, and at a known distance. Granted that this form of shooting, which is seen at its highest development in prone .22 small-bore shooting, is still but the A B C of rifle work; nevertheless under certain conditions it will still kill a lot of game—antelope, sheep, woodchucks, any animal standing still for a certain length of time. The problem of the man behind the rifle is to squeeze off his shot with the sights aligned. If he does that, and the game is not too far away, he'll have meat in the pot.

But wing-shooting is something else. It compares with target shooting with a rifle as tennis compares with golf. The tennis player deals with a moving ball, which he hits with a moving racket, while he himself is often moving. His object is to put the ball where a moving opponent will *not* be when the ball gets there. He deals with a whole set of variables, just as the wing-shot does. The golfer, on the other hand, deals with a *stationary* ball which he tries to put on a stationary target—the green or a certain place in the fairway. His problem is similar to that of the target shot with the rifle.

The wing-shot, however, shoots with a moving gun at a moving target at an unknown distance and traveling at an unknown angle. Tennis and wing-shooting, then, are essentially alike. So, by the way, are wing-shooting and the shooting of running game with a rifle—which is why the often-repeated statement that a good rifle shot and a good shotgun shot are never found confined within the same carcass gives me a pain. Actually every shot the scatter-gunner makes is duplicated by the rifleman who takes his game on the run. The technique in both cases is much the same.

True, many riflemen who are good target shots and who do rather well on big game can't hit their hat with a shotgun, but those same riflemen would be found to be helpless on running game. Now and then one comes upon a good running-game shot who isn't so hot with the shotgun, but in every instance the explanation is that this particular rifleman isn't *interested* in the scattergun.

We have said that our wing-shot shoots with a moving gun at a moving object at unknown and variable angles. His job is further complicated by the fact that the shot pellets his gun throws lose velocity at a very rapid rate. A lead that will knock a duck cold at 40 yards will miss him clean as a whistle at 50 yards, because the pellets are losing their velocity so rapidly. Complicate this problem, too, by the well-known habit of birds to vary their speed as well as their angle. One dove may float in at 25 miles an hour, the next may be hitting 50, and the lead that centered the slow bird will miss the fast one by feet.

Wing-shooting sounds like a complicated problem by now. You haven't heard half of it! The beginner at wing-shooting, unless he has done some reading beforehand, always attempts to shoot ahead of the bird with a more or less stationary gun. This system is called snapshooting. Most gunners use it on upland game where many of the birds are flushed by dog or hunter and are angling gently away. Using this system, a few hunters get to be fairly good on crossing birds; but it is exceedingly difficult to learn and very, very unreliable. The gunner must decide instantly where to put the charge so the bird will run into it, flash his gun to his shoulder, and fire. Now, a good all-round shot should be able to snap at crossing birds in an emergency, when even a fast swing might be too slow; but for a *system* snap-shooting isn't so hot.

Instead, it was long ago discovered that a moving bird should be shot with a moving gun; that the gunner *has to swing.* Now let us see what swinging does:

1. It more or less automatically corrects for variations in the speed of the birds, because the faster the bird flies, the faster the muzzle of the gun must move to catch up and pass it.

2. It minimizes the effects of the interval from the time when the brain of the hunter says to press the trigger until the shot charge leaves the muzzle. That interval is longer than most of us realize, by the way. The firing pin must fall, the primer must ignite, the powder charge must burn, and the shot must get going. But first of all, the message must travel from brain to finger—and that, my friends, is by no means instantaneous. If the muzzle of the gun is swinging when all this is going on, the time lag doesn't matter much; but it would if the muzzle were stationary, for then a mathematically correct lead would throw the charge feet behind.

3. Another thing which the moving muzzle does is to add the speed of the

swing to the velocity of the shot charge. Suppose the muzzle is swinging at the rate of somewhere between 10 and 25 feet a second when it is fired. Then the shot charge is not only traveling forward at an average velocity of about 900 foot-seconds over 40 yards, but at the same time it is traveling *sidewise* at the rate of drift given to it by the swinging muzzle. This factor, though seldom mentioned in connection with wing-shooting, further serves to cut down lead.

A bullet dropped from an automobile speeding at 60 miles at hour will not drop straight to the ground. Instead, traveling forward at an initial velocity of 60 miles an hour, it will curve forward and down with the same trajectory as if it were fired from a gun at that speed. In an airplane traveling at, say, 300 miles an hour, the effect is proportionately greater. World War II side gunners, handling their twin .50's on B-24 and B-17 bombers, learned that to down Zeros and Messerschmitts coming straight toward them for a run, they had to shoot *behind* because of the drift imparted to the bullets by the speed of the plane from which they were fired.

So all these factors add up to the fact that wing-shooting is a complicated and variable art, and that it is up to the hunter to overcome these variables or make use of them by the way he swings the gun.

How to go about it? Well, there are two schools—those who believe in the "sustained lead" and those who believe in the "fast swing." Let us see how they work.

Here comes a duck, let us say. The believer in sustained lead says to himself, "Here comes a bluebill. He'll cross at about a right angle to the gun and at around 45 yards. A 10-foot lead will get him." He points the muzzle at what looks like a distance of 10 feet ahead of the duck, then keeps the muzzle that far ahead of the duck by swinging with it—and presses the trigger, with the muzzle still moving. If all goes well, down comes the duck.

That system is used by thousands. It has killed hundreds of thousands of birds. Some gunners even use it at fast-moving skeet targets.

Let us compare it with the fast swing. Here comes the same duck, let us say. The gunner flashes his shotgun to his shoulder, starts with the muzzle *behind* the bird, swings on the line of the bird's flight, passes it with muzzle swinging much faster than the bird—and pulls the trigger when he thinks the muzzle is the right distance ahead, which in this case would be 5 or 6 feet. Here too the muzzle must be kept swinging after the trigger has been pressed. If everything has worked, down will come the bird.

Now, what are the advantages of the two systems? The sustained lead is a bit more exact and it will probably kill more birds when the gunner has plenty of time, as in the pass-shooting of waterfowl and the flight-shooting of doves. The cool, cold-eyed pass-shooting expert with his magnum 12 or 10 gauge nearly always uses it. However, it is slow.

The fast swing, though less exact, is much faster and much more adaptable to various conditions. The fast swinger will kill a duck while the sustained leader is still thinking about it, and in certain circumstances the fast swinger will get game where the sustained leader will go home empty-handed.

When I lived in Tucson I was not far from a famous mourning-dove and whitewing haunt. The birds flew over a river forest of cottonwoods and mesquites low and fast, then rose, to fly across an open flat. Most of the gunners preferred to shoot from the flat, where they could take their time about shooting because the birds were in sight for some time. Competition was pretty keen there and often three or four men would shoot at the same bird. Back in the forest, however, it was another story. The birds came low over the tree tops and were in sight for only 20 or 30 feet. To get them, one had to swing fast. To me that was ten times as much fun as the more deliberate open shooting on the flat, and even on crowded days I could go up into the trees and get first crack at the birds with plenty of snappy shooting.

An extremely important aspect of any kind of swing, and one not very often mentioned, is that swinging along the line of flight establishes the angle of flight. At least half the time the bird is not flying exactly parallel to the ground. He may be rising a little or dropping a little. Unless this angle is allowed for, even though the lead is correct, the shot will be a miss, with the charge going over or under the bird. The swing that starts behind the bird, picks it up, and passes it, automatically detects this variation from the horizontal and allows for it.

I often get letters asking me to tell how far a crossing duck, say, must be led at a certain distance. I can't answer that. Neither can anyone else. It depends on too many factors—the gunner, the load, his speed and style of swing, the species of duck, the duck's state of mind, the velocity and direction of the wind, etc.

Even the most skillful and hardened gunner will occasionally run into a sour stretch when every bird he takes a pop at sails merrily on, and he begins to suspect that some clown has hijacked his few treasured shells and has substituted blanks.

What's the answer to that one?

Our hero may be failing to cheek his comb and is shooting *over* his birds. That is a common failing, even with the best shots, and is usually brought on by a little excitement—those Opening-day Jitters. Again, our gunner—wanting to be extra sure, extra precise—may slow down or stop the rapidly moving muzzle of his gun . . . and he MISSES!

I remember one time when the dove season opened right after a stretch when I had been hitting the typewriter pretty hard. I was tired and tense. There was nothing difficult about the shooting, but I missed six birds and barely scratched another. My companion began to twit me. The combination of his twitting and my own lousy shooting finally made me so angry that all I could think of was killing the birds as fast as they came speeding in over the mesquites. Whereas before I had tried to be extra careful, and as a consequence was unconsciously stopping my swing, I simply forgot all about seeing that the lead was *exactly* right. I quit stopping my swing. I swung fast and shot fast—and killed twelve birds with fifteen shots, including three sets of doubles.

Correct lead is a long way from easy; and though it may seem strange, often the way to lead correctly is to do as I did that day—forget about it! As long as I worried about it, I slowed that gun up. When all I could think about was wrapping that Ithaca around my pal's neck, I hit them!

HITTING STRAIGHTAWAYS

The straightaway *appears* to be the easiest shot in the book. Actually it is one of the most deceiving and most difficult, and it is probably responsible for at least 50 percent of the shells that are annually wasted in the open air. The sharply angled crossing shot looks difficult and *is* difficult. Knowing this, the gunner is far less likely to miss it than he is the easy-looking bird which gets up so close to him that he could hit it with his hat and which drives away at a gentle angle.

Let us take a look at the reasons for this curious phenomenon. (And before we go farther, let it be said for the record that I can set myself up as an authority on the missing of straightaway shots, because I have missed them for every reason known to man.)

The cause of about 50 percent of the misses is the almost universal habit of failing to get the cheek down on the comb of the stock. Excited by the sudden rise of the bird, the gunner holds the cheek away from and above the comb, and the pattern goes high and to the left. Watch any upland gunner who misses consistently, and nearly always you will see that he isn't "cheeking" his gun.

This fortunately is something that can be corrected by practice. The best remedy that I know about is a lot of "dry practice," something which can be done satisfactorily in the sanctity of one's own home. Stand gun in hand, and fix your eye on some object in the room. Then throw the gun to your shoulder. Train yourself to bring it up so your cheek is firm against the comb and your eye looks right down the barrel at the object you want to "hit." If you cannot do that, then your gunstock doesn't fit. It is surprising how much good this routine will do. It should be kept up until correct mounting of the gun becomes second nature, then you can concentrate on other aspects of shooting. Five minutes a day of this dry practice for thirty days will pay off handsomely in the field.

One reason why good rifle and handgun shots are far more common than good performers with the scattergun is that few people have any illusions that skill with either of the rifled weapons can be acquired without plenty of practice. The average field shot, though, never touches his gun from one season to the next. Then he wonders why he is sour.

In many cases psychological factors are responsible, in part at least, for failure to check the gun properly. Some of us are jittery and jumpy by nature, and when a quail or a grouse goes up unexpectedly we leap a foot into the air and every muscle in our body twitches. Cure for that? Nothing but experience in the field, plus the self-confidence which comes from knowing we are going to knock the next flushed bird as stiff as a poker.

All this is more or less elementary; also, it assumes that the field shot's gunstock fits him so that correct and speedy gun mounting *can* become automatic and mechanical.

Let us get down now to the more esoteric reasons for missing the straightaway, that most deceptive of all field shots. Why is it that the man who correctly cheeks his gun, who automatically looks right down the barrels, can still register a goose egg on the bird which appears to be driving directly away and which looks as though it could be hit with a rifle?

One reason is that the "straightaway" usually is only a word, rather than an actuality. In upland shooting, many a shot looks as if it were a true straightaway—with the bird flying directly away from the gunner on a horizontal path—but almost none of them is. Consequently the hunter shoots right at the bird, and misses. If the angle is gentle and the bore is open, he will kill birds he really should miss; but the usual result is a missed bird, or a cripple hit with from one to three pellets on the edge of the pattern.

The human eye has decided limitations. (At least the pair which God gave me to carry through life has, and it is the only pair I know anything about from first-hand experience.) One limitation is that the eye tends to make an instant and inaccurate diagnosis of a bird's flight as "straightaway" when it is nothing of the sort.

A bird, let us say, gets up 15 feet to the right of the gunner and 25 feet in front. Its line of flight is a 10-degree angle to the left. The eye sees the rear end of the bird, notes the buzzing wings, and flashes the message "straightaway" to the gunner's brain. He holds right on the end of that bird—and the shot charge passes just to the right.

Another bird gets up right at the gunner's feet, rises sharply. Again the eyes say "straightaway." The gunner holds dead on, and by the time the shot charge gets there the bird is above its path. Or suppose the gunner is walking due west. A bird gets up 15 yards to the right and 15 yards in front, flies due west, on a line that parallels the gunner's. Bingo—and another miss!

Possibly one reason why the eyes do such a sour job of diagnosis in upland shooting is that the birds—unlike ducks or a flight of doves—are seldom outlined against the sky. Pheasants, quail, and grouse are usually seen moving swiftly against a background of anything from jack oaks to cornstalks, and their angle of flight is not so readily estimated as in the case of a bird seen against the sky.

Actually, most upland shooting comes within sort of a twilight zone between snapshooting and "swing" shooting. Most gunners hold right on the bird while snapshooting. If the bird is a true straightaway, they hit. Unfortunately, though, true straightaways are rare. If, on the other hand, the bird goes off at a decided angle, the fact that it is doing so becomes apparent and the gunner swings through, gets ahead, and hits.

How then should one learn to hit these difficult straightaways?

Simple, my friend! By aiding the eye with the brain, by using the brain to temper the eye's first message with skepticism. "Forewarned is forearmed," says the old proverb. So it is with upland shooting. If you go out *knowing* that most "straightaway" shots are really angle shots, you will be able to interpret better what those imperfect eyes of yours tell you.

You will miss at least seven out of eight of those easy-looking shots if you hold on the bird, unless you are using a gun throwing a very wide pattern. With an improved cylinder having just enough constriction to round up the pattern a bit, you will kill more birds with a dead-on hold than you will with a 55 to 65 percent pattern, say; but even with the spreader tube on a Cutts Compensator you'll do a lot of missing.

You must allow for the angle of the bird's flight—holding, for example, a bit high and to the right for a bird rising and angling slightly to the right. One reason why shooting in hills is so tough is that it presents to even the most experienced wing-shot a set of angles entirely different from those with which he is familiar. The bird flushing away from the hunter above it is, I think, the hardest one in the whole book to hit.

Watch those gentle angles, then. Diagnose those apparent straightaways. Remember that if the bird's path of flight is anything but a true straightaway at gun level, you'll miss far more than you will hit with a dead-on hold.

TIMING

Wing-shooting has many points in common with the game of baseball. The shortstop who comes in for a hot grounder, picks it up, and makes the throw to first with no waste motion is giving a beautiful example of what is known as "timing." So is the tennis player who connects with a swiftly moving ball and puts it away in the far corner of his opponent's court.

Both are dealing with movement. The shortstop's body is moving, his hands are moving, the ball is moving, and often he must make the throw to the place where the moving baseman is going to be. The tennis player hits a rapidly moving ball with a moving racket, often while he himself is moving, and he tries to put it where he hopes his moving opponent is not going to be. The batter tries to hit with his moving bat a moving ball thrown at various speeds and cunningly manipulated so it will twist, dodge, and duck.

Likewise, our honest shotgunner shoots at moving game (which can also dodge, twist, and duck, and which also comes over at various speeds) with a moving gun. Like the baseball player who throws the ball to the place where the baseman is going to be, the shotgun shooter "throws" the shot charge out of that moving gun of his to the place where he thinks the bird will be.

Often he guesses wrong, and the bird sails on unscathed. Even a simple change of pace will fool the best of us, just as it will in baseball. I have seen league-leading batters, after looking over a couple of fast ones, miss by feet a slow one thrown with the same motion—balls that any school kid should have knocked for a loop. I remember seeing some good shotgun shots, who had been knocking down fast-flying doves with reasonable regularity, completely flub a young whitewing that wobbled over at about 15 miles an hour. The bird got their timing off, and they all overled it.

The ball player that bats .350 is a very hot fellow indeed. He is a skilled athlete, the pick of many thousands. He practices constantly. The keenness of his muscular coordination, the sharpness of his eyesight are things to marvel at, these Reggie Jacksons and Pete Roses.

Yet John B. Smith picks up his gun less than a dozen times a year and wonders why he doesn't make a better average!

Very early in World War II the skeet club where I used to shoot folded up because the boys couldn't get any more shells. For five years I did not shoot a round of skeet—not one. Then some Air Corps officers asked me to come out to their base and shoot a few rounds with them. I had a good gun that fitted me. My form was O.K. I knew how it was done. That first round, though, I just couldn't do it. The birds seemed to go out of the houses at a terrific speed. My gun felt heavy. My muscles were slow to respond, and I felt terribly hurried. The first round I broke, if I remember correctly, sixteen birds.

On the second round, my gun began to feel light. Instead of traveling at impossible speed, the birds seemed much slower. Instead of being rushed, I began to feel I had time to spare. I broke twenty-two birds. Why? My timing had begun to come back.

This business of feeling that there is plenty of time, even when small fractions of a second are involved, is, I believe, a universal experience when anyone is hot, in the groove, on the beam, or whatever expression one wants to employ.

I believe that anyone who does much shooting with shotgun or rifle at flying targets or moving game notices this apparent stretching out of time, this slowing up of moving objects as his timing develops. The big-league shortstop comes in on a darting grounder, gauges it just right, and makes his throw. To the spectator this looks almost incredibly difficult—and I am one to agree that it is tough. To that keenly trained baseball technician, however, who is magnificently equipped with the finest muscles and the finest eyes, that ball appears to be moving much more slowly. When he is *right,* the most difficult grounder appears easy. So much has he stretched out the fractions of a second that he knows he'll make the stop and the throw.

All shotgun men with whom I have talked agree that when they are shooting their best, they have the same experience. The buzzing quail that to the novice looks as if it had been shot from a cannon appears almost to float along to the expert who is right that day. Even the roaring ruffed grouse headed for a hole in the foliage appears so slowed down that bouncing him is easy.

The first time the average shooter tries the No. 8 low-house bird at skeet and sees that clay saucer zipping right at him with an initial speed of around 60 miles an hour, he can hardly get his gun to his shoulder. Then as his timing becomes better, the bird apparently travels much slower, and he finds it relatively easy to break.

The only way anyone can perfect his timing is by practice. All of us would like to become good shots, if it didn't involve too much trouble. Few of us are willing to practice enough. The shotgun man who picks up the old pump about half a dozen times a year simply cannot be a first-rate performer.

I know dozens of shotgun-owning, license-buying sportsmen who would no more think of shooting trap or skeet or practicing on clay pigeons thrown by a handtrap during the off season than they would of beating their wives or forging a check. Without exception, they are bum shotgun shots. They kill some birds and have a lot of fun, but they are poor shots nevertheless.

I know other dozens of rifle-owning deer hunters who never fire a shot from deer season to deer season, yet who are disappointed when they fire a fusillade at a buck bounding up the other side of the canyon and don't connect.

Some highly gifted individuals can get their timing down with relatively little practice, just as some people take easily to music, writing poetry, or walking on their hands. But the average guy has to practice and practice if he is going to shoot well in the field. Practice does wonders, and with enough of it we ordinary citizens can learn to be very creditable shots and get the kinks out of our timing.

Shooting is a curious business. Anyone's timing can go haywire for both physical and emotional reasons. In the fast game of skeet—or fast wing-shooting at game birds—a gun that doesn't fit will throw anyone's timing into a tail spin.

Try a gun with a stock a bit too long or a bit too short. It will not come exactly to the shoulder. The timing will be destroyed, and the difficulty of hitting the clay saucers enormously increased. The wrong pitch of the butt will do the same thing. So will a shooting coat with a slick surface that makes the butt slide at the shoulder when the gun comes up fast—or a coat that is too thick and which apparently increases the length of pull.

Shifting to a gun of different balance and different barrel length will cause the same thing. The man used to handling a heavy 12-gauge pump with a 30-inch barrel will almost always overlead when using a lighter gun with shorter barrel. Likewise the man who shifts to a gun heavier than he is used to and with longer barrels will shoot behind until his timing becomes adjusted.

The mental attitude of the man behind the gun is also enormously important, and for dozens of purely emotional reasons a man's timing can climb to new heights or go into a tail spin. Once I took a double-barreled skeet gun out to shoot Western quail. I knew that I would have to hit the birds within 25 yards with the right barrel if I wanted to kill them cleanly. I tried to shoot faster than I ordinarily did, and the result was that the birds flew merrily away.

What I was doing was destroying my natural timing. I wasn't getting my face down on the comb and my shots were flying high and to the left of the birds. I finally sat down, thought it over, and then went back and did better.

Another time I saw three good skeet shots get into an argument as to who would break the birds fastest. All tried to speed up their natural timing with the result that they put on as ragged an exhibition as could be imagined. It is the same thing as good shots missing running deer because they are afraid the other guy will beat them to the kill.

The "competition jitters" will raise Ned with a man's natural timing in the opposite way, too. He will try to be extra sure of every target, with the result that he will slow and stop his swing and shoot behind. I have seen good shots who simply could not do well in competition because of some mental quirk. One chap I knew years ago was a fine tennis player as long as he was behind, but he simply could not win in tight competition because as soon as match point was in sight he tried to be extra careful. His timing went haywire, and he lost.

Competition jitters are caused by overeagerness, which is also an ailment that often besets the gunner when he first hunts a new species of game. A pal of mine who is a crack quail shot made his first hunt for South Dakota pheasants many years ago. All his life he had wanted to hunt those big gaudy birds, yet on the first day he did miserably. When those great cocks would come threshing out of the cornstalks, cackling and looking as big as pianos, he simply froze to his gun and shot feet behind them. Not until his second day did he start killing them neatly.

The man who goes out into the uplands for a bit of shooting while he is worrying about unfinished business at the office isn't going to do very well, since timing, at least in part, is a product of concentration. On the other hand, emotion may sometimes work just the other way. Some years ago I went out on the first day of dove season very angry about something or other. In that case my anger expressed itself in absolute concentration. I never shot so well before and haven't shot so well since. It was practically impossible for me to miss.

Often I read such sentences as this: "He saw the flash of a grouse through the timber, *instinctively* threw his gun to his shoulder, and fired. An instant later he heard the bird hit the ground."

Such stuff makes young shooters think that shooting is instinctive, that skill and timing are things that some are born with and others are not. It is true that some people are so equipped that they can learn faster than others, but timing comes from practice, *practice*, PRACTICE!

21

Buckshot, Ball, and Slug

THE USE of the shotgun on deer in the United States has increased in recent years. Both whitetail deer and human beings have been enjoying population explosions and often in the same areas. Deer are adaptable creatures. If they have a patch of brush and forest here and there to give them a minimum of privacy and they can find food they will survive. The food may be a farmer's new sprung wheat or leaves from somebody's orchard or flower bed but the whitetail doesn't care.

Because of the presence of deer near human habitation the use of rifles is forbidden in many areas. Instead deer hunters must use shotguns, under the theory that because shotguns do not have as much range as rifles they are less dangerous. The shotguns are used with buckshot or with rifled slugs. Even slugs are forbidden in some places and only buckshot can be used.

Deer have long been taken by shotguns in the South, where there is a great deal of brush and swamp. The deer are generally driven past stands by dogs or human beaters, and the shooting is mostly at short range. I first hunted in the South in 1945. I was a guest on a South Carolina plantation and the people I saw hunting deer used 12- and 16-gauge double-barrel shotguns bored improved cylinder and modified. It was the belief that the open-bored guns patterned buckshot better than full choke barrels. Well-heeled sports down there usually had at least two guns—one a 16 or a 20 for "birds" (quail) and with buckshot for deer, and the other a full choke 12 for ducks and wild turkeys.

If the gun used were a 12 gauge, the loads were 9 No. 00 buckshot or 12 of the smaller No. 0 buck. If the gun was a 16, the load was 12 pellets of No. 1 buck. Many 20-gauge doubles including some very fine ones—Winchester Model 21's, Parkers, Smiths, and even Purdeys—were seen in the hands of the gentry but they were seldom used for deer. If they were the load was 20 pellets of No. 3 buck.

Those buckshot loads were not so hot. Many deer were wounded by them, and if good deer dogs hadn't been along a lot of deer would have been lost. Many buckshot loads are very unreliable with the result that at 50 yards a deer may be hit with one buckshot, with 3 or 4, or maybe with not any. The deer hit with one pellet usually escapes to die—particularly if it has been gut shot.

However, at close range (up to 25 or 30 yards) a shotgun loaded with buckshot is one of the world's deadliest weapons. In Africa professional hunters use buckshot in 12-gauge shotguns when they go after wounded leopards, and some claim that if the hunter does not panic, has a shotgun and buckshot, reserves his fire to the last minute, he can stop the charge of any lion.

Since the end of World War II the quality and deadliness of buckshot loads has improved. All the loading companies now turn out "magnum" buckshot loads in 2¾-inch cases. These are in 12 gauge and are loaded with 12 No. 00 buck instead of 9. A 3-inch Magnum shell is also loaded in 12 and 20 gauge with buckshot—15 pellets of No. 00 buck or 41 pellets of No. 4 in the 12-gauge shell, and 18 pellets of No. 2 buck in the 20. The most potent of all buckshot loads is the 3½-inch 10-gauge Magnum, which throws 18 No. 00 buck pellets or 54 No. 4 buckshot.

In addition Winchester-Western made a real breakthrough in buckshot loads some years ago when the firm introduced Mark 5 buckshot loads. In these the buckshot are nestled in plastic "sawdust" and are protected from distortion against the barrel by a polyethylene collar. Other manufacturers soon followed suit. These loads pattern very well and sometimes they will throw a 100 percent pattern at 40 yards. I have never killed a deer with the loads since I live in rifle country, but those who have report kills to 60 yards regularly.

For the most part, though, buckshot is a pretty sad excuse as deer medicine. If it were used only by gunners who were cool enough never to shoot unless the animal was within certain range, it would be all right. However, these cool and collected customers are among hunters about as rare as 10-footers are among tigers and 40-inchers are among bighorn rams. I have seen hunters banging away with buckshot at deer at 100 yards. Presumably most Hindus will not eat meat, but I have seen few who wouldn't eat anything in the way of game meat you could throw down a hole. The jungles of India are full of meat-hungry town dwellers with cheap Spanish shotguns loaded with buckshot. They blast off at anything they see, and a high proportion of deer one shoots in India have old buckshot wounds. The more sporting Indian types will also bang away at tigers (if they themselves are safely up trees or in automobiles). They often cripple the big cats so that they become man-eaters.

The old-fashioned lead sphere called a "pumpkin ball" is no longer made in the United States, but it is still made abroad. In the days when shotgun barrels were bored straight cylinders throughout their length, these balls gave fair accuracy to maybe 50 yards. When choke boring came in, however, the balls had to be made smaller than the constriction of the smallest full choke. If the balls were bore diameter they would of course damage the choke. The result was that the balls rattled around in the bore and gave very poor accuracy. An all-purpose gun once used by French farmers for an occasional pheasant

and a crop-raiding wild boar now and then had a choked barrel on one side
and a barrel with the last three or four inches rifled on the other. These rifled
muzzles gave the balls a spin and fairly good accuracy. The now obsolete British guns of the "Paradox" type are now no longer made. They were odd
crossbreeds—heavy shotguns with barrels rifled their entire length with shallow segmental rifling. They had rifle sights and gave pretty good accuracy
with pumpkin balls or with special cartridges with special bullets. I understand these barrels had a slight choke and gave improved cylinder patterns
with shot shells.

The rifled slug is much more sporting to use on deer since it is more accurate than buckshot and kills well if the hit is in the heart-lung area. The most
commonly seen type of slug was invented by Karl Foster along in the 1930's.
These slugs are manufactured and loaded by all American loading companies. Whether Foster patented the slugs and received royalties or not I cannot say. The Foster-type slug is also loaded in Canada, England, and Czechoslovakia, and Lyman Gun Sight Company furnishes a slug mold for those who
want to make up their own.

The Foster slug is a short, round-nosed hollow shell of pure soft lead with
"rifling grooves" swedged into it. I have read here and there that the rifling
causes the slugs to rotate slowly when they are fired, but one of the Winchester

Winchester shotshell with rifled slug

Winchester 12-gauge No. 00 super buck load.

ballisticians told me that the only function the "rifling" performed was to reduce slightly the bearing surface and to give the slugs a modicum of sales appeal. The slugs fly with reasonable accuracy because they are heavier at the
front end. In writing up the slugs many years ago I said at the time that they
flew point on like a sock with sand in the toe. Various writers have copied the
description. Whether they rotate slowly or not is beside the point.

The important thing is that the slugs produce surprisingly good accuracy
and if a gun firing them has adequate sights the slugs shoot well enough so
that they are practical on deer within the limits of their rather round-house
trajectory. The slugs shoot best in barrels with little or no choke, poorest in
full choke guns as these give maximum deformation. The most accurate gun I
have ever used with slugs was a Remington skeet bored automatic with ventilated rib and two beads, a large front bead and a small bead midway on the
rib. That darned gun shot like a rifle. Aiming by putting the top of the front
bead on what I wanted to hit and the middle bead behind the front bead, I
could from the sitting position keep all of my shots in a 100-yard small-bore
target at 100 yards with at least half of them in the 6-inch black. That combination would certainly knock off any deer at 100 yards.

Starting along about 1960 various companies began bringing out shotguns
designed especially for use on deer with rifled slugs. I believe Ithaca was the
first but now all the major manufacturers have got into the act. These "slug
specials" have short cylinder-bored barrels and are fitted with a front sight
and an open rear sight. I have tried out several and all of them will stay on a
100-yard small bore target at 100 yards when I shoot from the sitting position.
Shot from a benchrest, some will group into 2 or 3 inches at 50 yards.

Inexpensive adjustable peep sights can be fitted to pump and automatic
shotguns, so the guns can be precisely sighted in for slugs. It is not often that
one runs across a field or skeet gun that will handle slugs as flawlessly as the
Remington skeet gun I wrote about above. Another excellent idea for the man
who has to hunt deer with slugs is to fit a scope—either a 1X Weaver K1 or
one of the 2½X big-game scopes. The inexpensive Weaver side and top
mounts do very well. Double guns are generally not satisfactory with slugs as
the barrels more often than not crossfire—shoot the slug from the right barrel
to the left and from the left barrel to the right.

Here is a list of companies that turn out shotguns especially designed to
handle slugs with barrels of various lengths from 18 to 26 inches: Remington,
Ithaca, Marlin, Browning, Mossberg, Winchester and Smith & Wesson.

As manufactured in the United States the Foster-type rifled slugs perform
as follows:

For the record, No. 00 buck are .33-inch in diameter and run 130 to the
pound. Statistics for other buckshot sizes are as follows: No. 0—.32 and 145,
No. 1—.30 and 175, No. 3—.25 and 300, No. 4—.24 and 340.

Various shotgun slugs have been made, some with attached wads and
some without. Of these the most famous is the German Brenneke. It is solid,
has swedged "rifling." It is made under bore diameter, but it is gas-tight be-

RIFLED SLUGS (APPROXIMATE BALLISTICS)

		VELOCITY In Feet Per Second		ENERGY— In Foot/Lbs.		DROP— In Inches		Barrel*
Gauge	Weight Ounces	Muzzle	50 yds.	Muzzle	50 yds.	50 yds.	100 yds.	Length
10	1¾	1280	1080	2785	1980	2.9	13.2	32
12	1¼	1490	1240	2695	1865	2.3	9.8	30
12	1	1580	1310	2425	1665	2.0	9.0	30
16	4/5	1600	1175	1990	1070	2.1	10.4	28
20	3/4	1600	1270	1865	1175	1.9	9.5	26
410	1/5	1830	1335	650	345	1.6	8.2	26

* All calculations based on full choke barrels of this length. (Courtesy Federal Cartridge Corp.)

cause of an attached wad that is over bore diameter. The Brenneke slugs are made in 12, 16, and 20 gauge. They are reputed to give good penetration and have been used on game as large as tiger. The slugs are not only more accurate than the old "pumpkin balls" but they have greater penetration and killing power. I am a bit skeptical of the killing power of the 20-gauge slug. The 93-grain slug for the .410 is useless and should never be used on game larger than rabbits.

To sum up: A shotgun with buckshot is a fearful and devastating weapon, but only at short range. Even with the best loads with the buckshot protected by plastic collars and nested in plastic "sawdust," shots should not be attempted at over 60 yards, generally at not over 40 or so.

With a cylinder-bored barrel and good sights, a shotgun used with slugs is a makeshift rifle. Even the relatively efficient Brenneke slug loses its velocity (and energy) rapidly and at 100 yards the energy of 1049 foot-pounds is on the order of that of the .222 at the muzzle or the .243 at 300 yards. Neither of these are powerhouses. However, within 40 yards there isn't much a well-placed 12-gauge slug won't knock off.

VI

Trap and Skeet Shooting

Alex Kerr

22

Trap Shooting

ONE OF THE EARLIEST mentions of trap shooting in print was in 1793 in an English publication known as the *Sporting Magazine.* The sport was said to be a "well established recreation." It was probably an English sport exclusively in those days. Live pigeons were the only targets. The pigeon was encased in a box, or trap, as it was later called. At the call of the shooter, the lid was pulled off the box by means of a string and the pigeon was released. Passenger pigeons as well as some quail were used in those days when game was plentiful and no one could foresee a future scarcity.

The first mention of a trap club in the United States is contained in the records of the Sportsmen's Club of Cincinnati, Ohio, for 1831. In 1840 a club was formed on Long Island, New York, with about thirty members. Most of the members were all good field shots and used trap shooting as a method of keeping in practice in the off seasons. By 1875 this sport of pigeon shooting had taken hold in several large cities in the U.S. and on occasion 100 straight kills were recorded.

In 1866 Chas Portlock of Boston, Massachusetts, introduced a "glass ball" as the first substitute for a live pigeon. This new sport gained considerable popularity in a short time.

The English had already introduced "glass ball" shooting, but the traps were so poor and gave so much trouble that the sport never really caught on until the improved mechanisms were introduced by Portlock. Many improvements were made in the traps as time progressed and "glass ball" shooting became popular throughout the country but never quite surpassed the popularity of live pigeon shooting.

The first National Championships were held in New Orleans, Louisiana, in 1885. Only forty shooters attended but it was the beginning of competition. "Clay Pigeon Shooting" was the name given to the sport, and it is still so called by many today.

In 1880 George Ligawsky of Cincinnati, Ohio, invented the first clay pigeon trap, marking the beginning of a new era in the sport of trap shooting.

With this trap and the clay targets, the true flight of a bird was simulated whereas the glass balls were merely thrown into the air. Ligawsky's trap and clay pigeons became an immediate success and imitations sprang up. The original targets were made of real clay and were baked in an oven. These early targets were quite hard, and it took a well-aimed shot to break them. Today targets are manufactured from pitch and other ingredients which break more easily. Traps too have improved considerably, and today one may see traps which load, cock, and reset their direction automatically.

Today the Grand American Handicap, which is regarded as *the* championship by most trap shooters, is held at Vandalia, Ohio. This is one of the largest sporting events in America, with over 2,500 individual entries, a far cry from the original Grand American Handicap held at Dexter Park, New York, in 1893, when only twenty-one contestants competed.

The Amateur Trap Shooting Association, founded in 1918, today serves as the governing body of all registered trap shoots. Its office and permanent home is in Vandalia, Ohio (P.O. Box 458, zip code 45377). The rules and regulations of trap shooting are governed by this body. At the beginning of each year every paid-up member receives an average and handicap card. It will show at what yardage the shooter will shoot from in handicap trap and also contains spaces for posting the shooter's scores that are made during the year.

The official publication of the A.T.A. is *Trap and Field* magazine. It is published monthly and is available by subscription. The magazine may be obtained by writing to *Trap and Field,* 1100 Waterway Blvd., Indianapolis, IN 46202. The magazine contains reports of every major shoot throughout the country and the scores of the shooters that have competed, as well as articles by top shooters and notice of coming shoots throughout the country.

SELECTION OF GUNS FOR TRAP

Most persons shooting trap for the first time usually use their favorite hunting gun. This gun most likely has a "field" stock and is not too suitable for trap. These "field" stocks are all quite similar in dimensions as most manufacturers have standardized their guns. Although these stock measurements are suitable in the field for most hunters, they will not do the job at trap. Field guns shoot where the shooter is looking, and this will result in a miss at trap if the target is shot at in the general area at which most targets are broken. Trap targets vary in height from the ground level to approximately 15 feet above it. As trap targets are always rising, it is necessary for the gun to shoot above the target so by the time the shot reaches the target they are both there at the same time.

All trap guns manufactured today have "trap" stocks with much higher combs than one finds in field guns. Trap shooters term them much "straighter." The shooter cannot get his head down as close to the barrel as he can with his field gun so the gun shoots at a point above where the shooter is looking. There is no one trap stock with suitable dimensions for all of us and it is best for the shooter to experiment until he gets the right measurements in a stock for himself. There are competent gunsmiths throughout the country who can assist you considerably in this direction. They should also be consulted in regard to getting the proper length on the stock at the same time.

It is not possible to say that one particular gun is the best for trap shooting. The best way to determine which type of gun is best for you is to try the different types and you will soon get a good idea which one is the most suitable for you. You have a choice of several different types and makes. Pump guns and autoloaders are the most popular today. Autoloaders have less recoil than other guns and so are increasingly popular. Over-and-under doubles and single-barrel guns are next in that order but the fact that they are less popular than the repeaters is due to their higher cost. The double-barrel gun is last in popularity. Most trap shooters prefer the over-and-under style over the side-by-side. All of our major American gun manufacturers produce guns specifically for trap shooting and a wide variety of types and prices are available.

Most trap guns in use today of the single-barrel variety have full choke 30-inch barrels. There are a few shooters who prefer the modified choke for 16-yard shooting and there are also a few who prefer the 28-inch barrel. A shorter barrel handles a bit faster and the modified choke is ample for 16-yard shooting. However, I would not recommend the modified choke for most handicap shooters. A trap target is flat, and although it is not likely that the target will slip through the pattern, it will not break the target with the smashing effect of a full choke. A well-hit target adds to one's assurance. Some shooters lose confidence when they are not smashing their targets, wondering if they may be doing something wrong, which in turn causes them to shoot poorly. Over-and-under and double-barrel shotguns are usually bored full and modified. There are a few companies who make an improved modified barrel in place of the modified. There is so little difference between the two that only a few are used in this combination.

Over-and-under shotguns enjoy their greatest popularity in the doubles event. This is due mainly to the fact that there is no time lost because of pumping the action and less chance of a gun malfunction. With the importation of some foreign guns at fairly low prices, this model gun should increase in popularity.

All trap guns manufactured today come equipped with ventilated ribs. The flat surface of the rib over the barrel is much easier to point with than no rib at all.

LAYOUT OF THE TRAP FIELD

A trap field consists of a trap situated in a trap house and five shooting positions spaced 3 yards apart. All five positions are 16 yards from the trap. Five shots are taken by each shooter at each of the five positions. This makes a total of twenty-five shots and this is referred to as a round of trap. Each shooter takes his turn in shooting and upon completion of his five shots moves to the next position. Each time the shooter on the fifth position completes his five shots he goes to the first position, and so on.

Targets are thrown from the trap and must go a minimum of 48 yards and not over 52 yards. The targets must be thrown between 8 and 12 feet high at 10 yards in front of the trap. Each of these traps moves automatically to a position unknown to the shooter; therefore, the shooter never knows where the target will be thrown. In singles shooting, the trap shall be so adjusted that within the normal distribution of angles as thrown by the trap, the right angle shall not be less than straightaway from position five and the left angle shall not be less than straightaway from position one.

There are three different events held in trap shooting. The first type is known as the "16-yard event." This event is held in classes and each shooter is placed in a class according to his ability.

The second event, probably the most popular, is known as "handicap shooting." Each shooter is given a shooting position at a certain distance from the trap. These distances are from 18 to 27 yards, depending on the shooter's ability. The intent of this handicapping is to make the shooters compete on an equal basis. There are no classes in these events and all shooters are competing against each other.

The third type of shooting is known as "doubles." This is a most difficult event as two targets are thrown simultaneously. Unlike 16-yard and handicap shooting, the flight of these targets is fixed, and the left and right targets follow the path of the exteme left and right 16-yard targets.

Almost all shooting is done with the 12-gauge gun. There are no minimum restrictions but the maximum is no more than 1⅛ ounces shot and no more than 3 drams of powder. No shot larger than 7½'s nor any gun larger than a 12-gauge may be used.

All traps must throw unknown angles. Some do this by mechanical means and are powered by electrical motors. The most modern traps load the targets and reset the angles automatically.

Clay pigeons are all of a standard size. They are basically black with a yellow, orange, or white trim. Some are made all black. These color variations are used depending on which has the best visibility. This varies at different gun clubs based on the background of each field.

An area of 1,000 feet deep by 1,000 feet wide is sufficient for safety purposes for a trap field.

TECHNIQUES OF TRAP SHOOTING

In my early days of shooting I once heard trap shooting described as rifle shooting with a shotgun. I have never heard a better description at any time than this. To be a fine trap shot you must point the shotgun. Some persons believe that because of the pattern the shot throws that this should be fairly simple. Once he has tried it he will discover there is a lot of room around the moving target.

Targets are thrown at varying angles; consequently, the shooter must be prepared to shoot anywhere within that given area. The first thing a shooter does when he prepares to shoot is to plant his feet properly. He must be able to turn to the right or left with ease in order to hit targets flying in different directions. A shooter shooting at the first station will get no more than a straightaway target for his extreme right. He can also get an extremely wide angle to the left. Knowing this he should face halfway in between both extremes. Obviously, a shooter should face in the center of both extreme right and left targets on all five stations. If for some reason or another he faces too far in one direction, he will find his body winding up like a spring when he tries to move to the opposite direction. This causes him to slow down or even stop his swing, and he misses or barely hits the target.

The next step in shooting is for the shooter to start his gun in the proper place. The gun should be started halfway between the two extreme angles of the targets. At station one the gun should be pointed on the left corner of the trap house, at station two halfway between the left corner and the center of the trap house, on station three the center of the trap house, on station four halfway between the center and the right corner, and on station five on the right corner of the trap house. Under certain conditions it is advisable to start the gun higher because of wind conditions. A target will sometimes climb considerably even though it is thrown from the trap at the legal height. The amount the gun should be raised should be determined by the shooter based on the amount of climb of the target. There are many shooters who normally start higher simply because they have to move the gun less to get to the target and it is easier for them to shoot in this manner.

Most new shooters are more concerned with the recoil of the gun than anything else. Their first thought is to get the gun on their shoulder comfortably so it won't kick. They place the gun on their shoulder, then try to bring their head down on the stock of the gun. This tends to stretch the neck muscles and pulls the head off the stock. The proper way is to bring the gun up to the face and line up the gun with the eye. Then the shoulder is raised to the gun. With constant practice this becomes a natural act.

When the shooter has accomplished the foregoing, he calls for the target. As he does not know in which direction the target will fly, he must let it get a sufficient distance from the trap house before starting to move the gun. He must never try to guess where the target is going.

Once the direction of the target is determined the next step is to visualize where you want to point the gun in order to break the target. The gun should be held firmly but not tightly by the hand on the grip. The other hand should grip the fore-end lightly, and the arms should be relaxed. Too tight a grip causes a jerky swing on the target. Trap targets take very little lead and the amount of this lead can only be determined by the shooter through his experience. Of course, the targets flying straightaway from the shooter take no lead at all. I have known some very fast shooters who claim they do not lead any target.

SHOOTING AT EACH STATION

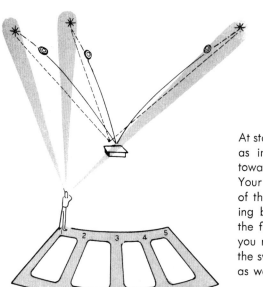

At station one, your feet should be placed as indicated with the left foot pointed toward the left corner of the trap house. Your gun should point at the left corner of the trap house, indicated in the drawing by a black dot. Solid lines indicate the flight angles of three typical targets you may encounter; dotted lines indicate the swing and follow-through of your gun as well as the target breaking point.

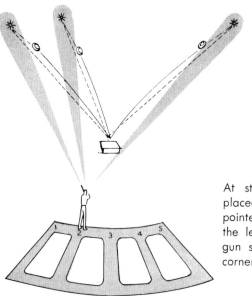

At station two, your feet should be placed as indicated with the left foot pointed one quarter of the way in from the left corner of the trap house. Your gun should point halfway between left corner and center of the trap house.

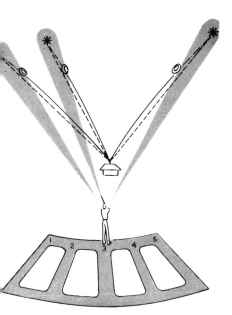

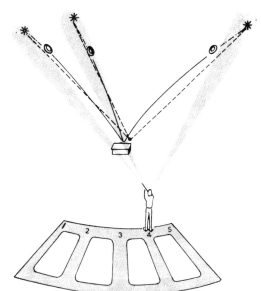

At station three your feet should be placed with the left foot pointed slightly to the left of the center of the trap house. Your gun should be pointed toward the center of the trap house.

At station four, your feet should be placed as indicated with the left foot pointed one-quarter of the way in from the right corner of the trap house. Point your gun halfway between the center and the right corner of the trap house.

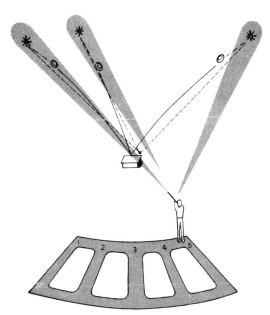

At station five, your feet should be placed as shown with the left foot pointed toward the right corner of the trap house. Point your gun at the right corner of the trap house. (All drawings courtesy of Winchester News Bureau.)

Never try to hold a certain lead on the target. The instant you have the gun pointed where you want it, pull the trigger. If you stay with the target, it will drop away from you and you will shoot over it. Try to swing the gun smoothly up to the target.

Eventually you will develop a sense of timing and you will shoot at your targets with a fairly consistent rate of speed. This varies with each person depending on how well co-ordinated he may be. Most beginning shooters shoot too slow; but by shooting with faster shots they will eventually increase their speed. Unlike upland game birds, trap targets are moving at their fastest rate of speed when they leave the trap house. This does not leave much time to think about a shot. Game birds start slowly and increase their speed as they go, giving the shooter more time.

One of the most common errors is to raise one's head off the gun stock. Sometimes this is caused by shooters wanting to get a better look at the target and sometimes by not bringing the gun tight enough into the face. In either case it causes the shooter to shoot over the target.

Handicap trap is the same as 16 yards except the ranges are greater—depending on the shooter's ability. Everything that applies to 16-yard shooting applies to handicap. The gun is moved to a lesser degree but you have to point finer on the targets. You can be a little sloppy in your 16-yard shooting and still get some fair hits but that same sloppiness will cost you targets when shooting at the longer ranges. The more your skill increases the farther back you will shoot. The wind, if it is a strong one, can even blow the target away from where you may have pointed before the shot even gets there. Most good handicap shooters who shoot from 23 to 27 yards are fast shooters. Their speed gives them better chances at these long ranges. As you increase your range yard by yard in handicap, you have to learn to make slight changes in your shooting. Your mental attitude becomes a problem just because you know it's tougher to shoot from there than it was a yard closer. Handicap shooting takes a lot of practice and most regular trap shooters realize this and do most of their practicing there.

Shooting doubles is the most challenging phase of trap shooting. First of all, you must face in a direction equally distant from both targets. You have the advantage of knowing where both of these targets are going so you are able to do this without any difficulty. Because you know where the first target will be you can start your gun much higher, which will give you a very short swing. This enables you to move to your second target much faster than you would if you started your gun where you would when shooting singles on that particular station. All of the top doubles shooters are fast shooters. Remember, you are shooting at two targets both going away from you, and the more time you take in shooting, the farther away they will be. Most doubles shooters widen their stance and point their toes farther apart. This prevents their knees from locking the body and preventing their swing to either side.

23

Skeet Shooting

SKEET SHOOTING was developed between 1910 and 1915 by C. E. Davies, of Andover, Massachusetts, his son Henry, and William H. Foster. Foster and Henry Davies were boyhood friends with a keen love of hunting. Henry's father, proprietor of Glen Rock Kennels in Andover, was also an avid hunter and was rated as an extremely fast and smooth wing-shot. Sometimes he would have a bad day in the field, however, and would return home determined to improve his shooting, particularly the shots he had missed that day. He set up a trap bolted to a plank and would duplicate the shots he had missed. The boys would help by operating the traps and throwing the targets. This was the beginning of skeet shooting, which is merely the creation of artificial shooting situations that match those encountered in the field.

All three men improved their shooting considerably, which led to the addition of more difficult shots and the start of competition. Davies Sr. mapped out a skeet field which would have shooting positions for more than one person. The field layout was a full circle with a 25-yard radius. The circle was marked off like the face of a clock with shooting positions at each hour. The trap was positioned at 12 o'clock and threw the targets at 6 o'clock. Two shots were fired from each position, making a total of twenty-four shots, the remaining twenty-fifth shot to be taken in the center of the circle with the target flying directly over the shooter's head. Thus the shooters were firing at targets both going away and coming towards them in addition to shooting both to the right and left. The shooting was referred to as "shooting around the clock." Thus the basic idea for skeet was founded. Clock shooting was kept up for a couple of years and was enjoyed by all who took part in it.

William Foster became editor of *National Sportsman* magazine in 1920. Although this magazine is no longer in existence today, it played a major role in popularizing skeet shooting. In the November, 1920 issue, clock shooting was recommended to the public. More and more hunters tried their skill at the new game and those using tighter-choked guns seemed to have an advantage over those using open-bored guns. Most of the shooters using upland game guns found they were at a disadvantage and did not make scores comparable to those with the tighter guns. In 1923 it was felt that it would improve the game to shorten the radius of the circle to 20 yards. Scores improved considerably from then on.

Those who wanted to install the new range found that too much land was needed. This resulted in the first changes made in the new sport. The first skeet fields required an area of roughly 500 square yards as the shooting was done in every direction and the spectators had to move along behind the shooters as they progressed from station to station. In 1923 William Foster conceived the idea of two traps set within a semicircle rather than a full circle. Thus the same shots were made but only half of the space used previously was taken up by this arrangement and the spectators did not have to move. This development brought the game to the form that we know today. Instead of twelve positions plus the one in the center we now have seven positions plus the one in the center.

After trying the game with its new changes, it was felt that the shots taken still did not duplicate all of the types of shots in the field because the targets were all at the same elevation. The solution was to elevate one trap about 15 feet off the ground. This was done by cutting a tree to this height and placing the trap on a platform atop the trunk.

The sport became so popular that *National Sportsman* ran an article showing full layout of the field and explaining the rules. To create interest a $100 cash prize was offered for the most acceptable name for the new sport.

During the following months inquiries poured in for additional information about the construction of the fields, cost of traps, etc., and over 10,000 name suggestions were received. After due consideration the name "skeet," suggested by Mrs. Gertrude Hurbutt of Dayton, Montana, was chosen. Skeet was considered to be a short, catchy name. It is derived from a Scandinavian word for "shoot."

The first National Championship match was held in 1927, and the winning team missed only eight targets out of 125. Today it is necessary to miss less than eight out of 1,250, and on several occasions perfect team scores of 500 out of 500 have been recorded. This National Championship did not attract a great number of shooters. Most of them were from the general area of Massachusetts. The first true National Championship was held in 1935 in Cleveland, Ohio, and was well attended by shooters from all over the United States.

SKEET SHOOTING TODAY

The National Skeet Shooting Association is the governing body of all skeet shooting in the United States. Its headquarters are located at P.O. Box 28188, San Antonio, Texas 78228. Any questions concerning skeet may be directed to this organization. Rule books are available as well as some shooting supplies.

Most states have their own state associations. These associations are responsible for conducting all registered matches within their state. Information about officers, and mailing addresses of any of these state associations, may be obtained from the National Skeet Shooting Association. Each state association has the address of each club within its state, and information about any of these clubs may be obtained through the association.

National Championships are held annually, usually in the month of August, in a different part of the country every year in order to give more shooters an opportunity to attend.

Most skeet matches are conducted with four events. The most popular is the 12 gauge. The other three events are the 410 gauge, known as the sub-small bore; the 28 gauge, known as small bore; and the 20 gauge. These events are held in various classes and each shooter is placed in a class based on his ability. The combined score of all four events is known as the high over-all and the winner is considered to be the champion of the shoot. Events are also held for ladies, juniors, sub-juniors, seniors and sub-seniors. Five-man and two-man team events are also held, usually in conjunction with the 12-gauge event, and are quite popular.

Intersectional and state championship shoots are held throughout the year during spring and summer. In the fall very few shoots are held as the hunting seasons are open at that time.

A monthly magazine known as the *Skeet Shooting Review* is included in the membership dues of the National Skeet Shooting Association. Results of shoots and information about changes in rules are covered each month. Tips on shooting are also featured.

Guns for Skeet

The originator of skeet planned the game around field shooting and used his hunting gun. Today skeet has become a specialized game. A hunting gun of the type used for upland game shooting would still fill the bill, and most skeet shooters use their skeet guns for hunting doves and quail.

Unlike trap, in competitive skeet four different gauges of guns are used. This may sound like a lot of duplication to some but it has proved otherwise. Most skeet shooters start with the 12 gauge, which is the most common and therefore the most popular with the beginner. After a shooter feels he has mastered the 12 he graduates to the smaller gauges. He finds out that the game becomes considerably more difficult and that it takes practice to become proficient with the little guns. Browning, Remington and others offer matched sets of skeet guns in the various gauges. The weights of these guns differ according to gauge, but similarity of balance is more important than identical weight. Still, some shooters have weights added so that guns in different gauges will be alike. This different "feel" in our smaller gauge guns has as much to do with the difficulty in shooting them as the lesser amount of shot.

Automatic shotguns are the most popular of all the skeet guns available today. Pump guns run a close second with over-and-unders running third.

Side-by-side double-barrel guns are seldom seen around the skeet field. There are some advantages to each type of gun. Automatics have the least recoil, pumps are the least expensive and over-and-unders have the best balance but cost the most. It is impossible to state that one type of gun is the best. For the beginner I would recommend that he try all of the different kinds and see which one he can handle the best, and if he chooses to become a competitive shooter, he should stick with the same type of gun in all gauges.

Guns with 26-inch barrels are considered to be best by most shooters and this length is accepted as standard by all manufacturers. Over-and-unders are made with a choice of 26- or 28-inch barrels. I have always preferred the 28 inch on an over-and-under as it makes the gun the same over-all length as a 26-inch pump or automatic.

All skeet guns have chokes that are made for skeet and most manufacturers' standards call for a 30-inch pattern at 25 yards. This is comparable to an improved cylinder bore in a field gun. Many shooters desire to add a choke device such as the Cutts Compensator or the Poly-Choke. This helps reduce the recoil as well as add muzzle weight to the gun. Chokes may also be changed with these devices. Thus the same gun may be used in field shooting.

Gun stocks on most skeet guns are about standard in drop (1½ inches by 2½ inches) and length (14 inches). These measurements may be changed in most guns without too much difficulty and very definitely should be if the gun does not fit the shooter properly.

OTHER EQUIPMENT

No one should shoot without using shooting glasses. There are occasional instances of shooters getting hit with a pellet that has ricochetted off a target. Your eyesight is worth protecting and glasses will do the job. Glasses are offered in many different colors and shapes. As our eyes are not all alike, each person must determine which color provides the best visibility.

Shooting sweaters, jackets, and coats are available with a shoulder patch on which to mount the gun and pockets to hold a box of shells. Some shooters prefer leather pouches attached to the belt which will hold a box of shells.

Ear plugs are available, as are acoustic muff-type protectors to prevent a shooter's ears from being damaged by constant shooting. Years ago, some shooters considered such devices "sissified." Today nearly every competitor wears them. They not only preserve precious hearing, but also help improve a shooter's comfort—and his scores.

For recoil-sensitive shooters, scores may also be improved by one of the several available recoil-reducing devices. These devices are generally built into the stock. Venting and muzzle brakes can also be effective in taming recoil, but they do increase noise levels—particularly for the other shooters standing next to you. Recoil pads help considerably and are advisable on the larger gauges.

Gun cases are essential for shooters to protect their guns. Most shooters prefer luggage-style full-length cases as they eliminate the necessity of assembling the gun and taking it apart each time they go out to shoot. Soft cases are not recommended if you travel by commercial transportation to attend shoots. There is no substitute for a solid gun case of hard leather, aluminum, high-impact plastics, or wood. I have seen baggage piled on top of my guns and have learned the hard way that they can be damaged in this manner.

LAYOUT OF THE SKEET FIELD

Skeet fields were originally full semicircle, but as mentioned earlier, it was necessary to make some changes for the safety of the shooters. The fields are now altered slightly and the targets are thrown at a slight angle from each trap house. A target must travel a minimum of 55 yards.

There are two trap houses. One is known as the high house and is located immediately behind station one. The targets emerge from this trap house at a height of 10 feet. The other trap house is known as the low house and the target emerges from a height of 3½ feet.

There are eight stations marked out on the field. Seven are an equal distance apart (26 feet, 8 inches) and are placed on the semicircle. The eighth station is in the center of the field midway between the two trap houses. Each shooting station is 3 feet square. Any part of both of the shooter's feet must touch the station.

A single shot is taken at targets from both houses on all eight stations. A target from the high house is always shot first. After finishing the single shots, doubles are fired. At stations one, two, six and seven, two targets are thrown simultaneously and the going away target is fired upon with the first shot and the incoming target with the second shot. This makes a total of twenty-four shots. The twenty-fifth shot is taken immediately following the first target missed and the identical shot must be made. If no misses occur, the shot may be taken from any station on the field. Most all twenty-fifth shots are taken at the seventh station, usually at the high house target.

Shooting is conducted with groups of five persons or less. Each group is known as a squad. Each shooter takes his turn on each station in the order in which they are signed up and continue in that order.

Each group of twenty-five shots is known as a round and is also the amount of shells in each box.

For safety reasons it is considered necessary to have an area 1,000 feet deep and 2,000 feet long for a skeet field. No No. 9 shot can travel this far and this amount of room is more than ample.

There are two types of traps available. One type is hand loaded and the other is automatically loaded. Most targets used are black with a yellow, orange, or white band.

Techniques of Skeet Shooting

Skeet offers a greater variety of shots than any other shotgun game. You know where each target is going; but, in spite of that advantage, you still have to hit them. The beginner has to learn he cannot break targets by shooting at them. After he learns to break a few he gets the general idea that you must shoot in front of each target in order to break it. Lead is the common term for this. The next step is to learn just how much lead for each shot. This will come from practice and from help of other shooters. It is best to try to learn to master one shot at a time, but this is possible only if you can get a skeet field to yourself.

It is reasonable to assume that a target flying at a given rate of speed and a load of shot fired from a shotgun at a given range will meet *if* the proper amount of lead is given. The confusing thing to many new shooters is what amount of lead is necessary for each shot. Years ago shooters' reaction time was checked by one of the universities and they found that it took approximately two-fifths of a second from the time the mind registered that that was the proper time to pull the trigger to the time the shot left the end of the shotgun barrel. Obviously a fast-swinging shooter is going to move that gun barrel farther in that period of time than a slow-swinging shooter. Because of this we get different answers from different shooters on just how much a target must be led.

Although getting the proper lead on each target is the ultimate objective, attention must be paid to stance and proper gun mounting. Position the feet correctly for each shot by facing the general area where you expect to break the target. The next step is to place the gun at a position in front of the trap house. Many new shooters will place the gun directly even with the trap house. This results in the shooter having to move the gun too fast in order to catch up with the target and he ends up with very poor control of the shotgun. As a rule of thumb a spot approximately one-third of the distance from the trap house to eight post would be about right. Some youngsters with very fast reactions can come in a little closer to the trap house, whereas some of us who are considerably older and find our reactions are slowing down must do just the opposite. The height of the gun should be approximately a couple of feet below the path of the target. This will allow ample room to see a target go downward if the wind happens to push it below its regular flight. Going up with a target that rises presents no problem; but if the target gets below the gun, we lose sight of it entirely.

After we get our feet placed right for the shot we are making and the gun started in the right place in relation to the trap house, the last thing that comes into our minds is to get the correct lead for the shot we are about to make. These three steps are the basic steps for each shot.

Next we must call for the target; the word "pull" is used by most shooters. Do not start the gun moving until the target appears. Bring the gun up to the shoulder at the same time you are moving the gun after the target. It is best to

The following illustrations show the shooter's position, aiming point, and suggested lead for each station on a skeet field. The aiming point is indicated by a black dot, the path of the gun's swing by a dotted line, and the point at which the target is broken by a star. (All drawings courtesy of Winchester News Bureau.)

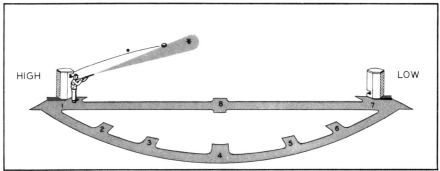

STATION 1 HIGH HOUSE   *Lead: 6" under*

STATION 1 LOW HOUSE   *Lead: 1'*

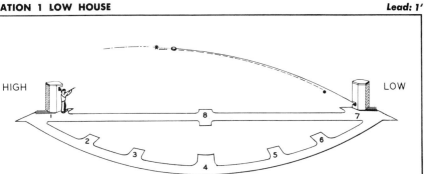

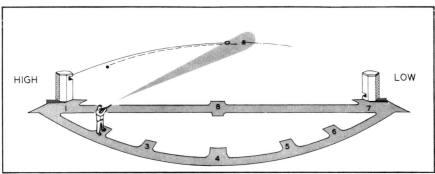

STATION 2 HIGH HOUSE   *Lead: 1'*

STATION 2 LOW HOUSE   *Lead:* 1½'

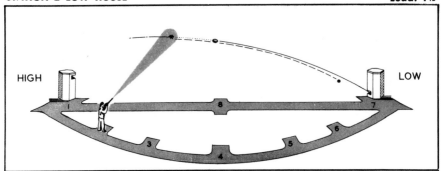

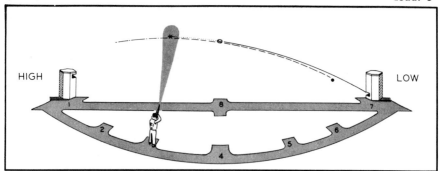

STATION 3 HIGH HOUSE   *Lead:* 1½'

STATION 3 LOW HOUSE   *Lead:* 3'

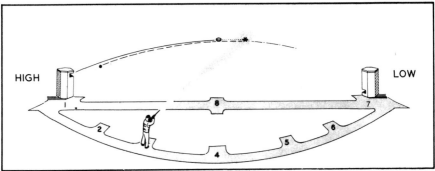

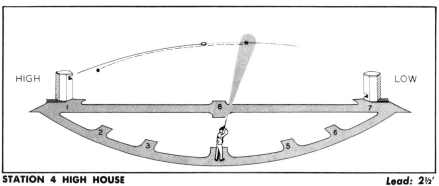

STATION 4 HIGH HOUSE   *Lead:* **2½′**

STATION 4 LOW HOUSE   *Lead:* **2½′**

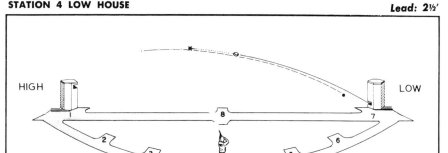

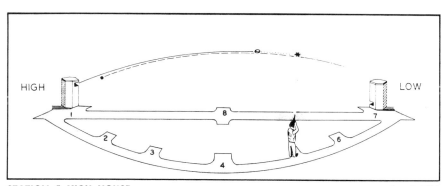

STATION 5 HIGH HOUSE   *Lead:* **3½′**

STATION 5 LOW HOUSE *Lead: 1½'*

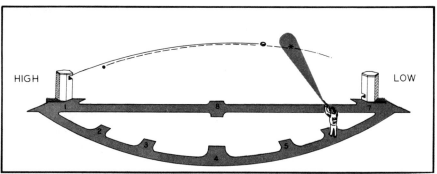

HIGH   LOW

STATION 6 HIGH HOUSE *Lead: 1½'*

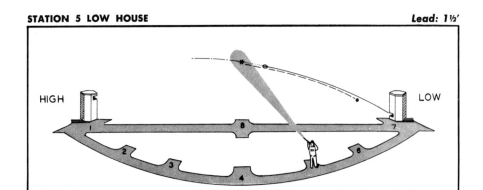

HIGH   LOW

STATION 6 LOW HOUSE *Lead: 1'*

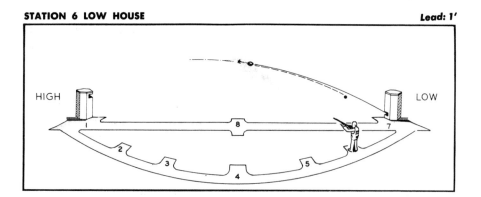

HIGH   LOW

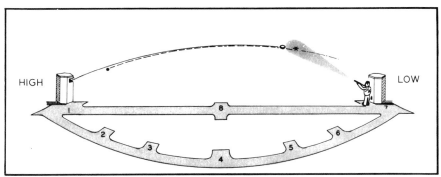

STATION 7 HIGH HOUSE   *Lead: 1'*

STATION 7 LOW HOUSE   *Lead: Point Blank*

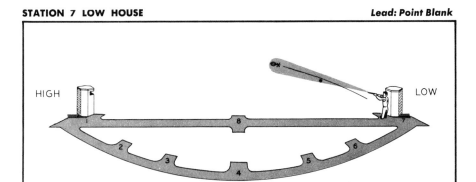

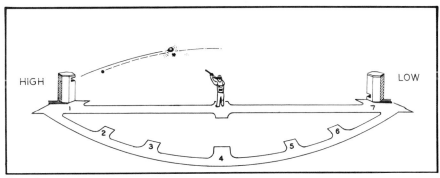

STATION 8 HIGH HOUSE   *Lead: Blot out target with muzzle and
                                                    slap trigger at same time*

STATION 8 LOW HOUSE

Lead: Blot out target with muzzle and slap trigger at same time

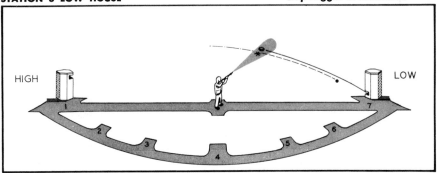

STATION 1 DOUBLES

Break High House Target First

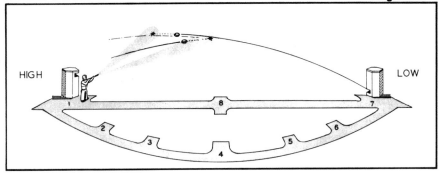

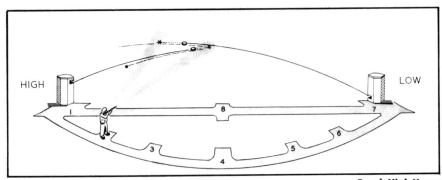

STATION 2 DOUBLES

Break High House Target First

try to keep the gun moving with the target and continue moving out to the correct lead. The instant this lead is reached pull the trigger. Never try to hold a lead in order to break a target at a certain spot on the field. Pull that trigger the instant that lead is reached. One of the two most common faults of experienced shooters is to stop swinging their gun after the lead is reached. You are not apt to make this mistake if you do not try to hold the lead. It is always best to "follow through" with your swing just like the golfers, tennis players, and baseball players do. Beware of the shooter who advises you that the shot you just missed was the result of shooting behind the target. This leads you to believe you did not have enough lead when in reality you stopped swinging your gun.

The other common fault of the experienced shooter is that sometimes he does not "get his head down on the stock." This means he is looking above his barrel instead of down the barrel. This results in shooting over the top of the target.

It is impossible to learn all of these steps at one time. If you try to, you will only confuse yourself. Learn them one at a time. These are the basic steps of becoming a good shooter. Try to memorize the leads for each shot and in time you will automatically remember them. This will also help tremendously with your field shooting. Every shot you make at skeet with the exception of those at eight post are identical to shots you will make in upland bird shooting. It will surprise you how much your field shooting will improve after a few rounds of skeet.

Safety and Care

Jack O'Connor

24

Safety with Rifles and Shotguns

MANY YEARS AGO a friend and I were visiting a picturesque old character who took hunting parties into northern Mexico for desert bighorn sheep, mule deer, and antelope. My friend was inspecting the old boy's battery and a scope-sighted 7 mm. Mauser took his fancy. Not many rifles were equipped with scopes in those days, so my pal was sighting at objects at the other end of the large room. On the top of a bookcase perhaps 40 feet away was a little figure of a bighorn ram. My amigo trained the scope on the ram. "This rifle isn't loaded, is it?" he asked. The outfitter said it wasn't so he worked the bolt, got the figurine of the ram in it, and carefully squeezed the trigger. There was a roar, the figure of the ram disintegrated, and the bullet plowed into the plastered adobe wall behind the bookcase.

This is one of many cases of "unloaded" guns causing mischief. I think that the first law of safety with firearms is for everyone who has occasion to handle a gun to form the habit of ascertaining the moment he picks a gun up whether it is loaded or not. A firearm that is actually unloaded is simply a piece of wood and metal no more dangerous than any other piece of wood or metal. A loaded gun is a deadly thing which should be handled with the utmost care.

If someone hands me a gun to look at I always ask, "Do you mind if I open this gun to see if it is loaded?" If he says he would rather I would not open it I hand the gun back to him.

Never take anyone else's word. Always see for yourself. The old outfitter thought his 7 mm. was unloaded. He had put it away unloaded. However, one of his hired men had seen a coyote. He had loaded the rifle but the coyote was gone by the time he got back outside. He put it away without unloading it.

I once read somewhere of a chap who brought an old cap-and-ball muzzle-loading rifle at a secondhand store to class up the decor of his summer cabin. He hung it over the fireplace and it stayed there gathering dust for years. Then one day a visitor took the old rifle down from its pegs, cocked it, aimed it at a corner of the cabin, pulled the trigger—and blew a hole in it. The old rifle had probably been loaded for decades.

I have always been a little suspicious of the adage that no one should ever point a gun at anything he does not want to shoot. It is not a very realistic instruction. If this were taken literally it would mean no one should do any dry-firing, for example. I know a chap who squeezes off 100 "shots" every day at a miniature target in his house. He does not want to shoot it.

Once I was on a hunting trip with some people I knew slightly. I had whittled a running buck down that morning, and that afternoon I was cleaning my rifle. The bolt was out and lying beside me. The rifle had been giving me some trouble with metal-fouling, so after I had run two or three patches through it I held it with the breech toward the light so I could look into the muzzle for fouling. This, of course, put the muzzle toward my head. Suddenly one of my companions jumped at me, grabbed my rifle, and almost knocked me down. "Don't point your rifle at your head, you damned fool!" he shouted.

I reminded him that the bolt had been removed from my rifle, that there were no cartridges in the magazine, and that in this condition the old musket might be useful as a club but not as a firearm.

All who handle guns should remember that the very first rule of safety is to know whether a firearm is loaded or unloaded. This should not be left to chance but should be made a routine as definite as the check an airplane pilot makes before he takes off. No one who isn't a law enforcement officer on duty should ever bring a loaded firearm into a house. No one who isn't a law officer, a soldier, or someone seeking to defend himself should ever carry a loaded firearm in a car. No one should ever carry a rifle in a saddle scabbard on a horse with a cartridge in the chamber. A firearm with an empty chamber is harmless, as there is no way for the firing pin to reach the primer of a cartridge in the magazine. But if there is a cartridge in the chamber, the arm is potentially dangerous—even in some cases if the safety is on.

Safety with firearms is largely a matter of good habit formation. The man who always unloads his gun before he enters a house or a car, who always ascertains whether a gun is loaded or not when he picks it up is doing a lot toward staying out of trouble.

Around others the safe man demonstrates that his gun is safe. He carries his double-barrel shotgun open, his pump or automatic with the action open, his rifle with the action open. When the safe man is hunting he should form the habit of taking the cartridge out of the chamber of a pump or automatic shotgun when he crosses a fence, climbs a tree, goes up a hillside that might cause him to fall. Every year hunters shoot themselves and shoot others because they do not unload their guns when they cross fences. When I was a lad two acquaintances of mine managed to kill themselves that way. They left their guns loaded and cocked and then shot themselves by pulling their guns toward themselves by the muzzles. Pulling a loaded firearm out of a car by the muzzle is another favorite way for the careless to bump themselves off. One hunter blew the foot off of a companion by leaning his cocked and loaded gun against a barbed wire fence. As he climbed the fence the gun fell, went off, and shot his companion's foot off. A good friend of mine has gone through most of his life with one arm because when he was a kid he jumped a ditch while carrying a loaded shotgun. The gun went off when he slipped and fell. The double-barrel shotgun is going out of style in this country, but in some ways it was the safest of shotguns since when the gunner opened it, there was no doubt either to him or to bystanders that it could not fire.

Then when the loaded gun or rifle is used in hunting, the person carrying it should know every instant just where the muzzle is pointing. I have seen hunters going in a line through a field and half of them had their guns pointed at companions most of the time. I have walked down a path behind a companion and I have had him lower the muzzle to point it right at my head. In such a situation the hunter should tell the person he is with to watch it and if he doesn't he should refuse to hunt with him again. A gun's safety should always be engaged until the game is sighted and the hunter is ready to shoot. But not even a mechanical safety is infallible, so the experienced sportsman always knows exactly where his gun's muzzle is pointing.

Let us say once more that everyone should know the exact status of every gun he handles, whether it is loaded or unloaded. If it is loaded is there anything in the chamber and how many cartridges are there in the magazine. A friend of mine recently almost got into trouble with a leopard. The gunbearer presumably had filled the magazine. My friend took a crack at a leopard that was dining on an impala, a small African antelope about the size of a hungry whitetail. The leopard went down and he thought he had killed it. As he approached to inspect it, the leopard rose to his feet and acted nasty. He raised his rifle to fire and all he got was a click. The only cartridge in the rifle had been the one in the chamber. The professional hunter bumped the groggy leopard off before it could spring.

When I take a rifle or a shotgun out of the rack before I shoot it I always look down the bore to make sure it is clear. About 999 times out of 1,000 the bore will be clear but about 1 time in 1,000 it will contain an obstruction. Once when I was on safari in Africa I found that the gunbearer who had cleaned the rifle had got a patch on the end of the rod cockeyed. The patch had stayed in the barrel and would have caused trouble. On another occasion I was hunting from a ranch in Mexico and while I was out shooting some quail a four-year-old boy had industriously filled the barrel of my .30/06 full of twigs.

Hunters are always getting snow and ice down barrels, and I suppose every year hundreds of men ruin good guns by taking a tumble, getting the muzzle plugged with mud, and then shooting the gun. Little rubber caps that cover the muzzles of rifles and keep snow out of them are sold at sporting goods stores. They should be helpful. I know that not a year goes by but what I get several letters from readers who are put out because some factory properly will not replace free a barrel that has been shot with an obstruction in it. Depending on the obstruction and the load, barrels are sometimes merely bulged and sometimes they are blown to bits. Incidentally, a good way to ruin a barrel is to "shoot out" a stuck cleaning patch.

A very lethal type of obstruction is a 20-gauge shell that has inadvertently been dropped into a 12-gauge chamber and then goes on up the barrel. Generally this happens when a man has guns in both gauges. He gets a 20-gauge shell mixed up with his 12's. In a hot corner he slipped the 20-gauge shell into the chamber. The gun does not fire because the 20 has gone up the barrel. He then puts a 12-gauge shell on top of it and touches it off. Few shotgun barrels survive it. At best it is generally a bulged barrel. At worst it is a barrel with a big hole blown in it. A 28-gauge shell can ruin a 16 gauge that way and a .410 can wreck a 28, as a .410 shell will stick in the muzzle of a full choke 28 gauge and the next shot will blow the muzzle out.

To be safe with a firearm, a gunner should make sure that he is using the correct ammunition. Those with old shotguns with twist or Damascus barrels should not use them with any modern smokeless-powder load, even low brass loads. Damascus barrels were made to stand about 5,000 pounds pressure per square inch and even trap loads give about twice that. The man with an old gun with twist barrels may shoot it for years and he may blow it up tomorrow. Furthermore, many old guns have short chambers (2⅝ inches for the 12 gauge, 2⁹/₁₆ inches for the 16, and 2½ inches for the 20 and the .410) and today most shells are 2¾ inches in length, except the .410 which is loaded in both 2½- and 3-inch cases, and the 12- and 20-gauge Magnum loads in 3-inch cases.

Shooting long shells in short chambers raises pressure, but just how much I cannot say. If the chamber is too short the end of the shell extends into the forcing cone of the chamber and the wads must be compressed the thickness of the mouth of the shell. Most old guns with Damascus barrels are also short chambered.

Once I went into Mexico for a deer hunt with a friend who was an enthusiastic hunter but by no means knowledgeable about guns. I was using a .270, he a .30/06. I was going pretty well, but he couldn't hit anything. After two days of futile bombardment I discovered he had been shooting my .270 reloads. I had them in .30/06 boxes with a little piece of paper pasted to the outside reading, ".270—120 Barnes, 52 grs. No. 4320." All this meant nothing to my pal. All he saw was the box that said ".30/06." In this case he was in no danger as the .270 and .30/06 have the same measurements from head of case to shoulder, but the .270 bullets rattle around in that .308 bore.

The danger in using the wrong rifle cartridges comes when someone manages to shoot cartridges too short and too small and sometimes with an over-size bullet in a large chamber. This can happen if the extractor holds the small cartridge so the firing pin can ignite the primer and also when a cartridge is of such size that it can wedge into another chamber. Some pretty weird notions go around about various calibers. Recently several people have written me or called me up to ask if it were true that the 7.65 Mauser and the 7 × 57 Mauser were so much alike that they were interchangeable. Of course they are not: the 7.65 case is 2.105 inches long and the bullet measures .311. The 7 × 57 case is 2.235 inches long and the bullet is .284.

Right after World War II many thousands of 6.5 and 7.7 Arisakas were brought back by G.I.'s who had served in the Pacific—but very little ammunition came along with them. A great deal of misinformation came along with the rifles. The 6.5 was usually called a .25 caliber, whereas a 6.5 has a bore diameter of .256 and a groove diameter which is supposed to be about .263 but which sometimes runs as much as .270. Tales were told of its high velocity, whereas the Japanese military round was a 139-grain bullet loaded to 2,500 feet per second. The M-2 cartridge used by the Americans drove a 150-grain bullet at about 2,825. The 7.7 Arisaka was called the ".31 Jap." Some lads fired .300 Savage cartridges in 7.7 rifles and apparently got away with it. The extractor usually held the case so the firing pin would touch off the primer. The powder gas expanded the case to fit the chamber and the fired cases were blown out straight and looked like oversize Colt Auto cartridges. The .308-inch bullets from the .300 Savage went through the somewhat larger bore. Actually the 7.7 Arisaka is a .303 caliber with a groove diameter of .311–.313. I have heard that even .35 Remington cartridges have been fired in a 7.7 chamber. If that is so it says a lot for the strength of the Arisaka action. Incidentally .35 Remington cartridges have wrecked quite a few .30/06 rifles. Some people formed 7.7 cases from .30/06 brass, shortened and resized, loaded them with .30 caliber bullets and sold them at high prices. The .30/06 cases are .020 inch smaller at the head than the 7.7 chamber. Mostly these cases expanded in the 7.7 chamber without letting go. But not always. Some made of brittle or possibly extra soft brass blew out. Several people were hurt and one lad was killed.

Much confusion about calibers comes from two misconceptions. One, which dates from muzzle-loading days, is that all cartridges bearing the same caliber designation can be fired in the same rifle. Any .30 caliber *bullet* can, of course, be loaded into any .30 caliber muzzle-loading barrel. I have received hundreds of letters from people who wanted to fire .300 H. & H. and .300 Weatherby cartridges in .300 Savage rifles and others have wanted to fire .308 Norma Magnum cartridges in .308 Winchester rifles. I once got myself in trouble when I wrote that the .257 Roberts cartridge took standard .25 caliber bullets and any .25 caliber bullet could be used for reloading. Many of my customers took this to mean that they could use any .25 caliber cartridge in a .257 rifle.

Another misconception is that there is the exact American equivalent for every metric cartridge. I have been told that the 7 × 64 and the .270 are identical, that the .30/06 and the 8 × 60 are one and the same and that the 9.3 × 62 is the same as the .35 Whelen. None of these things is true. After World War I many Model 95 Winchester lever-action rifles in .30/06 caliber were blown up because it was possible to get a military 8 mm. Mauser cartridge into a Model 95 .30/06 if the throat happened to be worn and the headspace on the generous side. Then the Model 95 came apart.

No one should ever shoot at signs, at telephone cables, insulators, power lines. It is the sign-shooters who have done much to give gun owners a bad reputation and shooting at power lines and telephone equipment is vandalism of the worst sort.

No one should ever fire a shot unless he knows where it will land and is 100 percent sure it won't harm anyone if it misses its intended mark. The bullet that misses the woodchuck on the skyline or the crow in a tree may travel a mile or more and kill a cow or a human being. An Arizona friend of mine was once seated by a beautiful picture window reading a book and thinking noble thoughts when he heard a noise and a .22 bullet fell in his lap. It had broken his picture window and must have traveled not far from a mile to get there. Some months ago I read of someone who was killed by a stray bullet fired so far away that no one heard the shot.

Just as no one should send a shot into the wild blue yonder by firing at something on the skyline, it should also be a rule never to fire a rifle bullet against a flat, hard surface or where bullets will ricochet. When I lived in Tucson, Arizona, varmint hunters pecking away at jackrabbits with .30/06 rifles and using full-metal-jacketed bullets because they were cheap caused no end of ill feeling. If anything bugs a rancher or a farmer it is to have ricochets whistling past his ears.

Some years ago a full-grown man with a .22 rifle and a little boy came out to the gun club to which I belong. He put bottles on the top of a trap house and every time he or the kid would miss a bottle the bullet would sail about a half mile and land in the back yard of a house on a hill. When I suggested that he find something other than bottles to shoot at and that he shoot into a bank which was available, he was furious.

And no one should ever shoot at any target he has not completely identified. A chap I knew once almost put a bullet into what he thought was a cow elk bedded down about 250 yards away. Something held his trigger finger— and presently a hunter wearing a brown sweater and tan pants got up and walked away. This hombre didn't quit shaking for fifteen minutes.

Even in country where both bucks or does were legal I have seldom shot a deer without knowing not only the sex but also having a pretty good idea as to the head. The hunter who never shoots until he knows for certain if the animal he is shooting at is a buck or a doe, a bull or a cow, is not going to shoot a human being by mistake.

Poor vision gets the blame for many hunting accidents and undoubtedly it is a factor. This is one of the reasons I am a firm believer in the scope sight. I think every hunter should also carry binoculars. But excited hunters shoot at sounds and movement of brush. They also can turn does into bucks, stones into rams, other hunters into bull elk.

Many years ago in Washington a hunter shot a young woman who was sitting on a rock looking for deer. He said he thought she was a cougar. If this man had been carrying binoculars and had taken time to use them he would never have made this tragic mistake.

Some of these accidents simply defy logical explanation. Some years ago here in Idaho one elk hunter shot and killed another elk hunter who was wearing a suit of white coveralls lettered something like "Joe's Service Station" on the back. The man who was shot was out in the open in a little mountain meadow building a fire. In another Idaho case a nonresident hunter shot the arm off another hunter at a distance of a few yards. The man who was wounded was wearing a red shirt and a fluorescent yellow vest. The man who shot him was convinced he was an elk.

In yet another Idaho case a friend of mine, an Idaho guide and outfitter, was shot on a deer hunt a week after he and I had got run out of the elk country by an untimely snowstorm. The lad who killed him was no tenderfoot, no excitable dude, but a young man who had been raised in the woods and who had hunted deer from the time he was knee high. He fired at a movement in the brush and killed the outfitter.

The man who always knows the exact status of any firearm he has in his hands, who always knows exactly where a loaded firearm is pointed, who never takes a loaded firearm into a car or a house, who always makes sure he is using the correct ammunition, and who always knows exactly what he is shooting at and where his bullet will wind up if he misses isn't going to cause much trouble.

25

Care of Rifles and Shotguns

Some people cannot carry a fine rifle or shotgun across the room without denting the stock and scratching the blue. Others (and I am among them) would just about as soon break a leg as mar the checkering or put a bad gouge in a fine walnut stock.

I have a friend who is a real gun nut, a crack shot, and a fine hunter. He appreciates a good-looking gun but he simply will not take the small amount of necessary trouble to keep a gun in good shape. When we come into a camp site and prepare to unsaddle our horses, take the packs off the pack stock, and make camp, I always look for a good stout tree with a projecting limb from which I can hang my rifle by the sling. I also hang my binoculars on the same limb. Then they are out of harm's way.

My pal leans his rifle against a stone or a spindly little sapling right in the midst of the pack animals. He generally throws his binoculars on the ground. I once saw a 1,200-pound pack horse step on his excellent pair of 12X Hensoldt roof prism binoculars. He worked the horse over with a club, but although this act no doubt eased his tensions it neither taught the horse a lesson nor repaired the binoculars.

Once he whittled down a bull elk and the animal was lying still feebly alive at the bottom of a canyon about 400 yards away. As he had run out of ammunition he asked if he could borrow a fine rifle I was carrying so he could finish off the elk. With misgivings I lent it to him. When he returned after field dressing the elk he had put more nicks and scratches on the fine stock of the rifle than I had put on in ten years of use.

Collecting and using fine firearms has been a hobby of mine ever since I could afford a hobby. I have a relatively small but, I believe, well chosen collection of rifles and shotguns which I use to hunt with. Some are in better shape than others. All show some signs of use. None show signs either of carelessness or neglect. One .270, which I have taken on several pack trips and with which I have done a great deal of hunting, has had a lot of the blue worn off the floorplate and at the muzzle and a few minor scratches and dents on the buttstock. All of this is unavoidable scabbard wear. Another, a thirty-year-old .30/06, has been used in Mexico, the Yukon, Idaho, Wyoming, and Tanganyika. Like the .270 it is in what is sometimes called "gun crank" condition—a term which means that the weapon shows use but has been properly and lovingly cared for.

So the first step in preserving firearms is nothing but the willingness to take some pains. The gun should never be flopped down on rocks or stones that will mar the metal and scratch or dent the stock. It should never be set up carelessly where it can fall down or be knocked down. It should never be carried where anything hard can bump it—in the back seat of an automobile next to another gun, for example. All the gun owner needs to forestall 90 percent of all bumps and gouges is a little care and common sense. The other 10

Winchester News Bureau

An example of proper gun care in the field. These hunters have avoided leaning their shotguns against the tree where they could be knocked over by the dog and have placed them on jackets instead of next to the ground.

percent of gun casualties comes from use. No one can avoid a certain amount of scabbard wear, and he who carries a rifle in a saddle scabbard through heavy and thorny brush is going to get some scratches on the buttstock.

Many gun users simply do not give a damn how a gun looks, just as long as it shoots. Some of my best friends feel that way. This essay is not for them. A friend of mine is a real shotgun aficionado. He married a gorgeous girl who was a fine bird shot and who could trim her husband at skeet. She did her skeet shooting with a mouldy old Model 12 Winchester skeet gun and her quail and pheasant shooting with a 16-gauge Parker D.H.E. that looked as if it had come over with Columbus. When my pal was courting this dish he was blinded by young and ardent love and had thought that his dainty little doll had simply been neglected by a cruel and calloused father who had given her the guns. It used to burn him up to think of that sweet and underprivileged little thing tramping through the wheat stubble behind a brace of German shorthairs knocking off upland birds with that horrible old Parker. He and the gal went to Europe on their honeymoon and at a gun store in Rome he picked up for her a veritable dream gun—a 20-gauge Beretta side lock over-and-under that was beautifully checkered and lovingly engraved. After she had hunted with it a few days it looked as bad as her Parker. The fact that this lovely creature was scratch and bump prone and was actually indifferent to the appearance of a gun shook my pal up. "I was never so shocked in my life!" he told me. "It was a real crisis. I thought for a while of leaving her, but she is otherwise a fine person. Now I have steeled myself against it and look the other way, just as one does when he sees someone being cruel to a horse!"

One of the best ways to avoid bumps, gouges, and scratches is to keep the gun in a case when traveling, as putting a gun in the back seat of an automobile with another gun is one of the commonest sources of bumps, dents, and scratches. Full-length cases for rifles and shotguns are not very expensive and they are certainly important in preserving the finish of a gun. Pains should be taken to see that they fit the guns they are intended for. They are made of tanned sheep hide with the fleece left inside, of canvas, of imitation plastic leather, cowhide, or if you travel with the excellent hard luggage-style cases, plastic or aluminum. They are lined with fleece, cotton flannel or protective foam padding. In damp weather, some of the lined cases may attract moisture and cause rust. As a consequence guns should not be stored in them for a long time.

The man who travels with a gun or rifle should have some sort of a hard case that will protect the firearm from rough handling on trains and on planes. In the old days when every well-heeled American had a good double-barrel shotgun as a status symbol, he carried the gun from place to place taken down and in a leather leg-of-mutton case. If he was particularly ritzy (and if he had a British double) he carried it in a trunk-type, oak-and-leather case lined with red or green billiard cloth and with brass corners, compartments for cleaning equipment, a box of shells, square oil bottle.

The British trunk-type cases made today use plywood instead of oak, and

These Weatherby Gun-Guard cases, in sizes for handguns, rifles, and shotguns, are typical of the popular high-impact gun cases which have ample cushioning and secure locks. Whether you're traveling to a distant skeet shoot or off on a hunting trip, you'll need a solid, batter-resistant carrying case.

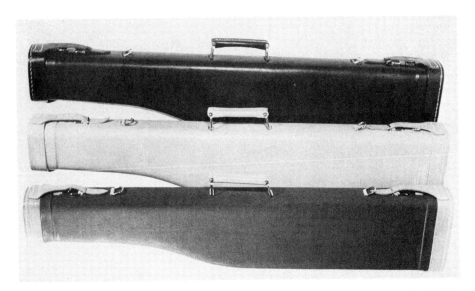

Leg-of-mutton case, named for its shape, is a classic piece of luggage designed to hold a take-down gun — traditionally a side-by-side double. They are excellent but expensive. Shown here are two leather-covered models and one in canvas with leather lids and trim.

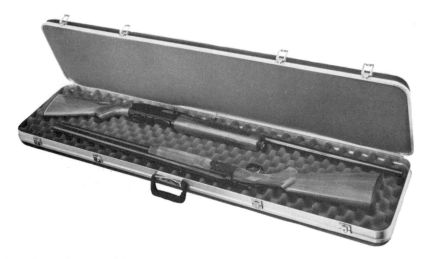

Polyurethane foam padding protects guns and holds them snugly in high-impact plastic transportation cases — today's most popular type. The same padding protects firearms in aluminum or wood transport cases.

often they are covered with canvas instead of leather. Like everything else in the British gun trade they have gone up enormously in price. Back in 1955 I ordered from Jeffery (a London gun maker which folded some years ago) a trunk-type leather case for my Winchester 12-gauge Model 21 with two sets of barrels. With canvas cover to protect the leather, the case cost about $65. I understand that today such a case costs in London over $500. I had a leather trunk case with brass corners and lined with billiard cloth made by Rigby in London for my pet .30/06. It has compartments for detachable scope, cleaning rod, oil bottle, two boxes of cartridges. I paid $75 for it at the time. I shudder to think what such a case would cost today.

Few leg-of-mutton cases are sold these days, as hunters generally transport their guns by automobile, don't take them down, and if they use a case it is a full-length job. Molded plastic luggage-style cases are much more popular today. They are lined with polyurethane foam and give complete protection. Various outfits also make cases for the competition shooter for transporting a whole flock of handguns. For some years I have used an aluminum case lined with polyurethane foam. It holds two scope-sighted rifles tied down by leather thongs and protected by the foam as well as assorted oddments like cleaning materials and ammunition. I have shipped rifles to both Africa and India in this case with perfect results. This case was made by the Saf-T-Case Mfg. Co., Inc., P.O. Box 5472, Irving, Texas 75062.

Bumps, scratches, and gouges can ruin the appearance of a firearm quicker than anything else. The second bad enemy is rust. When I bring a rifle or shotgun into the house I always wipe off all the outside metal parts with a slightly oily rag. The various silicone cloths are also good. At one time cleaning the bore of a .22 or a high-power rifle was an absolute necessity if rust were to be prevented, but nowadays (for the past forty years actually) just about all rimfires, shotshells, and centerfire rifle and pistol cartridges have been loaded with noncorrosive primers. These do not cause rust as the old potassium chlorate primers (which were used in U.S. .30/06 military ammunition until after the war) did, but they do not in themselves prevent rust. A rifle or a shotgun fired and left with a fouled barrel will eventually rust when the weather is damp, just as clean metal will rust. A .22 rimfire rifle that has been used with greased or waxed bullets can be kept uncleaned indefinitely even in damp weather and the bore will not rust.

Guns that have been out in extreme cold should never be brought directly into a warm house. If they are moisture will condense on them and cause rust. They should be left outside in the cold. It will not hurt them.

The shotgun, the .22 fired with gilding metal or cadmium-plated bullets, and the centerfire rifle fired with jacketed bullets must be cleaned and the bore protected by oil or rust is a possibility. The gun owner should have a variety of rods for this purpose. I have two shotgun rods, both ordinary maple rods with wool swabs and brass brushes for the various gauges. Best rods for rifles are the one-piece steel rods sometimes sheathed in plastic. A shorter rod of the same type does for handguns. On hunting trips the rifleman can use a jointed rod (although most are wobbly) or a flexible pullthrough.

Before we go farther, I am a firm believer in buying cotton flannel patches already cut. They come in various sizes for rifles, shotguns, and handguns. The worst type of patch is the one sawed off of somebody's shirttail with a pocket knife. The rifleman should also have bronze or brass brushes of suitable calibers, some bristle brushes, a powder solvent such as that old standby, Hoppe's No. 9, Outer's solvent or something of the sort, a bottle or a can of some good lubricant that will not gum and will not congeal with cold, a small bottle of linseed oil, and a can of lighter fluid to clean off recoil pads. It is likewise important to have good screwdrivers ground to fit guard and scope mount screws. Few things mar the appearance of a good gun more than screws chewed up by poorly fitting screwdrivers.

If it is possible all rifles should be cleaned from the breech so the rifling at the muzzle will not be damaged and care should also be taken not to damage the rifling at the breech. To clean a shotgun, I put a dry flannel patch on the end of a wool swab of the proper size and push it through the barrel or barrels. I then throw the patch away, put some powder solvent on a clean patch and run it through the barrels. If I see no leading and the gun is to be used within a few days that is all I do, except to go over all outside metal parts with an oily cloth.

When I have fired a rifle I remove the bolt, put a bristle brush saturated with solvent on the end of a cleaning rod and run it through the bore several times. I follow this with a clean, dry patch. Then if I see no signs of metal fouling, I saturate a clean patch with solvent and push it through the bore. If rifle or shotgun is not to be fired for some weeks, I follow the patch saturated with solvent with one that has on it several drops of oil with good body.

Minimum contents for a good gun-cleaning kit include rod, bristle brush, bronze or brass brush, patches, solvent, and lubricant. Kit shown here is an English import.

Leading in shotgun barrels and metal fouling in rifle barrels are not the bugaboos they used to be. Leading used to be annoying in many shotguns in the days when soft drop shot was used. Leading simply shows that some of the shot is rubbing off against the bore. It shows as a silvery looking deposit just forward of the forcing cone of the chamber at the breech. If a gun leads badly it means that the barrel is a bit rough or that the shot is quite soft or both. Generally the shot passing through the bore will eventually lap (smooth out) the barrel so that it no longer leads. Harder and plated shot have made leading a rarity and the use of plastic wad columns and plastic shot protectors has about done away with leading. However, leading is usually easy to remove. I put a brass or bronze brush of the proper size on the end of a cleaning rod, work it back and forth, and the lead generally wipes out. If it is bad the bore can be coated with mercuric ointment (blue ointment) which can be obtained at any drug store. The inside of the barrel can be coated with this and left a few days. Then the barrel can be wiped out when the mercury has amalgamated with the lead. This stuff should be handled very carefully, and with rubber gloves to prevent the mercury from poisoning you through your pores. And don't breathe the vapors!

When I was a young sprout shooting a Model 1903 Springfield, metal fouling (along with rusting) was a serious problem because we used bullets jacketed with cupro nickel (German silver) and when such a bullet was pushed through the bore at a velocity of over 2300–2400 foot-seconds, the stuff rubbed off on the lands, often forming big lumps near the muzzle where velocity was highest. We used to take to it with brass brushes, and when it got bad we dissolved it with ammonia dope.

The curse was taken off metal fouling when bullet jackets made of guilding metal or the similar Lubaloy came into use. Instead of forming lumps on the lands near the muzzle, the stuff rubs off as a very thin coppery wash which can be seen if one looks into the muzzle at a slant. This does not build up, interfere with accuracy, or anything else. Sometimes if a bore is rough because it was not lapped or because it was once slightly pitted by rust the guilding metal will rub off on the lands. When the rifleman looks through the barrel at the breech he can see that the lands are dark in contrast to the silvery sheen of the grooves. Generally three or four passes with a brass brush soaked in solvent will remove the metal fouling. If either leading or metal fouling persists, the rifle owner can do a bit of mild lapping himself. I used to use Winchester Rust Remover, a very mild abrasive in a heavy grease, on a tight patch. This product is no longer made, but there are other abrasive rust removers that can be similarly employed.

In cleaning a gun, the owner should take care to see that the chambers are clean. For rifles I use a slightly oily bristle brush on a wire handle, the same sort that is used to clean the chambers of large-caliber revolvers. Gas-operated automatics should be taken apart and the accumulated carbon and whatnot wiped out of the gas chambers now and then.

Most people over-oil their guns. Not only do they leave the actions dripping with oil but they grab an oil can and squirt oil into every crack and crevice. Then they go over the wood of the stock with an oil-saturated patch. Oil derived from petroleum is no good for wood. I have seen many old guns with the wood spongy and rotted from excess oil. Working parts should occasionally be anointed with a few small drops of good lubricant. A rifle to be used in cold weather should have all working parts carefully cleaned with gasoline so that all traces of grease are removed. Then they should be lightly oiled with one of the cold-resistant oils developed in recent years or with powdered graphite.

There are many reasonably satisfactory finishes for gun stocks. Today most factory finishes are sprayed-on lacquer, urethane or synthetic varnish. All of them glitter like the mouth of hell and some of them flake off badly when they are bumped. I am a very tender guy with a gun but a factory rifle I took with me to Mozambique in 1962 looked as if it were suffering from leprosy when I got it back. Some makers of fine gun stocks use several coats of spar varnish, brushed on, dried, and then sanded down between coats. Others use varnish and linseed oil and some nothing but linseed oil. If I am going to refinish a gun stock, I remove the original finish by softening it with varnish remover and then scraping it off. I then carefully sand the stock with No. 400 grit wet-or-dry sandpaper on a large eraser. Between sandings I raise the grain with water, make the whiskers pop up by exposing the damp wood to sudden heat such as that of a gas or electric burner. For the last sandings I use No. 600 grit. This is so fine it polishes the wood.

I then cover the checkering with masking tape and brush on marine spar varnish. I let the stock alone for a week or 10 days until the varnish is bone dry. I then use No. 600 grit wet-or-dry sandpaper used wet on a large eraser to sand the stock down to the bare wood with the varnish remaining only in the pores. I then put some GB Linspeed or ordinary boiled linseed oil on my hands and carefully rub the stock. I then take a dry cotton rag and rub off all the oil I can. I let the stock sit until the oil is thoroughly dry. I then repeat the performance. This way the finish is built up in microscopically thin and dry layers. People get into trouble with linseed oil finishes because they put one coat on top of another that is not dry. Then the oil never dries and the finish remains sticky.

Very dense wood with small pores can be finished with straight linseed oil, but most wood looks best if the pores are filled with spar varnish or some other filler before the coats of oil are applied. Open-grained, spongy wood that has not been filled never gets through absorbing oil and it turns almost black.

Factory lacquer or urethane finishes can be wiped with an oily rag to make them shine. They can even be polished with wax. "Gun oils" should never be used on a linseed oil finish. Neither should the oil finish be waxed as the wax will prevent a subsequent coat of linseed oil from adhering. Now and then the finish can be renewed by putting a few drops of linseed oil on the hands, rubbing the stock well with it, then rubbing off all surplus with a dry cloth. If in time the stock becomes scratched and slightly dented, the thing to do is to go over it with No. 600 grit sandpaper used wet and take the old oil off almost down to the bare wood. The scratches will disappear with the old finish. The finish can then be built up again as described above.

Care should be taken to keep linseed oil and oil of any kind out of the checkering. In time the checkering of a much used gun will fill up with dust, blood, dirt, grease, and dead skin from the hands. Then the stock should be masked off from the checkering and the checkering cleaned out with varnish remover and an old toothbrush or one of the little brushes sold by variety stores to clean suede shoes. Any kind of oil is poison to a recoil pad made of natural rubber, but today all American pads are made of synthetic rubber. Oil does not hurt these. They can be cleaned with lighter fluid on a rag or on a flannel patch.

A very wonderful way to mar and dent a good rifle or shotgun is to stand it in a corner or store it in the hall closet along with overshoes, wet raincoats and umbrellas, the kids' skates, and whatnot. A gun should have a place of its own. The shotgun, properly oiled and protected against rust, can be stored in a leg-of-mutton or trunk-type case, or better yet in a gun rack or cabinet. Guns should not be stored in cases lined with foam or fleece, as any moisture that may condense will be trapped and cause rusting.

If the sportsman has his own den, study, or trophy room he should have a place to display his guns, as firearms are handsome and suitable decorations in any masculine decor. Various types of gun racks are on sale at sporting goods stores, some holding one or two guns, some several. Some like glassed-in gun cases of pine, walnut, or maple.

My combination gunroom-trophy-room office is paneled in walnut. Desk, bookcases, cabinets are walnut. In one corner is an open walnut gunrack with cut-out space for gun butts and barrels to rest in lined with green billiard cloth. The rich sheen of the walnut stocks goes very well with the walnut paneling behind them. The guns also go nicely with the dark-red wall-to-wall carpet.

A gun with an unmarred stock and the blueing intact doesn't necessarily shoot any better than one that looks as if fourteen horses had stepped on it, but believe me it is a lot more fun to own and to look at.

Handgun Shooting

Jeff Cooper

26

Types of Handguns

THERE IS A FASCINATION about a pistol. All weapons appeal strongly to men and boys, but there is an individual, personal quality about a handgun that sets it apart from the others. The pistol is the personal defensive arm of the individual. The man who seeks a fight, or who is forewarned of deadly danger is not well advised to use it, for he has better choices. However, for one who wants no trouble but is prepared to finish what another starts, a reliable handgun—well used—is hard to beat.

While a pistol is primarily a combat arm, for use by man against man, it has many other uses. If fighting were its only utility it would be difficult to justify its inclusion in a book like this. Therefore, the additional uses of handguns should be understood by all shooters.

There is, of course, formal target shooting, as organized in this country by the National Rifle Association. This is a very challenging pastime; somewhat stylized and inflexible, but nonetheless interesting.

Sport shooting with the pistol has taken some very advanced steps in recent decades in all parts of the free world. "Practical pistol shooting" has become organized and promoted in such diverse areas as Australia, Norway, South Africa, and the United States, with somewhat less acceptance in continental Europe. In 1976 the International Practical Shooting Confederation was founded for the purpose of organizing practical pistol shooting competition throughout the world. Practical shooting is diverse, realistic, largely unrestricted as to style and equipment, and, unlike conventional target shooting, it accentuates speed and power as well as accuracy.

The use of the pistol as a hunting weapon has been stimulated by the introduction of the magnum revolvers, and with proper equipment one can now take both small and large game reliably and humanely with a one-hand gun, providing he is a very fine marksman.

Also, in particular circumstances, the pistol may be a useful auxiliary tool for the rancher, trapper, fisherman, surveyor, or hiker as both a source of meat and a defense against pests.

Lastly, there is "plinking," the common term for informal shooting at inanimate targets such as tin cans, clay pigeons, pine cones, or milk cartons. (Please, no bottles! Broken glass will always become somebody's problem.) Plinking, while it cannot be recommended as a good practice for the aspiring marksman, does little harm to the already good shot. It is far and away the most popular and widespread form of pistol shooting, and is the natural sport for the fixed-sight .22.

Handguns come in many types, styles and degrees of usefulness. They are designed to perform certain tasks, and in only a minority of cases are they really well adapted to more than one such task. For this reason it is well to know exactly what you intend to do with a pistol before you buy it. There is little question but that a .22 rimfire pistol is the best weapon to start with, but beyond that the issue becomes complicated. Action types may be classified as single-shot, revolver, and semiautomatic ("full-automatic" action is that of a machine gun). Revolvers may be further divided into single-action and double-action, while the autos come in locked-breech and "blow-back" designs. In power, handguns range basically between the .22 rimfire cartridge, suitable for training, target shooting, plinking, and the smallest game; and the .44 Magnum, which can take all but the heaviest game reliably with one shot. There are less powerful pistols than the .22 Short, and more powerful pistols than the .44 Magnum, but they are experimental and not production arms. Since portability and concealability are elements of a pistol's usefulness, its degree of compactness may render a given weapon more efficient for defensive purposes than another. Thus most handguns may be also classified as either "pocket pistols" or "holster pistols" for lack of better terminology, though even those pistols small enough to be pocketed should properly be carried in a good holster. The little ones are sometimes referred to as "snubbies."

However, I prefer to classify handguns by purpose. The characteristics of any tool are best described in terms of what the tool is intended to do. The following description is prepared on this basis.

Target Pistols

These instruments are made for one purpose, and that is to provide the shooter with a means of placing bullet holes as close together as possible on a piece of paper. They are designed for one-hand use on specific courses of fire and to conform to certain standardized rules. If the rules say "sight radius not to exceed 10 inches" and "trigger pull not less than 3½ pounds," such weapons appear with 10-inch sight radii and 3½-pound pulls. Thus they provide maximum accuracy within prescribed limits, regardless of the artificiality of such limits. This is a fairly important point to bear in mind, for some of the most highly developed handguns now available are not target pistols. One-hundred-yard performance is not important in a target pistol, since the longest standard range used in formally conducted pistol shooting is 60 yards. Trajectory is not an issue because courses are fired at known ranges. Power is a drawback rather than an asset, so target pistols are designed for the lightest possible loads.

Thus it is that a target pistol is a very specialized instrument, only coincidentally a weapon. It relates to a duty sidearm as a fencing foil relates to a rapier.

Most target pistols take the .22 rimfire Long Rifle cartridge. They offer superb accuracy, fine triggers and sights, very cheap ammunition, ease of control, and a weight generally between 2½ and 3 pounds. They tend to 6-inch barrels, broad sights, and light (but not feather-light) trigger pulls. The .22 target pistols are practically all semiautos, as the revolver has almost disappeared from this scene. Not that some excellent .22 target revolvers are not made; it's just that they are rarely seen any longer in the formal matches which are the reason for their existence. This is largely because of the greater ease of the auto in timed and rapid fire, though its solid, single chamber and generally better fit into the hand are also factors.

Colt, Smith & Wesson, Hi-Standard, and Ruger all make fine target .22 autos in this country; and Browning, Beretta, Walther, and Hämmerli pistols are imported. They are all good, and can win any match in the right hands, but choosing the best grade of each mark is a good idea if you wish to excel.

In U.S. competition the shooter engages one target only and he shoots at both 25 and 50 yards. This requires the trajectory and accuracy of the long-rifle match cartridge. The negligible recoil of this round is no problem, and a long, heavy barrel is an asset. However, if you go in for the international matches, you run into the "Olympic Rapid" course which calls for the placement of five shots on five different targets at 25 meters—in four seconds on the fast stage. Here even the very slight nudge of the .22 Long Rifle can be disturbing, and the inertia of an excessive muzzle weight can cause undesirable

The Colt Match Target, a very successful .22 target pistol.

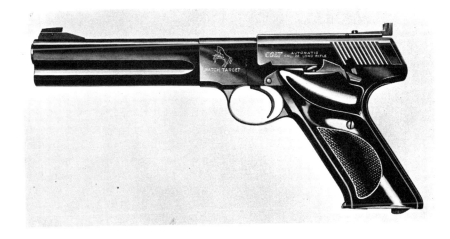

wrist flexion as the pistol is whipped sideways from target to target. Since the 10-ring measures just under 4 by 6 inches, hair-splitting accuracy is not as vital as total absence of recoil. These factors have created the demand for a .22 target pistol which is semiautomatic in action, chambered for the .22 Short cartridge, and weighted farther back in the hand. In many cases it is even fitted with a muzzle brake to reduce the pop of the Short still further. Such highly specialized pistols are made chiefly by Hämmerli, Hi-Standard, and Smith & Wesson, the latter offering an adapter kit to transform its conventional target auto (.22 L.R.) into an International Rapid auto (.22 Short).

Further along the road of particularized perfection lies the "free pistol," so called because it is made for a match which is supposedly free from restrictive specifications. Actually, there are restrictions—a free pistol may not have optical sights and you have to shoot it one-handed. The course of fire is simple—sixty shots slow-fire at 50 meters, at a 1.96-inch 10-ring. Hence the pistols are single-shot, hand-fitted, precision instruments capable of one-inch ten-shot groups at their stipulated range. Their trigger actions are fantastic, adjustable to a point at which the piece will discharge if the muzzle is raised. They all take the .22 Long Rifle cartridge. Such devices are not now made in the U.S. Versions from Hämmerli, Schultz and Larson, and Anschütz are imported.

The Centerfires

Target pistol shooting with centerfire weapons is a regular part of the U.S. sporting scene, and we have a number of excellent handguns available for this purpose. The activity is not popular abroad so there are not many imports to be considered.

Centerfire target pistols are "rule-beaters" just as are the .22's, though not to the same extent, for while the target .22 has no purpose apart from punching small groups on paper, the centerfire is at least vaguely derived from a duty weapon. Here again the leading lights are semiautos, made for the revolver-derived .38 Special cartridge. Cartridge development takes time, and this means that, as a rule, greatest accuracy is available in rounds that have been around for quite a spell. Thus the .38 Special, introduced shortly after the turn of the century, combines the most accuracy with the least recoil of any centerfire pistol cartridge. Stuffing its rimmed case into a semiautomatic action and making it still feed reliably is not easy, but both Smith & Wesson and Colt have been able to do this, and used to offer the Master and the National Match Mark III respectively. It is interesting to note that both take the .38 Special target wadcutter ammunition, *not* the police service or any other full-power version of the .38 Special cartridge, and that both take only a five-shot, rather than a full-capacity, magazine. They shoot brilliantly, but the only thing they do that a good .22 auto doesn't is qualify technically as centerfire pistols.

Since the U.S. uses the .45 auto as a service arm, we have formalized con-

The Colt "Gold Cup" .45, a service target pistol.

tests for weapons taking the .45 ACP (automatic Colt pistol) cartridge. This round is as accurate as the .38 Special but it kicks harder, so it is usually placed in a different category in competition. For a while a number of very sophisticated *revolvers* were made to take it, notably the still available Smith & Wesson Model 25, but the main effort has been to "tune" the standard 1911 auto to the absolute ultimate in precision. This is an uphill pull, for John Browning's magnificent man-stopper was not meant to be a paper punch. Its action is designed for reliable service and long wear under brutal conditions, not for tight groups.

The .45 target autos shouldn't shoot as well as they do, but they don't know any better. A 6-inch five-shot group at 50 yards is good performance in a duty sidearm—few men can hold that well under pressure—but the fanciest tune-ups on the .45 auto will put ten shots into 2 inches at that range quite often, and 3 inches is normal. Such tuning jobs are both expensive and subtle. They may cost up to $500 and even then not every smith who will take on such work can really deliver.

The Gold Cup version of the Colt .45 auto is presumed to be ready for competition as it comes out of the box, but not everyone finds this to be true. Also, the Gold Cup seems to be set up specifically for light target loads, as extensive use with full charges batters off its sights and knocks out its trigger stop. Naturally it may be advanced that one should use only target ammunition in a target pistol, but it is possible to set up a standard-grade pistol which will shoot as well and still stand up to full loads for a long time. Unfortunately, the finest edge of accuracy will not last indefinitely in any pistol, and the heavier the loads used the sooner this edge will wear. Men who shoot a

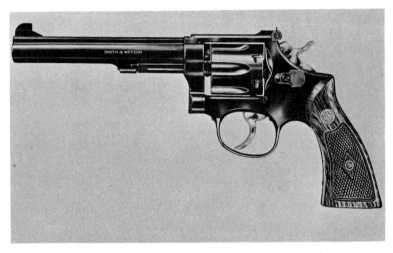

The Smith & Wesson "K-38", a popular police target revolver.

great deal must resign themselves to periodically retuning their pistol, but this is no great cross to bear.

The sort of weapon we have been discussing may be called a "service target pistol," and there is another conspicuous member of this class. American police departments favor the .38 Special revolver as a duty sidearm, for reasons which may have merit even though I can't see them. A revolver *is* somewhat safer than an auto in untrained hands, but the .38 Special cartridge is not one to stake one's life on. However, police matches are held with .38 revolvers, and the superb accuracy and mild recoil of the round suit it for use in

The Smith & Wesson big bore target revolver, in .44 Special or .45 ACP.

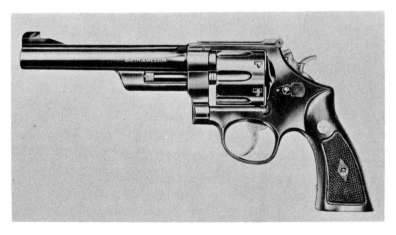

some very refined weapons. The Smith & Wesson Model 14 (K-38) and the Colt Python are very satisfactory examples of this breed. Some claim that the Python's long throat (it takes both the .357 and the .38 Special cases) impairs its accuracy a bit when the shorter case is used, but I have seen no reliable tests of this idea. It may be academic in any case, since if the absolute maximum in accuracy is desired one is better advised to use one of the specialized .38 target autos.

There is a third but rather rare example of the service target pistol, and that is the big-bore target revolver. Any cartridge may be lightly loaded, and if accuracy does not suffer, a .44 or .45 caliber bullet plopped softly into a paper target cuts a hole that is just enough larger than the .38 to pick up an extra point now and again on a "liner." In the long run this can win matches, but since it applies only to competition which is confined to revolvers, and since nearly all such competition is police sponsored, and since police in general require a .38, the big-bore service target revolver is not common.

HUNTING PISTOLS

Hunting with a pistol is a fine sport, but since it is only for the expert it is both traditionally and legally frowned upon. In a good many jurisdictions it is prohibited—on fairly mysterious grounds, for most places allow hunters to use a bow, and it seems to me that anything that is wrong with a handgun is even "wronger" with a bow. The subject is treated more fully in Chapter 33, so all that is necessary here is to say that the general suspicion of pistol hunting has hampered the development of the hunting pistol. Nevertheless we have some splendid examples available for consideration.

The .22's

Most pistol hunting is small-game hunting, and the .22 Long Rifle high-velocity hollow-point cartridge is a pretty fair harvester of small beasties—say up to about 5 pounds in weight. It has killed much larger animals, including deer, bear, and men, but then the Atlantic has been crossed in a rowboat.

Since game shooting is precision shooting, the .22 hunting pistol should be a highly refined arm. The cheap, crude, "economy" .22, with its gritty trigger, fixed sights, and doubtful accuracy, is often seen afield but it is not the proper tool for the job. Actually, the prime difference between a target .22 and a hunting .22 is weight. Formal target shooting is confined to one hand (which is about as sensible as confining swimming contests to one arm) and this calls for a moderately heavy weapon for the sake of stability.

Hunting shots are two-handed, except under the most peculiar circumstances, and with a two-hand hold weight is very much less important. Consequently, while any good .22 target pistol, other than a free pistol or a short, is a good hunting pistol, there are a number of excellent hunting pistols that

The Colt Woodsman is an excellent pistol for the smallest game.

are never seen in serious target contests. The 4-inch light-barreled autos are examples, along with the small frame revolvers.

It is quite important that any hunting pistol be fitted with accurately adjustable sights. It is possible for fixed sights to be "right on" for an individual shooter, but it is rare. Small game offers small targets, and very minor sight adjustments may be critical. Changing ammunition may cause a slight difference in point of impact, and anticipated hunting conditions may require a different sight picture. For example, head shots on rabbits at 15 yards call for a new zero in a pistol that has been set up for waterfowl at 75.

Also, a hunting pistol of any caliber must have a crisp, delicate trigger release if it is to be effective. A coarse trigger may be acceptable under certain conditions—either in benchrest or quick draw, at opposite ends of the scale, for example—but in a hunting weapon a "wish-off" is what is needed.

Thus it is advisable to select a hunting .22 from among the more expensive models of any line. It may be pertinent here to repeat a principle I have long propounded—skimping on the cost of any firearm is nearly always false economy. Price differences in the cost of high- and low-grade pistols, for example, are less than the cost of even a modest amount of ammunition. Guns do not go out of style or become obsolete, even in this era of rapid change, and the service rendered by a high-quality weapon over the years will bring satisfaction out of all proportion to the extra money it may cost. When I see a man choose a $100 pistol over a $400 one, I can only wonder if he can match the price of four second-line auto tires or a night out on the town against a lifetime of superior performance in his sidearm.

In any case, the hunting .22 may be either a medium-heavy target pistol or a featherweight trail gun for a backpacker who begrudges each ounce. For the latter, the standout is the Smith & Wesson Model 43 (Kit Gun Airweight), which provides fine accuracy, micrometer sights, and a superb trigger action all in a package that weighs just 14½ ounces.

Generally speaking, the .22 hunting pistol takes the .22 Long Rifle cartridge, but there are some others to be considered.

The .22 W.M.R. (Winchester Magnum Rimfire), which is *not* interchangeable with the Long Rifle, is offered in several good revolvers, no autos having been chambered for it as yet. Such pistols are, in my view, neither fish nor fowl, but do have one use. Their ammunition is quite small and light, and for the rare backpacker who plans to spend months, rather than days, afield without resupply, they provide a somewhat beefed up .22 without the penalty of bulky centerfire ammunition. The excellent S & W Kit Gun is supplied in this caliber, though not at present in an airweight version. Called the Model 34, it weighs 24 ounces. Ruger furnishes an optional cylinder for the W.M.R. in his Single-Six, allowing the use of either it or the long-rifle cartridge in the same gun. This pistol, however, weighs 35 ounces and has fixed sights.

The Centerfires

The heavy-caliber service pistols, from .40 inches on up, make very satisfactory hunting arms, within certain limits. Cartridges include the .38-40 (a true .40), the .44 Special, the .45 Colt, and the .45 ACP. When loaded with proper bullets these pistols will do nicely for deer-sized game at ranges under 50 yards—always providing they are expertly used. When properly main-

The Ruger "Single Six", at 23 ounces, makes a nice trail gun. It may be much improved by a set of adjustable sights.

tained they can be amazingly accurate, especially the .44 Special and the .45 ACP, and their curved trajectories are no hindrance up close. Their thick, blunt, half-ounce bullets strike hard and go deep, causing both shock and hemorrhage. And since they are essentially intended for defensive use, they are true dual-purpose arms.

In the lighter calibers, such as .38 Special, .38 Super, and 9 mm., accurate service pistols make fine small-game guns, and the super-light models, particularly the 18-ounce, 5-inch barreled version of the Colt Cobra, make splendid trail guns for those who need more power than that of a .22.

I must emphasize that service pistols qualify as hunting weapons *only* when using properly designed bullets. Plain, round-nosed ammunition, particularly if fully jacketed as in the military calibers, simply will not do. The Keith form of semi-wadcutter, or a truly quick-opening soft- or hollow-point, is absolutely essential to dependable stopping action. An animal no bigger than a jackrabbit can take a round-nosed full-jacket .45 ACP bullet right through the vitals and keep on running. The exception here is the service pistol which is carried as a defense against very large and dangerous beasts. This is by no means a recommended procedure, but if there is no other protection available and there is a real risk of unprovoked attack by such animals as crocodiles, bears, big cats, or buffalo, a hard-nosed armor-piercing bullet such as that of the .45 ACP Super X load may be all that will be able to penetrate the vitals. Such a wound would be most unlikely to stop a determined charge unless it reached the brain or the cervical portion of the spinal cord, but it could be fatal in a matter of some minutes, which would be important if the shooter could arrange to stay out of reach for that long.

The magnum revolvers, beginning with the .357, were intended partly as a means of increasing the combat efficiency of the police and partly as hunting weapons. They never quite made it (as fully loaded) as police weapons because of their excessive penetration, which is risky in metropolitan squabbles,

The Ruger Super Blackhawk .44 Magnum.

The author's veteran Smith & Wesson .44 Magnum, with a tie-slide made of boar's teeth taken with the pistol.

and also because of a certain difficulty of control which intimidates rooky policemen. However, they do well as sporting arms.

Three-fifty-sevens are now made by Colt, Ruger, and Smith & Wesson; and .41's and .44's by Ruger and Smith & Wesson. There are also some fly-by-night single-action revolvers in both .357 and .44 as well as a rather terrifying derringer in .357, about which I'd rather not speak.

When well made, with a good trigger and micrometer sights, the magnums are very fine arms. I prefer them with long barrels, which provide a long sight radius, an extra measure of velocity, a certain versatility in loading, and distinctly reduced muzzle whip.

The .357 will do very well for game of up to 100 pounds in weight and the .44 is reliable up to 400. Both can and will exceed these limits quite substantially, but this should be classed as emergency action only.

At risk of offending some very good friends in the arms trade, I consider the .41 Magnum, in its high-velocity loading, a pointless weapon. It offers slightly less than the .44 (15 percent less frontal area, ⅛ less bullet weight, and 100 f/s less velocity) in a weapon of exactly the same bulk and an ounce greater weight; but its recoil is not enough less to notice except in a side-by-side comparison. No one who is upset by the blast and belt of a .44 is going to find the .41 easy to shoot, or, put the other way, anyone who can handle a .41

can handle a .44. The .44 does the same job better, so why bother with a .41? This does not apply to the factory combat load for the .41, which is much milder than the high-velocity load, but the .44 can be loaded down, too, and keep its edge all the way.

The .44 Magnum is the king of hunting pistols, beautifully made and finished, superbly accurate, and powerful enough for any task to which a sidearm may reasonably be put. It will shoot flat out to as far as you can hold on the vitals of a deer, it will drive right through both shoulders of a prime Kodiak bear and out the other side, and with the right ammunition it will print ten-shot 5-inch groups at 100 yards. However, it is a man's gun, not for the timid. It kicks five times as hard as a police service .38, and its report is that of a major-caliber hunting rifle. Loaded light, it can double as a combat pistol, though it is really too bulky for continuous comfortable wear. Altogether it is a lovely instrument, but for experts only.

COMBAT PISTOLS

These may properly be termed "defensive pistols," for a pistol plays a completely defensive role in combat. Its purpose is to stop what somebody else starts.

A combat pistol should be easily controllable, small, light, and handy. It must be as reliable as technology can make it. It must be safe for its user and yet capable of going into action from a safe condition in a split second. It need not be able to place tiny groups on a piece of paper, but it's better if it can. Above all it must be able to stop a strong, determined man instantly with one solid hit. These things are not easy to combine in one weapon, but we have come very close to the answer. Since the requirements are often conflicting, certain compromises must sacrifice a measure of one quality in the interest of another, and thus the choice of a combat pistol will depend upon which requirements are most important to the chooser.

It has always seemed to me that the single most important quality of a combat pistol is adequate stopping power. The power to prevent an adversary's continuing with a course of action which absolutely must not continue is the only reason for the existence of the weapon. Well, perhaps there is another. Perhaps the power to intimidate must be considered, for merely brandishing a pistol, without firing it, may upon occasion achieve desirable results. However, since one pistol is about as intimidating as another when you are looking down its muzzle, there is little point in dwelling upon the matter. I have heard that a nickel-plated .45 takes first prize in this contest, but fortunately I can't say from experience.

The most careful analysis of the stopping power of pistol bullets was made by the late, illustrious General Julian Hatcher, U.S.A., based upon the Thompson-La Garde tests of the early 1900's. Anyone wishing to go deeply into this matter must start with a careful study of the chapter entitled, "Bullet Effect and Shock Power" in his *Textbook of Pistols and Revolvers*. Greatly simplified, General Hatcher's conclusions are that stopping power is a function of (1) bullet momentum, modified by (2) frontal area, modified by (3) the bullet's shape and material. Momentum is mass times velocity, while energy is mass times the square of velocity. Hence tables of energy give a misleading view of stopping power since they greatly overvalue velocity.

Maximum stopping power is therefore achieved by balancing the heaviest bullet against the highest velocity which can be controlled by an average man in a light pistol, giving it the largest frontal area consistent with ballistic efficiency over a fairly short distance, and giving it a shape and material which will maximize destructive effect in tissue. In selecting a weapon the last factor may be largely disregarded since a bullet of almost any shape or material can be fired from any given cartridge. But the greatest momentum and frontal area consistent with controllability remain the vital elements in the choice of a defensive handgun.

For there is never "enough" stopping power. Men have been hit with far more lethal missiles than can be fired from any pistol and still kept their feet. There is a skull in the Harvard Medical Museum of a man who had a crowbar blown through his head without losing consciousness. This very fact leads a certain faction among combat pistolmen to claim that since *complete* stopping power is unattainable, degrees of stopping power are meaningless. With this General Hatcher did not agree, and neither do I. Police records compiled at Los Angeles State College indicate very positively that the efficiency gap between the various popular police and service cartridges is very great, and that doubling the calculated stopping power of a pistol does in fact double its value as a life saver.

All of which leads to a decision in favor of the big bores. While tests have shown that the capability of a light bullet at high velocity to produce "secondary missiles" (flying bone fragments) gives it the possibility of very great stopping power, this only occurs if bones are struck, and this is not to be counted on. The big bores are, in general, the .44's and .45's. There is also the .41 Magnum and the .38-40, the .455, and the .476 (almost obsolete). A "full-house" .357, loaded up to its pressure limit and with a barrel at least 6 inches long, will also qualify, but if this cartridge is loaded down and fired from a short barrel it becomes marginal, along with the 9 mm. Parabellum and Super .38, and the .38 Special in its full combat loadings. The .38 Special, in its "police service" loading, is not even marginal, as any thorough study of police records will show.

With this in mind, I do not propose to discuss the great mass of inadequate defensive pistols. Since there are plenty of good models available, there is no need to examine the inferior types.

On another point, only semiauto pistols and double-action revolvers need be given serious consideration as combat arms, for while it is undoubtedly true that the single-action revolver is amazingly efficient in the hands of one or two super experts, such performance is more of a theatrical novelty than a practical attribute. The single-action is very fast from the leather, and it can be accurate and powerful, as well as slightly more compact than a double-action revolver or equivalent power. However, it is extremely difficult to handle accurately in rapid fire or multiple target situations, and it is murderously awkward to reload. Its vaunted reliability is an illusion, as it breaks down somewhat *more* frequently than a good double-action under heavy use, and there is nothing mystically perfect about its "feel." Any hand can be trained to any grip, and un-aimed, waist-high fire can be delivered with equal accuracy from a single-action, double-action or auto-pistol with the same amount of practice.

The Autos

In any general view of defensive pistols, it would be futile for me to try to conceal my preference for the .45 automatic. A good .45 auto, properly loaded and skillfully used, is distinctly superior to any other defensive sidearm yet to appear. The .45 auto cartridge has its limitations, as has the basic 1911 Browning action still in use, but no better combination has been offered, and as it stands the combination is rather splendid.

The original and for long the only available .45 automatic pistol was made by Colt and some subcontractors. Today a good many other makers provide weapons in this caliber including Browning, Heckler & Koch, AMT, Llama, Detonics and others. Despite this profusion the Colt remains the outstanding example of the type still. It displays a few drawbacks which are only to be expected in a design perfected in 1911, but these defects are minor and the price remains comparatively low.

The Colt .45 auto, slightly modified by the author for combat competition. Over fifty years old, this is still the world's best combat sidearm.

A presentation set of Browning combat pistols. The P-35 at the top is good, the .380 in the middle is marginal, the .25 at the bottom is best used as a watch fob.

A .45 automatic offers a comfortable amount of stopping power, eight shots quick and an instantaneous reload, extreme ruggedness, simple maintenance without recourse to a gunsmith, compactness for its power, readily available ammunition, and great reliability. Slightly modified, it is also capable of extreme accuracy and a boost in stopping power, the latter by way of "throating" it to feed semi-wadcutter lead bullets. Against it is the fact that it is a weapon to be used only by a well-trained man. In unfamiliar hands it is hard to shoot well and, as with any self-loading weapon, more liable to accidental discharge than any hand-operated repeater. It is also sensitive to variations in ammunition. With the wrong loads it may misfunction.

A standard .45 auto weighs 39 ounces and measures 8½ by 5 by 1¼ inches. The Commander weighs 26 ounces and is ¾ of an inch shorter.

There are a good number of .38 automatics (I include the 9mm pistols in this class) all of which suffer from the limitations of their caliber. The P35 Browning (called for some curious reason the "Hi-Power", though it is no more powerful than any other pistol taking the 9mm cartridge) has a long and distinguished history of service. It remained probably the best of the heavy duty 9mm automatics until the introduction of the Czech '75 in that year.

The Swiss S.I.G. .210 was the most luxurious of the group until its discontinuance, offering marvelous workmanship and very superior accuracy as delivered. More recently Beretta of Italy, Steyr-Mannlicher of Austria, Heckler & Koch and Walther of Germany, Llama of Spain and Smith & Wesson of Springfield, Massachusetts, have produced 9mm pistols of modern design. All of these pistols offer certain technical advances but the most interesting of the lot is the P7 of Heckler & Koch (previously called the PSP). This remarkable little gun offers all the power that can be had from the cartridge in much more compact and simplified form than any of its competition. Anyone who is content with the marginal power of the 9mm should look hard at the P7. Its gas-delayed blowback system, together with its squeeze cocking mechanism, combines with its remarkable compactness into the most advanced pistol of its type.

The Revolvers

If one prefers a revolver, or for some reason is required to forego an auto pistol as in many police departments, there is a wide choice available in excellent combat arms. Here again I see no point in discussing the entire range for there is little reason to select something "almost as good" when the best may be had. An important point is to concentrate on double-action performance, for cocking a double-action revolver in a combat situation is the mark of a novice. The two great combat revolver men are Elden Carl and Jack Weaver, and while Carl may occasionally sight-in single-action, neither ever cocks his piece with his thumb in a serious situation. Therefore a slick, smooth, reliable double-action is a primary requirement in a combat revolver.

A double-action revolver is bulky for its power and almost the first problem in selecting one is the choice between adequate power in a huge weapon, or manageable size in one of dubious power. Oddly, the best compromise of these alternatives is no longer being made. The solid-frame, round butt, five-shot, double-action .455 revolver made by Webley for the Royal Irish Constabulary had a 2¼-inch barrel and weighed only 21 ounces, yet it threw a solid blow. Its 265-grain bullet didn't move very fast, but then neither does a medicine ball. If you can find an R.I.C. .455, keep it!

But turning to current production, we find that the large-caliber revolvers are awfully big and heavy, running upwards of 40 ounces in weight and overall dimensions of 12 by 6 by 2 inches; and that the small revolvers are not offered in calibers which can put a man down with any real authority.

There are a number of fairly compact .357 revolvers available at this time which attempt to provide adequate stopping power in reduced bulk. The M19 Smith & Wesson was the first of these but now we have the Ruger Security Six and the French Manhurin. Constructing a compact .357 is something of a problem because of the high pressures developed in full loads in this caliber. A continuous diet of full charges has a reputation for wearing the small versions

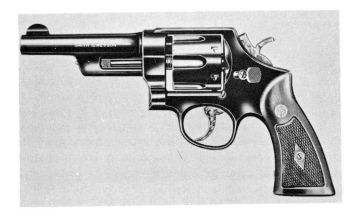

The Smith & Wesson Model 21 in .44 Special is the best combat revolver for those who can put up with its bulk.

loose in a fairly short time. This type of piece is one in which it is probably well to conduct most practice with light loads and reserve full charges only for full duty occasions.

On the upward side of the Model 19 lie the .41, .44 and .45 revolvers of the Smith & Wesson line. Colt does not make, at present, a big-bore double-action revolver, but they did at one time and fine weapons they were. All these Smith's are pretty huge for regular wear but they do a fine job once the whistle blows. The .44 Magnum is the bruiser of the lot, but it is somewhat extravagant as a combat arm. Happily, I have never seen a man shot with one, but from the way its full load whistles through a robust mule deer without any noticeable slowdown, I suspect that only a fraction of its awesome power would be soaked up by a man, unless he were standing on the other side of a 12-inch pine tree. It seems a bit unsound to pack such power into a handgun, and to put up with the resulting control problem, in order merely to tear up great hunks of the landscape on the far side of your antagonist. (If you are expecting him to wear a steel vest that's another matter.) I do not wish to exaggerate the difficulty of shooting the big .44. It can be shot, slow fire, with the precision of a target pistol, but its recoil does make rapid fire and multiple targets something of a problem, and a sensible man does not pose himself problems just for kicks—not, anyway, in a life-and-death situation.

Loaded down to about 1100 f/s in a 6-inch barrel, the .44 Magnum becomes a fine combat load, though the pistol itself remains cumbersome. These same ballistics may be had in a .44 Special (Models 21 and 24) which can be trimmed down to below 40 ounces in weight, as against almost 50 for the Magnum.

The .41 has the same exterior dimensions as the .44 and weighs about an ounce more, due to the smaller holes in barrel and cylinder. As a combat round, its high-velocity hunting load has the same shortcomings as the full-house .44, though to a very slightly lower degree, but it has the advantage of a factory-loaded combat round, which the .44 has not. This combat round has a momentum area factor of 56 in a 4-inch barrel and 60 with a 6-inch barrel, plus the feature of a very good bullet shape, so it will obviously be a good cartridge for defensive use. If it could be used in a neat, compact, five-shot, 35-ounce, double-action revolver with a 3½-inch barrel and a bird's-head grip, it would considerably surpass the Combat Magnum. As it is, it's hard to see why anyone would favor a .41 over a .44, since the latter is just a bit better in every respect other than an almost imperceptible difference in controllability.

The Snubbies

There is another class of combat revolver which deserves consideration, as it affords a maximum of portability and concealability while still retaining at least a measure of stopping power, if much attention is paid to proper loading. This is the "snubby," or "two-inch" as it is known in police circles. Such weapons are made by Colt (the Cobra and Agent) and by Smith & Wesson (the Chief's Special, Bodyguard, and Centennial) and this diversity of models shows how popular they are. While a couple are offered in the short .38 revolver calibers (.38 S & W or New Police) they should only be considered in caliber .38 Special, which is little enough at that.

These little revolvers are very unobtrusive, running about 6 by 4 by 1¼ inches over-all and weighing about as much as twenty rounds of rifle ammunition. The Colts carry six shots to the Smiths' five, but this very fact allows

The Colt Cobra, an aluminum "snubby" in .38 Special.

the Smith cylinder to be slimmer, which is a point in favor of concealability. They are tricky to shoot, for their feathery lightness lets even a .38 kick sharply, and their tiny butts are not easy to grasp in a full-sized hand. Hand-filling custom stocks are almost a necessity here. Nevertheless, as emergency or "hide out" guns they are much favored by detectives and off-duty policemen, and they have merit as protection for important public figures whose duties call for an unarmed appearance.

They should be loaded with a flat-point or semi-wadcutter bullet with a brisk charge of quick-burning powder such as Bullseye, with the hope of getting about 900 f/s at the muzzle of the abbreviated barrel. The m. a. (momentum area) factor of these pistols is not high, being about 30 or a little less, but it's still a great deal better than that of James Bond's celebrated PPK, which weighs about the same. Neither, of course, can be compared with a Colt Commander with its m. a. factor of up to 75, but the Commander, while handy, still weighs nearly twice as much when fully loaded.

Spares

There are great numbers of other types of combat pistols; that is to say, they are designed and sold as defensive arms, but there is not room here to catalog the second rate. The derringer, the Peacemaker (especially in its cut-down "storekeeper" version), the masses of "pocket" autos in .25, .32 and .380, and the dainty .32 revolvers, may indeed suffice upon occasion. A .45 derringer (emphatically not the old original .41 rimfire) or Peacemaker is a formidable weapon in skilled hands, but I cannot recommend its choice as "original equipment." Nor can the minor caliber sidearms ever be trusted with your life. They will all kill, in some circumstances, but they will rarely stop, and stopping, not killing, is the mission of the combat pistol.

MISCELLANEOUS PISTOL TYPES

Trainers

The use of .22 caliber rimfire ammunition for practice is sufficiently desirable to suggest the acquisition of a subcaliber handgun. The Colt and Smith & Wesson service revolvers have traditionally been paralleled by .22 caliber pieces of nearly the same size, weight, and action. It may seem an extravagance to buy a pistol only for training, but when one considers the necessity for continuous practice and compares the cost of ammunition it may be seen that the trainer will quickly pay for itself.

The auto pistols are fairly easily converted from one caliber to another, and most of the major versions have offered a .22 conversion adaptation which may be fitted to the service pistol for practice and removed when full service is called for.

The Smith & Wesson Model 18, in .22 rimfire, is an understudy for the police service revolver.

Plinkers

Plinking pistols, which are intended mainly for tin-can shooting, are another class that deserves mention. Most .22's fall into this slot, and the majority of them are simple, unpretentious, satisfactory instruments for their price. As a rule they do not make good training weapons, for they may discourage a beginner, or worse, induce a flinch by reason of a gritty trigger action. But, though I know it is swimming upstream, I must inveigh against plinking on the part of beginners. As I will try to explain later on, if you wish to become a good shot, stick to paper until you really are good.

I don't suppose I need point out that any good target or hunting .22 is a fine plinking pistol—it is the reverse that is not true. The appeal of a plinker lies mainly in low cost, and stinting on the cost of weapons is never a good idea.

A .22 plinker can be had for a very low price, and naturally the most inexpensive versions of the type are of very poor quality. In some cases they are so badly made as to be dangerous to anyone using them. It is a good idea to spend a little more money and get something that will be serviceable. One hundred dollars is about the lower limit for a plinker which will give satisfaction, and two hundred may be a better figure than that.

Cap and Ball

In recent years there has developed a vogue for the shooting of nineteenth-century firearms, both long and short. The emphasis has been upon the muzzle-loading, black-powder weapons, both cap and flint lock. As a result, quite a little industry has been promoted in Western Europe for the sole purpose of supplying replicas of antique firearms to the mysterious Americans. Clearly the serious collector of old guns will not usually risk his treasured originals by shooting them. These replica weapons are fully as serviceable as the originals were when they were produced for serious use, and sometimes better made. They sell for what the traffic will bear, which is occasionally a touch on the high side, but they make attractive den ornaments as well as offering interesting sporting possibilities. And they are not to be disregarded as fighting tools, for they can be both accurate and powerful.

While some single-shot dueling-type replicas are available, most interest centers around the .36 and .44 caliber revolvers of Colt and Remington design. Experimenting with these can be quite good fun, and there is a nostalgic glamor about using our grandfathers' weapons. Actually a cap-and-ball re-

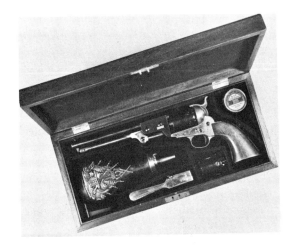

The Navy Arms Company's replica of the Colt Navy .36 of 1851.

The author's presentation Commander. This little gun also shoots, averaging 2¾-inch groups at 50 yards.

volver is a dreadful nuisance to load and to clean (the fictional "stink" of gunpowder refers specifically to black powder, which contains sulphur) and some people, including this writer, prefer to use one only when there is a staff available for the non-shooting tasks, but to many this is an enjoyable part of the game. And ammunition costs are really vastly less. It is estimated that you can shoot a "Navy" (Colt .36 Model of 1851) all afternoon for $1.00—and that can't be said of a .45 auto.

Barrel Length

There is a good deal of misunderstanding, and resultant argument, about this subject. It hardly affects the major-caliber autos since, except for the Luger, they offer no option, but most .22's and nearly all revolvers may be had with barrels of various lengths.

Clearly, the shorter the barrel, the handier the weapon. A short pistol may be drawn a bit faster, and it packs into a smaller space. It also may be somewhat easier to flick between targets. Why, then, a long barrel?

The readiest answer of the layman is increased accuracy, but this is not necessarily true. Accuracy, or more precisely, hitting ability, can be thought of as either intrinsic or practical. Intrinsic accuracy is the ability of the weapon and ammunition to group shots in the same place. Practical accuracy is the ease with which the weapon lends itself to this purpose in the shooter's hands. Intrinsic accuracy may be measured in a machine rest. Practical accuracy is a subjective combination of gunner and gun.

In this light, barrel length has little or no effect upon intrinsic accuracy. Pistol bullets are short and thick, and such bullets, carrying a large portion of their mass at a relatively great distance from their axes, do not need much spinning for stability. Once such a bullet has traveled a few lengths in a straight line, and is spin-stabilized, it will fly as accurately as it will from a fifty-diameter tube. Thus the basic grouping ability of a pistol is far more dependent upon the quality of its manufacture than upon the length of its barrel. The notion may even be taken that the longer the barrel, the more chance of a flaw in it, and hence the greater probability of accuracy in a short barrel. However, modern manufacturing methods rather invalidate this view.

On the other hand, a long barrel may indeed affect practical accuracy, and oddly enough in both directions. A long barrel provides a long sight radius, and it is geometrically undeniable that the greater the distance between the sights the greater precision of the sighting process. The drawback is that a long sight radius emphasizes his errors to the shooter, and may demoralize him. The sight picture of a snubby looks rock solid to the eye, and brings a feeling of confidence which may be of greater importance in achieving hits than such technical imprecision as may accompany it. All this is most difficult to test with any real validity, and becomes eventually a matter of subjective preference. I think I can hit a little better with a long barrel, but there are plenty of good shots who feel otherwise.

Apart from accuracy, a long barrel has other and more positive advantages, especially in weapons of great power. The longer a bullet remains in the tube, the longer its duration of thrust. This means something to a handloader, for while factories must load for a compromise of barrel lengths, the home-loader can match his powder to his barrel and gain quite a lot of velocity in a long tube. For example, Hercules #2400 was intended as a small-case rifle powder, and is quite slow-burning for use in a pistol. It will not burn completely in 4-, 5-, or 6-inch barrels, but it works just fine in the long, Smith & Wesson 8⅜-inch option. It shoves all the way down the tube, achieving full velocity without a nervous pressure curve. A shorter barrel calls for a quicker push, which is achieved at the cost of higher stresses and sharper recoil. Various velocity tests have been conducted to determine the measurable velocity changes caused by varying the length of a pistol barrel, but I have as yet seen no tabulations which take all variables properly into consideration. There is some power advantage to a long barrel; how much is still open to question. As an oversimplified rule of thumb, you may take it that, in a high-velocity magnum revolver, you gain 100 f/s for each 2 inches of barrel between 4 and 8 inches. Specifically, a .41 shows 1500 f/s from the 8⅜-inch muzzle, 1350 from 6-inch, and 1250 from 4-inch (high-velocity, jacketed, soft-point, hunting round; factory loaded). Coincidentally, the .357 factory load, which claims 1430 f/s in the ballistic tables, shows 1105 f/s from the muzzle of a 2½-inch Python, which is somewhat short of a high-velocity .38 Special fired from a six-inch barrel. Velocity changes due to barrel lengths seem proportionately much less with standard-velocity loads.

A further matter, which also is important only with high-powered pistols, is blast. Both the noise and the flash from the muzzle are reduced by increasing barrel length, and both are serious with a full-velocity magnum.

And lastly, a long barrel increases a pistol's weight, and increases it out front where it best serves to dampen vertical rotation of the weapon on recoil. For this reason the 8⅜-inch Smiths are noticeably easier on the shooter than either the 6's or the 4's.

For these reasons I think a long barrel shows up well in a hunting pistol, where high velocity and extreme precision are important, and ease of portability and concealment are secondary. In a combat pistol these considerations are reversed, and the 4- and 5-inch barrels have the advantage.

RELIABILITY

Before leaving the subject of pistols proper, one more point should be made. There is a notion in some circles that the only reliable handgun is a revolver. This was true up until about 1900, but it has not been for a long time. The auto pistol was adopted by both the German and the U.S. Armies in the first decade of the twentieth century, after elaborate and rigorous testing. A properly made and maintained handgun, of any type, will function almost every time, and on very rare occasions it will fail. Autos will fail to feed and revolvers will skip. Autos will fail to extract and revolvers will pull bullets. A revolver will override a primer failure with a second pull on the trigger, but a jammed cylinder is usually harder to clear than a jammed slide. There is little to choose, for both weapon types are almost, but not absolutely, reliable.

The reason for the police use of revolvers is not reliability; it is safety. The auto user must be a little more familiar with his weapon than the revolver man if accidents are to be avoided, and a firearms accident involving a policeman seems harder to justify than one in the armed forces.

27

Ammunition

THE CARTRIDGE IS the heart of any firearm, and the most beautifully designed and built pistol can be no better than its ammunition. Furthermore, the power and efficiency of any handgun are completely dependent upon its particular cartridge design, and to a very large extent its accuracy also is a function of its cartridge. Naturally, for any particular round there are better and worse weapons; but, in general, the cartridge is a more significant element than the weapon itself.

It is therefore important that the shooter understand a few fundamentals about cartridge design, so that he may both select the most efficient caliber for his hands, and also use the proper ammunition in his piece once he has acquired it.

Except in the case of the rimfire .22's, which are used in both short and long guns, pistol ammunition is small in comparison with rifle ammunition. It is essentially less powerful, though the most powerful pistol loads overlap the lower zones of rifle power. Pistol cartridges are mainly straight-cased, as opposed to the bottle-necked rifle rounds, since they must work efficiently in short barrels, and efficient powder burning requires far greater proportional length when the bore is smaller in diameter than the case body. (In terms of volumetric efficiency the 5-inch barrel of a .45 auto pistol is equivalent, at 12½ expansions, to a 42-inch barrel in a .30/06.)

Pistol cartridges in use today may have been designed either for black or for smokeless powder. Since smokeless powder can be produced in a great variety of volume-to-power ratios, while black powder is fairly constant in this respect, the black-powder designs have larger cases than are efficient for smokeless, and give a false impression to the uninformed. For instance, the 9 mm. cartridge—a smokeless design—is quite a bit smaller than the .38 Special—a black-powder design—yet the 9 mm. is considerably the more powerful cartridge in standard loadings.

Centerfire pistol cartridges come in three basic patterns: those for revolvers, those for semiautomatics, and those for varminters (which are chiefly, but not necessarily, single-shots). The basic revolver design is straight-cased, seats on its rim, and is intended to fire a homogeneous, lead-alloy, inside-lubricated bullet. The basic auto design is straight-cased, but seats on its case mouth as its rim is of case diameter and its extractor groove is recessed. (One prominent example, the Super .38, is "semi-rimmed," with an extractor groove and a rim only slightly greater than case diameter. This permits it to seat on its rim and still feed efficiently in a box magazine.) The typical auto pistol cartridge uses a jacketed bullet made to take the bite of very shallow rifling, and is round-nosed or semi-pointed to assure reliable funneling into the breech. Both types have been successfully adapted to the "wrong" actions—the .45 auto cartridge to the service revolver, and the .38 Special cartridge to the target automatics—but these are specialized oddities.

The "varminters," still quite rare, are small-caliber, bottle-necked, high-velocity cartridges which attempt to make a rifle out of a pistol. Since they are both new and somewhat experimental, they do not classify readily, but they naturally need jacketed, pointed bullets to achieve their rifle-like performance.

Pistol ammunition is ignited by the same sort of primer used in rifles and shotguns, but since case length is much less, the length of the primer flame need not be as long. However, it must be hot and strong, particularly if the modern "ball" powders are used. Pistol powders must obviously be so composed as to burn properly in a short distance. In either rifle or pistol, powder which "burns out" before the bullet leaves the muzzle is inefficient in overcoming bore friction. (It is not generally known that with the .22 Long Rifle cartridge, any barrel longer than about 15 inches is wasteful, except as it increases the distance between the sights. On the other hand, a powder which takes longer to burn than bore time is also wasteful, since it simply blows part of its potential out into open air, making a large flash to no purpose. The arms companies naturally load for the average barrel length in general use for each cartridge type, and lean slightly in favor of too quick, rather than too slow, a rate of burning. The handloader traditionally uses very quick Bullseye for 2- to 4-inch barrels, medium Unique for 5- and 6-inch barrels, and #2400 for the long ones.

BULLETS

Pistol bullets are a problem. Not for target shooters, it's true, for if accuracy is the only need, it can be satisfied. But there are other purposes besides target shooting to which a pistol is suited, and these demand a tricky series of compromises if the weapon is to do all that it can.

Any bullet must meet three essentially different sets of requirements. First, it must seal the bore with a minimum of friction, taking all the powder's thrust without raising pressure unduly, take a firm and stable spin from the rifling without stripping or leading, and resist deformation of its base due to the heat and impact of discharge (interior ballistics). Second, it must fly straight and true in the air, without yawing or tumbling, retaining as much as possible of its initial velocity over its accurate range, overcoming the resistance of the air as efficiently as possible by its momentum and aerodynamic shape (exterior ballistics). And, third, it must transmit its impact energy to its intended target in a way best calculated to immobilize that target (terminal, or impact, ballistics).

It is clear that the foregoing requirements are largely contradictory. A thick, shallow projectile—almost a disk—is best inside the barrel. A long, pointed, streamlined needle flies best in air. And anything from a cupshaped meat chopper to a tungsten carbide drill bit may be needed on impact, depending on the characteristics of the target.

In dealing with pistol bullets, we have, fortunately, relatively little difficulty with exterior ballistics, since pistols, except for the varminters and an occasional magnum in the hands of a specialist, are short-range weapons. Flight characteristics (in 100- to 400-grain missiles) begin to affect performance seriously out beyond normal pistol ranges. There is room for opinion here, but while I can hardly accept the 50-foot outside limit suggested by many as the maximum effective range of a handgun, I do feel that a pistol has "run out" at 150 yards. On my old home range we set up a generous, though armless, steel silhouette at a measured 162 yards. I watched several of the world's best pistol shots engage this target over the years. Even with such masters, while it was not "safe," neither was it doomed, at least on the first shot. (I do not include the scope-sighted varminters in this observation, as they are not typical and their ballistic and functional characteristics are different.)

A glance at any service pistol bullet will confirm this idea, for they are without exception short and blunt, designed for good interior behavior and larger diameter, rather than for velocity retention at long range. Where 120–160 grains is standard for .36 caliber pistols, exterior ballistic tables call for an optimum diameter of .28 or less for this weight in rifles. While our .45 caliber pistol bullets weigh about 250 grains or a bit less, a rifle bullet of this diameter intended for use at long range crowds 550 grains.

So, in practical terms, pistol bullets are studied almost entirely from the view of interior and terminal ballistics, with exterior ballistics taking a rear seat.

Generally speaking, "plain lead" bullets are easy to make, easy on barrels, provide fine terminal behavior, and tend to leave portions of themselves in the barrel when driven hard. Conversely, jacketed bullets are more expensive, somewhat more accurate, harder on barrels, will not "lead" or strip, will not deform at the base, and tend to inefficient action on impact except as to penetration.

It may be well to point out here that deep penetration may or may not be desirable in itself. Obviously a bullet must get well into its target to do its job, but if it goes too deep it squanders its limited energy on the far side, and, in police work, this constitutes a public hazard. A handgunner can rarely predict whether a given bullet will be required to interrupt a thin, un-armored bandit's career, or to drive clear through a car body, and one bullet cannot do both jobs equally well. A popular answer to this, in police circles, is to alternate "stoppers" with "piercers" in cylinder or magazine. This is probably a better solution than a full measure of compromise bullets which can do neither task especially well.

As noted, revolver rifling is cut deep for plain lead bullets, while that of autos is meant for copper jackets and is consequently shallow. A lead bullet fired in shallow rifling may simply strip, ramming straight ahead while slivers are shaved off its surface and left in the bore. Such behavior loses both power and accuracy, and quickly fouls a bore, with progressively deteriorative results. Also, even deep rifling holds a lead bullet only up to a velocity of around 1200–1300 foot-seconds, beyond which trouble arises. Of course, this limit may be raised by hardening the bullet alloy with tin, antimony, or zinc, but the harder the bullet the less efficient its action on impact, so in some cases the solution of one problem creates another. In any case an auto pistol bullet at anything over about 900 foot-seconds, and any handgun bullet at more than 1200, is going to need a skin harder than soft lead, so we can proceed from there.

The so-called "gas-check," a base fitting of harder metal which takes the powder's thrust, has been used from time to time, but without any great success, to my knowledge. It does prevent base deformation, but it does practically nothing about leading or stripping since this occurs forward of the gas-check. Also, in revolvers, there is a distinct possibility of separation as the bullet jumps the gap between barrel and cylinder. This is also true of half-base-jacket bullets, on which the gas-check extends part way up the body of the projectile; and even of full cylinder base jackets, which continue forward only to the beginning of the bullet's forward taper. It appears that, to bond

A selection of jacketed pistol bullets (left to right): metal piercing, military service, Shooting Associates' Double D, Speer half-jacket Keith.

Bullets may be jacketed from the nose (left) or from the base (right).

jacket and core reliably, the jacket must actually constrict at the point, though not necessarily to the degree found on soft-point rifle bullets. A slight "crimp," starting the jacket inward, seems to suffice. Of course none of this applies to military-type jacketed bullets, which are jacketed over the nose and are open at the base.

General Hatcher states flatly that a jacketed soft-point bullet cannot be made to expand at pistol velocities. I think that statement should be qualified. It is certainly true that ordinary pistol bullets rarely upset, or "mushroom," under ordinary circumstances. In Sir Sydney Smith's great book on forensic medicine there are photographs of a number of .32 automatic bullets involved in a political assassination. Each is deeply cross cut at the point, the intersecting cuts extending back almost to bore contact, and yet the bullets taken from the body of the victim are indistinguishable from those unfired except for the rifling grooves. On the other hand, one can easily force even a nose-jacketed bullet to deform by firing it into a very resistant substance such as "wet pack" (slick paper soaked in water and then pressed into blocks). I think it is true that a rifle-type soft-point, or hollow-point, will not usually expand at impact velocities of under 1800 foot-seconds on a small amount of soft animal tissue, but expansion may well occur on massive targets, and specialized pistol bullets may be constructed which will expand on comparatively light resistance, though they are not readily available for sale.

Hollow-pointing is not the panacea that many believe it to be. I have known it to cause serious accuracy problems—whether due to air turbulence or a misaligned center of gravity I cannot say—and it does not insure expansion at pistol impact velocities. I have seen exit holes in husky mule deer hit with the 225-grain hollow-point from the .44 Magnum that measured a neat .43 inch in diameter. I have also recovered .38 Super jacketed hollow-points that hit small game, passed through, and simply mashed the cavity shut on the ground beyond.

Thus it is that quick and reliable expansion in pistol bullets, especially in those of normal impact velocities (below about 1400 foot-seconds), is hard to get.

Progressive expansion of the .44 Magnum bullet, as resistance is hardened.

In revolver bullets we are much more fortunate, for revolver ammunition need not function in a self-loading mechanism, and revolver rifling is deep enough to hold up to about the speed of sound without trouble. This permits the use in revolvers of the semi-wadcutter, or Keith-form, bullet which combines most of the characteristics desirable in a handgun projectile. The Keith bullet is a cylinder with a conical point which is cut off flat at about two-thirds bore diameter. In addition, at the commencement of the cone's taper it is not quite bore diameter, which leaves a sharp shoulder of full diameter to back up the reduced caliber flat-point. Such a missile provides flight characteristics good enough for pistol ranges, together with really excellent terminal behavior. Whether or not impact velocity is sufficient to upset it, a Keith bullet chops its way into a target, transmitting its energy rapidly to target tissue from the point of entrance on. The sharp shoulder does not press aside a blood vessel or a nerve trunk; it cuts a chunk out of it. According to the Hatcher researches, such a bullet has nearly 40 percent more stopping power, assuming adequate penetration, than a round-nosed hard-jacketed bullet, and 25 percent more than a round-nosed lead bullet.

I repeat that the Keith bullet achieves its terminal effect regardless of any disruption, expansion, or "mushrooming." If a round-nosed bullet may be so deformed by impact on tissue as to increase its diameter to any great extent, the situation changes. Bullet expansion naturally increases stopping power in direct proportion to the cross-sectional area of the wound channel, which increases as the square of its diameter. However—and this is important—a bullet does not expand instantly on impact. It takes a little time, and, in the case of a powerful cartridge, such time may exceed its time in target. In the first inch of penetration a Keith bullet is transmitting as well as it is likely to; whereas if it takes 6 inches of soft tissue to mushroom a soft point, the bullet may reach its proper diameter only at exit. Such a bullet recovered from the woodwork might look extremely efficient but actually be much less so than a flat point which did not deform at all. Of course if the target is big enough to stop the bullet, all the bullet's energy is transmitted regardless of expansion or lack of it. Even so, a short, thick wound channel—provided it reaches the vitals—is usually more damaging to the nervous system than a long, thin one. Clearly, neither a thin penetration nor a shallow flesh wound is likely to suffice in any situation desperate enough to call for pistol fire.

The excellent Keith form of bullet is now almost standard in the more serious revolver cartridges as factory loaded, and it is very common also in handloads for both revolvers and auto pistols. The auto must be modified to feed it reliably, and this may be the first thing one has done when he acquires a 1911 .45.

In the .357, .41, and .44 Magnums velocities may be reached which lead bullets will not handle. Leading—leaving small chunks of lead soldered to the bore—has always been a nuisance with high-velocity pistols, even when various sorts of gas-checks are used. Though the magnums have fairly deep rifling there comes a point where a full jacket is indicated. Some researchers maintain that a proper alloy and correct lubrication can make homogeneous bullets satisfactory at any pistol velocity, but jackets seem to be necessary for the rest of us at 1400 foot-seconds or better. These jackets must cover the base and extend the full length of bore contact and beyond. Recent laboratory tests sponsored by the N.R.A. indicate that plain cylinder jackets, with no forward crimp, give unsatisfactory performance. Properly designed round-nosed, jacketed, soft-points and hollow-points are now offered by the factories in .357, .41 and .44. Such ammunition needs full velocity for efficient terminal behavior, and I feel that it's best used for hunting. For combat use in a short barrel the Keith-form semi-wadcutter is probably superior.

One notable bullet that should be mentioned here is the Norma .44. This Swedish product had a truncated cone for a point with no bore shoulder. Its point was flat and fairly large. Its core was of soft lead, but its jacket was of mild *steel,* coated inside and out with what appears to be cupronickel. This jacket extended almost to the tip, providing plenty of crimp onto the core. This was a bullet for heavy game, as it would expand only on severe resistance. It would mushroom perfectly in 17 inches of wet pack, which is roughly equivalent to 4 feet of solid muscle. On light resistance it did not upset at all, behaving like a "solid." (One was recovered from the hindquarters of a trophy moose, having entered the chest. It showed only rifling marks to indicate it had been fired.) This Norma bullet was wonderfully accurate, showing consistent 5-inch groups at 100 yards. Either as factory loaded or in handloads, it was the first choice in .44 Magnum target competition, as long as it was sold.

HANDLOADING

Centerfire ammunition is expensive. At around 40¢ per round it effectively precludes adequate practice except on the part of range personnel and the very wealthy. One hundred rounds a week is about the right amount to keep a master shot in trim, and at retail rates a year's supply of ammunition can work out to nearly ten times the cost of a good pistol. (This is a fairly clear-cut explanation of why most of the best shots are range officers, for pistol shooters are, in my experience, a remarkably poverty-stricken lot.)

One answer to this problem is to load your own ammunition, as hand-loading not only lets you make up custom ammunition for your particular needs, but can get your ammunition costs down to a manageable figure. Ray Chapman, a combat master who is *not* a range officer, once worked out a cost analysis on his .45 loading operation, since he expends ammunition at an impressive rate. With all equipment paid for, using reclaimed cases, getting his lead free (wheel-weights from an auto shop), and not counting his time, he came up with a figure of .08 per round—which is about half of the retail cost of a .22 Long Rifle cartridge. That was twenty years ago, but today it could be done for 2¢.

Now of course, his complete "factory" had to be bought—at the equivalent of about three high-grade pistols—and his brass must be replaced from time to time, and his time must also be evaluated; but still the saving is huge. What's more, the ammunition is superb. Ray's "select grade," in once-fired uniform brass, is fully up to match specifications.

Handloading is a field in itself, and I do not feel that a detailed study of it should be included here. Various good technical manuals exist which will guide the student in his efforts, and I think it better to confine these observations to the general aspects of the operation.

Loading equipment varies greatly in type, all the way from a simple, one-at-a-time tong tool to a highly sophisticated home factory. Since the main reason for a pistol shooter to load is quantity, I think it false economy to select a slow and laborious rig even if it is cheaper. A rifleman may wish to make up ten of this or twenty of that, for experimental purposes, but the pistol shooter thinks mainly in terms of thousand-round lots. Thus the big "repeaters," notably the Star, which perform half-a-dozen functions at each stroke, are well worth the initial outlay.

Loading is a tedious, monotonous business which appeals to some and not at all to others. It requires unflagging concentration, and must not be interrupted by phone calls, screaming children, door-to-door salesmen, or chit-chat. One does not smoke while loading, for fairly obvious reasons. Each round must be *exactly* like every other, in every way, or accuracy vanishes. *One* mistake, such as a reversed primer, a skipped charge, or a double charge, can be serious. It's not an exaggeration to say that an error in loading could conceivably cost you your life, so if you are prone to errors, or find concentration a bore, loading may not be for you. I know a pharmacist who loads as a form of relaxation—he would actually rather load than shoot. On the other hand, I find it a dreadful drag.

And the actual loading is only part of the exercise. Reclaimed cases must be washed and should be polished. Bullets must be cast, sized and lubricated. Bullets may be purchased ready made, or swaged one-by-one in a press, but both of these courses raise costs.

So you see that assembling one's own ammunition has both advantages
and drawbacks. If you shoot a lot it is almost a necessity, for even an elaborate
layout will pay for itself in less than a season.

If you shoot only now and then, or if you can afford military ammunition
(nobody can afford commercial ammunition), or if you can work out a satisfactory barter arrangement with a custom loader, you may do well without
loading your own. But be thankful if you are one of those who really likes
loading ammunition, for it is probably inevitable and you might as well relax
and enjoy it.

A LIST OF PISTOL CARTRIDGES

The following is prepared as a summary of the basic characteristics of the
various pistol cartridges now in use. It is not entirely complete for there are
many odd examples which are out of production or so rare as to be collectors'
items. There are too many different types available as it is, and we could do
without most of them. Important cartridges, which serve a useful purpose, are
marked with an asterisk.

*The .22 Rimfire Short

First introduced in 1854, this is the oldest small-arms cartridge still manufactured for sale. It propels a .224-inch, 29-grain bullet at 865 foot-seconds
from a 6-inch barrel, or at 1035 in its "high-velocity" loading. A high-velocity
load in a .22 Short seems to be about like a supercharged lawnmower. If you
want more power you should have started with something else. However, the
"hot" load is often all you can find in the stores, and at least it does no harm.

The short is an accurate round, though not quite so much so as the long
rifle, and is very popular with shooting galleries and shooters of the International Rapid Fire course. It should not, however, be used on live targets larger
than starlings or mice.

Short, Long, and Long Rifle .22 rimfire ammunition is largely interchangeable in the same weapon, but there are exceptions. An auto pistol will
not feed the three rounds through the magazine, though all may be fired single-shot from the breech. A revolver usually takes all three equally well. (The
.22 WMR does *not* fit in this family.)

The .22 Rimfire Long

This was an interim experiment of the past century and should have died
at birth. However, it is still made for hardware store clerks who do not wish to
explain about the long-rifle cartridge. It combines the short bullet in the
long-rifle case and lacks the accuracy of either. Forget it.

*The .22 Rimfire Long Rifle

This modest little round is the backbone of the firearms trade. It is highly sophisticated and superbly accurate. As a match cartridge it takes its .224-inch 40-grain bullet to some 950 foot-seconds from a 6-inch barrel, and to 1125 in hot form. A high-velocity long-rifle cartridge makes some sense, because it may be used in a trail gun where a little edge in power may be most desirable in anchoring a cottontail or an iguana. Probably it should be produced only in standard-velocity-solid, and high-speed hollow-point forms—one for the range and one for the trail—but you can get almost any combination you desire. Fifty rounds, at about 3½¢ each, take up little more space than one 12-gauge shotshell.

The .22 Winchester Magnum Rimfire

This is a souped-up .22 rimfire cartridge taking a jacketed 40-grain bullet to 1550 foot-seconds from a 6½-inch barrel. This is all right except that each round now costs 10¢. A .22 centerfire can be reloaded to greater velocity for considerably less. This may be a fine back-packer's cartridge, but I find it very limited in purpose.

The .22 Fireball

This is a rifle cartridge, specifically the .222 Remington, shortened .30 inch. In a 10½-inch barrel it gives a 50-grain bullet an honest 2650. Since it is at present adapted only to bolt actions, it is difficult to fit into the handgun picture. It is neither a target nor a defensive cartridge, and as a varminter it is surpassed by most rifles with only a bit more bulk.

The .25 ACP (6.35 mm.)

This is a 1906 design which should never have happened. It is adapted to cheap, blow-back, pocket pistols which are useful only as threats. Anyone shot with this cartridge is apt to become emotional and resort to violence. The .22 Long Rifle is a better defense cartridge as well as being otherwise useful. Ballistics of the .25 are 50 grains (fully point jacketed) at about 800 foot-seconds.

The .30-Caliber Auto Pistol Cartridges (7.62 mm., 7.63 mm., 7.65 mm.)

When the famous old "broom-handle" 7.63 mm. Mauser pistol of 1896 appeared (and subaltern Winston Churchill blooded it at the Battle of Omdurman some weeks later) it introduced a new breed of handgun cartridge—the small-case, small-bore, hard-jacketed high-velocity military cartridges of the twentieth century. The Mauser spat its 85-grain bullet at the unheard-of velocity of 1400 foot-seconds from its 5½-inch barrel, and while this is not exactly the answer to all defensive pistol design problems, it was certainly a departure.

Shortly thereafter, the .30 Luger (7.65 mm.) was announced with similar but lesser ballistics (93 grains at 1200 in a 4½-inch barrel). The designators for the two cartridges differ, and because of case shape they do *not* interchange, but they are both of exactly .309-inch caliber.

The Tokarev pistol used by the Russians in World War II—called 7.62 mm. just to confuse things—takes a cartridge of the same outside specifications as the Mauser but loaded about 300 foot-seconds light. The Mauser ammunition works reliably in the Tokarev, though it strains it a bit, but the Russian ammunition may not operate the slide on the Mauser.

All three cartridges are bottle-necked and intended for use in locked-breech pistols or in submachine guns. They must not be confused with the small, straight-cased .32 auto cartridge (7.65 mm. Browning).

The .30 autos have a good potential as small-game cartridges though they must be loaded with properly expanding bullets to do the job. In any case, the pistols are increasingly rare and the ammunition, while still being manufactured, is an unlikely item on a store shelf. For defensive use, these rounds are marginal, though if bone is hit the Mauser's high short-range velocity can make it a stinger.

The .32 ACP (7.65 mm. Browning)

This is a semi-rim small-case smokeless design of practically no utility, though it is enormously popular, especially in Europe. Like the .30-caliber U.S. Carbine it is much more popular with those who have never seen anyone shot with it than with those who have. It is adapted to small, light, cheap, blow-back, pocket autos which are marvelously easy to carry and conceal, but

A pair of .30's, the old .32-20 (left) and a wildcat cartridge made by necking down a .44 Magnum.

which serve only to give the wearer a false sense of security. 71-grains, full jacket, at 950 foot-seconds.

The Short .32 Revolver Cartridges (.32 Short Colt, .32 Long Colt, interchangeable and .32 Smith & Wesson, .32 Smith & Wesson Long, .32 Colt New Police, interchangeable)

Except for the .32 Smith & Wesson Long, which is an accurate light target load, these rounds are a complete waste of time. These are the cartridges for the bureau-drawer-specials with which badly trained children have accidents. They cannot be recommended for any serious purpose. (As a rather conclusive testimonial to the effect of a .32 revolver, General Hatcher was once struck in the gun hand by an adversary who was using one. He felt only a slight numbness which in no way affected the accuracy of his return fire.)

The .32-20 (.32 W.C.F.)

This is rather a good small-game cartridge, using a 115-grain bullet at up over 1000 foot-seconds and factory loaded with a well-designed expanding bullet. No pistol is now made to take it, though ammunition is still produced for sale. It's quite similar in impact effect to the .30-caliber auto pistols. High-velocity ammunition was once made in this caliber for use in rifles only. Such ammunition is unsafe in revolvers, and the boxes are so labeled.

The .380 ACP (9 mm. Browning Short)

This is an attempt to produce a cartridge for a light, low-pressure, blowback auto that still has some modicum of stopping power. Its 95-grain bullet at 950 foot-seconds is quite a bit superior in this regard to any .32 auto, and nearly any pistol which may be had in .32 ACP is also available in .380. If one simply had to have a minimum pistol for purposes of concealment, a .380 might do. I wouldn't stake my own life on it, but then I don't ride on bald tires either, while many do.

The 9 mm. Makarov (.38 Russian)

This is the new service round of the U.S.S.R. Of .36 caliber and taking a 94-grain bullet at 1033 foot-seconds, it lies somewhere ahead of the .380 but quite a way short of the 9 mm. Parabellum or the .38 Special. The pistol to take it has an unlocked breech, as evidently the saving in machine work thus obtained is more important to the Russians than the efficiency of the weapon. Its cartridge does not interchange with any other standard round.

The Short .38 Revolver Cartridges (.38 Smith & Wesson, .38 Colt New Police, interchangeable and .38 Short & Long Colt)

These are old cartridges of low power, relating to the .32 Short revolver cartridges as the .380 relates to the .32 ACP. That is, they are used in weapons of the same type and size, but with a larger bore diameter. They are not satisfactory as target, hunting, or defensive loads and should be allowed to become obsolete.

The .38 Special

This is the standard U.S. Police cartridge, and undoubtedly the most popular revolver round in America. It is extremely accurate, and has been loaded to so many different requirements that its ballistics are problematical. Its basic "service" load is not much—158-grains round-nosed at 870 foot-seconds—but it can be loaded with Keith bullets of the same weight at over 1100, which is more like it.

Its prime uses are three: It is a superb target cartridge, it is a nice short-range small-game load, and it is the most powerful round you can feed into a two-inch aluminum snubby.

The .357 Magnum

This is a hot .38 Special. Bore size and bullet weights are the same, but velocity is increased, if you wish. The original figures for the cartridge were

Some .38's (left to right): the 9 mm. Parabellum, the Super .38, the .38 Special, and the .357.

A sampling of the great variety of ammunition available for the U.S. Service pistol (left to right): government service, commercial standard-velocity target, commercial mid-range target, general purpose handload, Western 230 metal-piercing, Remington 173 metal-piercing, base jacketed combat handload, Shooting Associates' custom combat and hunting load.

158 grains at an enthusiastic 1510 in an 8⅜-inch barrel. This was pretty fierce, and provided accuracy, energy, flat trajectory, and stopping power equal to that of a big bore—more if bone was hit. Immediately the cartridge was loaded light, and barrels were shortened. Today a factory load in a 4-inch barrel shows 1245 foot-seconds, practically the same as a .38 Special loaded hot in a 6-inch revolver. Still, a hot .38 Special is not entirely to be sneezed at, especially if that's all that's to be had, and the .357 stands as the most powerful load that can be crammed into a medium-framed revolver. If you want more steam from a sixgun you must go to a considerably more cumbersome piece. Any .357 revolver will chamber and fire .38 Special ammunition.

The 9 mm. Parabellum (9 mm. Luger)

This is a small-case, smokeless-powder cartridge of almost universal popularity. It is *the* caliber for Europe's pistols and submachine guns, and it may

The Magnum family (left to right): the .357, the .41, and the .44.

even become ours if we standardize with NATO. It's a good round, showing an average of 1120 foot-seconds for its 125-grain bullet, with the usual military handicap of very poor bullet design. The Parabellum is generally comparable to the .38 Special, with a little more velocity and a little less weight for the same caliber. Some fine pistols are made for it, but it must always fall short of real stopping efficiency as compared with a big bore pistol. Its relative stopping power is about half that of the .45 ACP.

The Super .38

This is a sort of hot Parabellum, delivering a little more weight (130 grains) at somewhat higher speed (1300 foot-seconds). Only a few guns are made for it—principally Colt and Star—and its ballistic advantage over the Luger cartridge is offset by the rarity of its ammunition. Remington at one time made a fine jacketed hollow-point for the Super, but it is no longer in production. It is very popular in Mexico, where the .45 is restricted, and it offers specific trajectory advantages over the latter. It's a fine cartridge for a trail gun which may be called upon to double as a defense weapon.

An earlier and lesser cartridge, the .38 ACP, has exactly the same exterior dimensions and will usually operate in a Super. However, Super ammunition is dangerous in a pistol intended only for the .38 ACP.

Note: All .38's mentioned up to this point are actually .36's, measuring around .357-inch in groove diameter.

The .38-40 (38 W.C.F.)

This is the middle member of the Winchester Center Fire series, designed long ago on the rather foolish concept that one cartridge could serve equally well in both pistol and rifle. The .38-40 is a true .40 caliber. It is a powerful round, hurling its 180-grain bullet to nearly 1000 foot-seconds. It may be considered the smallest of the big bores, with about the same relative stopping power as a .357. No weapons are now made for it, which is a pity, for while we do have better loads, lesser items have been introduced since its demise.

The 10 mm. Auto Pistol Cartridge

This is a new development intended to supplant both the 9 mm. Parabellum and the .45 ACP. It is a very powerful cartridge, essentially similar to the .41 magnum in its police loading, yet it is compact and adaptable to the double-column magazines which are now fashionable. It fires a .40 caliber JTC bullet of 200-grains at an experimental velocity of 1165 foot-seconds. In production trim this will probably be reduced to about 1100 foot-seconds. Its recoil is very slightly greater than that of the .45 ACP, but in return it delivers more energy at 100 meters than the .45 does at the muzzle. It can be fired initially only from the Bren Ten auto pistol, but it would seem to have an additional future in the very advanced P7 pocket pistol.

The .41 Long Colt

This obsolete round is mentioned only to point out that it was never actually .41 caliber and that it cannot be used as sub-caliber ammunition for the .41 Magnum, as the .38 Special is for the .357 and the .44 Special is for the .44 Magnum. The .41 Long Colt is actually a .388 while the .41 Magnum measures a true .410. No weapons are now made for this cartridge, which pushes a 200-grain bullet at 730 foot-seconds, but the ammunition is still in production.

The .41 Magnum

This cartridge is factory loaded in two power levels, one a high-speed jacketed hunting round and the other a medium velocity combat load with a Keith-form, lead bullet. Both bullets weigh 210 grains, but the h. v. load starts at 1500 foot-seconds from an 8⅜-inch hunting barrel (1350 in a 6-inch) while the combat load shows 940 foot-seconds in a 4-inch combat barrel (990 in a 6-inch).

This is obviously a very powerful cartridge, but in its hunting load it is less all around than its big brother the .44 Magnum, while in its combat version it is not quite up to its predecessor, the .44 Special, when the latter is properly loaded. Besides, a .44 Special can be had at 39½ ounces, while a .41 with the same length of barrel will go a full 48.

In fairness, it should be noted that the .41 light load is the best *factory* combat pistol cartridge now available. The fact that almost any big bore pistol could be loaded to similar specifications, without bringing out a new caliber, tends to obscure this fact.

The .44-40 (.44 W.C.F.)

This is another obsolete cartridge for which weapons are no longer made, but it is interesting to note that its ballistics, dating from black-powder days, are nearly identical with those of the new .41's combat load. The .44-40 takes a 200-grain bullet at 935 foot-seconds in a 6-inch barrel. It has not the inherent accuracy of the .44 Russian-Special-Magnum tribe, so it becomes redundant, but it is too good a cartridge to throw away.

The .44 Russian

No longer made, this is the ancestor of the .44 Special, and the Russian cartridge may be used in .44 Special and Magnum cylinders. It was a light load, suitable for top-break revolvers, and showed 750 foot-seconds with a 246-grain bullet.

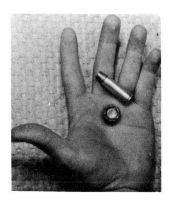 

Perfect expansion of a Remington gas check .44 bullet
obtained on sand.

Magnum options: .357 combat and metal-
piercing; .41 combat and hunting; .44 steel-
jacketed soft-point; full-jacket solid.

The .44 Special

According to Elmer Keith, this is "by far the best designed of the large-caliber revolver cartridges." The .44 Special is a superb caliber. It is brilliantly accurate, comparatively mild to shoot, and may be loaded to as great a power level as a man can control in rapid fire. It is available in the excellent Smith & Wesson Models #21 and #24, which are in my opinion the ultimate in large-frame police revolvers, and in its 4-inch version it weighs a manageable 37 ounces.

Factory loadings for the .44 Special leave a good bit to be desired, pushing a round-nosed 246-grain bullet to about 750 foot-seconds from a 6-inch barrel, but this is essentially gallery ammunition. Eighteen-and-a-half of 2400 will get a 250-grain Keith bullet up to a spry 1200 foot-seconds in the same gun, and cut back to about 1000, this provides splendid stopping power with enough docility for precise burst control. If a man prefers a revolver for self-defense this is the cartridge he should probably settle on. All the .44's of this tribe are, actually, of .43-inch caliber.

The .44 Magnum

This is the powerhouse—the big-game pistol cartridge. It is more completely discussed in connection with the revolvers that use it, but here we should note that it is a long-case .44 Special. Specials may be shot accurately from a magnum cylinder, though the reverse is not true. The .44 Magnum is as accurate as the Special and quite considerably more powerful. In fact its power is somewhat difficult to employ, for it goes right through almost anything, from bears to bulletproof glass, so fast that it hardly has time to transmit much of its thunderous energy to its target. I do not favor it as a combat round, as it is hard to use rapidly and accurately at the same time. Loaded down a bit, the .44 Magnum is just like a .44 Special for combat use—that is, just great.

Note: Any .44 Magnum will chamber both .44 Special and .44 Russian ammunition. Any .44 Special will chamber .44 Russian. Magnum ammunition, however, will not chamber in a Special cylinder, nor Special in a Russian.

The .45 ACP

This is the biggest of the small-case, rimless, smokeless-powder, military-type auto pistol cartridges, and it is one of the outstanding developments in small arms. It combines accuracy, stopping power, and mild manners in a way only duplicated by the .44 Special. The military load is both a bit light, at 860 foot-seconds, and attenuated by its Geneva-Convention bullet, but military ammunition is useful mainly for practice. Frontier Ammunition now loads a 230-grain bullet of "Jacketed Truncated Cone" (JTC) form, which is probably the best factory option. Loaded 100 foot-seconds faster and with a proper combat bullet, the .45 auto comes on like a well-trained rhinoceros. Stopping failures are rare even with the military load: they're just about out of the question with proper ammunition.

While the .45 ACP cartridge may be used in the 1917-type service revolvers, rimless extraction without the easily lost half-moon clips poses a problem. Because of this the .45 auto-rim cartridge is made, duplicating the forward structure of the ACP round but with a rim to engage the extractor of the revolver. Naturally, while ACP ammunition may be used in both revolvers and autos, auto-rim ammunition is only for revolvers.

The .45 Colt

This old black-powder cartridge was introduced with the original 1873 Single Action Army Pistol, now affectionately known as the Peacemaker. The original load was a 255-grain bullet and 40 grains of black powder, which came on at a vigorous 910 foot-seconds—as solid a man-stopper as anyone could wish. Modern smokeless loads go out at about 860 foot-seconds but this is still a fearsome pistol cartridge. It's a pity that only old-fashioned single-action revolvers are now being made to take it; but only emotionally, for in modern revolvers the .44 Special is a little better in every department.

The .455 Webley

This is a small-case, big-bore revolver cartridge of excellent defensive characteristics. It takes a 265-grain bullet at about 600 foot-seconds and is thus mild enough for a small gun and yet a vigorous man-stopper. It was the British service cartridge for many years and, while now obsolescent, it is a very superior round for its purpose. In the R.I.C. "Bulldog" snubby it is possibly the best undercover revolver ever made.

28

Holsters and Accessories

HOLSTERS

The essential quality of a handgun is readiness. A handgun may be kept in readiness in a desk drawer, a glove compartment, a headboard, or on a muzzle peg beneath a cash register, but all such arrangements depend upon the shooter's being in a certain place when trouble comes. Far better is a good holster.

Good holsters are not common. This is not to say that good leather and good workmanship are rare, but that good design is. This is because very little comparative or competitive work is conducted in this field, and consequently most shooters, outfitters, and holster makers simply do not know what is required. Take the matter of trigger exposure. A majority of standard holsters are cut to expose the trigger to the shooter's finger as the weapon rides at rest. This is wrong. Proper technique requires that the trigger finger stay straight, and outside the trigger guard, until the piece is nearly on target. In a good holster the trigger guard is completely covered, both to prevent leg shots and to develop proper drawing habits. Likewise a good holster allows the rest of the hand to slide into its firing position before the pistol starts to move, yet most designs require the pistol to be well underway before a proper grip may be taken.

Holster selection, therefore, calls for thought. Just anything available will not suffice.

The purpose of a holster is to carry the weapon comfortably on the person, safe and ready, secure against loss. Other considerations, such as protection from the elements, accessibility to either hand from any position, and concealment, may also matter. Speed is always a factor, for the chances are that if you need a pistol at all, you need it immediately. However, some of the speed refinements found on competition holsters, such as cutaway fronts, exaggerated set-outs, and tie-downs, offer very small speed increments in exchange for rather severe limitations on practicality, and are thus not usually indicated in a full-duty holster. Let's say that if an experienced man, with a bit of practice, can get off a controlled shot (a sure torso hit at 10 yards) in around one second, including reaction time, his holster is fast enough for general use. Competition, of course, is another matter, for contests are sometimes won by speed differentials which would be of consequence only if two adversaries started on the same signal, a virtually impossible coincidence.

As to method of carry, holsters may be generally classified as waist-band, gun-belt, and shoulder harness.

Waist-Band Holsters

The waist-band holster is simple, cheap, and fairly concealable. Worn under a coat it affords good protection to the weapon. It is not especially fast, but with practice it can be fast enough for noncompetitive shooting. When the kidney position is used, as favored by the F.B.I., it is a bit dangerous if hurried. (A friend of mine once drilled himself neatly through the right buttock trying to speed up an F.B.I. draw.) It is also quite awkward to reach while sitting in an armchair, and miserably uncomfortable in a car with seat belt fastened. It also interferes with a pack.

The appendix position (forward of the hip on the strong side, with the muzzle raked about 15 ° forward) is both faster and safer than the kidney position, but it is a bit more obvious. It's rather good for a plainclothes policeman who doesn't particularly care whether his sidearm is spotted or not.

The spleen position, or waist-band cross-draw, has most of the qualities of the appendix position, and in addition is quite a bit more accessible when seated and to the weak hand as well. I favor it if a waist-band holster of any sort is to be used.

The appendix position.   The spleen position.

I have not yet found a way to construct a waist-band holster which allows a solid shooting grip to be taken on contact, since the pistol rides snugly against the body. This is a serious disadvantage. All waist-band holsters must ride rigidly on the belt, which means that a wide loop and a rather broad belt are required. If fashion or inconspicuousness dictates a flimsy belt, it will be necessary to have a belt made which is narrow at the buckle but widens immediately to about 1¼ inches. This may necessitate alteration of the belt loops on some trousers. Obviously, the holster's belt loop must fit the belt exactly, for any sort of smoothness in drawing.

Gun-Belt Holsters

A gun belt holster can be very safe and very fast, but only uniformed personnel can normally wear a weapon on a gun belt. The defensive pistol is

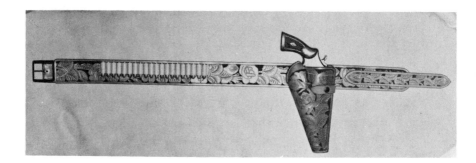

The Berns-Martin split-front gun-belt holster

The author's "full-race" competition rig, by Alfonso.

Ray Chapman's competition rig, by Andy Anderson.

The set-out on the Alfonso "Western Police" rig, showing a solid gun-hand contact with thumb on the safety and trigger finger straight.

much more often and more usefully carried on the trouser belt; therefore the gun belt holster is largely restricted to military and police situations, and formalized competition.

While practical shooting competition is as free from regulation as possible, it finally became necessary to specify that all holsters used in practical competition be truly practical. This pretty well rules out the gun belt holster except for policemen who choose to wear the equipment that they are required to wear on the street.

Shoulder Holsters

A shoulder holster, if properly designed, has many important advantages. It is safe, concealable, accessible to either hand from any position, highly protective, and fairly fast. It is especially handy when seated and it works well when the shooter is belted into his car. It is particularly comfortable to wear except in the tropics, as it supports the weapon at two points, which splits the weight. It permits a solid, shooting grip on contact while keeping the trigger covered. It is not costly.

However, the shoulder holster has three drawbacks: It is intolerable in extreme heat, as its harness shuts off air circulation beneath the shirt. It takes much more practice to use well than a belt holster. And it is difficult to get a good one.

Shoulder holster design is very subtle, and one that is almost good enough may be no good at all. At the present time, Milt Sparks of Idaho makes the

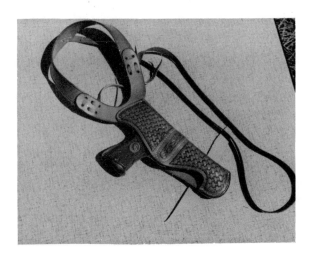

The Hardy-Cooper shoulder holster.

only shoulder holster that I consider suitable for serious use. It is patterned after the original design by A. H. Hardy of California and is called the "Hardy Heritage."

From the foregoing it is clear that it is difficult to get by with just one holster unless you have only one use for your sidearm. One's lifestyle has a good deal to do with this. A detective does not need much protection for his gun since he wears it under his coat. A uniformed police officer (in the U.S.) is concerned primarily with the security of his piece against snitching. A man whose daily activities involve violent physical action will be concerned about the security of his weapon against loss, while if one works on a ranch amidst flying hay and blowing dust it will be necessary to wear a weapon in such a way that it is not deactivated by the intrusion of foreign matter. McBride tells us that the favorite holster position for the trench raiders of WWI, who often carried out an entire mission belly down in the mud, was right in the small of the back.

A practical holster must be, above all, *comfortable*. If the weapon is not within reach it is useless, and a holster which is taken off as soon as convenient is likely to be a positive danger to the wearer. Let us say that a holster that does not permit you to wear your pistol in complete comfort, every day of your life, it is not a practical device.

Any good holster will necessarily afford a solid gun-hand contact before the pistol starts to move. If one must start the weapon out of the leather, and then shift his hand in order to obtain a firing grip, he is giving away too much. A properly designed holster always permits solid placement of the second finger of the shooting hand on the butt and prevents the trigger finger from entering the trigger guard until the weapon has started into battery.

If a retaining device is used it should permit instant release on gun-hand contact. If friction is used for retention it should hold the weapon against its own weight and a bit more.

ACCESSORIES

Ammunition Carriers

Probably the first extra that should accompany any pistol not intended solely for target work is some means of carrying spare ammunition. With the auto pistol, spare ammunition is always carried in fully loaded magazines, and one's equipment is not complete until it includes an ammunition carrier to be worn on the belt. These magazine carriers may be single or double, but they should permit the quick accessibility of at least one spare magazine without the release of any catches or snaps. One spare magazine will usually suffice in any situation in which the auto pistol may be necessary. (I have never heard of a case in which a man was called upon to reload his auto quickly twice in the same action.) Reserve magazines may be carried in any way that is comfortable and secure, but the shooter must be able to get a solid grip on the number one magazine between his thumb and second finger, and should retain the magazine against a load of at least one G.

Revolvers are most easily reloaded from speedloaders, but since these devices are of approximately the same size as the revolver cylinder, they are difficult to wear comfortably on anything but a duty belt. It may be unwise to assume that one will always have a speedloader necessary when he needs to load a revolver. Among other things, it is often advisable to reload a revolver with one or two rounds rather than with six. Therefore while carriers for speedloaders are good under some circumstances, the shooter should always be aware that single or double or triple loading with individual rounds may also be called for. A few old-fashioned belt loops may be the best answer to this.

Cleaning Kit

The next extra that comes to mind is a cleaning kit. I like to keep this as compact as possible, so it can be tossed into a pack or an overnight bag along with my shaving gear and toothbrush. It should include a rod—jointed for convenient packing, a bristle brush, about ten cut patches (the whole box is too large), a small can of solvent and one of oil, and a small screwdriver or combination tool; the whole wrapped in a soft, clean cloth. A solid rod, a brass brush for leading, a toothbrush for nooks and crannies, a drift punch for detailed stripping, and cleaning materials in bulk may be kept at home but they just add to the clutter while traveling.

Spare Parts

I like to carry a small supply of spare parts for the auto when far afield. Revolvers, of good quality, are selectively assembled and broken parts can often not be installed without hand fitting; parts for autos are quickly replaceable by hand, without tools or any special skill. Consequently I usually carry a spare of any moving part which might conceivably fail. Actually the only part that ever did require replacement was an extractor of the old type which sheared when I tried to use some wartime steel-case ammunition without lubricating it, but I've got the other parts in the kit just in case. The inventory includes an extractor, a firing pin, a hammer and strut, a trigger spring (3-leaf), a sear, and a nice stiff recoil spring. This last may be cut down more easily than it can be beefed up. Naturally a drift punch goes along as it is needed to get inside the lock work. This set is for a 1911 auto, but a very similar selection will do for any other self-loader. A spare barrel with link and pin may be added for travel overseas. A hone is also handy for touching up a trigger, providing one has been carefully trained in its use.

Lanyard

A last little item that I have found very comforting is a lanyard. This is simply a cord by which the pistol is attached to the shooter. It used to be standard in the military service and I think it still should be. A bad fall, a heavy blow, or a fumble in a touchy spot may effectively separate you from the pistol in your hand at a time when you particularly need it. And we don't all awake like cats, completely aware of our surroundings. The older service pistols, except for the Peacemaker, usually came with a lanyard ring in the butt. (The one on the .45 auto makes a fine bottle opener when the magazine is partly ejected.) The lanyard should be about 72 inches long and worn diagonally over the shoulder by day. When you're sleeping, it should be shortened by half and looped around the right wrist.

Shooting Glasses

Turning to the more sedate uses of the handgun, in training and practice, we find some other extras that are useful. The N.R.A. recommends that shooting glasses be used at all times with all three weapons, though the chance of a blown pistol's damaging the eye is far less than that with a rifle. In shoulder-to-shoulder competition one can be struck in the eye with an empty case. And when firing at steel targets at close range there is always the risk of lead spray. Shooting glasses are a good idea in general, but I know a good many people who find them distracting.

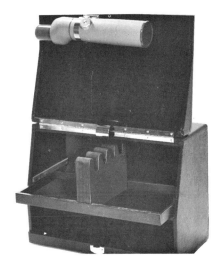

A target shooter's pistol case, with spotting scope in place.

Some shooters like to wear Mickey Mouse ear protectors.

Spotting Glass

For fixed-range competition and practice, a spotting glass is almost a necessity, particularly with a .22. Good ones are available in 15 to 20 power, and are almost always found fixed into the lid of the target shooter's pistol box.

Ear Plugs

Many shooters have recently discovered that shooting is hard on the ears. The older generation simply used cotton, but the young guard frowns upon anything so uncomplicated. Custom-made ear plugs and bulbous headsets are the new thing, and I suppose they do much good in preventing deafness.

Custom Stocks

Because of the shape of the butt, the revolver is more in need of a customized stock than the auto pistol. We have come full circle on auto-pistol stocks, and most of us now use something very much like John Browning's original design. The rubber stocks popularized by Pachmayr of Los Angeles are highly regarded by many, but they do make the butt somewhat larger than standard, and the problem for most people is making the butt feel smaller rather than bigger. Rubber stocks are certainly nonskid, but I have never known of a situation in which a weapon was too slippery in the hand to be useful, regardless of what type of stock was attached to it.

Revolvers need more attention in this area. A conventional revolver butt is badly constructed to mate with the human hand, being narrow at the top where it should be broad, and broad at the bottom where it should be narrow. Probably the best stock design was pioneered by Fuzzy Farrant and Walt Stark of California. Their stocks reverse this relationship, but they require some cutting of the revolver frame.

In no case is it wise to become accustomed to ornate and elaborate finger grooves and thumb rails, since these may develop into a crutch which will make the shooter less efficient if he must do without them. If ornament is desired a whole area of cosmetics is involved. Some people like their personal weapons to be beautiful, and there is nothing wrong in that. If one chooses ivory, precious metal, or other embellishment, that is a matter of personal choice and has nothing to do with the shooting qualities of the weapon.

29

Grip, Stance, and Position

THE PURPOSE of shooting is hitting. If you can hit—hard, fast, and consistently—you are doing everything right. Style and form are means, not ends, and anyone who claims that there is only one way to shoot hasn't been around very long. The principles we present will work. They are used by men whose pistol shooting is so good that it is literally hard to believe, but they are not necessarily the only correct methods. I have a photograph of a man shooting a free pistol in a way that would be laughed off any conventional range. The man was champion of the world in 1930. So we do not claim that we know *the* solution. We offer *a* solution which we know can produce a master marksman.

GRIP

Perhaps the first thing the aspiring pistol shot should realize is that the weapon recoils in the hand while the bullet is still in the barrel. This means that the movement must be uniform for every shot if any accuracy is to be achieved. Thus uniformity of grip is absolutely essential to good shooting, the more so as recoil increases. A solid gun-to-hand contact, consistent both as to the position of the hand on the gun and as to the amount of mass and muscle tension employed, is the attribute of a good pistol shot. This was emphasized to me a while back when I was checking out an accuracy job on a Colt Commander. The shop master where the work was done is an old-line target shot, accustomed to very precise work with light loads. However, I was setting up the pistol, which kicks a third harder than the standard .45 using service ammunition, for heavy combat loads. This confounded my target-shooting friend, who fired a 25-yard group that was impressively narrow but about 8 inches deep. The startling recoil of the little gun had caused him to alter his grip tension, with distressing results. In my hands the pistol shot splendidly—not that I am necessarily a better shot, but I am used to the recoil problem.

The essentials of a good grip are high placement of the hand and linear alignment of the axis of the forearm in the vertical plane of the barrel. The first is easy, though it's odd how beginners tend to hold a handgun way down toward Patagonia. On a revolver the web between the thumb and forefinger should ride just at the recoil shoulder of the butt, while on an auto the hand should be thrust solidly up into the curve of the backstrap. The idea here is to place the base of support up as close as possible to the axis of recoil, so as to reduce rotary movement and consequent muzzle whip. It is most important to place the heel of the hand directly behind the piece, so that there will be no lateral twisting action on recoil. The most common error of the novice is to place his hand to one side of the butt, especially if he has short fingers. To illustrate this principle, I have often shifted a recruit's group center from one side of his target to the other by simply causing him to shift the mass of his hand slightly to one side as he grips the weapon.

Behind the hand lies the wrist, and the human wrist is marvelously unsuitable as a gun-mount. It is essentially too flexible, and must be trained into rigidity by a conscious effort.

With the hand high on the weapon, the first-finger pad is placed directly in the center of the curve of the trigger. By choice, the thumb of the shooting hand should point either straight forward in the direction of fire or somewhat higher. With weapons of the Colt/Browning configuration the preferred place for the thumb is on top of the safety. A good many marksmen for years have favored sliding the thumb under the safety, but we have now seen too many cases in which a grip of this type resulted in the safety's being knocked on by accident—to the considerable discomfiture of the shooter. If the high thumb position results in occasional failure to depress the grip safety, it can easily be deactivated by tape or an interior clip. (This in no way renders the gun less "safe." John Browning never intended that both thumb safety and grip safety be used together, since in designing the grip safety he was complying with a requirement specified by a government contract. If one uses the grip safety he does not need the thumb safety, and vice versa.)

Support

Under normal circumstances the pistol is fired two-handed. (This will naturally be protested, since a two-hand hold is prohibited in I.S.U. competition, but I do not consider such competition the normal use of the pistol.) The two-hand hold is not the crutch of the duffer, as some traditionalists claim; it is rather the technique of the master. I shot for twenty years in the conventional fashion with one hand, until I found that while one hand is satisfyingly accurate, it is not strong enough for the control of heavy loads in quick shifts between targets—at least not against serious competition. I know of a prominent police rangemaster who maintains, with some scorn, that the two-hand hold is all right for those who need it. He can outshoot his recruits with one hand, but he is conspicuously absent from big-time combat competition.

The supporting hand—the left in the case of a right-hander—is brought up beside the pistol, palm vertical, fingers joined, and thumb up. The fingers

The basic auto pistol grip.

The basic revolver. grip.

The basic revolver grip.

A variation of the revolver grip, for use in deliberate fire.

overlap those of the gun hand, with the index directly under the trigger guard (though some auto shooters slide it forward into the outer curve where the guard joins the frame). In no case does the supporting hand grasp the wrist, for the wrist is the weak point and additional stiffness is needed forward. Likewise it is wrong to place the pistol and gun-hand into the horizontal palm of the supporting hand, as this supports the gun arm, which does not especially need it, without helping the wrist, which does. The pistol should be "clapped" between the palms, for only so can the full potential of the supporting hand be realized. The reason this point is not entirely clear in most police and military circles is that in such places the two-hand grip is thought of more as an aid to accuracy than to recoil control. Letting the piece fly loose under recoil is acceptable in slow fire, but not in burst shooting.

It is critical that the proper grip, once learned, be used in all positions. Thus only can the same center of impact be obtained. The illustrations show the basic grip of four masters of the pistol, and while there are slight variations, each grip is consistent throughout each individual's selections of positions.

SHOOTING POSITIONS

The Weaver Stance

If only one method of shooting is to be learned, it should be the Weaver Stance, invented by Jack Weaver, of Carson City, Nevada. It is basically a two-handed standing position, but not the fully erect, straight-armed position of the target range. The big difference is that the Weaver Stance is fast, while the other is deliberate. Jack had to defeat his share of quick-draw artists to prove it, but prove it he did. Tests have now shown that a master can keep all his shots on the international target at 25 meters, starting with the weapon holstered and safe, and including reaction time, *in one second per shot.* At three full seconds, which is the regular time allotted to Olympic competitors starting with the pistol ready in the hand, he can keep all his shots in the nine ring. The Weaver Stance may be used with deliberation, but it is essentially a position for fast shooting.

To assume the Weaver Stance, face the target squarely with the left foot leading just a little. The right arm may be either perfectly straight or slightly flexed at the elbow, but if it is flexed the flexion should be straight down and not out of line with the thrust of recoil. The supporting hand is placed, palm vertical, along the side of the pistol with the fingers by choice beneath the trigger guard. The left elbow is dropped and the left shoulder is advanced. The essence of this Weaver position is the strength achieved by isometric pressure between the right and left hands. The pistol is thrust forward by the right hand into the left, and the pressure between the two hands can be mea-

Two views of the author shooting from the Weaver Stance. Note how left elbow is dropped and left shoulder advanced. Pressure between right and left hands holds pistol steady.

sured at about 15 pounds. This "push-pull" effect is what makes the Weaver Stance so much stronger than any other two-handed position, to say nothing of any position which uses one hand only. Strength in a gun mount may not be important in slow fire or when firing single rounds, but it becomes vital when rapid shots and quick engagement of multiple targets are desired. This element of the Weaver Stance is what makes it possible for weapons of very considerable recoil to be mastered by people who are not especially strong. The notion that service pistols "kick too hard" for servicemen is due to ignorance of this principle.

In the Weaver Stance the head is preferably held erect. A good many old-timers (myself included) tend to dip the head slightly to the right. This mannerism is permissible but should be avoided at the beginning of training if possible.

We should note that whether right or left eye is used matters very little. If a right-hander wishes to use his left eye as master he need move his hands only about half an inch to the left, and his head about half an inch to the right, and he will be as comfortable as he would be shooting right-eyed.

In using the Weaver Stance it is important to train the fingers, hands, wrists, arms, shoulders, and head into a single, rigid unit so that any change of target—up, down, or sideways—is accomplished by action of the shoulders and back. If the shooter never allows his "gunmount" to go limp, he will never have to find it again in a hurry, and his kinesthetic sense of direction will be acquired much more quickly.

The Weaver Stance is the best system to use in most pistol situations. It is fast, strong, and versatile. While there are modifications to be seen among the top shooters of the world, they all use some version of the Weaver Stance when the chips are down.

Braced Kneeling Position

If a situation occurs in which it is necessary to lower the line of sight to reduce the silhouette of the shooter, or to promote some increased degree of accuracy, the braced kneeling position can be used. Once understood it is scarcely slower than the Weaver Stance and one can bound out of it as quickly as he can drop into it—which is not true of any version of the sitting position.

The first act in the assumption of the braced kneeling position is the alignment of the feet toward the target. As the hand locks onto the pistol, the left foot is pointed directly at the target so that a line between the balls of the feet will intersect the point of impact. These two actions take place together, and then as the right knee flexes the holster is, in effect, pulled off the pistol which comes straight forward into line as the right knee hits the ground. The right knee is placed well out to the right and the shooter sits upon his right heel with the toe turned under. The axis of the right foot should be vertical and the right buttock seated squarely upon the right heel. The spine is fairly erect and the left elbow is placed just forward of the kneecap. The hands

Braced kneeling position.

on the pistol are placed exactly as in the Weaver Stance but here a vertical line dropped from the pistol will include the elbow, the knee, and the ankle of the left foot so that the weapon is supported entirely by bone without muscle tension. The right arm is straight or nearly so, and the head is held erect.

The braced kneeling position is not as fully understood as it might be because the great pistol champions, who are copied by the aspirants, are so good from the Weaver position that they gain nothing by going to kneeling. Consequently you will sometimes see a class A shot drop to both knees and shoot from what amounts to a shortened Weaver Stance. This can be done, but it shows lack of education since the braced support of the left elbow on the left knee is an advantage that should not be ignored.

Prone Position

In cases where a shooter feels he should take complete cover, or lower his silhouette as much as possible, or shoot beneath an obstacle such as a parked car, or obtain all the accuracy of which the weapon and cartridge are capable, he should go to the prone position. While permitting extreme accuracy the prone position is not slow and can be assumed in less than two seconds by a trained man.

Rollover prone position.

The rollover prone position, now used by all senior marksmen, was the invention of Ray Chapman, to whom credit must be given for its perfection. Its advantage lies in the rolling of the torso to the right so that the head may be supported by the deltoid of the right arm, relaxing all muscles in the neck. To test it the shooter goes absolutely limp, turning off all muscles in his body. If anything, from his pistol to his head, moves at all the position is not properly assumed.

To get into the rollover prone position quickly, the shooter faces at least forty-five degrees to the right of the line of sight as he puts his hand on his pistol and drops to both knees, placing his left hand forward so as to catch himself as he goes on down. As the pistol comes out of the holster and points forward, the left hand hits the ground, catching the weight of the shooter. The body is then thrust forward and right, landing upon the right forearm, which extends toward the target, though the spine assumes an angle of at least forty-five degrees to the right of the line of sight. The safety comes off as the pistol lines up, and the finger enters the trigger guard as the left hand is swung forward to catch the pistol. The edges of both hands are on the ground, as are both forearms. The right cheek rests on the upper arm, relieving the muscles of the neck. The torso is rolled to the right to take the weight off the diaphragm, and the right toe is turned under as the left ankle crosses over behind the right knee.

From prone one can shoot a pistol as accurately as the pistol will, as long as proper trigger control and sighting principles are observed. The disadvantage of the position is that when one is down that low it is difficult to see over intervening obstacles. It will rarely suffice in brushy country or broken ground.

Speed Rock Position

This is the gunslinger's position, so called because it is the fastest way to get off a shot and because most practitioners rock the body slightly backward by bending the knee in order to start the barrel up toward level even before the weapon clears leather. In the rock—as used by a man (not a blank-shooter) who must hit a target—the grip is naturally one-handed, but the wrist and forearm are solidly locked. The pistol is pointed at belt level and fired as it lines up. This is a technique that calls for much practice and one that, to my knowledge, is never officially taught. Its speed advantage is perhaps a half second over the Weaver Stance, and its accuracy potential is limited to large targets at 20 feet or less, but it has saved lives. For the policeman who makes a traffic stop and is greeted by unexpected gunfire at 10 feet it is a most comforting skill to acquire.

F.B.I. Crouch

Related to the rock, but less useful, are the F.B.I. crouch and the so-called "lock-on." In these the pistol is drawn and pointed with some deliberation, but not from higher than diaphragm level. Good shooting may be done this way, but not as accurately as from the Weaver Stance and not much, if at all, faster. It is sometimes used in competition to split a difference against a specific antagonist whose abilities are known. It is also the only way that so-called

Speed rock position.

hip shooting can be done with an improperly designed holster, as the speed rock works only from a speed holster. However, in practically all cases, if you aren't wearing a speed holster you had best settle for the Weaver Stance.

Sitting Position

The sitting position is not as useful to the pistolero as it is to the rifleman, since the accuracy differential between sitting and kneeling is pronounced with a rifle and negligible with a pistol, and the kneeling position is quickly and easily assumed while the sitting position is awkward to get into. Nevertheless, the sitting position is taught by the F.B.I. and has some usefulness in the field, especially when shooting from a forward slope across a canyon. To take it, sit down facing the target and assume the basic two-hand grip, with both arms straight. The torso is forced well forward so that, on level ground, the elbows are forward of the knees, which support the upper arms lying between them. This position is easily varied to suit different angles of elevation, from about 30 degrees downward to 45 degrees upward, which gives it its main usefulness. For firing horizontally from level ground it is not very practical; not as accurate as prone and hardly faster, and not as fast as kneeling and hardly more accurate.

If a backrest is available, such as the trunk of a tree, the braced sitting position may be taken, which is fully as accurate as prone or a bench rest. In this one the torso leans well back, somewhat as in a modern racing car, and the pistol hands are pressed between the knees, the feet being placed somewhat outboard for extra stability. From this you can shoot as well as the pistol can, but obviously conditions must be just right. It should be pointed out that a revolver fired from this position may scorch the trousers severely, as its flash gap is not clear of the shooter's legs.

Offhand Position

Offhand is the official target-shooter's position. Highly trained specialists can shoot brilliantly from it, but it is likely to discourage the ordinary man, since it is the least accurate sighted method of shooting a pistol. A conventional offhand position is taken by facing 30 to 45 degrees to the left of the direction of fire (depending upon the individual build), with the feet about a half pace apart, and extending the unsupported arm straight at the target. This traditional stance serves no useful purpose that I can see—though I used it unquestioningly for twenty years—and should be confined to traditional target shots and people with one arm.

A variation of offhand—the one-hand point—does have value in rough and tumble situations where one hand is necessary to hold on. Short-range unsighted fire is delivered in this manner when riding a horse, riding postilion on a motorcycle, or hanging onto a bouncing jeep or a speedboat. The left hand holds the controls or a support, the body is placed as necessary, and the

Offhand position.

The one-armed point is used at short ranges when you have to hold on to a support.

right arm is extended not quite fully, since a completely extended arm lacks directional strength. The pistol is held about chin high, and the eyes focus on the target. The weapon appears as a vertical black bar just under the target, and the sights are not used. This is a wild way to use a pistol, but it works, especially from motorbikes, ATC's and speedboats.

30

Shooting the Handgun

The Sight Picture

Pistol shooting, unlike rifle shooting, may be either sighted or unsighted, but since nine out of ten times it is sighted, it is well to understand the principles involved. Telescope sights work the same way on any weapon, so there is no need to repeat a discussion here that has already appeared in the rifle section, but conventional iron sights are completely different in operation on rifle and pistol. A rifle's rear sight is quite close to the eye, and the distance between front and rear sights is much greater than eye relief. This is reversed with a pistol, on which the front and rear sights are closer than either is from the shooter's eye. Thus the rifleman cannot focus on front and rear sights at once, and his front sight is far enough out to begin to approach the infinity setting which is needed for a clear view of the target. The pistol's sights are close enough together to be held well in the same focus, but this is too near the eye to work for the target too. Since the short sight radius of the handgun makes even the most minor misalignment a very serious matter, the pistol shooter focuses on his sights and lets the target blur. The training posters are prone to show a correct sight picture thus:

with all elements black and sharp, but such a picture is optically impossible. You can see this:

299

or this:

but not both at once.

The last is the one you must strive for, but it is not easy. There is an understandable urge to focus on the target, which must be overcome by an effort of will. One way to help this is to shoot at a plain paper on which there is no bullseye and on which shot-holes cannot be seen, shooting only for the center of the area. With nothing definite to freeze on at the target, there will be less difficulty in focusing on the sights. This trick has been responsible for a good many breakthroughs on military and police ranges.

Pistol sights today are almost exclusively of the square-cut patridge type, though in the past various sorts of blades and beads have been tried. We have found that the patridge sight is the only one to give a really precise index of elevation with a radius of 10 inches or less. Some feel that front post inserts of contrasting colors aid in picking up a quick sight picture. The recent trend in target sights has been toward a broad ⅛- to ³⁄₁₆-inch front sight which leaves only a narrow line of white on each side, thus:

This may be very precise but it is slow, and it also covers a lot of countryside if you ever want to use your pistol in the field. For cobat competition and for hunting most of us have come to favor a rather narrow (¹⁄₁₀- or even ¹⁄₁₆-inch) front sight which provides a positive elevation but provides it much quicker, thus:

Even if this is a bit less precise as to deflection, it is a small matter since the main problem is that of elevation.

It is one of the annoying facts of ballistics that bullets travel in a curve, not a straight line. This curve, called the trajectory, is formed largely by the force of gravity, which acts on the missile the instant it leaves the muzzle. No bullet can, in the nature of things, shoot absolutely flat, even for a short distance, though some may seem to. Thus it is that the line of sight and the axis of the bullet's initial direction are not parallel, but slightly convergent. A close look at any revolver will reveal that the line of sight and the axis of the bore are slightly *divergent,* but this is to allow for the rise of the muzzle in recoil while the bullet is still in the barrel. The direction of the bullet is slightly upward into what was the line of sight at the instant of firing. Rising slightly, the trajectory intersects the line of sight shortly after leaving the muzzle—10 feet more or less depending upon the type of pistol—travels above it for a distance, drops back and intersects again, and then falls away below. The second intersection occurs at the range for which the weapon is said to be "zeroed."

Because a pistol's sights are set up to relate a straight sight line to a trajectory which curves in a plane intersecting the center of the earth, tilting the sights, or "canting," will disrupt this relationship. Canting is not very serious in small increments or at short ranges, but it can build up. A striking way to illustrate it is to assume the fetal position, lying on the side with the pistol gripped between the knees, and fire a 50-yard group. The position is rock-solid, and the group will probably be small, but it will be way off in the direction of the side on which you lie, because of the convergence of the line of sight and the angle of departure; and it will be way low, because it was fired horizontally without any compensation for drop.

From all this it should be clear that the sight picture must be related to the trajectory, as seen from the rear, thus:

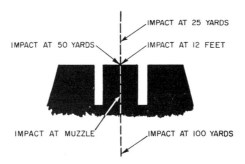

For target work the pistol may be sighted either for dead center or for six o'clock. Those who favor six o'clock claim that a minimal line of white between the black bull's-eye and the black front sight provides an exact index of elevation.

The six-o'clock hold.

However, since the front sight and the target cannot be in the same focus, this point may be more theoretical than practical.

The dead-center hold is favored by others on the theory that since the front sight is held in sharp focus while the bull's-eye (or other target) blurs, it is more natural for the shooter to let the sight seek the center of the bull, thus:

The dead center hold.

Some experts use one and some the other. Personally, I use six o'clock for zeroing and group shooting from a bench, but I use a square bull, which offers a much more precise line of white than a round one. For combat and field shooting I try to adapt the hold to the trajectory, but known-range combat competition on blank targets naturally calls for a dead center sight picture.

The axiom in pistol sighting remains *look at the sights, not at the target.* Easy to say—not easy to do.

SIGHTING IN

Naturally, while pistol sights are usually set to some sort of zero at the factory, if they are exactly right for any given shooter, range, and ammunition, it will be only by coincidence. (However, one prominent factory supplies its pistols with the sights screwed solidly down to botton setting to protect them during shipment.)

Consequently a pistol should always be sighted in by its individual user before it is put to serious use. This may be done by firing three-shot groups from prone, braced-sitting, or a bench rest, taking care that grip and tension in the sighting position are exactly the same as those used in less solid positions. If the pistol has adjustable sights, the group center is easily moved to the desired point of impact, in relation to the line of sight, by moving the rear

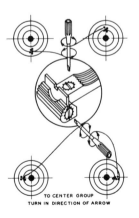

Adjustment of a micrometer click sight.
Courtesy Smith & Wesson.

sight in the direction you wish the group to move. If you wish the shots to print to the right, move the rear sight to the right, and so on. If the sights are not adjustable you have a problem. The top of the rear sight (not the bottom of the notch) may be ground down a bit to lower the point of impact, but it is impossible to raise it without welding. To raise a group the *front* sight may be ground, since the front sight movement changes impact in the reverse direction. Deflection changes may be achieved by drifting sights laterally in their slots, or by bending and re-squaring the front sight blade. This is a good reason for getting a pistol with adjustable sights to begin with.

A satisfying 50-yard group fired on the 100-yard rifle target with the .45 auto.

Of course, really precise shooting may not be demanded of a sidearm, and for predominantly coarse shooting with one kind of ammunition, a slightly wayward center of impact may be endured. Also it is quite feasible to drift a rear sight back and forth until a correct deflection setting is found, and then simply to memorize any elevation errors and hold accordingly. Still, if you're serious about your shooting, you'd best stick to adjustable sights.

Horizontal band of red across a silhouette target provides a sharp elevation index for sighting in.

And here are a few tips for the sighter-in:

(1) Make corrections in only one plane at a time. Often a lateral change will produce an unexpected vertical change, and vice versa.

(2) Start on a big paper, and fairly close up, to be sure you're approximately on before moving out to critical range.

(3) Make large corrections, in order to "bracket" the desired center of impact on the first try. Creeping up on it can waste much ammunition.

(4) Do not extrapolate. Test your zero at the true range desired.

(5) Sight in on a still day, and shade your sights.

A square bull's-eye used as a target for sighting in.

UNSIGHTED FIRE

As we have seen, there are certain circumstances in which a pistol may be shot without the sights. It has been asserted by people who presume to instruct in these matters that in a majority of cases in which police officers use their pistols they do not use the sights. This may be true, but when one considers that in the majority of cases in which police officers shoot they do not hit, it would seem to be irrelevant. We are not interested in the techniques of missing. Nevertheless there *are* situations in which the sights cannot be seen, such as in the narrow light band between enough light to discern details and insufficient light to identify a target. Under these circumstances, if the shooter has perfected his kinesthetic stroke he will find that if he uses the system that works in broad daylight, his ability to hit his target will not be affected, as long as the range remains short. A practiced hand can stay consistently inside a 10-inch circle in almost full dark at ranges up to about 30 feet, and these are the ranges at which most pistol confrontations occur.

When two shots are fired as quickly as possible with the auto pistol it is not possible to pick up the sights for the second round. In this case a stroke is used which has come to be called the "Double Hammer." Here the sights are used for the first shot but not for the second. When the shooter has cultivated sufficient strength in his arms he will find that the two shots may be placed very close together by muscular "feel," and that while he cannot use the sights for the second shot he can still place his round quite well. Since it is always tactically advisable to fire two shots in any case where a pistol may be needed to save one's life, the Double Hammer is a valuable technique.

And then there is the matter of hip shooting—of rolling the pistol out of the leather and firing as the muzzle clears the holster. This sort of thing is great fun and with practice it can be quite effective at short range. A man who devotes his life to it may obtain amazing proficiency even at middle ranges. However, since it works only from a holster designed for the task, and since it is only fractionally faster than the Weaver position, its use must be considered more of a stunt than a useful tool.

TRIGGER CONTROL

"Hold and squeeze!" is the traditional chant of the firing line. To "hold" is to steady down with a solid firing position and take a perfect sight picture; to "squeeze" is to control that trigger. With rifle or pistol, a man who holds and squeezes—every time without fail—is a man who wins matches, fills the freezer, and is deadly in a fight.

The object of trigger control is to cause the weapon to fire at a time when the sights are properly aligned—and at no other time. This may be managed in three ways.

If, when the sights are perfectly aligned, pressure is steadily increased between thumb and forefinger, without any knowledge of the rate of increase, sooner or later the hammer will fall. And since the sights are aligned as the pressure is being increased, and at no other time, the shot will be perfect. In most rifle shooting, and in such pistol shooting as is conducted deliberately, the pressure is increased gently as long as the sights are on target. It is held firm when the sights drift off the target and increased again when they are lined up, causing—eventually—a perfect shot. This method of fire is referred to as an "open-end surprise break," in that the ignition comes as a surprise to the shooter, and during a time frame which was not important to him.

If a quicker shot is indicated, the same system is used, except that the increase of pressure on the trigger is confined to an anticipated time span. The pressure increases gradually, but the shooter forces himself to make sure that the hammer will fall within a space of time which he selects in advance. This system is known as the "*compressed* surprise break," in that the ignition is still a surprise but the time in which it is allowed to take place is compressed into limits set by the shooter. This can be done with great speed, and it is the system used by the master pistol shot. *No matter how fast he fires, the exact instant of ignition will come to him as a surprise.*

The compressed surprise break is not easy. It constitutes a major portion of the reflexive skill needed in a good shot. I have heard it said by masters that a man who has learned it needs to learn nothing else. I am not sure that this is entirely true but I think we can admit that if you learn the compressed surprise break you will be a good shot, and if you do not learn it you will not be. It is as simple as that.

A third system of trigger control is sometimes used by people whose experience warrants it. It is called "the nudge," and it is practiced by applying the exact amount of pressure for ignition at exactly the moment the sights are where they should be. It is the system which is usually tried, with disastrous results, by beginners, but it should not be thought that it cannot be used at all. The majority of slow-fire target pistol shots use the nudge, but I do not recommend it for beginners. Without a very great degree of nerve control the nudge will result in a flinch, and a flinch, once developed, may be impossible to correct.

Whatever method of trigger control is chosen it is important to remember that the pressure occurs between the pad of the trigger finger and the thumb, or between the pad of the trigger finger and the fork of the thumb and the first carpal. *It is never exerted by closing the entire hand.* It is difficult for the novice to separate the flexion of his index finger from the other three fingers of his hand, but this must be learned or the trigger will never be mastered.

Trigger management is affected to no small extent by the mechanical action of the trigger itself. A good double-action revolver should operate with a glassy-smooth trigger stroke of about 9 pounds' weight, while single-action pulls should be crisp and apparently motionless at from 2½ to 4½ pounds. The weight of a trigger pull is not nearly as important as its crispness, for a trigger that creeps is very hard to use well. Revolvers can usually be set up with better triggers than autos, for the latter have to withstand the slam of the action as it returns to battery. Nevertheless some very fine triggers may be found in autos of the basic Browning design. A good trigger action on a Luger is almost out of the question, due to the elaborate linkage between the trigger and the firing pin.

BREATH CONTROL

Breath control in pistol shooting is little different from rifle work, as long as the shooting is deliberate. For a very precise shot, the breath is inhaled, let out, inhaled, let half out, and held during the squeeze. This is done from prone, braced sitting, a bench, and also for a very careful shot from standing.

In coarse shooting breathing is simply allowed to take care of itself, though we occasionally hear a judoesque "Hiyei" on an obstacle course or the Flying-M. Staccato shouts are apparently helpful in fencing and other combat sports—it's possible that they help in the more violent forms of pistol shooting as well.

One breathing technique is most helpful on an assault course or during a hunt when the shooter may find himself rather crucially short of wind. When the lungs are laboring at the point of exhaustion (as they sometimes are in combat competition and may well be in a live situation) it is still possible to shoot well. The trick is to stop the breath for an instant as the lungs fill, and to press off a shot at this moment. Then let the lungs exhale, refill, and hold again for another shot.

Developing Familiarity with Your Pistol

One facet of pistolcraft is rather overlooked by those who favor stylized over practical shooting. This is familiarity. In my primary training days, I was carefully taught how to jam a pistol into my right hand with my left, being sure that each part mated with each other part according to the book. This was a way of forcing the pistol to feel right as I held it—a comrade rather than an awkward and unfamiliar tool.

Actually, the true pistolero doesn't need this treatment. As long as he knows the fundamentals of grip, stance, sighting, and trigger control, he can progress toward true mastery by much handling. This is apart from dry practice, which is also very necessary. The more your pistol is in your hand, the more familiar it becomes. Safety checks, operation of the action, operation of the safety, hammer, magazine release, cylinder latch, or whatever can become reflexive and natural, along with the general feel and balance of the weapon, through regular and carefully programmed play.

I used to use a .45 auto as a paperweight on my desk, where it was always ready to slip into my hand when I laid down my pencil. I am aware that this might cause some embarrassment in most jobs, but it is an example of what I mean. Most of us have a chance to relax in privacy for a little while each day. The aspiring pistolero should work a bit of gun-handling into this period, for only in this way will he succeed in making his pistol a part of his hand, to which he never need give conscious thought.

The Presentation

The "presentation" of the pistol is the term for the movements which place it on the target from a condition of unreadiness. Since the condition of unreadiness is normally holstered and locked, the presentation is often referred to as the "draw," but it should be remembered that a presentation can be made when the pistol is placed in the desk drawer, or on a mantelpiece, or in any other condition in which it may be seized prior to firing. The presentation, when properly learned, becomes reflexive and automatic so that the body places the pistol on the target and the sights are used not to align the

barrel but to verify an alignment already obtained. This naturally takes practice, as does any motor skill. It is not mysterious but it must be learned in
proper sequence, because if the draw is conducted improperly it can be dangerous to the shooter. All leg shots which have come to my attention have
happened to a shooter who attempted to learn the presentation without dis-
covering the proper sequence of events. When done properly the presentation
is quite safe. When done improperly it is hazardous.

While there are various kinds of draws in use we will describe the most
common type, which is that from the strong side practical holster with the
Colt/Browning type of auto pistol.

On the count of *One* two things happen. The right hand establishes solid
firing contact with the pistol in the holster—index finger straight, second finger wrapped tightly around the butt, thumb on top of the safety without
moving it. The left hand moves straight forward to a position about a hand
breath in front of the belt buckle—fingers extended, palm vertical, thumb up.
The safety is not depressed and the finger does not enter the trigger guard.

On the count of *Two* the pistol is drawn straight upward until it breaks
contact with the holster, and no farther. The muzzle is just clear of the
leather. The index finger remains straight alongside the weapon and the
thumb remains on the safety without depressing it.

On the count of *Three* the pistol is advanced halfway from the holster to
the waiting left hand—and at this point the safety comes off. The thumb remains on top of the safety. The index finger remains straight.

On the count of *Four* the hands come together and the index finger enters
the trigger guard. The right hand, wrist, and forearm are now in a full firing
grip, with the barrel an extention of the right forearm. The muzzle is depressed about forty-five degrees and the eyes remain on the target.

On the count of *Five* the right hand is forced into the left, building isometric pressure, and the pistol is raised into the line of fire by the action of the
shoulders. The eye shifts focus from the target to the front sight, and the pistol
stops for a split second at the top of the stroke in order to allow the eye to obtain a clear, sharp, focused picture of the front sight. Anytime after the count
of Five the shooter may gently let the hammer fall.

These stages in the strong side presentation to the Weaver Stance must be
learned in sequence so that the reflexes never get out of order, but when the
stroke is delivered properly it will flow from one stage to the next without any
hesitation or jerkiness. This is the reason why, though we say the finger should
never enter the trigger guard until the sights are on the target, in this case the
finger does enter just as the stroke is completed so that when the sights arrive
on the target the compressed surprise break may be initiated.

Note that there is no way that a shooter can get a shot anywhere but down
range using this stroke, if he executes it in proper sequence.

In revolvers, which have no safeties, the trigger finger enters the trigger
guard between Two and Three and rearward pressure on the trigger com-
mences as the pistol is pressed up from Four to Five. High-speed photos of

STRONG-SIDE DRAW WITH AUTOMATIC PISTOL

Start. Arms may be held in any position before the draw. In this sequence they are at shooter's sides.

1. Right hand takes a firm firing grip on pistol, with thumb on top of safety and trigger finger straight. On this count, the left hand is placed directly in center of body and about 12 inches forward.

2. Pistol is drawn and freed from holster. Safety has not been actuated and trigger finger remains outside trigger guard.

3. Pistol swings toward left hand and thumb depresses safety. Trigger finger, however, does not enter trigger guard.

4. After muzzle has cleared left hand, trigger finger enters trigger guard as hands come together.

5. Pistol is pressed forward and upward into alignment as isometric pressure is exerted between right arm, thrusting forward, and left arm, pulling rearward. To exert this pressure, left elbow must be kept low. Straight left arm is sign of inferior gun mount.

master revolver shots indicate that the hammer is about halfway back by the time the sights arrive on the target. This is one of the reasons why it is somewhat more difficult to shoot a revolver than an auto pistol. The coordination of the trigger stroke and the presentation must be infallible, since there is no way to cancel the stroke once achieved.

When using the Heckler & Koch P7 pistol, which has no safety but which is actuated by squeezing the grip, the pressure on the squeeze member is exerted between Four and Five. As the hands come together the squeezer is relaxed. As the right hand presses the pistol up into the left the grip is compressed, cocking the striker. The finger is on the trigger at this time and considerable coordination is necessary to make sure that the pressure does not exceed that necessary to drop the striker before the focus on the front sight is obtained.

In drawing across the body from the weak side the left hand is not advanced quite so far and the palm is more nearly horizontal than vertical. The piece is drawn on the count of Three, underneath the left arm so that it may be rolled into position to be grasped at the count of Four. Otherwise there is little difference.

If the pistol is to be cocked this should be accomplished with thumb of the supporting hand as the weapon moves from Four to Five.

In practicing remember to strive for smoothness and consistency before working for speed. To be smooth is to be fast. Make the stroke perfect, without regard for time, until everything works as intended; and then the application of increased amounts of muscle pressure will build up such speed as you need.

It is well to remember that the presentation need not be practiced at the range, and that it is not necessary to go shooting to perfect this part of your skill.

A TRAINING PROGRAM

Learning to shoot a pistol well is a major project. While I have supervised the training of thousands of service people, who had no choice, I have also known some scores of individual civilians who asked my help only to give up in dismay when they found out how much work was involved. I would estimate that it is about three times as hard to shoot a pistol well enough to make it serve any practical purpose as it is to achieve the same skill with a rifle. This is, of course, subject to considerable discussion, but my point is that if you're not prepared to work, quite hard, at your pistol shooting, you had better take up something else.

However, assuming that you really are interested, and that you have obtained the necessary equipment, how should you proceed?

Your first step should be to study the theory of the pistol. You should gather a full working knowledge of sighting, grip, position, and trigger control. You should know not only what you must do, but also why. You can apply this theoretical knowledge by using your pistol in dry practice at home.

CROSS DRAW FROM BELT WITH DOUBLE-ACTION REVOLVER

Start. Arms are at sides.

1. Right hand grasps pistol in firm firing grip, but with trigger finger straight and outside the trigger guard. Left hand is held lower and closer to body than in strong-side draw.

2. Pistol is drawn, clearing leather, but trigger finger does not yet enter trigger guard.

3. Pistol is rotated forward below left arm and trigger finger enters trigger guard.

4. As hands come together, pressure is exerted against the trigger.

5. Pistol is raised into alignment as pressure on trigger cocks hammer. As sights arrive on target, shooter verifies alignment exactly as hammer falls.

This sequence illustrates how increasing pressure is applied on the trigger in the double-action presentation. When shooting this pistol, extra coordination is required to dominate the trigger-cocking mechanism.

(Snapping a pistol when empty will not hurt it unless it is a cap-and-ball or a rimfire model. The Browning Medalist .22 has a dry-firing device, but other .22's should be snapped with an empty case in the chamber.) Work on this until you feel familiar with the weapon and reasonably steady in sighting and

MILITARY DRAW TO LOCK-ON POSITION

1. Thumb releases holster flap and continues up and over the tang as fingers come onto the butt.

2. After clearing the leather, pistol is thrust forward under left hand, which grasps the slide. Right arm continues forward, left hand remains still, loading the pistol in one motion.

snapping. Do all your initial work from the Weaver Stance, unless your goal is formal target shooting, in which case use offhand.

Your first firing efforts should be single, deliberate shots delivered at a large, blank paper at short range. A .22 is very desirable at this point unless you are already familiar with high-power rifles or shotguns, and even then if money is a consideration. A 2-by-3 foot cardboard at about 10 feet is a good starter. Shoot exactly for the center, rest, and try again. This is a confidence-building exercise, designed to familiarize you with the recoil and report of the weapon, its sight picture and trigger action, and to convince you that it really will hit where you point it. Unless you have a serious nerve problem, or have not understood the section about trigger control, all your shots should go into a group the size of a teacup. If you have natural talent or are already a good rifle shot you should soon be able to put ten careful shots into a fifty-cent piece. Keep at this until you can.

(If you favor a double-action revolver, I feel you should start right out shooting double-action. This may sound radical, but it is similar to the practice of starting a beginning skier on the parallel method. It avoids shifting styles later on and gives the student less to unlearn.)

The next step is to increase the range to 30 feet. Still using the Weaver Stance, still shooting deliberately with a rest between shots, work at this range until you can stay in a 3-inch circle. This may not come in one- or two-range sessions, but do not let this discourage you.

Be careful of two rules:

DO YOUR HOMEWORK. Ten careful squeezes each morning, and ten each evening. Aim for the center of a light switch on the opposite wall, and make each squeeze a perfect surprise break.

DO NOT PLINK. I know it's great fun to raise puffs of dust all around a beer can, and to hit it occasionally, but doing this before you are thoroughly grounded may ruin your chances to become a good shot.

Now that you can shoot a slow-fire ten-shot group into 3 inches at 10 yards, it is time to take up the compressed squeeze. At the same range, on the same target, and from the same position, try this: When your sight picture is exactly right, chant, in a slow cadence, "ONE for the money and TWO for the show and THREE to make ready and FOUR to go." On each numeral fire one shot. Now see how your group looks. At this point you will encounter your greatest hurdle, for the ability to squeeze unhurriedly to a surprise break is far easier than to be able to limit the time in which it occurs. There is a formidable tendency to jerk the trigger on the signal, and if it can't be overcome all is lost. Some like the call, "Let the GUN do it, let the GUN do it, let the GUN do it," on the theory that this helps dominate the forcing of the hand at the instant of firing.

By the time you have got back into that 3-inch circle, now taking about 2½ to 3 seconds per shot, you're off to a good start. Without slighting this same exercise on every range session, you may now branch out in two directions. One is slow fire at 25 yards on a bullseye, using the kneeling position; and the other is drawing to the Weaver Stance for single shots at 10 yards. In each case keep working toward that 3-inch circle.

With one range session every two weeks, plus conscientious homework, you may be able to fire all three of the preceding exercises in respectable fashion, placing thirty shots in three 3-inch groups by the end of six months. This is twenty-four hours of careful range practice, which may of course be compressed into a much shorter time if your way of life permits. However, range sessions of longer than two hours' duration are not advisable as it is nearly impossible to concentrate with sufficient intensity for longer than this. Two hours of maximum concentration are too much for most people as it is.

By this time you have completed step one. If all your work up to now has been with a .22, shift to a middle-sized weapon (not a fully-loaded magnum) and see how you do. Continue until you can print those same 3-inch groups with the duty gun.

Now you must decide what you want to do with your skill. If target shooting is your aim, go directly to the standard courses (listed in the first section of

Chapter 32) and take it from there. You can spend the rest of your life on these, and it may give you much pleasure.

If hunting is your purpose, start extending the range, using deliberate fire from the braced positions, until you can produce reliable 6-inch groups at 50 yards. Then shift to a 1500 f/s pistol and work back up toward your eventual goal of 6-inch groups at 100 yards.

If you want to be a combat shot, duplicate the hunter's exercise and add the following:

(1) Work on multiple targets until you can place two shots on each of 3 silhouettes at 10 yards in four seconds, including reaction and draw time.

(2) Work on moving targets until you never miss the running man at 25 yards.

(3) Learn to reload completely in two seconds using an auto, or three using a revolver with a speed loader.

When you can do all these things 90 percent of the time, you have completed step two, and are ready for competition. You won't win, but neither will you look foolish, and step three is the establishment of a respectable record in combat competition.

At this point you may plink, but don't let it go to your head.

The foregoing is just one of many programs, but it is a good one. It should take about two years and about 4,000 rounds. Perhaps you can do it in less, which is splendid, but don't be upset if it takes more. In three years several men have become really superb pistol shots, while others can never hope to be better than just good. It's up to you.

A Practice Program

After achieving a decent level of skill, you must practice. Unlike several other abilities, pistol shooting cannot be learned and then tabled for future reference. But just shooting is not necessarily practice, which must be properly programmed if it is to reward the expense of ammunition with the maintenance of skill.

If you are fortunate enough to belong to a well-run practical pistol club (or a generalized sporting or shooting club that conducts practical pistol competition) you have no problem. Just keep practicing for the next monthly match, shooting it three or four times for record, and you will stay in good form. This is assuming that any good program varies its courses widely. Continuous practice on any one course of fire is detrimental to overall ability.

However, if you do not have a program handed to you, you must make your own. You can do this in any way you choose, but for a generalized range session intended not to prepare you for a specific contest but to keep your

THE SPEED LOAD

This system for reloading the auto pistol was devised by Ray Chapman and is used in practical matches.

1. As empty magazine is discharged from pistol, left hand moves upward with loaded magazine obtained from belt holder.

2. Left hand inserts magazine carefully in butt opening and slams it home briskly.

3. Pistol is immediately regrasped with both hands. Secret is to move quickly, then carefully, then quickly.

hand in, I suggest the following:

(1) Five rounds slow fire at 50 yards on a standard bullseye, or at 100 on a silhouette. Check and repeat for a better group. (10 shots)

(2) Five individual draws to braced kneeling, on a silhouette at 50 yards. (5 shots)

(3) Set out three silhouettes, the center at 25 yards, the two sides at 10. Face 90 degrees from the direction of fire, hands over your head. On signal pivot, draw, hit each target twice, reload, and come back. If someone can time you, repeat and beat your time, but get all hits. (24 shots)

(4) Draw and fire five rounds from standing at a silhouette at 50 yards, allowing 10 seconds. Repeat. (10 shots)

(5) Ten individual rounds at improvised moving targets. Bowl a wornout softball, or start a tin can down the back-stop and hit it while it rolls at 10 to 15 yards. (10 shots)

31

Sharpening Your Skill

PISTOL SHOOTING is an odd practice, in that it is basically very simple, but even the most minor error or failure will ruin it. Driving a car is a much more complex activity, but one can drive like a clod, with no knowledge of or interest in the niceties of the art, and still arrive at one's destination. On the other hand, all you need to know about shooting a pistol may be taught you in twenty minutes, but unless you learn to practice *exactly* what you have been taught, without even a trivial or momentary deviation, you might as well not have learned at all. A very slight misalignment of sights will put you off the paper. A very small flinch will put you into the ground halfway to the target. A tiny relaxation of concentration will produce a group like a shotgun pattern at 60 yards. So it is well to respect the game, for, while simple, it is *not* easy. To be a good pistol shot will take all you've got.

I know of no secrets, tricks, or short cuts in the mastery of the pistol. It's the doing that's hard, not the knowing. The essence of the thing is concentration, and concentration is largely a product of determination.

So, if you wish to become a real pistolero, *concentrate.* Get the principles well in mind, work out regularly at home, get to the range at least every other week, and concentrate.

PISTOL HOMEWORK

Homework consists of three phases: snapping, drawing, and handling, often in combination.

Snapping, or dry firing, should be a daily activity. Pick out a target of appropriate size and squeeze off a shot from your empty gun as carefully as if your life depended on it. Call the shot each time, until range corroboration proves that you know exactly where every shot goes without looking at the target. Use the squeeze or the double-action pull until you complete step two, and then try the press. If you have a view of a well-traveled street, use the hubcaps of passing cars as press targets. Passing cats and dogs also serve well as snapping targets. But do your dry firing carefully. Fight down the tendency to feel that precision does not matter since the gun is empty anyway.

I suppose character enters here. The kind of person who cheats will never be able to resist cheating himself, since no one will ever know. He slacks his concentration and pretends to himself that every squeeze was good, knowing perfectly well that such was not the case. Such a man, fortunately, cannot become a really good shot, as he can't do anything that takes self-discipline.

Calling each shot should be a regular practice when live firing on the range, especially in deliberate fire. At distances where the strike is not visible, it's well to have a partner use a spotting glass, and to log each call without verifying it until the end of the string. This will avoid subconscious compensation for an incorrect hold, which can spoil a group. I suppose it is clear that small groups are more important than high scores, for sights may be adjusted to bring a group to center, but in a widely scattered pattern an X is just an accident.

Drawing practice may be conducted in front of a mirror, in the case of unsighted fire, or against a regular dry target. Combat shots do almost all of their dry firing starting holstered, in order to combine two elements in one session. Drawing practice should be conducted with the hands in varied starting positions.

Handling practice goes right along with the other phases of homework, but should include safety checking, clearing, and loading. It is somewhat more important for the auto pistol, whose hammer, safety, slide stop, and magazine release must become as familiar in location and feel as the shooter's own body. Another extra exercise for the auto is blind loading, to enable the shooter to change magazines instantly without looking at his piece. It should become a reflex for the auto shooter to swap magazines in any combat situation on the instant of any lull. This way he knows he's got a full weapon in hand without having to think about it. Such a reflex comes only with constant practice. It is less useful with a revolver, which must be taken out of action to load, and thus requires a conscious tactical decision of its user.

Homework is absolutely necessary to good pistol shooting, and it is the hardest single chore to get a trainee to do. At each range session with a novice I always ask, "What have you done since you were out here last?" And the answer is too often a sheepish "nothing." However, homework is a supplement to, not a substitute for, range practice. As the shooter progresses, there are a number of advanced techniques he should work on, among which is the pivot.

Most people, from a firm Weaver Stance, can fire 90 degrees to the right and about 75 degrees to the left without discomfort or unsteadiness, leaving the feet planted. This is because the left foot leads. With some slight difficulty, one can expand this arc to include all of a full circle except for about 35 degrees dead astern. To shoot straight to the rear, in the Weaver Stance, the 180-degree pivot is best executed as follows. On the first count establish a solid, firm gun-hand contact and place the left hand in its proper position in front of the belt buckle. At the same time cross with the left foot behind the right, taking a full step to the right and not allowing the left foot to drop back. The two feet should be planted flat on the ground with the toe of the left foot no farther rearward than the instep of the right. It will be necessary to bend the right knee in order to get into this position. The step should be as long as can be comfortably achieved. On the count of Two start the pistol out of the holster as the left quadriceps pulls hard. The weight remains on the balls of both feet and the body is snapped completely around to the rear into a proper Weaver Stance. When this is done properly the muzzle never covers the ground any farther away from the shooter's feet than about a foot. There is no danger to spectators since the pistol never points anywhere but either down or toward the target.

When this pivot is executed from a crossdraw holster, great economy of motion is effected by simply allowing the body to pull the holster off the muzzle of the pistol, which then just rises slightly from its holstered position to its position on target.

In drawing to a braced kneeling position facing directly to the rear the left foot is dropped straight backward as the right hand hits the pistol, and then as the pistol is drawn the whole body pivots on the balls of the feet as the right knee comes to the ground. This is a very simple move to execute and permits some people to shoot rearward more rapidly from kneeling than from standing.

MOVING TARGETS

Moving targets are definitely part of any advanced training, and lead estimation can get to be a whole art in itself. For example, using a 900 f/s load and firing at a target moving 50 feet in 5 seconds your correct sight picture would look like this at 7 yards:

like this at 15 yards:

and like this at 25 yards:

With different ammunition, different ranges, and different target speeds, everything must be reset, and the best estimator, assuming he can also shoot, wins the day.

Hitting thrown targets is also good fun, and though it is hard to see how it relates to any foreseeable use of the weapon, it sharpens both a quick sight picture and a very precise press. The trick here is to press just as the target checks at the top of its arc.

A modification is to set a 12-ounce can on top of a 2-pound coffee can filled with water at about 7 yards. Draw and hit the coffee can, which action will fire the smaller can straight up. Catch the second can with your second shot at the top of its flight.

All moving target shooting calls for swing as well as lead, just as in shotgunning. You must be sure to follow through, holding steadily on target after the shot as well as before, for stopping your swing is fatal.

As you progress you should work about 15 percent of your time with your weak hand, for you might conceivably need to use your handgun after your dominant arm was disabled. And practice drawing, as well as shooting, this way. You never know. An expert can draw, place five hits at 7 yards, reload, and place five more, in less than twenty seconds—using only the weak hand.

FLINCH

It is probably beyond argument that the greatest single enemy of pistol marksmanship is flinch. It is common, natural, and devastating. While it is also a hazard to riflemen and shotgunners, it is more so to pistoleros. It is the

Ray Chapman taking a thrown tin can while drawing to the Weaver Stance.

Thell Reed using the one-arm point from a moving jeep on a motorized assault course.

direct cause of those horrible "grounders" you see on the boot range, which make the perpetrator want to crawl down the nearest gopher hole.

Naturally, then, to become a good pistol shot you must lick flinch, but before you try you must get your terms straight. "Flinching" is the accepted term for that nervous twitching of the hand which accompanies the poor shot's final pressure on the trigger. It is concealed by the recoil of a loaded weapon, but, of course, it is visible to both the shooter and his coach if the

weapon is empty. However, since the action is caused by the shooter's antici-
pation of recoil and blast, it will not take place if he knows there is no cartridge under the hammer. The coach's answer to this is to present the weapon
to the shooter for each shot, sometimes loaded and sometimes not. Since the
shooter does not know whether to anticipate a click or a bang, he must now
release uniformly, producing either humiliating "dry-flinches" or properly
directed shots.

However—and this may come as a shock to some—we have uncovered
something which would appear to confound the foregoing. Specifically, we
have seen inadvertently unloaded pistols (bad primers, skipped chambers,
etc.) dip sharply on let-off, *in the hands of masters.* Question: How can a man
"flinch" like this and still fire the fantastically precise groups necessary to hold
his own in today's level of competition? Answer: "That was no flinch, that was
a P.I.P."

The explanation lies in the nature of combat competition, which, unlike
ordinary target shooting, often demands almost instantaneous recoil recovery
for succeeding shots. The conventional target shot never has to fire faster than
five shots in ten seconds (which is sluggishly deliberate to a combat shot) and
he normally uses just as light a load as will pass inspection. The only conventional course which calls for really quick recovery is the International Rapid,
in its fast stage (five different targets in four seconds). The I.S.U. solution to
the problem thus posed lies in completely eliminating all disturbance of the
gun hand by the use of an auto pistol chambered for .22 Shorts and equipped
with a muzzle brake. This is rather like a matador's raising the level of his performance by tackling goats.

Combat shooters fire the International Rapid Course with heavy-caliber
handguns, starting holstered and safe (a good score is 280 x 300 or better), and
many other courses in which quick recovery from heavy recoil is essential to a
respectable performance. What has developed from this is the need to get the
weapon "back on" just as fast as humanly possible. This requires a powerful
hold, and a definite muscular response which must take place immediately
after, not before, the explosion of the cartridge. The interval between the fall
of the hammer and this recoil recovery is so small that to an observer it looks
like flinch. But of course it can't be flinch when it is accompanied by record
scores. Hence I have called it Post-Ignition-Push, or P.I.P. for short.

P.I.P. is not found in a slow-fire shooter. My daughter is a fine slow-fire
shot, and her let-offs are absolutely motionless—wet or dry. I take some pleasure in proving this to bystanders by spinning a partially loaded cylinder for
her, so that no one knows what lies under the hammer, and then watching the
gun. On the empties that muzzle doesn't budge—even with the .44 Magnum.
But Christy is a slow-fire shot. She can't place a burst with precision, or even
limit a single round to a specific second. I have also observed target shots with
national reputations who made no attempt to recover, allowing a heavy load
to point the weapon straight up. No flinch—and also no P.I.P. But such a
person has a bad time on a combat course—he just doesn't have enough time.

All this study, practice, and concentration is directed toward the end of making you into a really capable pistol shot, and if at times it threatens to become a nuisance, remember that the ultimate reward is sweet. A master marksman knows powerful satisfactions that are both the result of the domination of a difficult art, and the realization that he has achieved the classical power of Zeus—the control of the thunderbolt in his fist.

32

Matches and Courses

IT IS SAID that competition is the life of trade. It is equally true that competition is the life of marksmanship. Not only does the universal drive to excel spur us to prove our shooting to be better than the next man's, but contests bring us into contact with the best men in the field, show us what our standards of performance must be, and test new developments in equipment and technique.

The man who works alone, or who completes a standard training program, may develop a useful degree of skill, but he will be most unlikely to discover more than about 50 percent of his potential unless he competes regularly and formally with his peers. For this reason, any sportsman's association or gun club is remiss unless it conducts regular local matches for its members, with all three weapons.

Pistol competition was sponsored in the United States, up until the middle twenties, by the United States Revolver Association (U.S.R.A.) whose program favored local competition with national records to be amassed by mail. Today the National Rifle Association (N.R.A.) is the principal arbiter of the sport, and the emphasis is on shoulder-to-shoulder competitions working up from locals, through regionals, to the Nationals held annually at Camp Perry. N.R.A. rules conform to those of the International Shooting Union (I.S.U.) and are rather stately. The rule book is about fifty pages long and I will not reproduce it here, but I will quote the following excerpts since they are critical to anyone wishing to enter any N.R.A. match:

3.1 Service Pistol—U.S. Pistol, caliber .45 M1911 or M1911A1 or the same type and caliber of commercially manufactured pistol. The pistol must be equipped with issue or similar factory standard stocks (i.e., without thumb rest). Trigger pull must be not less than 4 pounds. The pistol must be equipped with open sights. The front sight must be nonadjustable, will not be undercut, and will not exceed five sixteenths of an inch in height. The pistol may be equipped with an adjustable rear sight with open U or rectangular notch, the distance between sights measuring not more than 7 inches from the apex of the front sight to the rear face of the rear sight. The fore-strap of the grip may be checkered. The mainspring housing may be either the flat or arched type. Trigger shoes may be used. Trigger stops, internal or external, are acceptable. Otherwise, external alterations or additions to the arm will not be allowed. The outside dimensions and design of the arm may not be altered in any way which would prevent it from being holstered or carried in field service in a normal manner. The internal parts of the pistol may be specially fitted and include alterations which will improve the functioning and accuracy of the arm, provided such alterations in no way interfere with the proper functioning of the safety devices as manufactured. All standard safety features of the weapon must operate properly. It is the competitor's responsibility to have his weapon checked prior to the firing of the match.

3.2 .45 Caliber Semi-Automatic Pistol—Any .45 caliber semi-automatic pistol, trigger pull not less than 3½ pounds, sights may be adjustable but not more than ten inches apart. All standard safety features of weapon must operate properly.

3.4 Any Center-fire Pistol or Revolver—Center-fire pistols (single shot or semi-automatic) or revolvers of .32 caliber or larger (including .45 caliber pistols and revolvers); barrel length, including cylinder, not more than ten inches; trigger pull not less than 2½ pounds, except .45 caliber semi-automatic pistols not less than 3½ pounds. Sights may be adjustable but not over ten inches apart. All standard safety features of weapon must operate properly. Programs may specify particular calibers or types of center-fire weapons which will be permitted or not permitted in stated event.

3.5 .22 Caliber Pistol or Revolver—Any pistol (single shot or semi-automatic) or revolver using a .22 caliber rimfire cartridge having an over-all length of not more than 1.1 inches and with lead or alloy bullet not greater than .23″ in diameter and weighing not more than 40 grains; barrel length, including cylinder, not more than ten inches; sights may be adjustable but not over ten inches apart. Trigger pull not less than 2 pounds.

5.15 Firing Position—Standing, gun held in one hand only, the other hand and arm being used in no way to assist; all portions of the shooter's clothing, body and gun clear of artificial support. Competitors will take their positions immediately to the right of their numbered FIRING POINT markers and immediately to the rear of the designated firing line. No portion of the shooter's body may rest upon or touch the ground in advance of the firing line.

In addition, the following rules are quoted as standard in any pistol match, whether conducted by the N.R.A., the military services, the police, or the local chowder and marching societies:

14.3 How to Score—A shot hole, the leaded edge of which comes in contact with the outside of the bullseye or scoring rings of a target, is given the higher value. A scoring gauge approved by the NRA will be used to determine the value of close shots. The higher value will be allowed in those cases where the flange on the approved gauge touches the scoring ring.

14.5 Early or Late Shots—When stationary target frames are used if any shots are fired at the target before the command "Commence Firing" or after the command "Cease Firing" the shots of highest value equal to the number fired in error will be scored as misses.

14.6 All Shots Count—All shots fired by the competitor after he has taken his position at the firing point will be counted in his score, even if the pistol is accidentally discharged.

14.7 Hits on Wrong Target—Hits on the wrong target are scored as misses.

14.8 Ricochets—A hole made by a ricochet bullet does not count as a hit and will be scored as a miss. It must be noted that a bullet which keyholes is not necessarily a ricochet.

14.9 Visible Hits and Close Groups—As a general rule only those hits which are visible will be scored. An exception will be made in the case where the grouping of three or more shots is so close that it is possible for a required shot or shots to have gone through the enlarged hole without leaving a mark. In this case the shooter will be given the benefit of the doubt and scored a hit.

14.10 Excessive Hits—If more than the required number of hits appear on the target, any shot which can be identified by the type of bullet hole as having been fired by some competitor other than the competitor assigned to that target or as having been fired in a previous string will be pasted and will not be scored. If more than the required number of hits then remain on the target a complete new score will be fired and the original score will be disregarded, except (a) if all hits are of equal value the score will be recorded as the required number of hits of that value (b) if the competitor wishes to accept a score equal to the required number of hits of lowest value, he shall be allowed to do so (c) if a competitor fires less than the prescribed number of shots through his own fault, and there should be more hits on the target than the shots fired, he will be scored the number of shots of highest value equal to the number he fired and given a miss for each unfired cartridge.

The targets used in N.R.A. Competition are round black bull's-eyes, except for the international rapid-fire target which is uncommon. Their dimensions are as follows:

50-foot slow fire—20-yard Standard American reduced to 50 feet. 7, 8, 9, and 10 rings black.

10 ring	.90 inches	6 ring	4.16 inches
9 ring	1.54 inches	5 ring	5.56 inches
8 ring	2.23 inches	4 ring	7.33 inches
7 ring	3.07 inches		

50-foot timed or rapid fire. 9 and 10 rings black.

10 ring	1.80 inches	7 ring	6.14 inches
9 ring	3.06 inches	6 ring	8.32 inches
8 ring	4.46 inches		

20-yard slow fire, 7, 8, 9, and 10 rings black.

10 ring	1.12 inches	6 ring	5.04 inches
9 ring	1.88 inches	5 ring	6.72 inches
8 ring	2.72 inches	4 ring	8.84 inches
7 ring	3.73 inches		

20-yard timed or rapid fire. 9 and 10 rings black.

10 ring	2.25 inches	7 ring	7.46 inches
9 ring	3.76 inches	6 ring	10.08 inches
8 ring	5.44 inches		

25-yard slow fire, 7, 8, 9, and 10 rings black.

10 ring	1.70 inches	7 ring	5.50 inches
9 ring	2.77 inches	6 ring	7.40 inches
8 ring	4.00 inches		

25-yard rapid or timed fire—Exactly the same target as the 50-yard slow fire except that only the 9 and 10 rings are black.

50-yard slow fire. 8, 9, and 10 rings black.

X ring	1.70 inches	7 ring	11.00 inches
10 ring	3.39 inches	6 ring	14.80 inches
9 ring	5.54 inches	5 ring	19.68 inches
8 ring	8.00 inches		

50-meter (164-feet ½-inch) international target 7, 8, 9, and 10 rings black.

10 ring	1.97 inches	5 ring	11.81 inches
9 ring	3.94 inches	4 ring	13.78 inches
8 ring	5.91 inches	3 ring	15.75 inches
7 ring	7.87 inches	2 ring	17.72 inches
6 ring	9.84 inches	1 ring	19.69 inches

50-meter international target reduced for firing at 50 yards. 7, 8, 9, and 10 rings black.

10 ring	1.80 inches	5 ring	10.80 inches
9 ring	3.60 inches	4 ring	12.60 inches
8 ring	5.40 inches	3 ring	14.40 inches
7 ring	7.20 inches	2 ring	16.20 inches
6 ring	9.00 inches	1 ring	18.00 inches

The military services use the "L" target for training and qualification, which measures as follows:

10 ring	5.00 inches	6 ring	19.13 inches
9 ring	8.63 inches	5 ring	22.63 inches
8 ring	12.13 inches	4 ring	27.13 inches
7 ring	15.63 inches	3 ring	46.13 inches

Balance of target 4 feet by 6 feet scoring two.

The international rapid-fire target, used in the Olympic Games and sometimes elsewhere, is a sort of pseudo combat target in the shape of a stylized
human figure marked off into vertically oblong scoring rings which have no
anatomical significance. It is rather difficult to use, as it comes in upper and
lower halves which must be joined on a long carrier. Actually the lower half
may be dispensed with—if you get down in there you're out of contention
anyway. This target is used at 25 meters. It is 63 inches high by 17¾ inches
wide. The "head" is 8¾ by 5⅞ inches. The center section, from shoulders to
hips is 25 inches high. The ten-ring measures 5⅞ by 4 inches, the nine-ring
11¾ by 7⅞ inches, and the eight-ring 17¾ by 11¾ inches.

Left to right: The N.R.A. 50-yard pistol
target; the International Rapid Fire target; and an early combat silhouette.
The pistol is shown for size. The X-ring
in the combat target is not normally
visible to the shooter.

The large, or "Colt," silhouette.

The reduced, or CHP, silhouette.

Hanging a steel silhouette. Steel targets have many advantages as they avoid the necessity of pasting, but there is a risk of lead splash at very short ranges.

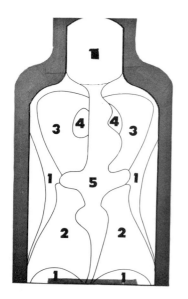

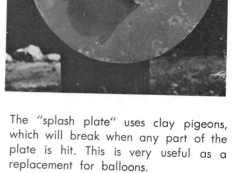

The "splash plate" uses clay pigeons, which will break when any part of the plate is hit. This is very useful as a replacement for balloons.

An anatomical target designed by the medical staff at the U.S. Air Force Academy. Head shots get lowest score.

STANDARD COURSES OF FIRE

National Match Course

Range	Type Fire	Time per 10 shot string slow fire or 5 shot string timed and rapid fire	Strings	Target
50 yds.	Slow	10 minutes, 10 shots	1	50 yd. SF
25 yds.	Timed	20 seconds, 5 shots	2	25 yd. TF
25 yds.	Rapid	10 seconds, 5 shots	2	25 yd. RF

NRA Short Course

Range	Type Fire	Time per 5 Shot String	Strings	Target
25 yds.	Slow	5 minutes	2	25 yd. SF
25 yds.	Timed	20 seconds	2	25 yd. TF
25 yds.	Rapid	10 seconds	2	25 yd. RF

Camp Perry Course

Range	Type Fire	Time per 5 Shot String	Strings	Target
25 yds.	Slow	2½ minutes	2	25 yd. TF
25 yds.	Timed	20 seconds	2	25 yd. TF
25 yds.	Rapid	10 seconds	2	25 yd. RF

Marksman League Course

Range	Type Fire	Time per 5 Shot String	Strings	Target
25 yds.	Slow	5 minutes	2	25 yd. SF
15 yds.	Timed	20 seconds	2	25 yd. TF
15 yds.	Rapid	10 seconds	2	25 yd. RF

Gallery Course (May also be fired outdoors)
(50 feet or 20 yds.)

Type Fire	Time per 5 Shot String	Strings	Target
Slow	5 minutes	2	Slow Fire
Timed	20 seconds	2	Timed Fire
Rapid	10 seconds	2	Rapid Fire

Single Stage Course

Any number of strings (10-shot at 50 yards slow fire, or 5-shot at timed or rapid fire) fired at a single distance as specified in the conditions of the match and in the regular time allowance for that type of firing.

International Slow Fire Course

60 shots (6 series of 10 shots) with a break of 30 minutes after 3rd series of 10 shots. Time limit 20 minutes for each series of 10 shots. 50 meters.

International Rapid Fire Course

60 shots i.e., 30 shots once repeated.
30 shots in 6 series of 5 as follows:
    2 series of 8 seconds each
    2 series of 6 seconds each
    2 series of 4 seconds each
25 meters.

The really rough parts of the conventional courses are the 50-yard slow-fire stage of the National Match Course and the whole of the International Slow Fire Course. These are so hard that you can spend your life on them and get nothing for it but frustration. Don't let this bother you, though, for they represent a completely impractical use of the handgun. If you have all that

Firing the International Rapid Fire course with a .45 auto from the leather, using the two-hand grip.

time in any live situation you would scarcely shoot from offhand. Actually there are quite a few pistol shooters who feel that the whole notion of shooting at bull's-eyes from offhand is what leads most people to under-value the handgun as a weapon. The conventionalists counter by saying that any criticism of the classical style is merely sour grapes on the part of people who simply can't shoot well. There is some merit in this, for offhand shooting *is* difficult, and quite a few people who can use a pistol very effectively from a practical position may indeed never be able to shoot a decent score on the National Match Course. In all due respect, however, I must point out that practical shooting, while undoubtedly not as intimidating to the beginner as offhand slow-fire, takes a bit of doing too. A couple of years ago I wheedled a national champion of the Camp Perry school into entering a local Mexican Defense contest. He placed sixteenth out of twenty-four entries. It would not have taken much practice for him to work up in this league, for he is a superb shot, but it would have taken some.

So it is that practical competition is beginning to be appreciated, its essential differences from the conventional being that it is freestyle, it is much faster, it is diverse, it calls for drawing, and it is confined to full-power handguns. It is becoming fairly standardized at this writing, and the following courses are often encountered.

HUNTING COURSES

The Field Course. 15 Rounds

This is a simple but illuminating course of fire. It was first used as a contest course for the .44 Magnum revolver only, but it is equally good for any of the high-velocity handguns generally referred to as magnums.

Stoeger deer targets are normally used, but any similar game targets will do, or even police silhouettes if necessary.

There are three stages, of 100, 50, and 35 yards. Five shots are fired at each stage.

At 100 and at 50 the standing deer target is used.

At 100 yards there is no time limit and no restriction on position, except that no artificial rest may be used.

At 50 yards the shooter starts loaded and holstered, and is given three seconds per shot, freestyle, from the leather.

At 35 yards a running deer target is mounted on a trolley, to move 50 feet in five seconds. Five individual runs are made, each with one round from the leather.

Differences in weapons make scores relative on this course, but any man who can shoot 135 × 150 on it with a .44 Magnum on a deer target is a deadlier brush hunter than most riflemen.

The Stalk (Deer Hunt). 10–15 Rounds

This is similar to an archer's "roving range." It is a very challenging and enjoyable course of fire, but it is time consuming, very difficult to administer, and it requires more terrain than is available to most gun clubs. Deer or other game targets are used. Ideally, a fairly steep, wooded canyon or draw is found, with a trail along its bottom. From 300 to 500 yards of this trail are marked off, with the ends designated as start and finish points. The targets are placed in such a way as to be visible from the trail, but not obvious, at ranges of from 25 to 125 yards.

It is the shooter's task to cover the trail as rapidly as possible, and still locate and hit each target. Since game rarely offers a stationary second shot, only one shot per target is permitted. Positions are naturally freestyle, but the shooter may not leave the trail to approach a target nor shoot to the rearward of his position.

Secrecy is necessary in setting up this course, as a major part of the problem lies in finding the targets. A judge accompanies each contestant to record his time, and he should be careful to pick up all empty cases left in the trail lest they betray the firing points of previous shooters.

An indefinite number of targets is used, not less than ten nor more than fifteen, and the scoring rings are not used except to define the target's vital zone, for each shot is either a kill or a miss for scoring purposes.

In order to rule out complete and tedious deliberation, a maximum time is established, and each shooter is notified when he has exhausted half his allowed time and also when he has covered half the distance to the finish line. Time is recorded from start to finish, unless the shooter does not reach the finish in the allowed time, in which case he is halted and quits.

Scoring is simply the number of targets hit adjusted by the time taken to run the course. If two or more contestants make the same number of hits the lowest time wins. The tasks are, "Find 'em, hit 'em, hurry!"—in that order.

This course favors a flat-shooting, very accurate pistol with excellent sights and trigger action; exactly what is needed in a hunting weapon. It calls for somewhat different skills than true combat shooting, but it is interesting to note that while not all good combat shots do well on the stalk, those who do are always good combat shots.

Combat Courses

Next we come to what are properly known as combat courses. That is, they test the use of the pistol as a fighting tool. They are interesting, challenging, and varied. The targets always represent a man, or the vital zone of a man, since minor differences in placement at short range are inconsequential. Such targets may be the 43-inch Colt Silhouette, the 27½-inch reduced silhouette, or the standard combat target. This last is a buff cardboard 30 by 18 inches, with a 10-inch X-ring in the center and 6-inch shoulder cuts.

The Practical Pistol Course (F.B.I.) 50 Rounds

This is the grandaddy of them all, and while there is a lot wrong with it, I list it as example only, as it has been largely expanded.

Ranges are 7, 25, 50, and 60 yards. The large police silhouette target was normally used.

The course was intended for training only. It is not well suited to competition, owing both to its artificial restrictions and the fact that a really good shot usually fires a perfect score on it and thus some sort of tie-breaking system must be added.

It is shot in two stages, as follows:

In stage one (10 rounds) the shooter stands at the seven-yard line. On signal he draws, fires five shots (one-handed and belt-level), reloads and fires five more, in twenty-five seconds. This is so easy that it is only for beginners. To clean it in ten seconds takes a good marksman, but twenty-five is the official time.

In stage two (40 rounds) the shooter stands at the 60-yard line, with five rounds in his pistol and thirty-five rounds on his person. On signal he draws, drops to prone and fires five rounds. He loads in prone, holsters, runs forward to the 50-yard line, assumes the prone position, fires five shots, reloads in prone, assumes the free-sitting position, and fires five more. At the 50-yard line there is a barricade about the size and shape of an ordinary door, placed upright. After firing his five from sitting, the shooter rolls behind this barricade, reloads under cover and then fires five shots using the right-hand barricade position; reloads under cover, fires five from the left-hand barricade position, reloads, holsters, and runs forward to the 25-yard line. Here he originally assumed the sitting position but now normally goes to kneeling. Some departments call for offhand here with the shooter on one knee, but unsupported, which is pointless. Properly the shooter should take the braced kneeling position. After five shots he jumps behind the barricade, which is the same as that at the 50-yard line, reloads, and fires five right-handed-barricade, reloads, and fires five left-handed-barricade. He must fire the whole stage in 5 minutes and forty-five seconds.

Because of the regularity with which good shots "go clean" on the P.P.C., inter-departmental contests usually use a small x-ring in the center of the silhouette to break ties. A better system, making for better competition and better gun-handling, is to cut the time allowance drastically. Ten seconds on stage one and three minutes on stage two makes for a pretty fair match.

Requiring the shooter to use the barricade position is a bad point in that the more modern Weaver Stance is faster, more accurate, safer from return fire ricocheting off the barricade, less prone to bark up the shooting hand, and just about as protected if the feet are properly placed. The barricade position may be of some use in steadying down a novice, but it certainly should not be required for half the sighted shots on a standard course. If the P.P.C. is used for a contest it should be shot freestyle in much shorter time increments, with the shooter required only to keep his body within the marked-off shooting stations.

Naturally, with all that reloading, the P.P.C. strongly favors the auto pistol.

The Advanced Military Combat Pistol Course.
50 Rounds

This was designed in 1947 at the Marine Corps Base at Quantico, Virginia. It is very generalized, and an excellent test of over-all skill, but rather complicated and hard to administer. It also requires "bobbing" (disappearing) targets, which are always available on a military range but rare elsewhere. It is fired in six stages.

Stage One. This stage tests the maximum accuracy of the shooter and his weapon. As this is not a particularly vital factor in the use of a handgun, five shots are fired, accounting for a possible of 50 points, or one-tenth of the total score.

Range: 50 yards. Target: N.R.A. 50-yard pistol target. All hits inside the "8" ring, i.e., "in the black," count ten. Hits inside the "5" ring but outside the "8" ring count five. Hits outside the "5" ring count zero. Shots: five. Strings: one. Position: Any position which does not employ an artificial rest. Prone or sitting is recommended but not required. Time: no limit.

Although time and position are unrestricted, the shooter will not be permitted to "spot on" with optical instruments, since to be effective in combat, the shooter must know where his weapon shoots before he opens fire.

Stage Two. This stage tests the effectiveness of deliberate fire at what is considered to be a long combat range. Since this employment of the weapon is not common, only five shots are fired, with a possible score of 50 points.

Range: 50 yards. Target: Military Silhouette. Shots: five. Strings: one. Position: freestyle. Time: 15 seconds from the leather.

Stage Three. This stage tests the shooter's ability to draw rapidly and shoot carefully at mid-ranges. This is considered to be a useful skill and is given a weight of one-fifth of the total score.

Range: 25 yards. Target: Military Silhouette. Shots: 10. Strings: 10. Time: 2½ seconds per shot.

The shooter holsters his weapon and stands facing the butts. A "standby" signal is given and approximately one second later the target is turned or raised into the shooter's line of vision. It remains visible for 2½ seconds and then disappears without signal, during which time the shooter draws and fires one shot. After each shot, the shooter renders his weapon safe, reholsters, and signals "ready" to the line judge, who then repeats the process. Any stance, position or system of firing which fulfills the above requirements is permissible.

Stage Four. This stage tests the shooter's ability to draw and shoot very rapidly at short range, as well as his ability to reload his weapon and continue firing with speed and dexterity. It is given a weight of one-fifth of the total score.

Range: 10 yards. Target: Military Silhouette. Shots: 10. Strings: one. Time: 12 seconds.

The shooter stands facing the target with his weapon holstered. At the signal to fire, he draws and fires five shots, reloads, and fires five more.

Stage Five. This stage tests the shooter's ability to pivot and draw simultaneously, pick up targets rapidly, and engage several targets at once. It is the most practical and valuable part of the course, and is given the greatest weight of any stage, 120 out of 500 points.

Range: 10 yards. Target: 3 Military Silhouettes, 3 yards apart. Shots: 12. Strings: 2. Time: 4 seconds per string.

The shooter stands facing 90 degrees or more to either the right or the left of the line of sight to the center target. On the signal to fire the shooter draws, pivots to face the target and fires two shots at each target, in any order. He then reloads, reholsters, resumes his initial position, and signifies to the line judge that he is ready to commence the second string. Two identical strings are fired, requiring twelve shots and making possible a score of 120.

Stage Six. This stage tests the shooter's ability to combine maximum speed with the necessary accuracy to hit a man at close range. Since a relatively fast draw is also required in stages 3, 4, and 5, this stage requires only eight shots and is given a weight of 80 points.

Range: 10 yards. Target: Military Silhouette. Shots: 8. Strings: 8. Time: 1½ seconds per shot.

The shooter stands facing the target with his weapon loaded, holstered, and safe. At the signal to fire he draws and fires one shot. He then checks his weapon for safety, reholsters, and awaits the second signal.

Qualification Scores:

Expert 455
Sharpshooter 415
Marksman 375

Notes:

(1) Overtime: In stages 2, 4, and 5, any shots fired after the time limit has expired count as misses. In addition, the shooter loses the value of one additional hit (10 points) for the string in which the overtime occurred. In stage 6 if the shooter cannot fire in 1½ seconds, he is told to fire the stage at maximum speed and is given half credit on his resulting score. If the shooter can barely make the required time interval, he is given the choice of counting all overtime shots as misses or taking half credit on the whole stage.

(2) In competition, the time required for each string in stages 5 and 6 will be recorded for each shooter on his score sheet. In the case of tied scores, the average time for the two strings in stage 5 will be computed to the nearest ¹/₁₀

second, and this average will be added to the average time required for each of the eight shots in stage 6 to the nearest $\frac{1}{10}$ second. The sum of the two averages will be compared and the tie will be resolved in favor of the faster shooter.

(3) If this course is used as a test of general ability with the handgun, the shooter in question should be permitted to shoot it only twice, preferably on successive days, and his second score taken as an index of his skill.

The International Rapid Fire Course (modified).
30 or 60 Rounds

This is the course used in the Olympic Games, where it is shot from a 45-degree ready position with compensated, .22 Short, auto pistols. When it is shot from the leather, freestyle, with full-duty weapons, it makes a pretty fair combat course. When so modified it should be shot on a combat target (silhouette with a 10-inch X-ring) rather than on the somewhat "busy" international target; however, even on the latter, very respectable scores may be achieved by a good shot.

It is fired in three stages, all at 25 meters (about 27 yards) and all on a battery of five targets placed side-by-side one width apart. On signal (or upon appearance of the targets if you have the luxury of bobbers) the shooter draws and fires one shot at each target. On the first stage he is allowed eight seconds for each of two strings. On the second stage he is allowed six seconds, and on the third stage, four. This makes for thirty rounds in all, but the whole course is fired twice in Olympic competition to make a total of sixty shots for a possible of 600 points. 580 is an excellent score with a .22 short on the unmodified course, as is 560 with a combat pistol from the leather. Master shots often go clean using a combat target, using the X-ring to break ties.

The main drawback of this course is the varying time allowed to perform a single task. It is an artificial difficulty to have to memorize three different intervals, when the actual problem suggested is that of hitting five adversaries as fast as possible.

The Mexican Defense Course (modified). 36 Rounds

This is another old-timer, and a very fine course of fire for either training or competition, particularly as now modified. There are many who feel that it is the best single test of useful pistol skill. Its drawbacks are that it involves some fairly complicated footwork which is difficult to judge, and it is rather more dangerous for beginners than most.

As the name implies, it was invented in Mexico, but the last two "tie-breaker" stages were added in California about five years ago. These last are hard, and to my knowledge the course has never been "cleaned" under pressure, though it may have been in practice.

The course is laid out with six large-type police silhouettes, one width apart. (We still use them, armholes and all, because this is the way the Mexicans set it up.) Two firing lines are marked out, 8 and 10 meters from the targets. All strings are of six shots, and all strings are allowed five seconds.

The shooter stands, loaded and holstered, inside the 8-meter line, with his back to the targets. On the command "Walk!" he starts toward the 10-meter line, hands clear of his weapon. As soon as one foot touches the ground beyond the 10-meter line, the judge sounds a whistle and starts the clock simultaneously. At the whistle the shooter crosses the line with his other foot (jump turns, as in hopscotch, are not permitted), pivots, draws, and opens fire. The step, pivot and draw are simultaneous, and the shooter may touch his gun any time after the whistle.

On the first string the shooter stands fast and fires six shots at one target.

On the second string he stands fast and fires one shot at each target.

On the third string he fires six shots at one target, but must advance while firing. The first shot is fired outside the 10-meter line, the second is fired with at least one foot down inside the 10-meter line, and the sixth shot is fired with both feet inside the 8-meter line.

On the fourth string he fires one shot on each target, advancing as on #3.

This is as far as the Mexicans go, and it's hard enough for ordinary shots, but experts clean it up to here. Thinking of Billy-the-Kid's exit from the burning McSween house, when he ran to his horse under fire while beating down a group of riflemen at short range with his pistol, I added two lateral stages in 1959 which are not standard. Thus:

On the fifth string the shooter fires six shots on one target at ten meters, the first opposite #1 target and the sixth opposite #6. Two lines are marked on the ground perpendicular to the 8- and 10-meter lines and exactly between targets #1 & #2 and #5 & #6. The first shot must be fired with both feet outside the 10-meter line and to the left of the left-hand perpendicular. The second shot must be fired with at least one foot down to the right of the left-hand perpendicular. The last shot must be fired with neither foot on the ground to the left of the right-hand perpendicular.

On the sixth string the shooter fires one shot on each target, moving as on #5.

Any error in procedure, such as a foot fault or jumping the whistle, costs the shooter the value of one center hit, which is five on the police silhouette. However, since a shooter might elect to sacrifice 10 points to avoid the lateral running on the fifth and sixth strings, if he is not clear of the right-hand perpendicular at the five-second whistle, his score for the string is halved.

Since the maximum value of a hit is five, 36 shots made the possible score 180. The highest score recorded in competition so far is 179, and anything over 160 is very good.

The Night Shoot. 30 Rounds

Since a defensive handgun is very likely to have to be used in the dark, this standard course is both entertaining and enlightening. Buff silhouettes with a

10-inch X-ring are used. Ranges are 10 and 7 yards. The course should be shot in full dark on a moonless night.

On the first string the shooter stands facing the target at 10 yards, loaded and holstered, and with six spare rounds available. Lights are out.

The signal to fire is the illumination of the target by flood lights. As the shooter draws and opens fire the illumination continues for four seconds and then ceases. The cease-fire whistle sounds fourteen seconds after the lights go on, and ten seconds after they go out. In this period the shooter draws, fires six shots, reloads, and fires six more. This stage tests the shooter's ability to fire rapidly at a target illuminated by an uncontrolled source of light, to load quickly in the dark, and to reengage a darkened target located only by his bodily orientation. It is difficult but possible. It has been cleaned several times in competition.

On stage two, the shooter engages three targets, one width apart, at 10 yards. The shooter carries his own flashlight, turned off before the firing signal. Lights are out. The shooter is loaded and holstered, his hands are clear of his gun but may hold his flashlight. On signal, the shooter turns on his light, draws, and fires at each of the three targets twice, in any order. He is allowed four seconds. The string is repeated for a total of twelve rounds. This stage tests the very practical ability of a man to illuminate a target with one hand and hit it with the other.

On stage three, the shooter engages one target at 7 yards, with six individual draws. The shooter faces the target in the dark, holstered and clear, and the signal to fire is a single flick of the flood lights. On each flick he draws and fires one shot. The lights are out before his weapon can line up, so he must hit what he glimpsed before he drew.

The Running Man. 24 Rounds

This is a straightforward moving target course, without frills. Any competent gunhandler must be able to lead and swing, and this is the standard way of testing this skill.

The target is the standard silhouette with a 10-inch X-ring. It is mounted on a trolley and weighted so as to travel 50 feet in five seconds, and to be visible only when moving. Two trolley systems should be used, so that the shooter alternates on left-to-right and right-to-left problems. (The fifty-in-five rate is not based on any statistical study. It's simply an easy standard to remember. Variable rates are interesting, but not fair in competition.)

On the first stage, the shooter stands loaded and holstered, 7 yards from the center of the target's path. He may draw when he first sees the target. On the first run he fires six shots right-to-left; and on the second, six shots left-to-right.

On the second stage, the shooter fires at 15 yards; three shots right-to-left and three shots left-to-right.

On the third stage, the shooter fires two shots on each of three runs at 25 yards, alternating left and right.

On each stage the shooter's hand remains clear of his pistol until the target has started its run.

This one can also be cleaned, and the X-ring is necessary. Top score is 24 × 24 (23X) which was shot, incidentally, double-action with a K-38.

The Assault Course (Hogan's Alley). Rounds Unrestricted

This is a very fast course designed to sharpen the shooter's reactions to close-range, street-fight situations. It requires space and 160 degrees of safe shooting directions. Normally, fifteen silhouette targets are used. The shooter may fire as much as he wishes, but only two hits per target count for record.

The starting point faces a trail some 50 yards long, with a flag planted at the finish. The targets are spotted along both sides of the trail, from 5 to 15 yards out. They are in plain sight from some point on the trail, but as few as possible should be visible from any one point.

On his first run the shooter stands loaded and holstered at the starting line, carrying as much spare ammunition as he needs in any way he chooses. At the signal he draws and fires at the first target, which is visible from the starting line. At his convenience he holsters his weapon, in a safe condition, and moves out along the trail. Whenever he chooses he may stop, fire, load, and holster, but he may not move with his pistol in his hand. This simulates a series of unconnected emergencies, not a continuous assault. His time from the starting signal to the instant he raises the flag at the finish is recorded by the judges.

The second run is made with the pistol in hand, after the first draw, and the shooter may both shoot and load while in motion.

Since the targets are easy to hit, the issue on the assault course is speed. Scoring is by time among those with the same number of hits, i.e., the fastest man to hit all thirty targets wins, but a man with twenty-nine hits is placed lower than anyone who hits them all.

Another successful scoring method is to establish a par time by experiment and then to add the value of a hit for every second under par and subtract the value of a hit for every second over par.

It is not possible to standardize the assault course completely, due to variations in available terrain, but an expert will hit fifteen targets in 50 yards—drawing for each target and running holstered—in under forty seconds.

All the foregoing courses are scored contests in which the shooter fires a given score and is ranked in the match by its numerical value. The courses which follow are known as "man-against-man," and in these it is necessary to defeat a series of individual antagonists in succession, as in a joust, a fencing match, or a tennis tournament. Both scored and man-against-man contests have their place, as the scored match is a more accurate method of rating skill, but the man-against-man match calls for more nerve control. Any competition program should include both types, and in some circumstances it may be advisable to seed the field by a scored match and run off the qualifiers man-against-man.

All the following are true combat courses. All require an indefinite number of rounds. All have more spectator appeal than any scored match.

The F.B.I. Duel ("Walk-and-Draw")

This was invented at the F.B.I. Academy at Quantico, Virginia. It is the oldest of the man-against-man contests. Two targets are used, usually 12-inch circles or 12-by-20 inch ovals. They may be "electric sandwiches" (as used by the F.B.I.), steel plates with acoustic or impact trip switches, inflated balloons, or clay pigeons on 12-inch steel splash plates. All that is necessary is that there be a satisfactory method of determining which target is hit first. The electric systems are excellent as long as they work, but they are subject to breakdown and require a power source that is not always readily available. Visual judging on balloons and clay pigeons is more dependable but less accurate. Any electric system used must be able to read the time spread between two hits, since hits within .05 seconds of each other count as ties.

The two contestants stand side-by-side about 5 yards apart, facing the two targets, 35 yards down range. Each is loaded, holstered, and clear. At the command "Walk!" they start walking toward the target. At any time thereafter the firing signal may be given, at which they halt, draw, and fire until a target is hit. Ties may be called one hit apiece or no hit. When a hit is achieved the judge sounds a cease-fire whistle, announces which side hit first, and commands "Load and holster. Ready? Walk!" The process is repeated until one contestant achieves two clear wins over his opponent, or three in the prize bouts. The distances called by the line judge are irregularly varied, between 25 and 5 yards.

If, as sometimes happens with beginners, both contestants empty their weapons without a hit, they reload and continue without command.

The challenge in this course is to match speed against accuracy as the range changes. A fairly deliberate shot is necessary at 25 yards and a blistering quick draw at 5, and the winner must work out the correct balance as he moves.

The Leatherslap (Balloon-Bust)

This is a very simple contest, but one of great interest and gallery appeal. It's an excellent way to introduce combat competition to a new area, providing only competent hands are shown to the public. Bumblers are not only foolish-looking but constitute a danger to themselves and the spectators.

The traditional range is 7 yards (taken from F.B.I. practice) and the traditional targets are 12-inch balloons. The contestants "toe-the-line," opposite their targets, and on signal they draw and fire until a balloon breaks. It must be made clear to the spectators that it takes a *positive* edge on time to win a point, not a shading so close that, in a live situation, both men would go down. If the unanimous decision of three judges is used to make a point, the results are quite fair.

The Leatherslap poses a simple problem, but it is subject to all sorts of variations. The range may be varied, as well as the target and the starting positions; but what is given here is the classic version. While artificialities are often inserted by clubs with some special axe to grind, it may be said that a consistent winner of this match is a good man to have on your side.

The Balloon Option ("The Thinking Man's Shoot")

This is a course in which, unlike all others, the contestant is forced to make split-second tactical decisions under pressure, in addition to his other problems. It's frustrating for the shooter, but that doesn't detract from its merit as a test of combat proficiency.

Two 12-inch balloons are provided for each firing point, located one above the other about 3 feet apart. The range is 7 yards.

The Balloon Option target assembly.

Three different firing signals are used. On the *whistle,* the shooter draws and covers the target. On the *bell* he draws and hits the lower target only. On the *horn* he draws and hits both targets. He must do the correct thing before his opponent does to win a point. If he does the wrong thing, even though he does it first, he loses. If both contestants fault, it shall count as a point against each. Ties count as no hit, and the whistle counts as no hit unless a contestant fires on it. The signals should be selected by pure chance, such as a chuck-a-luck die, to eliminate any human preference.

This course is excellent police training, as it develops the ability to stop the killing stroke at will without inhibiting the shooter's efficiency.

The Flying M

This is the best of the man-against-man contests.

It requires a rather complex layout but it is by no means hard to administer.

At the firing line an opaque barricade is constructed, 7 feet high and 10 feet long, perpendicular to the direction of fire. Opposite the ends of the barricade three targets are placed, two standard paper silhouettes and one timed target (balloon, splash plate, or electric). The outboard target on each end is 15 yards out, of paper, and placed about 15 degrees outboard of directly down range. The middle target on each end is 25 yards out, of paper, and directly down range from the end of the barricade. The two inner targets are the timed targets, placed side-by-side 7 yards down range from the center of the barricade. Fourteen-inch balloons may be used on the 15-yard and 25-yard positions.

The two contestants start back-to-back, up range from the center of the barricade. They are loaded, holstered, and clear, and they must be touching heels (one heel each). On signal they leap forward, clear the barricade, pivot, draw, and fire. The paper targets must be engaged first and then the timed target. The man who hits both his paper targets, and then hits his timed target first, wins the point. If he hits his timed target first but has missed either of his paper targets, he loses; unless his opponent has missed, too, in which case no point is awarded. If both contestants miss one paper target neither wins, regardless of who is quicker. Contestants change sides between firings. Contestants may not touch their weapons until clear of the barricade, but they need not be firmly planted prior to drawing.

This is a very fine contest, but there is the danger of fumbling by inexperienced gunhandlers, so screening is advisable.

El Presidente—Twelve Rounds

This has become a standard qualification test throughout the world and was named by my colleagues as a result of some professional work that I did for the president of Guatemala in the 1960's. It is not a combat simulation, but simply a nerve exercise which tests various sorts of shooting skills. When I originated it it was thought to be impossible. Practice and application have caused it to become quite simple by today's standards.

The shooter places himself opposite three combat silhouette targets at a distance of 10 meters from the center. The targets are spaced 2 meters apart center-to-center, or 1 meter edge-to-edge. The shooter faces directly away from the targets, hands relaxed and (in the definitive test) with his coat on, concealing his pistol. On command the shooter executes a 180-degree pivot, draws, and engages each of the three targets with two shots apiece, then reloads his weapon and repeats the exercise for a total of twelve shots per string. Since the center ring on the combat target counts five points, the total score for each string is sixty points. Par time is ten seconds. To score, the targets are first examined for twelve hits. If any one of the twelve shots did not hit a target a double penalty of ten points is exacted. If there are no penalties the total score is divided by the time the shooter took to shoot the string, to the nearest tenth of a second. A perfect score of sixty points, divided by a par time of ten seconds, will result in an index of six. To obtain an adjusted score the index is multiplied by the factor necessary to convert six to one hundred, which is most easily done by multiplying the index by fifty over three. Thus a score of sixty, fired in ten seconds, will result in exactly one hundred points, which is considered par. It should be noted that a perfect numerical score is never considered to be the shooter's best performance, because if he can keep all his shots in the X-ring he is going too slow. A score of fifty-six, fired in eight seconds, will produce an index of seven, which, when multiplied by fifty over three, achieves an adjusted score of 116.7, which is considerably better than par.

If you can fire a Presidente on demand at par you may be considered to be a competent pistol shot. If you can fire 120 on demand you may join anybody's first team.

THE STANDARD LADDER

Man-against-man contests have many advantages, but they also have serious drawbacks, most particularly in scoring. The ordinary square, seeded ladder of a tennis tournament does not work well in a pistol match because (1) pistol matches are normally entered on the spot rather than in advance, and (2) a pistol bout may be over in two exchanges, which doesn't provide much sport for a man who trained hard, drove 100 miles, and saved up for his entry fee. Also, the element of luck is more important in a man-against-man pistol bout than in a ten-game set of tennis, and a man who suffers a comparatively insignificant stroke of ill fortune feels that he is entitled to keep on shooting, at least for a second chance.

Therefore, after many years of experiment, the J-ladder has now been accepted as standard. It is a modified double-elimination ladder which gives every man at least two bouts for his entry, and a chance to take as high as second place, though not first, even if he loses his first bout. Using this system, the only man who wins all his bouts is first, and the only man who loses only one bout is second. Everyone below second must lose at least twice. An exception to this is if the winner from the left-hand (losers') side has already been defeated by the number two man on the winners' side, then he may not challenge him for second place but must settle for third place over-all, even though he was only defeated once. The over-all winner does not necessarily meet every good performer in the contest, but the J-ladder is still the fairest paired system known.

It is important to note that any ladder must be "square," that is, it must have four, eight, sixteen, thirty-two or any doubled number of places thereafter. It cannot have any other number of places and be made to work. If you have more than eight entries you must go to sixteen places; if more than sixteen, to thirty-two, and so on. This means that only by coincidence, or by some system of qualification, will the number of entrants match the number of places. This difficulty is met, on an ordinary single ladder, by matching the most formidable contestants with "byes" in the first round; that is, granting them a forfeit until the second round, in which they will meet the victor of a first-round bout between two lesser lights. The bye system does not work on the J-ladder, since you cannot reasonably carry a nonexistent competitor into the losers' column. Therefore the J-ladder must be squared by elimination.

An objection to scored eliminations is that they cannot test the same skills which are needed for a man-against-man shoot, but it should be remembered that the essence of combat shooting is versatility, and hence a man who qualifies on a scored course and then wins a man-against-man contest is probably a better shot than one who excels in just one field.

Once the proper number of contestants is selected they must be "seeded," either by qualifying scores, or by a seeding committee on the basis of their competitive records. *Under no circumstances may they be placed at random.* The two top contenders are placed at the top and bottom of the ladder, and the next two on each side of the median, and so on. This is to preclude a lop-sided match in which the heavy-weights knock themselves out on one lobe of the ladder while an average competitor rides easily up to second place over the bodies of the mediocre.

The "Round Robin"

Somewhat fairer than any ladder is the contest in which each contestant meets every other contestant, commonly called a "round robin" for some obscure reason. It is simply scored by the number of wins each man earns and a two-way tie is ruled out because though two men may have the same number of victories, they will have met each other and settled the matter. There is, however, the possibility of a *three-way tie,* which will have to be broken by some system essentially unrelated to a man-against-man contest.

The other grave drawback of the round robin is that it involves so many bouts that it is necessarily confined to small entry lists. The formula for the number of bouts for a given number of contestants is: $B = \dfrac{C\,(C-1)}{2}$. Thus a three-man round robin will have just three bouts, but eight men will need twenty-eight, and a twenty-man list would take 190!

This system, therefore, is chiefly useful in matching the indefinite few highest scores in a scored match, as a sort of dessert in a day's program.

SURPRISE SHOOTS

An expert gunhandler must be able to meet any sort of challenge which his weapon can physically solve, and an expert combat shot must be able to handle any sort of short or midrange combat situation. While the standard courses, taken as a group, certainly pose a variety of problems, each can be practiced for in advance, and this creates a slight artificiality. Realism is what combat shooters should seek, and certainly one can never predict the circumstances of a live situation.

Therefore any complete program should include a number of contests which are as unlike the standard courses as possible, while still emulating actual combat, and in which the procedure is not announced until the contestants are assembled and the entries paid.

Such contests are challenging to create, and stimulating to shoot. Since you hit them cold they measure your ability to cope with the unexpected which is probably the most valid test of the pistolero.

In laying out such a course it should be kept in mind that simplicity is the keynote. Rules should be just as few as possible, and the shooter must be allowed to react just as he would in reality, using his equipment in any way consistent with the problem. In general, at least two shots should be permitted (not necessarily required) on any target, since it is normal battle procedure to fire twice at any adversary.

What we have come to call "combat logic"—the degree to which the course approaches a practical demand which might be made on a pistol shooter in a mortal emergency—is the measure of a surprise shoot. And it is in surprise shoots that we discover additions and improvements to combat shooting which may become standard in the future.

Naturally, secrecy in the preparation of a surprise shoot is essential.

THE POWER SCALE

The combat pistol expert must be able to hit not only fast and accurately, but *hard*. Pistols that strike an adequate blow let you know it when they go off, and combat shooting with reduced loads is a contradiction in terms.

If a contest is restricted to .357's and big bores, and allows only factory full-charge ammunition, there is no problem, as all such combinations are full-duty equipment and compete on an even basis. This is the preferred club policy.

However, since the medium bores are usually admitted, the spectacle of a man's using a practically recoilless .38 target automatic to defeat a man using a fully combat-worthy combination on a course, such as the Mexican or the International, where *recoil is an issue,* must be provided against.

Also there are those who claim they cannot afford factory ammunition even in a contest. Reloads are, for practical purposes, impossible to test at a contest.

One solution is to use the Hatcher scale of Relative Stopping Power, to adjust competition place points. For example, if 10 points are awarded for a first place, 10 is multiplied by the Hatcher rating of the cartridge used and this gives the adjusted score. This makes it virtually impossible to win a contest with a low-powered weapon, which is as it should be, but it involves a lot of cumbersome arithmetic.

A simpler way is to place loads in arbitrary categories based on the Hatcher scale, such as giving a value of one to the .38 Special and similar rounds, two to the .357 and the low-velocity big bores, and four to the .44 Magnums.

33

Hunting with the Handgun

PISTOL HUNTING has been called a stunt, which it is, but hardly more so than any hunting which is not conducted strictly for meat. It has been called inhumane, but it is no more so than any other hunting if it is done with proper care. I have been told that, since the average hunter can't hit his rifle, he should not be encouraged to go around wounding things with a handgun. But the average hunter wounds plenty of game with his rifle. With a pistol he is more likely to miss clean, to the benefit of the game. There is no practical way to keep the incompetent bungler out of the woods, and he can foul things up as well with one weapon as with another.

Actually, a proper pistol is both accurate enough and powerful enough for a great many types of hunting. It will not do for tiny targets, long ranges, or pachyderms. Neither should it be used on lions, tigers, buffalo, or the great bears. But there is plenty of hunting which does not fall into the foregoing categories, and a lot of it can provide excellent sport for the handgunner who is willing to work for it.

The three requisites for sportsmanlike pistol hunting are short range, proper equipment, and superlative marksmanship. A good range for a pistol is about 35 yards. Fifty yards is a long field shot; 80 is marginal; and 100 to 125 is strictly big league. Naturally this depends upon the size of the game—but the essence of handgun hunting is cover. The handgun is a "brush gun," and unless the cover is fairly thick it is not going to be the tool for the job. Certain game may be spotted from afar and then approached in cover—I'm thinking of the javelina—and this makes for good pistol situations, but the shot itself must always be a close one.

This range limitation is not, however, as serious as it might look. We do a lot of talking about those elegant 300-, 400-, and 500-yard shots but, if we're honest, we know they are exceptional. Most game is engaged at under 50 yards. At that distance an expert field shot with a good pistol can hit within 3 inches of his point of aim even under pretty adverse conditions. This will anchor a lot of game. On my last prowl into the backwoods of Guerrero, one of

Mexico's wilder regions, I had a rifle, a shotgun, and a pistol available. In seven weeks' time I fired the rifle three times, the shotgun seven times, and the pistol seventy-two times. This was thick country, and the largest game was small deer, a perfect setup for my old Super .38 and hollow-point ammunition. A .357 might have been even better for the rabbits, birds, iguanas and pigs which constituted the main targets, but I needed something to serve a defensive mission as well, and I appreciated my *cuatro cargadores*.

Proper equipment for the pistol hunter includes a weapon of adequate power and accuracy, a carefully obtained zero, a fine trigger action, and the right bullets. These matters are discussed in the sections on hunting arms, but I note them here again for emphasis. You should not blunder afield with a gaspipe under the impression that refinement is needed only on the target range. In the woods you stand to lose more than a high score.

Fine marksmanship is the ultimate key to handgun hunting, for while a mediocre rifle shot can do very well on a hunting trip, a mediocre pistol shot won't even get started. This corroborates the comparative efficiency of the two arms, for the master pistolero and the duffer with the rifle shoot just about in the same class—if you exclude such things as buck fever and mistaken targets, which will not bother the master. Theodore Roosevelt, who by his own admission was a very poor hand with a rifle, was a very successful hunter. I can't say how his hitting ability with a rifle would have compared to that of Ray Chapman with a pistol, who now has a string of seven clean, one-shot kills on big game to his credit.

As to standards, if a man can fire 135 x 150 on the field course he is ready to go hunting. This is not too hard with a .22 but it's a chore with a full-house .44. Which is why pistolmen should stick to small game until they have attained quite a high gloss with their magnums.

SMALL GAME

Obviously small game is the most common objective of the handgun hunter. There is more of it, more time to shoot it, it's closer to home, and it's practical with a .22. Tree squirrels and rabbits, both cottontail and jack, are the most common targets, and they all provide most excellent sport as well as fine meat for the table. And they're not easy. One can easily be "skunked" in a whole day's hunting in good territory, especially if he tries only for head shots, as he should.

The marmot family makes excellent pistol targets. I consider marmots small game rather than "varmints" because I like to eat them, and edibility seems to be the difference. Marmots seem to call for a little more steam than a .22 Long Rifle provides, and will often make it down a hole when hit squarely with a service-type medium-caliber pistol bullet. Most of my experience with them comes from the goldens of the high Rockies, and I find that a .38 Super needs an expanding bullet to anchor them.

Any animal that is ordinarily treed with hounds is probably best taken with a pistol, as any man who intends to follow a dog pack will do well to avoid the encumbrance of a long gun. The range is rarely over 30 feet, and at that distance a competent pistolero can hit a dime.

Treeable game in the U.S. includes the opossum, the raccoon, the bobcat, the cougar, and the lesser bears (*Euarctos*), and naturally the weapon used should be of adequate power for the game. Above all it must be loaded with proper ammunition. Brain shots are the most humane on a treed beast, but they are not always possible, and even the normally inoffensive black bear can work up a fair amount of justifiable indignation after being hazed to and fro across the countryside.

There are two major game animals which are often hunted with dogs but not into trees. These are the boar and the jaguar, and they are great prizes for the handgunner. I confess to a certain reluctance to popping a treed quarry—the dim-witted possum, the charming and mischievous 'coon, the lithe and elegant cougar, or the quaint and comical bruin—but a burly hog or a massive, cattle-killing *tigre* is something else. Both tend to "come on" when the hunter shows up, and then comes the big moment for the pistol shot. The shot must be delivered coldly but very quickly. The range is short—too short—but the bullet must be placed with surgical precision, for you can't blast a furious, 300-pound beast to a standstill with pistol fire; you have to hit the central nervous system. Any man who has stopped a charging jaguar with his pistol rates a special feather in his war bonnet. This feat is to the pistol hunter as beating the drop is to the combat shot.

Varminting with a handgun is popular enough so that special weapons have been built for it. The classical "varmints," in this country, seem to be woodchucks and crows, and hunting either with a pistol is a fairly specialized activity. As I said, I regard woodchucks as game, but I don't know about crows, as I have never eaten one. Both chucks and crows can get very cagey in regions where they are hunted extensively, and as a rule become essentially rifle targets, but in places where they are really pests they are fair game for a handgunner. A flat-shooting pistol is indicated, for distances can stretch out with either beast.

Rats are often found in large numbers in public dumps, and here is a really fine target for your .22. These repellant creatures are best jack-lighted at night, and can provide a lot of tricky shooting in the course of an evening. Of course one checks the local ordinances first, but quite often a rat-shooter has the blessing rather than the disapproval of the city fathers.

Game birds are excellent pistol targets, but, except for the wild turkey, they are banned to the pistol shooter in the U.S. I have hunted ducks with a pistol in both Mexico and the Yukon, and believe me it isn't easy. One works to leeward along the shore, hoping to recover the birds as they wash up, and a slightly bobbing target flat on the water, with ripples intervening, calls for a fancy degree of elevation control. A hair high is an over, and a hair low is a short ricochet. You can try them on the wing, too, but don't expect much unless conditions are just right.

The king of the upland birds, for the handgunner, is the pheasant. You'll have to look pretty hard for a locality where it's legal, but taking ringnecks over dogs from the holster is a sporting enough activity for anyone. The rule is to keep your hand off your gun until the bird rises, and then to draw and track him as he goes out. A brace taken this way with a heavy pistol is somewhat more of an achievement than the same taken with an ounce and a half of number fours. A load of 1000 f/s or less is indicated, to avoid meat spoilage.

Turkeys are the exception to the general prohibition on taking birds with a pistol, and often offer good sport. A fine account of a .38 Special on turkey may be found as the lead piece in the marvelous little book *Colt on the Trail*, published some thirty years ago by the Colt people as an encouragement to the field use of the sidearm.

MEDIUM-SIZED GAME

Of the medium-sized pistol quarries my favorite is the javelina of the Southwest and Latin America. Fast, excitable, diurnal, gregarious, and near-sighted, he is just right for the pistolero. When jumped, the flock is likely to explode in all directions, offering a series of difficult shots to several hunters at once. The .357 seems made to order for javelina.

However, when one thinks of American hunting one thinks of deer, and deer—whitetail, mule, or blacktail—are very satisfactory game for the hand-gunner. The best states are Alaska, Arizona, New Mexico, and Idaho; though Wyoming, Montana, and Florida are also good if you can get a positive ruling on pistol hunting out of their game departments.

One of the really fine deer parks for the pistolero is the Kaibab plateau of Arizona, a state that specifies the .357, .41, and .44 as legal deer cartridges. The Kaibab is a high, rolling timberland and one of the world's most beauti-ful forests. It is inhabited by a carefully managed herd of big, handsome, well-fed mule deer that is hunted just hard enough to make it wary. The con-ifers and aspens provide enough cover for close shots without developing into a tangle, and each little draw has a jeep trail in its bed to permit easy hauling for your kill. You can camp out or hunt from a lodge, and packing and freez-ing facilities are only half an hour to the north on a paved highway. Alto-gether a fine spot, marred only by a one-to-a-customer limit that forces the handgunner to take the first thing offered rather than to wait for a trophy.

For when you hunt deer with a pistol you can't be very selective about your animal unless you are prepared to risk total failure. Considering that a handgun is three times as hard to hit with as a rifle, and has only one-third its range, one must regard any full-grown deer as a prize, and take a trophy rack as a gift of the gods.

The deer hunter works the same way with pistol or rifle, except that he simply avoids terrain that opens out too much. Setting 100 yards as his limit (remember, only an expert should take the field) he prowls the timbered ridges, glasses the edges of clearings, and waits at saddles if the woods get too

The Stoeger deer target can help to sharpen your aim before a hunting trip.

full of other hunters. Particularly effective is an upwind course just below the crest of a main ridge, crossing the tributary ridges at right angles and searching the small bay at the head of each draw, where deer like to lie up in the middle of the day.

Such matters are better covered in a book for deer hunters. The handgunner who hunts deer must simply remember to stick to close shots, to master his weapon, and to use the right ammunition; and he will do very well.

The deer cartridges are the .44 and the .41, though any big bore, properly loaded, will do the job up close. The trajectory of the magnums is their big advantage, for the hunter has enough problems without having to lob his shot at 75 yards.

BIG GAME

The question must eventually arise as to whether the pistol may properly be used on game larger than deer. I confess to a lack of first-hand experience in this area, but I think the best answer is a qualified yes. After all, it isn't so much the size of the target as the range at which it is shot. The .44, using the right bullet, will shoot right through both shoulders of a moose and out the other side. Not at 300 yards, but at pistol ranges. If the hunter insists on close shots, and passes up the foolish ones, he ought to be able to take fairly large animals with humane, one-shot kills. On big animals the .44 does not deliver the instantaneous knockdown of a .30/06 on a deer, but for that matter few riflemen have ever seen a moose knocked off its feet by a rifle bullet either. As long as the quarry staggers and falls within 50 yards, the kill may be considered clean, and a .44 Magnum bullet, through the heart, will achieve this on animals quite a bit bigger than a deer. Thus I believe that elk and moose, together with the African antelope, may properly be taken with a handgun under special circumstances. By no means do I recommend this as a general pastime, but I hope I have made clear by now that pistol hunting is never a sport for the ordinary sportsman.

Since the pistol hunter is rather unusual to begin with, he has the advantage of being able to forget convention. Since he's not after a Boone and Crockett head anyway, he can branch out. There are a number of beasts which are not game animals in the strict sense, but which, in these days of diminished conventional hunting, may offer fine sport to men in search of the unusual. Particularly I have in mind the crocodilians—alligators, crocodiles, caimans and gavials. These are big, rough, not uncommon in the right regions, and can be dangerous. They are scorned by the riflemen as they lie in mesozoic sloth on the sandbar, but how about tackling a 15-footer with your .44?

Experts claim there is only one good place for your bullet, and that is in the center of the short neck directly from the side. This will anchor, while anything else will let the beast make it to the water. It ought to be feasible to spot downriver, then land and make an inshore approach to a point just at the edge of cover. Then, if you can hit a half dollar at whatever distance you can close to, a 240-grain steel-jacketed soft-point should net you enough leather to fill a shoe store.

And keep in mind that these latter-day dinosaurs come in several degrees of impressiveness. The king is the saltwater crocodile (*Crocodilus porosus*) of Oceania. Up to 10 yards long, agile and aggressive, and notably fond of human flesh, a prime *porosus*, taken with a pistol, would be a trophy of which any hunter should be proud.

Top Pistol Trophies

Just as the rifleman gleans the world for its best and finest trophies, the pistol hunter can endeavor to establish a set of grand prizes which could stand as testimony to the special qualities of the handgun as a sporting weapon. I don't feel that it would be right simply to duplicate the rifleman's list, for while it is technically possible to secure an argali, or a tiger, or a white bear, or even an elephant, with a handgun, it is not a sportsmanlike venture. I realize that sportsmanship is a matter of opinion, but in *my* opinion one can go too far in attempting to do a job with "an instrument singularly unsuited to the task," as Mark Twain said of a golf club. It may be that any pistol is unsuited to the pursuit of big game, but I don't believe this to be true. I think there is a compromise area, where rare, burly, beautiful, or dangerous animals are sought at short range under conditions that make them especially suitable as pistol targets. In preparing my own list of top pistol trophies I realized that I immediately pose a legal problem, for in many jurisdictions hunting with a handgun is not permitted. I do not suggest breaking the law, I simply suggest that laws, including game laws, can be changed. You can't win at Indianapolis without exceeding the speed limit. Likewise you'll find it impossible to collect the grand prizes of the pistol without securing certain legal dispensations. This can probably be done.

The following, then, is my choice of the royal five for the pistolero, listed by continents. Naturally all specimens should be prime examples of the species, as near to the record as possible.

Eurasia

For this area I'll pick the European wild boar (*Sus scrofa*), found from the Eastern Alps to the Tien Shan. He is a short-range target, rugged and quarrelsome, and he is quite capable of killing you. Taken with a pistol as you come up on the dogs, his 300 pounds must be stopped by the most careful use of the heavy handgun. Since most of his habitat is presently behind the Iron Curtain there are fairly difficult problems to be solved in getting at him. (Imagine trying to get a visa for your .45 auto!) But he has been imported into the U.S., so let's accept an immigrant, especially if he is outstandingly big and bellicose.

Africa

Here again the current political situation is so unstable that it's hard to say what the rules are or how they are enforced. In ex-English areas the pistol is probably still viewed with horror, but in some other areas people are more reasonable if they are approached politely. Skipping the giants and the traditional, I'll choose the gorilla. You'll need a museum permit to take him, but such can be had. If you threaten his group he will charge, and a charging gorilla is a fearful spectacle. To stand your ground with a handgun and flatten him at 15 feet is man's work.

North America

Again I will bypass the traditional, because the big bears are not humanely taken with a pistol. For a creature that is large, wary, noble in aspect, and a lover of the deepest forests where the range is short, I'll pick the Roosevelt elk (*Cervus canadensis occidentalis*). Bigger in body, darker in color, and with shorter but heavier antlers than the better known Rocky Mountain elk (*Cervus canadensis canadensis*), he is a beast of the dense, dank, rain forests of the Pacific Coast. He must be hunted with great skill, for you have to move in on him like a ghost to escape detection by his marvelously sensitive ears. And if you succeed in this, his massive body calls for very precise use of your .44 if you are to secure a clean kill. As of this writing, it is practically impossible to get permission to hunt the Roosevelt elk with a pistol, but this may change as handgun hunting becomes more respectable.

South America

There is no argument here, as the jaguar takes the prize. Not just any jaguar, but a really prime cat of 250 pounds or more. Such are hard to come by, and though Mexico's famed Enrique Job tells me that size is not a function of range, I feel the chances for a really massive *tigre* are best in the Mato Grosso and southward. Siemel, the spearman, has a photograph of one he took, the skin of which is so big that a tall man can just reach the ear when the hind legs touch the ground. This was Brazilian, but I understand that Paraguay, Bolivia, and Argentina claim some huge cats, too. Few English-speaking hunters penetrate the upper reaches of the Paraguay-Paraná river system, so there is not much written material available to us on the big cattle-killing jaguars, apart from rumor. This is one of the few remaining unspoiled hunting countries. Happily, there is no special problem about handgun hunting in Latin America, where the authorities seem more worried about rifles than pistols. If you can get a weapon permit at all, it is good for any sort of weapon.

34

Care of Handguns

A HANDGUN is not a particularly complicated instrument, and a good one is extremely rugged, but a certain amount of intelligent care is still necessary if you are to get from it the kind of service it is built to tender.

Firearms are made largely of ferrous metals, and, as the Hittites discovered, iron rusts. Consequently, your pistol must be protected against rust, inside and out. A nickel finish is quite resistant to corrosion but it covers only the outside of a weapon. I have found "satin" chrome plating to give a highly resistant flat-white finish, but this is strictly a custom proposition. Anodized aluminum alloy parts are rust proof, of course, but have no durability. Stainless steel is another answer, but not everyone likes its color.

Since the hand sweats, and sweat contains salt, any hand-held ferrous instrument must be wiped clean after use. Except under very sandy or dusty conditions it should also be lightly oiled. Remember that "bluing" is not rustproofing: it is a darkening process only. All jointed, moving parts must be kept free of foreign matter as well as corrosion, and lightly lubricated for smooth operation. Reliable operation of any pistol depends on this, and reliability can be important.

The bores of .22 Shorts and Long Rifles need not be cleaned, except to remove foreign matter, as experiment has shown that such residue as is left by these little cartridges is probably a better barrel preservative than a regular cleaning. However, .22 actions should be wiped or brushed clear of the "mud" that builds up with prolonged use.

There is some discussion as to whether or not a modern, smokeless-powder pistol should be cleaned at all. The powder residue and priming compound are noncorrosive, and the bullet should leave no rust-promoting material in the bore. Besides, disassembling an auto may loosen a tight accuracy job, and cleaning a revolver, as you must, from the front, may burr the muzzle. Nevertheless, I like to keep them clean. I have more confidence in the reliability of a clean weapon, I can keep track of the condition of the bore better when it is kept bright, and I just have an emotional prejudice against dirty firearms, as I think most men have who take pride in their equipment.

There are several systems for cleaning a gun, all of which are said to work. My own is as follows:

(1) Swab out the bore (and all revolver chambers) with a clean cloth, such as a precut patch, to remove loose residue.

(2) Wash the bore and chambers with a bristle brush and a solvent such as G.I. rifle bore cleaner or Hoppe's No. 9. Water will do as well but water gets into the action to promote rust. Let the barrel stand wet while you tidy up the rest of the piece. I often let my own weapons stand overnight with solvent in the bore.

(3) Wipe off, or scrub off, all parts where powder residue collects, such as the ramp, bolt face, and slide rails in an auto; or the cylinder front and barrel face in a revolver.

(4) Wipe out the barrel and inspect it. If leading is present remove it with a brass brush. Mild leading can be removed by firing a dozen or so jacketed rounds through the bore. Severe leading should not be allowed to build up.

(5) Lightly oil the bore with a cut patch, and then use the latter to wipe down all exposed parts. In very dry or sandy climates do not oil, as this will pick up grit. In such climates humidity is not a problem.

(6) Re-assemble, check the action, and tighten all screws.

In very humid regions use a little more oil, of heavier viscosity. Graphitic lubricants are especially good in extreme cold. Always clean any firearm from the breech, if possible. Completely disassemble and inspect any firearm in extensive use once a year. Any firearm that is to be put away for an extended period should be greased, inside and out, and labeled with a tag noting this fact so that it may be degreased before returning to service. Wood stocks deserve an occasional dressing of raw linseed oil.

After a dunking, your pistol needs attention—badly if the mishap occurs in salt water. Strip the weapon completely, wash with fresh water, dry, oil, and re-assemble. A freshwater bath is not nearly so bad, especially in a dry climate, but even so the weapon should be cleaned and inspected. On the Balsas expedition our pistols went completely under almost every day, yet, with proper care, they came through without a trace of rust. Interestingly enough, some recent laboratory tests showed that a .45 auto may be fired while totally submerged without damage to itself or the shooter, and even strikes a fair blow at 18 inches.

At home a sidearm should be stored clean and dry, and *not* in a holster, as leather tends to gather moisture. All pistols not designated for house protection should be stored on a dry, smooth surface, covered against dust, and under lock and key. I am mildly against display racks, as they invite burglary. I have been told by police friends that one must *never* leave a handgun in a car, locked or otherwise, as this is the first source a hood looks to for weapons. However, this is sometimes difficult advice to follow in jurisdictions where it is legal to transport a sidearm in a vehicle but not on the person.

35

Safety with Handguns

ALL HANDGUNS must be considered as deadly weapons. They cannot be treated lightly, and the safe and competent handling of his weapons is the first duty of the shooter.

Firearms are unforgiving. In a world in which we are usually granted a second (or third, or seventeenth) chance, we must face the fact that with guns we may not be allowed even one mistake.

The safe handling of all firearms may be summed up in four standard rules:

(1) ALL GUNS ARE ALWAYS LOADED. If everyone were raised to assume that any firearm he might encounter was naturally loaded, the plaint, "I didn't know it was loaded," would never be heard. It is true that a weapon may be empty, but never, *never* make that assumption. When a weapon is picked up, touched, or handed from one person to another, it is immediately cleared, before anything else. Each time it changes hands it is cleared again. Don't feel that it is discourteous to clear a piece that has just been cleared by another who presented it to you. It is good gun manners to do so, and it will not offend, it will impress. The courts have held that a person who clears a weapon and then hands it to another relieves the latter of responsibility for its accidental discharge, but this is a non-shooter's view. A gun in your hands is *your* responsibility, and a judicial opinion is a poor substitute for a human life.

To clear a handgun is to open its action, and leave it open. In a single-action revolver the piece is half-cocked, the loading gate opened, and the cylinder spun by hand so that all chambers may be inspected. A double-action revolver is simply cleared by swinging out its cylinder. With the auto pistol the magazine is removed, and the action opened gently while the breech is inspected. Slamming the action open will drop the cartridge in the breech on the ground, which is sloppy technique. The system illustrated is the swank way to clear an auto, with the magazine held by the little finger while the thumb and index finger of the left hand pinch the action open. Needless to say, the finger stays out of the trigger guard during all clearing operations.

361

(2) MUZZLE IN A SAFE DIRECTION. Point a firearm only at things you are prepared to see destroyed. When you point a weapon at a human being you imply that you are quite willing to see him dead. This has nothing to do with whether or not the piece is loaded, for, remember, the assumption is that it is *always* loaded. I notice that very experienced shooters acquire an obsessive compulsion about this. If, during handling or dry practice, anyone steps into the line of sight, there is an immediate and automatic deflection of the muzzle either up or down. All safety techniques must become automatic, for if you have to think about them you can be distracted, and distraction is no excuse for an accident.

(3) KEEP YOUR FINGER OFF THE TRIGGER till your sights are on the target. Every handgun accident I know of, with the exception of those which were caused by shooting at the wrong person by mistake, has been caused by a violation of this principle. Train your finger to stay straight. Keep it straight. Do not ever place your finger on the trigger unless you are about to drop the hammer, and know that you are about to do it on purpose. On a fast presentation your finger will enter the trigger guard at the count of Four as your hand swings up into Five. You are already down range and no more than a tenth of a second elapses between the entrance of your finger and the fall of the hammer. At all other times if your sights are not on your target your finger is outside of the trigger guard.

(4) BE SURE OF YOUR TARGET. Shoot only at what you have positively identified. A man who shoots at a sound, or a shadow, or into an area he cannot check, is criminally irresponsible. Hunters who shoot other hunters by mistake are violators of this principle. I have always held that such people are guilty of negligent homicide, not the innocent victims of a tragic accident. It is not enough just to identify your target; you must also be sure that what lies beyond it is not vulnerable either. This is especially true of aerial targets.

If these three basic precepts were always observed, there could be no firearms accidents. There is nothing complex or abstruse about them, so we must attribute all gun mishaps to a combination of ignorance and disrespect for the weapon.

In a fairly full shooting career I have seen perhaps thirty accidents some fifteen of which involved the attempt to clear a misfunction. There seems to be a tendency toward mild hysteria when a weapon fails to operate correctly, and even otherwise responsible shooters will often start working feverishly with the action in total disregard of their surroundings. In a mortal emergency this may be justified, but on the range it must be prevented. When a piece hangs up, *Stop.* Take a deep breath, keep the muzzle downrange, get your finger out of the trigger guard, and then consider the problem. Stay where you are and do not leave the firing line until your problem is solved. All this may seem pretty obvious, but apparently it is not.

There is a greater probability of accident with pistols than with long guns, because handguns are easier to point and because they are usually kept ready for action. It would be vacuous to say that one should therefore be *more* careful

Revolvers are maintained either loaded or unloaded. Double-action revolver (above) is shown unloaded, with chamber open. When loaded, hammer is lowered all the way and pistol may be fired by simply pulling the trigger. Single-action pistol (below) must be cocked first.

Automatic pistol has four conditions of readiness

Condition 1. Weapon is fully loaded, fully cocked, and placed on manual safe. This is the condition maintained when the pistol is worn. (The single-action auto pistol should never be worn in any other condition.)

Condition 2. Pistol is fully loaded and hammer is lowered all the way onto the action. Half-cock position in most auto pistols is not a safe condition and is so stipulated by manufacturers; one exception is the Tokarev Russian service pistol in which the half-cock *is* the safety. Condition 2 is for maintaining pistol in ready storage.

Condition 3. The piece is unloaded but with a full magazine in the butt. Hammer is usually all the way down. This condition is recommended by military services of the world, but it is not a good way to carry the weapon either in live or dead storage since the pistol is neither ready for a half-trained shooter nor safe for an untrained tinkerer.

Condition 4. Pistol is entirely unloaded, no round in the chamber and no magazine in the butt. Used by those who want to keep the pistol in a drawer or on a mantelpiece, but completely safe from undisciplined hands.

with a pistol than with a rifle or shotgun, for this would imply that it would be proper to use less care with the latter, which is not true. However, a pistol in careless hands is rather terrifying, and careless pistol handling is inexcusable.

When a handgun is used as a defensive weapon, it must be kept in readiness at all times, unlike a hunting rifle, which is never loaded until it is taken into the field. A safe ready condition must therefore be established in which the pistol may be carried or stored. With the revolver there is no problem, for a revolver has only one condition of readiness, which is loaded and hammer down. (The best modern revolvers cannot be fired by a blow on the hammer, so we can forget the nineteenth-century custom of leaving the top chamber empty.) The auto pistol, on the other hand, is somewhat trickier, since it has three acceptable ready conditions and the user must make a choice. When carried on the person, an auto pistol should be fully loaded, cocked, and locked (unless it is double-action, in which case it is carried hammer down). This is alarming to many, and one of the reasons for favoring a revolver. When the pistol is removed for any reason, such as while sleeping or for storage in a glove compartment or a desk drawer, the hammer is lowered fully. In this condition the pistol is still fully loaded, but the mainspring is released and it cannot be fired accidentally. There is no danger of accidental discharge due to a blow on the hammer, for the firing pin does not reach all the way from hammer to primer. (This is true of the basic modern designs. There are exceptions.) For a semiready condition of complete safety, the auto may be charged with a full magazine but with no cartridge in the chamber. This requires two hands to ready the piece for action (with most people) and reduces the capacity of the weapon by one shot, but increased safety may sometimes warrant it. If you ever need to use a defensive pistol you will probably need it instantly, and that half-ready is not good enough.

TREAT ALL FIREARMS WITH RESPECT.
YOUR FIRST MISTAKE MAY BE YOUR LAST.

INDEX